D1626117

The Holy
VEDAS

भूर्भुवः स्वः तत्सवितुर्वरेण्यं भर्गो देवस्य धीमहि ।
धियो यो नः प्रचोदयात् ॥

O Supreme Lord!
Thou art ever existent,
Ever conscious, ever blissful.
We meditate on Thy most adorable glory.
Mayest Thou guide and inspire our intellect
On the path of highest divinity!
May we be able to discriminate
Between truth and falsehood.

(Rig.3.62.10)

The Holy
VEDAS

A Golden Treasury

Pandit Satyakam Vidyalankar

Blessings
Svami Satya Prakash Sarasvati

Clarion Books
Associated with HIND POCKET BOOKS

THE HOLY VEDAS

Edited & prepared by

Pandit Satyakam Vidyalankar

© Clarion Books
First hardcover edition, 1983
Seventh Reprint, February, 2005
ISBN 81-85120-54-4

Published by
Clarion Books
(*Associated with* Hɪɴᴅ Pᴏᴄᴋᴇᴛ Bᴏᴏᴋs (P) Lᴛᴅ.)
J-40, Jorbagh Lane, New Delhi-110003
Tel: 24620063, 55654197 Fax: 24645795
e-mail: fullcircle@vsnl.com

Typesetting : SCANSET

J-40, Jorbagh Lane, New Delhi-110003
Tel: 24620063, 55654197 Fax: 24645795

Printed at Nutech Photolithographer, Delhi-110095
PRINTED IN INDIA
83/05/07/02/41/SCANSET/SAP/NP/NP

Contents

म␣हो अर्णः सरस्वती ␣ प्र चेतयति केतुना ।
धियो विश्वा वि राजति ॥ १२ ॥

Vast is the ocean of sacred words
Which enlightens the universe
With divine vision.

(Rig.1.3.12)

Foreword

FOR the last several years, Pandit Satyakam
Vidyalankar and myself have been busy on the English
translation of the Rigveda. This is only a part of our big
project in which we propose to bring out the translations of various other Vedic texts, particularly
the Vedic Samhitas. The Rig Samhita has 10,589
verses, the Yajur 1,975, the Samaveda 1,875, and the
Atharva 5,977 verses, and thus the total comes to
20,416 verses. Pandit Satyakam, with his great qualities
of head and heart and with his love for music and
poetry, is the right person to have been assigned the
task of selecting something like one thousand verses
out of this entire stock for the benefit of entire
humanity. We are very much obliged to the publishers
for the excellent production of this Vedic Anthology.
Humanity is proud of this most ancient heritage and it
has been the most amazing accomplishment of mankind to have preserved this divine literature to this day
under all hazards and vicissitudes of history.

The Vedas constitute the back-bone of our entire
culture and development through the millennia not
only in India but also abroad. For most of us, they
constitute the first literature that dawned on us at the
earliest time of man's appearance on this globe. In
India, we regard them as the revealed knowledge.
What the effulgent sun is to animate and inanimate
activity on the terrestrial earth, the Vedic enlighten-

The dawn receives her beams from beyond the rising place of the sun. Borne on a hundred auras of glory, the auspicious dawn advances on her way in different directions

(Rig. 1.48.7)

ment is to the prestigious life of man on this planet for the majority of humanity. Man with his most highly evolved physico-psychic complex is a gem in our divine creation, much above the animal level. For his fulfilment, the necessary code of conduct is incorporated in the Vedic texts. It is the most precious gift to humanity from our benign Creator and Lord.

Origin of Language

WE are told that the divine revelation came to man at a time when the world was in its infancy. I shall not take you to primitive man and his group as conceived by an evolutionist of the modern age—a society which was least conducive for the type of revelation we received from the divine source. Undoubtedly, the primitive and mentally unevolved man could have been least receptive to the highest type of enlightenment. I shall not refer you to the history or the geography of the event of revelation, for the time-space reckoning must have started very long ago in our history. I am talking of days when man had no language, though he had a complete set of vocal and hearing organs. Think of the days when man had existed without a vocabulary; he had not yet called the sun the *sun,* the moon the *moon,* and the earth the *earth.* How surprising it was that he was flourishing in surroundings to which he had not yet given names. He was moving, sitting, sleeping, eating and drinking but he had no terminology for these functions. His gesture had no words. He was enjoying colourful Nature, t he had no terms for white, red, pink, blue, green or black. In the midst of such a state of affairs now inconceivable, the divine knowledge was revealed to him through exceptional personalities with high receptivity, stupendous memory and superb understanding. The earliest contribution of men of this group was *to assign names* to the objects of surroundings in the most general terms. The language of the divine Rigveda itself has an astonishing stock of about 35,000 words in 10,000 verses with immense intrinsic potentiality for coining new terms. With the *revealed Vedas* starts the concept of human language in terms of which man not only talked with contemporary man, but also continued his link with posterity. Without having an instinct to communicate to posterity, man could not have made any history, culture, philosophy, science and technology. This communication could have been possible only through *a language*, as divine as Creation. Philosophy or science assumes the pre-existence of *orderliness* in Creation, the Rita, another name for eternal consistency. According to a theistic concept, there is a concomitant relationship between the Veda, Creation and science. A theist is one who submits or surrenders himself to the Divine Creator, the Divine Language (WORD) and the Divine Creation—the three *realities.*

Thousands of years have passed since the divine knowledge was first revealed to a small group of seers (the four Samhitas to the first four—Agni, Vayu, Aditya and Angiras, so named traditionally). There was another group of seers with stupendous memory, who passed on this knowledge to the successive generations. The art of script and writing was invented and developed at a much later stage.

Phenomenon of Oral Communication

IN the British Musuem, one may see a written Bible of the third and fourth centuries A.D.; the Holy Qoran of thirteen hundred years ago beautifully scribed, but one would rarely find a script of the Veda of such an ancient date. Such an amazing phenomenon of pre serving the most ancient texts of 20,000 verses through all the years of history could not have

occurred in any other land. The credit goes to the
traditional Brahmanas of India who against all hazards
of human history could keep the texts so well preserved with the right phonetic accents and accuracy to this
day.

Dynamism in the Vedic Period

MAN was very dynamic in the Vedic Age when he
for the first time domesticated cattle and developed
barley, rice and lentils. He with regularity introduced
innovations in agriculture. The Rishis of the days of
the *Yajnas* laid the foundations of the earliest physical
and life sciences including mathematics and astronomy. The places where these *yajnas* were performed
were known as *yajnashalas;* they were man's earliest
temples of learning, his academies and his open-air
laboratories and observatories. There could not have
been any limit to man's achievement and his col-
laborative accomplishments. The Veda stands for the
philosophy of *dynamic realism,* against that of static
mysticism.

Knowledge and Theism

IT was the Veda that inspired earliest man. In
other words, the ancients drew inspiration from God,
God's Words and God's Creation. You cannot think of
knowledge by eliminating God from His Creation. After
all, what is knowledge? What is physics? or metaphysics? Is it not with reference to our Great Creation?
It is just the study of a little activity in the dynamic
world in a particular parameter. The world is the
source-book of all such studies. In our own body
complex, there is something, the study of which is
beyond the dimensions of our physics—how does a
sense-organ function? How do the vital forces operate
and how does the mind work? These questions

pertain to that realm of creation which is also as real as the physical realm. Raising questions in their context, exploring mysteries and finding out the generalities take us to the disciplines of psychology and metaphysics and so, ultimately, it is our creation (ultra-micro, micro and macro) which has to be studied and explored. The Veda takes you even a little beyond this creation. While the Vedic texts present to you a little picture of the mysteries of this creation, they by and by lift you up a little beyond the physical or metaphysical reality. They raise you from creation to the Creator. They take you from the Sun to the Sun that shines behind the Sun, to the Fire that glows behind the mundane fire, they take you to Light that enlightens all the lights familiar to us. They take you to Beauty and Pleasure behind the so called beauty and pleasure that exist in our everyday life. And thus the Veda becomes the source-book of the *para vidya* (mundane knowledge) and *apara vidya* both (science of Ultimate Reality). In the lower stages, all the disciplines of knowledge are distinct and separate. What botany is is not physics; what hearing is is not seeing, what knowing is is not feeling but in the *apara vidya* (the knowledge of the Supreme), all these distinctive disciplines merge into one. The highest knowledge is merely one, the integrated knowledge, and this is the knowledge, not gained through our sense-organs, vital organs or through our mental behaviours. This is the final knowledge that we aspire for. This is then the establishment of a personal link between an aspirant and the Supreme One.

Beauty in Nature

THE Vedic verses enable you to enjoy the glory of God in His creation. May you enjoy to the full the charm of the damsel of Dawn a little before sunrise; some of the verses draw your attention to the glory of the rising sun, the vast luminary that enlightens our globe throughout the day. The verses take you to the thrilling evenings and to the calmness of night, cool and refreshing. The sky and the firmament have their own beauty with stars set like pearls and diamonds on a blue background

THIS is, however, one aspect of Nature's glory. The rays of the sun take away moisture from the surface of oceans; the moisture takes the form of dark clouds which during particular months of the year proceed with high speed thousands of miles at a height of 4,000 to 20,000 feet high in the firmament. Whilst the clouds move, the midspace wind also attains a stupendous velocity. The water particles of the clouds are surcharged with electricity. The result is thunder and lightning. The thunder, lightning and highspeed wind, all the three integrate themselves to provide dread to the living beings on the terrestrial globe. For days together, the sun is rendered invisible and is shrouded as if with layers of clouds. And finally the rain falls in torrents, and the sky again becomes clear. Man gets light and warmth both from the mighty sun. The clouds are known as *Vrittra* in Vedic terminology. More than a dozen names are given to these clouds; they are the demons, they are serpents (*ahih*); they are the *varahas* (meaning boars also). The sun is also given dozens of names. The Vedic verses take delight in referring to the eternal conflict between Indra or the sun and the shrouder, the clouds, which obstruct light and warmth of the sun. Ultimately, it is the sun that becomes victorious. But again the story is repeated everywhere. The Divine Poet of the Veda is never tired of narrating this parable; and He takes us to another conflict of the same nature which exists within the interior of all of us—a constant struggle between our divine tendencies and our devilish ones. The incessant conflict between Truth and Non-truth, between Good and Evil, or Enlightenment and Nescience, Knowledge and Ignorance. While the Vedas narrate this parable, their reference to the sun and clouds is merely symbolic. The real conflict which they intend to stress is between the self and the dark forces within our own personal make-up. On one side we have truth, light and immortality and on the other evil, darkness and death.

Theism of the Veda

IN the verses of the Vedas, we invoke the Supreme Lord, the Sole Master of Creation and the living beings. Man is also an architect or potter in certain respects, but his creation, his art, his pot exists at a place where he does not stay. But the Supreme Divine as an architect produces everything *within* Him, for there is nothing that exists outside Him and He is *within* all. For we have in a passage of the Yajur, where there is a reference to the Supreme Reality:

> It moves, it moves not.
> It is far, and it is near,
> It is within all this,
> And it is outside all this (Yajur.22.5).

In Vedic terminology, by *creation* we mean a purposeful well-ordained transformation of the un-manifest to the manifest form, from *asat* to *sat*. In that sense, all the rich and wonderful creation is *within* the existence of our Lord (in Time-Space parameters). He is also known as the *hiranyagarbha* or the Golden Embryo. We have in a Vedic verse:

> The Golden Embryo existed prior to all. It was the source of everything that was born. It was the sole Lord of Existence. It maintains or upholds everything that exists between earth and heaven. Only to that Lord, and to none else, shall we offer

our affection and homage   (Rig.10.121.1·
Atharva.4.2.7)

THIS Supreme Reality is not merely a philosophi-
cal abstract concept, it is a reality which we have to
invoke and evoke for our personal becoming or for the
fulfilment of our life. In this sense, Vedic Theism is a
concept of dynamic reality. The Supreme Reality is
our concern every moment. We might ignore Him,
and so we usually do, but He does not neglect us.

> While He is near, He leaves it not; though it is
> near, it sees Him not. Behold the Art of God, His
> Poetry that shall not die and shall never grow
> old (Atharva.10.8.32).

God Himself is unmanifest, but He is manifested
behind his Divine Art. The effulgence behind His
creation is His effulgence; the mighty force behind
Nature's force is His force. He is light behind the light;
terror behind the terror, the sweetness behind everything that is sweet, and the Supreme Activity behind
all activities. We admire His forces, invoke all bounties
of Nature, and through Nature, we proceed to the un-
manifest Reality, the Supreme Source of Enlightenment and Bliss.

We invoke our Lord in terms of attributes and functions, and we try to establish a personal relationship
with Him. In Vedic poetry, the tiny little soul and the
Supreme Self are both taken to be two birds (*Suparna*),
mutual friends and companions.

> Two birds, which are closely associated and
> intimate friends, perch on the same tree. Of
> them One (the lower soul) tastes of its fruits; the
> other (the Supreme Lord) shines resplendently
> without tasting (Rig.1.164.20).

Coupled with a few more verses of the Great Hymn (1.164, 21,22), one can enter into the depths of the mystic meaning of the intimate relationship of the two birds perching on one and the same fig tree.

The Supreme Reality is known by different names in regard to its functions, attributes and nature. Taken out of the context of its creation and suzerainty over souls, the Reality would have no name other than OM (=A—U—M), the all-comprehensive syllable, embracing the limits of the entire phonetic alphabet with potential creativity, sustenance and dissolution in it. (Om kham Brahma—Yajur.60.17).

The functional and attributive names of the Supreme Reality are numberless. Primarily, they are the names of our Lord; in their narrow connotations, they are the names of Nature's Bounties also— primarily the sun, and secondarily the bounties of midspace and the earth. Society is also a living organism, with its head, its shoulders, its eyes, and its limbs. The same functional terms as are used for the Supreme Reality may be used for offices in an organised society. Again, *man,* his entire body-complex, is a huge sovereignty by itself with the soul as the supreme ruler, and the sense-organs (and the functional organs) as his subordinates.

THE seers of the Vedic age not only discovered this fire, they devised the means of controlling and harnessing it. They finally introduced certain elaborate fire-rituals called the *yajnas*. Apart from small and big fire-rituals, the Vedic Samhitas refer to the *cosmic yajna* which goes on incessantly in Nature, producing sunshine, clouds, rainfall, vegetation, and completion of Nature's cycles of various types. In analogy to the benevolent and purposeful cosmic *yajna*, any activity of man, intended to contribute something to society with selfless intentions, came to be known as *yajna.* The entire 18th Chapter of the Yajurveda deals with this type of *yajna,* contributing to the general human good. Many of the verses end with a refrain *yajnena kalpatam.* This *yajna* is not a fire-ritual; it refers to man's dynamic activity to explore and utilise Nature's resources for our common good. Motivated by the spirit of these *yajnas,* our seers of yore explored the flora and fauna, surveyed organic and inorganic resources, and laid the foundations of a welfare state. The domestication of animals, the science and craft of agriculture, and the utilization of all types of resources for food, clothing and housing were some of the earliest undertakings of the Vedic age. These *yajna-shalas* were, in a way, the open-air academies, laboratories and observatories for the advancement of culture and enlightenment.

A concerted, coordinated well-planned effort for human good is *yajna.* This is a sacred act and hence is technically known as sacrifice, a selfless act.

Life and Living in the Atharvaveda

THE verses of the Atharvaveda stand unique for their own charm and spell on human life and day-to-day living. The learned author of this anthology has with care given to us the outstanding hymns and verses from this Veda, a collection of 5,977 verses. The Veda takes you to the topics of highest spirituality and theism on the one hand; on the other hand, it glorifies Mother Earth on which we are born—see the Bhumi-Sukta of Book 12. The hymn passionately ends with the lines:

> O Earth, my mother, set thou me happily in a place secure. Of one accord with heaven, O sage, set me in glory and in wealth (63).

Same more verses paying tributes to one's own existence on the wonderful planet of the Earth:

O Resplendent Sun, the performer of the cosmic sacrifice, may you, being invoked, come on a chariot driven by two, by four, by six, by eight or by ten horses. May you come to accept precious offerings, but do not scorch us to the extreme

(Rig.2.18.4)

I am victorious, I am called the Lord Superior
on Earth, triumphant, all o'er-powering, the
conqueror on every side (54).

> May Earth, the Goddess, she who bears her
> treasure stored up in many a place, gold, gems,
> and riches, giver of opulence, grant great pas-
> sions to us, bestowing them with love and favour
> (14).

> Rightly, I am the son of Earth, Earth is my
> mother (12.12).

In Book 10, we have an excellent hymn in support
of all (7), and another of the Loftiest Brahma (8).
Every verse of these hymns is meaningful and elevat-
ing.

IN the Atharvaveda, we have hymns for every stage
of human life. A full hymn (11.5) is devoted to
Brahmacharya, and the Brahmacharin, the young
avowed to study divine scriptures with penance,
austerity, dedication and full discipline. There is no
limit to the potentiality of this dedicated young man:

> Lighted by fuel goes the Brahmacharin, clad in
> black-buck skin, consecrate, long-bearded,
> swiftly, he goes from east to northern ocean,
> grasping the worlds, of bringing them anear him
> (11.5.6).

> Self-restraint is Brahmacharya:
> By fervour and by self-restraint the gods drove
> death away from them. And Indra brought by
> self-restraint heaven's lustre to the deities
> (11.5.19).

The hymns and verses selected for this **Anthology**
from the Atharvaveda would speak of the richness of
the variety of themes included in the Veda.

IN Vedic terminology, every little thing concerning the human body, the outer and innermost complex, is the concern of the subject of *adhyatma*. Book 11 of the Atharvaveda has a full hymn of 34 verses devoted to it (Hymn 11.8). Another *Adhyatma* hymn is the entire Book 13 of nine hymns. This hymn is devoted to Rohita, meaning red, the colour associated with fire or the rising and the setting sun. The entire hymn needs a careful and detailed study. Two verses are quoted here:

> The Earth became an altar; heat was Agni; and the butter rain. There Agni, made by song and hymn, these mountains rise and stand erect. (53)

Then having made the hills stand up, Rohita spoke to Earth and said: In thee, let everything be born, what is, and what is yet to be (54). (1.53,54).

The entire Book 14 is devoted to marriage and married life—the life of a householder and his wife. In the Rigveda 10.85, we have the details of the marriage of Soma, the youth, with Surya, the maiden, the daughter of the Sun, i.e., Dawn. Verses 6 to 16 are devoted to the marriage ceremony. Many of the verses of this hymn are still quoted in our marriage ceremonies, and they form the basis of the sanctity of married life.

In the Atharvaveda, Book 14, we have numerous other passages of importance in household life and marriage ceremony.

In Book 19 of the Atharvaveda, we have several hymns devoted to Shanti, or Peace (Hymns 9-11), quite in common with the verses of the Rigveda and Yajurveda.

The learned author of this Anthology could select roughly five per cent of the divine verses available in the Samhitas. Such selections have always personal touch. The editor has picked out a small number of representative verses at random without under-rating those which he has left out. There are thousands of verses still in the Samhitas, which you yourself would like to include in an anthology of your choice. May this Anthology draw you nearer to a literature which has been the proud possession of mankind since the earliest days of our history.

WHY we would like you to keep this Anthology with you in your home and on your shelves, in your drawing-rooms, and even by your side as a constant companion is for the following reasons:

O The Vedic verses are the earliest source of knowledge.

O They are in a language, prior to which there was no language of such a rich stock of literature. The Vedic language is the mother of Sanskrit, a language of great importance for comparative research. Sanskrit is regarded as *"the first daughter of the earliest mother tongue."*

O Vedic theism is pure and simple and most natural monotheism, invoking ONE GOD, the Supreme Lord, the mighty force behind all forces nd the Divine Light behind all effulgences. Just as the presence of the soul within a human body is recognized by the activity of the body or the life in it, similarly, the existence of the Supreme Reality in the cosmos is realized by looking at the purposeful dynamism in the Lord's creation. Hence the Vedic verses invoke the Lord by evoking Nature's Bounties, known as deities, the *Devah* or *Vishvedevah*.

O The Vedic verses refer to Nature's eternal history, but not the history of a human achieve-. ment. They do not bring any human personality between MAN and his GOD. The verses refer you to the glory of GOD in His Creation and ask you to establish a personal link with Him in the innermost core of your heart, where you can feel His throb, hear His voice and see His enlightenment. Man-based religions are of a later date, whereas man's natural religion is eternally with him.

O The Vedic concept of God is perfectly ethical, and hence the Vedic verses uphold high moral values of life. God is Truth personified, Activity personified, Purity personified, Love personified and Bliss personified. We crave to imbibe within us a bit of His qualities. The Vedic Dharma is thus the morality-based Dharma based on truth and its acceptance for life, i.e., faith (*Shraddha*), austerity (*Tapas*), piety (*Daya*) and selfless service and dedication (*Yajna*), generosity (*Dana*), peace (*Shanti*), friendship (*Mitrata*), fearlessness (*Abhaya*) and mutual understanding (*Saumanasam*). Above all, is the essential quality of complete reliance on God (the lone *alambana* or *skambha,* the pillar of strength).

O The Vedic verses refer to a type of coordinated life. Man is not an individual. He is a social organism. God loves him only who serves other beings: men, cattle and other creatures. His glory lies in being a member of a big family. On the one hand, man is bound by blood-kinship—his parents, his wife, his sons and grandsons, and on the other, he is linked with every individual of society, whether near or far from him. It is given to man to link himself with those who constitute his ancestry, and also think of those who would be his posterity. Man thus lives, works and dies for society. The Vedic verses refer to this dynamism. Man is expected to develop his craft, sciences and technology, and lead society from poverty to prosperity, with a happy today and a happier tomorrow.

O The immortal soul assuming a human form may be regarded as a purposeful benevolent bondage. It is through such a series of bondages that man is expected to attain his fullness. This is his liberation or emancipation. In that state, we are told, we shall be free from the shackles of body and sense-organs; we shall revert to our self-effulgent form and enjoy Divine Bliss. The mortal would thus become *amrita* or immortal.

We must express our gratitude to Pandit Satyakam Vidyalankar for his excellent Anthology of Vedic Verses, which would be read with all the reverence that it deserves, and would be enjoyed in our dark moments of desperation and difficulties when we need inspiration and enlightenment the most. We are also indebted to the printers and publishers for their excellent production of this volume.

The Veda is a symbol of Divine Light and Divine Happiness. May we all have divine blessings!

New Delhi,
October 15, 1983

SVAMI SATYAPRAKASH
SARASVATI

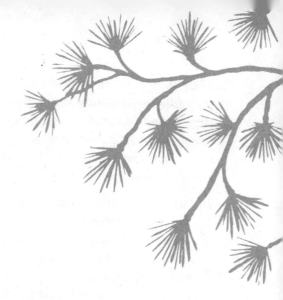

Preface

*T*he four Vedas contain the divine, infallible knowledge revealed to those primal men whose soul was specially illumined by the grace of God to receive and impart to humanity the words of Almighty God. The purpose of this revelation was to enlighten and spread Godly knowledge to man so that he may live a happy life in this world, be aware of his innate divinity and try to realise eternal bliss.

The Vedas are the sacred heritage not only of India but of all mankind. But however till now the translations and interpretations of these sacred books have been made use of mostly by historians and scholars. Modern man has not been able to draw inspiration and guidance from them to rise above the mundane, the physical and the metaphysical to achieve harmony with his Creator.

These simple and *lucid verses continue to inspire all, including contemporary lovers of philosophy. In matter, in form and in variety, Vedic hymns can claim a place among the most ancient and deep philosophies of any civilization and yet continue to have relevance to the world of today and tomorrow.*

In this book an attempt has been made to bring together such representative hymns which encompass all the aspects enshrined in the Vedas. I have also tried to retain the spirit of the original Sanskrit mantras in my English renderings and to impart some of the holy ambience of these sacred texts which are the fountain-head of Hindu philosophy and culture.

In order to place the Vedic hymns in their proper perspective, they have been classified into six sections as under:

○ *Hymns on Creation*
○ *Hymns on Devotion*
○ *Hymns on Revelation*
○ *Hymns on Action*
○ *Hymns on Splendour*
○ *Hymns on Positive Sciences*

The hymns of the Vedas are grouped under such headings as Agni, Indra, Varuna, Soma, Rudra, etc. The different names represent God's various powers and attributes. The Vedas have definitely stated that the manifested Devahs are only an aspect of the one Supreme Lord. Therefore in most of the places I have referred to them as the Supreme Lord only. The splendour attached to these Devahs attains special significance when one sees the divinity behind the splendour of all manifestations of Nature, the Creator behind the creation.

I would like to express my gratitude to all those who have helped and inspired me in doing this sacred work. I would like to mention first and foremost the name of Shri Shanand Satyadevaji of Durban, South Africa, who by his intense devotion to the Vedas initiated this project and made available the resources to accomplish this great work. Also I must thank Shri Dina Nath Malhotra of Hind Pocket Books, his editorial staff and printing press and all those who worked day and night in a spirit of dedication to enable this holy book to appear in an exquisite form. I also thank Shri D.D. Mehta for the excerpts taken from his book, Positive Sciences in the Vedas *in our science section.*

Pandit Satyakam Vidyalankar

Diwali
4th November 1983

HYMNS ON Creation

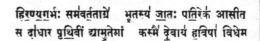

हिरण्यगर्भः समवर्तताग्रे भूतस्य जातः पतिरेकं आसीत
स दाधार पृथिवीं द्यामुतेमां कस्मैं देवाय हविषा विधेम

In the beginning was Hiranyagarbha (Golden Womb).
The seed of elemental existence,
The only Lord of all that was born.
He upheld the heaven and earth together
To what God other than Him, could we dedicate our life?

(Atharva. 4.2.7)

Vedic Concept of Creation

The theory of evolution is one of the greatest revelations of modern scientific thought. Various philosophers, physicists and scientific men, working independently of one another and in different domains of Nature, have, have established the truth of this theory, so that, instead of remaining a theory, there are evident signs of its soon becoming a proven fact. The theory enunciates the great truth, that all complexity came out of simplicity, heterogeneity out of homogeneity, perfection out of imperfection, variety out of uniformity. All this beauty and grandeur with apparent paradoxes is the result of the struggle which Nature wages towards the attainment of order and perfection.

In the beginning of the present order of things, in some far-off period, in some distant point of time, the whole universe existed in a state of *paramanu* (atoms), invisible, subtle and unmanifested. That which we know now as the earth, the sun, the moon and the stars was then, in the beginning of the Kalpa, but formless matter in its most elemental and attenuated condition—ether, no doubt our ancient Aryan philosophers called it—non-being (*asat*). We involuntarily exclaim with our glorious Rishis:—"Before, O child, this was a mere state of non-being (*asat*), one only, without a second. Thereof verily others says: Before this was non-being, one alone, without a second, from that non-being proceeds the state of being."

There is nothing, therefore, inappropriate in the name which the ancients gave this ether-spirit, viz., the anima mundi—the divine inflatus, the *Hiranyagarbha*. The Aryan title *Hiranyagarbha*—the womb of light—is far more expressive and scientific than the name ether.

The Evolution of Heat and Light

In the beginning, there was neither nought nor
    aught
Then there was neither sky nor atmosphere above.
What then enshrouded all this universe?
In the receptacle of what was it contained?
Then was there neither death nor immortality,
Then was neither day, nor night, nor light,
    nor darkness,
Only the Existent One breathed calmly,
    self-contained.

(Rig.10.121.1)

First in the beginning, therefore, was this *Hiranyagarbha,* one only without a second. The next step towards evolution was the generation of heat. The atoms of ether came closer together and united in different proportions and formed molecules. Thus the various elements were first evolved out of the homogeneous atoms of ether. This union necessarily implies the contraction of the primeval mass. Thus, these two processes, namely, of chemical union and contraction, gave rise to a great deal of heat.

This intense heat raised the elements to a state of gaseous incandescence, and the whole mass would be now a luminous vapour of all elements, iron, gold etc. This self-luminous vapour has been called by the Aryan Rishis Prajapati (the Lord of all creations) and modern scientists have called such incandescent vapours nebulae (clouds), from their resemblance to white clouds. Thus, there arose light where there was formerly only darkness.

The findings of astrophysicists of today have now reaffirmed the statements of the Vedic declarations, with the help of every sophisticated and ultra-modern scientific equipment. They have gathered information about the circulation of energy and material in space. Astrophysicists are studying how the universe began. Did it all begin with a terrific explosion, the "big-bang"? With the aid of the radio telescope, the scientists in Effelsberg can pick up signals that were sent 15,000 million years ago— when the "big-bang" is believed to have taken place. From these signals and what is now going on in space, it is possible to look back to the beginning of evolution, as if through a window in time: one can reconstruct the "big-bang".

Dr. Schmid-Burgk describes what is supposed to have taken place: "The cosmic material was originally densely packed and very hot. Because of the high temperatures, the atoms had been broken down into nuclei and electrons; even earlier, the nuclei of the atoms had been reduced to their elements, the protons and neutrons. During the hottest moments, the first few fractions of microseconds of the 'big-bang', not even individual protons and neutrons could exist, but only what they are made up of, the quarks." The signals from space, however, also tell how the universe cooled down, expanded, how stars were born and died. With the passage of billions and billions of years, the time lapse has resulted slowly but surely in the loss of heat, the cooling down of planets which were all a part of the "Fire Ball" once.

The moon was also at one time a part of the earth,

and of course being but a smaller body, it has lost almost all its heat. The sun, which was the nucleus of the primitive rotating nebula, still retains a great deal of its heat, but it is not so intense as it must have been in the beginning. However, a time will come when the sun will cool down to darkness and no more be a fountain of light and heat to its planets, when there will be perfect darkness and intense cold—in fact, when this present cycle will come to an end. Long, long before that time arrives, this our earth will become a desolate wilderness—lifeless, silent and obscure. Seas, rivers, lakes, and oceans will be congealed to ice, even the very air will be a mass of solid. That time, according to Aryan calculations, is 2,333,227,018 years distant.

Modern scientific findings have reaffirmed the statement of this Vedic declaration.

———•———

The whole of this Universe
Is stationed in the Omnipresent
And the Omnipotent God.
We see Him in various forms.
He brings to light
All these worlds.
Him they call the Kala, Infinite,
Pervading the infinite space.

(Atharva.19.53.3)

In the Beginning

(NASADIYA SUKTA)

The non-existent was not then,
Nor was the existent,
The Earth was not, nor the firmament,
Nor that which is beyond.
(When there was nothing then), what could cover
    what,
And where and in whose care did the waters and
    the bottomless deep then exist?

(Rig.10.129.1)

There was no death nor immortality then;
There was no sign of night, nor of day.
That one breathed without extraneous breath
    with His own nature.
Other than Him there was nothing beyond.

(Rig.10.129.2)

In the beginning there was darkness,
Intensified darkness, indistinguishable darkness,
All this visible world was reduced to its
    primordial nature.
This primordial world which was enveloped by the
    All-pervading power of One
Before whom the world of matter is a trifle
    became One (that is, came into existence)
Through the force of His intense activity and
    spiritual fervour.

(Rig.10.129.3)

In the beginning the Divine Will arose.
This was the first seed of the mind of the Creator.
Those who can see beyond by putting their mind
  and heart together
Found the binding link of the existent in the
  non-existent,
The non-existent existing in the existent.

(Rig.10.129.4)

The rays of the Divine Will spread across the
  whole world.
They spread below and above
And the result was that small and big organisms
  bearing seeds were born.

As the existence of Earth was dependent on the
  Divine Will of the Creator,
The position of matter was lower than the spirit
  which acted with the Divine Will.

(Rig.10.129.5)

Who truly knows, and who can declare whence
  it cometh
And whither it vanisheth?
The divine people who know were born.
Much after Creation came into being.
Who then knows whence it has come about?

(Rig.10.129.6)

Whence this Creation has come;
Who holds or does not hold;
He who is its surveyor in the highest heaven
He alone knoweth,
And yet doth He know?

(Rig.10.129.7)

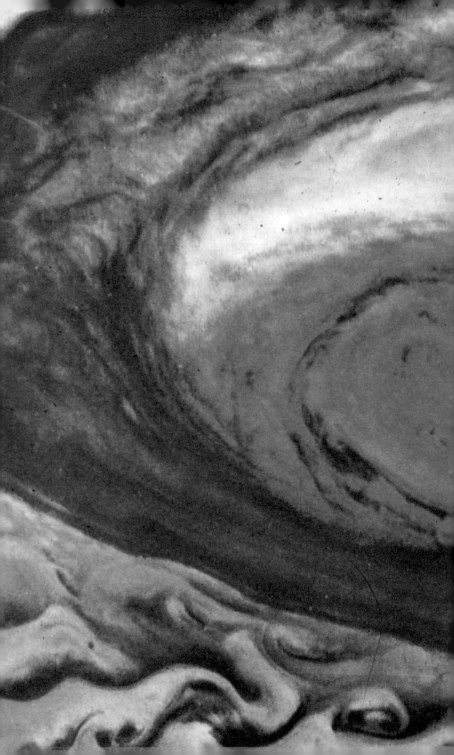

Bless that the sun,
With extensive radiance,
Rises for peace.
May the four quarters of the horizon
Be auspicious for peace and harmony.

(Rig.7.35.8)

Cosmic Yajna

(PURUSHA SUKTA)

The Supreme Being is thousand-headed,
Thousand-eyed, thousand-footed;
He pervades the Universe on all sides,
And extends beyond the ten directions.

(Rig.10.90.1)

He, indeed, is all this,
What has been and what will be,
He is the Lord of Immortality
Transcending through material existence.

(Rig.10.90.2)

Such is his magnificence, but
The Supreme Being is greater than this;
All beings are a quarter of Him,
Three-quarters make up immortality in the
   Supreme Region.

(Rig.10.90.3)

Three-quarters of the Supreme Being remain
   abstract,
One quarter part manifests again and again,
And, diversified in form, it moves
To the animate and the inanimate world.

(Rig.10.90.4)

42

Through the divine energy of the Supreme Being
This dynamic universe (Virat) came into existence
In the course of the evolution of the universe, the
    earth and other habitable planets came into being
And souls manifested themselves in the form
    of living beings and thus life came into existence.

(Rig.10.90.5)

With the coming into being of the dynamic
    universe,
The adaptation of the primordial matter was made
    in the primeval activities.
Thus began the changes in the atomic composition
    of matter.
In this colossal cosmic sacrifice, substances to
    sustain life were produced
As well as vegetation, grains, fruit, flowers and
    therapeutic substances that increase both energy
    and the life-span.
This made it possible for animal life to thrive.

(Rig.10.90.6)

In the course of the creation of the universe,
The Rig Veda, the Sama Veda, the Yajur Veda and
    the Atharva Veda were revealed.

(Rig.10.90.7)

Three kinds of animals came into being in the
    creation of the universe.
Belonging to the category of domestic animals were
    four types of animals:
1. horses, donkeys, etc, which possessed two sets of
    teeth, upper and lower.
2. cows, 3. goats, 4. sheep. These three possess
    only the lower set of teeth.

(Rig.10.90.8)

Because of his superior intellect, man is recognised
As the most advanced of all living beings
That came into existence at the creation of the
    universe.
Among them were also those who displayed divine
    qualities
Ascetics, hermits and sages
Well-versed in the knowledge of the Vedas
Who contemplated intensely on how to integrate
    and organise society.

(Rig.10.90.9)

The entire human race was visualised in the form
    of one human being.
Some of the questions were:
Into how many parts was this man-conception
    society divided?
What was his mouth? and what were his arms?
What represented his thighs and what were his feet?

(Rig.10.90.10)

In this conception of human society as a man,
    the highly intellectual Brahmanas (priestly
    class) were regarded as the mouth,
While the Kshatriyas, who were the administrators
    and warriors, represented the arms.
The Vaishyas who were artisans, traders and
    agriculturists corresponded to the abdominal
    region and the thighs,
While the Shudras of the society were associated
    with the feet of this man-conception society.

(Rig.10.90.11)

The moon denotes the mind of the Supreme Being,
While the sun His eyes.
The wind and breath issue from His ears,
While fire is produced from His mouth.
Similarly the moon is associated with the mind of
    the human being
And the sun symbolises his eyes.

(Rig.10.90.12)

This universe is conceived in the form of the
    intangible Supreme Being.
In the idealised schematic physical map of the
    universe, the central region, identical with the
    abdominal region, corresponds to the middle
    space, Antariksha.
The uppermost region, synonymous with the head,
    is depicted as the luminous outer space.
Its lowest region correlating with the feet is
    identified as the earth (Bhumi).
The entire planetary system of the universe
    gradually evolved according to this scheme.

(Rig.10.90.13)

The Supreme Being proceeded ahead with the
    symbolic yajna (task) of the creation of the
    universe,
A colossal, cosmic yajna in which solid
    substances displaying natural specific properties
    were offered as oblation, *Ahuti.*
In this cosmic yajna clarified butter or ghee
    symbolised spring, wood chips summer, and
    corn autumn.

(Rig.10.90.14)

In this cosmic yajna innumerable species of animal
    life came into existence
Of which the human race is most advanced.
Among mankind there were also seers and sages,
    hermits and ascetics, and intellectuals and
    scholars who set about the task of organising
    society by disciplining man, the animal.
In this imaginary symbolic yajna or sacrifice, there
    were seven enclosures or disciplines and twenty-
    one sticks, *samidha,* were utilised.

(Rig.10.90.15)

In the course of this symbolic cosmic yajna of the
    Supreme Being, the scholars and sages undertook
    the yajna (function) of organising society.
With this object they gave significance and priority
    to the formulation of fundamental laws and
    of behaviour that promoted social stability and
    cohesiveness.

(Rig.10.90.16)

The Creator is perfect
He possesses perfect power.
Whence is created perfect Nature?
The perfect universe derives life
From the perfect Creator.
Let us comprehend this perfect power
That bestows life on all beings.

(Atharva.10.8.29)

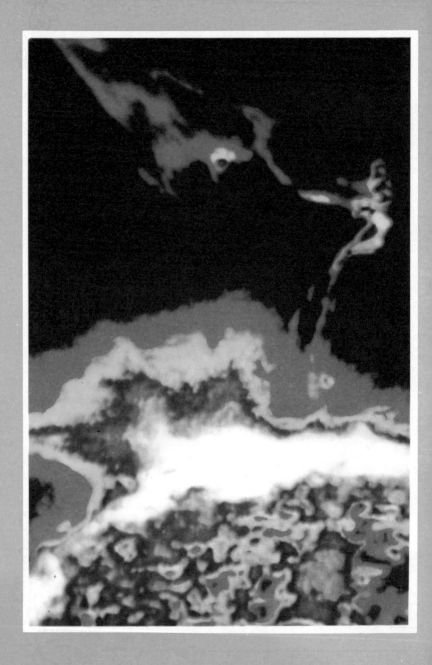

Cosmic Luminaries

Bringing with her life-sustaining blessings and giving life to the lifeless, the Divine Dawn imparts her brilliant lustre to the world. The dawn of today has appeared as the last one of the countless mornings that have gone by, but she is the first among the brilliant dawns that are to come.

(Rig.1.113.15)

Since the mighty cosmic vital powers procreate you in the womb of firmament, O cloud-bearing thunder winds (verily, these winds are vital), you shine like the starry heavens. You, the showerers of rain, illuminate the world with the flash of lightning.

(Rig.2.34.2)

The cosmic energy grows in space unbounded.
Many cosmic vapours impart strength to it.
The friend of mankind, it lies there within
The lap of nature's laws,
Enjoying the affection of sisterly cosmic rivers.

(Rig.3.1.11)

The cosmic energy is the generator of the
Universe, the embryo of waters, the leader of humans,
Most virile defender of the human race,
It remains ever illumined by its own radiance and
It provides sustenance for its beloved progeny.

(Rig.3.1.12)

Who knows what is the truth,
Or who may here declare it?
What is the proper path
That leads to the place of divine forces?
Only their inferior abiding places are perceived,
Not those which are situated
In superior mysterious locations.

(Rig.3.54.5)

The flames of this mighty cosmic energy descend
Like the hurled thunderbolt
Of the powerful Lord of Heaven.
Its fierce flame has the power of destroying
All material forms.
It consumes all dross
And superficial material forms,
As the fire consumes forests.

(Rig.6.6.5)

O Agni, the Cosmic Fire,
After deep contemplation and search,
The resolute seeker has discovered Thee
From the lotus-leaf lake, Cosmos,
Which is the head and support of the universe.

(Rig.6.16.13)

May Thy cosmic energy and cosmic radiations,
Which are discharged from heaven
And traverse the earth,
Leave us unharmed, when they pass by our
dwellings!
O appeaser of the wind,
Thou hast a thousand medicaments,
Inflict no pain upon us.

(Rig.7.46.3)

The Divine Poet
Holding the sweet melodious flute,
Reposing on the raging waves of the sea
Swiftly glides over the endless canopy of the sky.

(Sama.619)

This divine melody with uniforn. light
Spreads over the whole world.
It dissem␣nates the wisdom that inspires the brave.
And with this melody the pious devotees expand
Their field of knowledge.

(Rig.5.48.2)

The refreshing glow of Divine Consciousness sends
forth each busy man to his pursuit; she knows no
delay. O Dawn, rich in opulence, when you come,
birds that have flown forth rest no longer.

(Rig.1.48.6)

The dawn receives her beams from beyond the
rising place of the sun. Borne on a hundred auras
of glory, the auspicious dawn (physical and
spiritual) advances on her way to men in different
directions.

(Rig.1.48.7)

This immortal nature of the universe takes its place
In the hearts of mortal humans
And it also blesses them
In all their sacred aspirations.
With its spiritual radiance,
Reflecting by intense love
And knowing all secrets of wisdom,
It shines extensively.

(Rig.3.1.18)

Flute of Divine Love

Listen to the melodious music of the
divine poet.

He plays upon the flute of love, the
notes soar to high heaven and reach
the distant stars and dance on the
raging waves of the sea.

The earth, the sea, the sky, the stars are
all woven together by the soft strains of
the divine music.

Its vibrations echo through the
corridors of time in the endless
canopy of the sky.

(Sama.446)

The divine light of cosmic intelligence, which has golden radiance and a sweet voice, descends from heaven to inspire us thrice at our assemblies. Mayest Thou accept, O Lord of Divine Light, the praises recited by the eulogers and thereupon fulfil all our aspirations.

(Rig.3.54.11)

O the stream of consciousness divine,
These offerings are presented to you with adoration.
May you acknowledge and accept our praises,
And place us under your kind care.
May we ever take your shelter
As a traveller takes refuge under a tree.

(Rig.7.95.4)

O beautiful spiritual stream of divine light,
By your blessings people get both kinds
    of nourishment, physical and supramental.
May you be pleased, O protectress, to be
    considerate to us.
May you, the friend of the vital breaths, bestow
    riches on them who are sincere in devotion.

(Rig.7.96.2)

May the auspicious stream of divine light bestow
    spiritual fortune upon us.
May the faultless and active stream,
The giver of spiritual sustenance,
Think of us.
You have been already glorified

By people of divine vision.
May you be glorified by seekers of truth.

(Rig.7.96.3)

The constellations are set high
By Him in the heaven above us;
They are visible at night,
And disappear by day;
His laws remain always unviolated;
The moon during night moves on its splendour
By His command.

(Rig.1.24.10)

May those cosmic luminaries of equal splendour,
the sun, the dwarf-stars and the giant-stars, be
pleased today by our invocations, they who are sons
of Mother Infinity, luminous, purified by showers
of effulgence, who abandon none and are
irreproachable and unassailable.

(Rig.2.27.2)

The cosmic pair of day and night,
Come to cherish our noble deeds
Like two deers in a forest,
Like two wild cattle on fresh pastures,
Or like two swans flying in the sky.

(Rig.5.78.2)

Ruddy and luminous are the rays that bear the
auspicious expanding and illustrious dawn. Like a
valiant archer and like a swift warrior, scattering
enemies, she drives away the gloom.

(Rig.6.63.3)

The bright dawn heralds a new day,
Its rosy lances have opened
the golden gates of the Sun,
and lit up the path of action.

Awake, O man, the slumber
and darkness of the night are over.

May each dawn lead us from
triumph to triumph in the long journey of life!

(Rig.1.113.16)

O Lord of Solar Systems, may we be free from
   every bond!
O Lord of Cosmic Life, residing among Nature's
   bounties,
May Thy protection extend to mortals.
O Lord of Cosmic Light and Bliss, may we partake
   of Thy bounty.
O Heaven and Earth, may we live through your
   blessings!

(Rig.7.52.1)

May He, the showerer,
Be impregnator of the perennial plants,
For in Him rests the vitality
Of both the organic and inorganic worlds.
May the waters sustain me
For full one hundred years.
May you all shower blessings on us.

(Rig.7.103.6)

We solicit from you, O Divine Waters,
That pure, faultless, rain-shedding,
Sweet essence of the earth
Which the pious worshippers
Have first consecrated as a
Beverage of the Resplendent Lord.

(Rig.7.47.1)

O Divine Waters, the fire protects that wave,
Which is most rich and wherewith may
The sun and life-giving elements be pleased.
May we, devotees of Nature's bounties,
Share with you today your joy!

(Rig.7.47.2)

Unsoiled by dust, the golden cosmic chariots of the
clouds are shining like kindled flames, enlarging
themselves twofold and threefold at will. They are
invested with great strength and virile energies.

(Rig.6.66.2)

The clouds come in their colourful chariots
    with tremendous speed,
And of them, the brilliant ones shed the rains.

(Rig.8.7.28)

He is the one who shines without fuel
In the midst of cosmic waters,
And whom worshippers adore
At the place of worship.
May this Divine elixir,
Mixed with sweet celestial waters,
Be given to the soul to infuse vigour and heroism.

(Rig.10.30.4)

Knowledge, *Jnana*, is like the light of the sun.
The celestial region is equivalent to the ocean.
The sun is older than the earth.
Space has no dimensions.

(Yajur.23.48)

Perennial Flame of Life

See unity in diversity.
Behold one divine form appearing in
multiforms;

Immense is His vastness, unparalleled
is His glory.

All the countless earths, suns and
planets which are seen, and which are
beyond our perceptions exist under
His command.

Kindled in various forms, the perennial
flame is one;
Sprinkling the world with golden
beams at dawn;

Painting the evening clouds with
changing colours, the sun is one.

(Rig.8.58.2)

O Mother of Divine Powers, the life-force of the
earth, and the ensign of sacrificial works, may you
shine forth exalted. May you rise up, bestowing
reward for our devotion.
O, the Universally Respected Maid, make us
eminent among the people.

(Rig.1.113.19)

These stars, sons of Mother Infinity,
Are of huge dimensions, unparalleled
Provided with super brilliance,
Radiating out as if from innumerable eyes.
Whether far from or near to
The royal celestial bodies,
They appear as if beholding
From their innermost places
Both our vices and our virtues.

(Rig.2.27.3)

In this creation are held in balance the three
regions, terrestrial, interspatial and celestial, and the
three divine realms pertaining to body, mind and
spirit provided with three eternal functions—
physical, mental and transcendental. O sons of
Mother Infinity, the dwarf-stars, the sun and the
giant-stars, you are excellent and great since you
further the eternal law (of our Lord.).

(Rig.2.27.8)

The stream of spiritual awareness, limitless, shining,
issuing forth from the ocean of cosmic intelligence,
comes onward with a tempestuous roar.

(Rig.6.61.8)

May the solar systems, the Mother Infinity
The most loving sun, the ordainer,
And waters be extolled.
May the guardians of the world become our friends
And accept the elixir of devotion.

(Rig.7.51.2)

All the solar systems, all the vital principles,
All Nature's bounties, all the men of intellect,
The sun, the fire divine, the pair of twin divines,
Have been glorified by us;
May you all ever cherish us with blessings!

(Rig.7.51.3)

May He who augments the plants,
Augments the waters
And who rules with His divine magnanimity
Over the whole earth
Give us shelter and all sorts of felicity.
May He grant us the desired light at three seasons!

(Rig.7.101.2)

We use thee, O water,
So that thou makest us happy
By curing our diseases.
Thou rejuvenatest our potent energy,
To enable us to have more progeny.

(Sama. 1839

The brilliant stars, sons of Mother Infinity,
Are the upholders (of all gravitational bodies).
Movable or apparently stationary,
They are the protectors of the universe balancing
    the equilibrium,
Are provident in acts, dispellers of darkness,
True to eternal law, and acquitters of Nature's
    debts.

(Rig.2.27.4)

The divine cosmic embraces the entire Cosmic
    Creation.
For providing protection
Men crown Him alone with their offerings and
    hymns.
Possessed of golden flames, he distinguishes
Himself in both the regions of the universe
Like the minds hastily rustling
Through field of ripe corn.

(Rig.2.2.5)

May we prosper, invigorated by Thy cosmic laws,
which are generous, diverse in form, but with
similar functions.

(Rig.6.70.3)

The sky is like a barren cow,
And the earth is potent
The sky takes whatever shape it desires
The mother earth receives water from the father,
    the sky,
Who nourishes all living beings.

(Rig.7.101.3)

HYMNS ON Devotion

यो भूतं च भव्यं च सर्वं यश्चाधितिष्ठति
स्वर्ँयस्य च केवलं तस्मै ज्येष्ठाय ब्रह्मणे नमः

Most humbly we bow to Thee, O Supreme Lord,
At Thy command moves the mighty wheel of time.
Thou art eternal and beyond eternity,

(Atharva. 10.8.1.)

God Proclaims

"I am the prime source of contemplation and
   divine light.
I am the farseeing sage and centre of cosmic orbit.
I am the accomplisher of piercing intellect.
I am the past, the well-wisher of all
So many all behold me."

(Rig.4.26.1)

"I give the earth to the noble men;
Rain to the mortals who till the soil;
I set free the roaring waters;
The cosmic powers obey my orders."

(Rig.4.26.2)

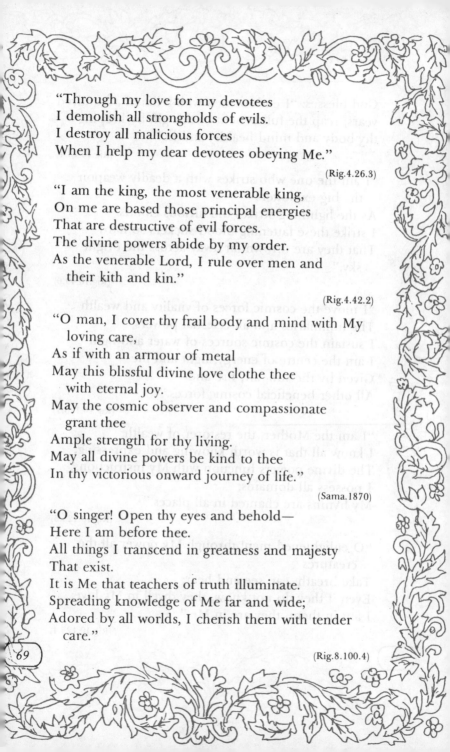

"Through my love for my devotees
I demolish all strongholds of evils.
I destroy all malicious forces
When I help my dear devotees obeying Me."

(Rig.4.26.3)

"I am the king, the most venerable king,
On me are based those principal energies
That are destructive of evil forces.
The divine powers abide by my order.
As the venerable Lord, I rule over men and
    their kith and kin."

(Rig.4.42.2)

"O man, I cover thy frail body and mind with My
    loving care,
As if with an armour of metal
May this blissful divine love clothe thee
    with eternal joy.
May the cosmic observer and compassionate
    grant thee
Ample strength for thy living.
May all divine powers be kind to thee
In thy victorious onward journey of life."

(Sama.1870)

"O singer! Open thy eyes and behold—
Here I am before thee.
All things I transcend in greatness and majesty
That exist.
It is Me that teachers of truth illuminate.
Spreading knowledge of Me far and wide;
Adored by all worlds, I cherish them with tender
    care."

(Rig.8.100.4)

God blesses: "I endow men with a life of a hundred years; reap the full benefit of this gift by keeping thy body and mind healthy and fit."

(Rig.10.18.4)

"I am the one who strikes with a deadly weapon the big exploiters
As the lightning strikes the furious clouds.
I strike these fattening blood-suckers so hard
That they are thrown far away across the bright sky."

(Rig.10.49.6)

"I move the cosmic forces of vitality and wealth
The luminaries and all celestial powers;
I sustain the cosmic sources of water and light
I am the centre of energy, light and life
Given by the sun, air, fire and
All other beneficial cosmic forces."

(Rig.10.125.1)

"I am the Mother, the restorer of wealth;
I know all that is worth knowing and expressing;
The divine powers function with My instructions;
I possess all domains;
My hymns are chanted in all places."

(Rig.10.125.3)

"O enlightened men! through My power all the creatures
Take breath, eat, see and hear;
Even if they do not know, they dwell in My love;
I am in them, they are in Me."

(Rig.10.125.4)

"Only I speak words that bring joy
To divinities and men;
I grant powers to men I favour;
I make them divine, the seer,
And men of perfection."

(Rig.10.125.5)

"I stretch the bow for the defender of cosmic life
So that his arrows may pierce the malicious powers.
I rouse the fury in the hearts of people
To battle against evils;
I penetrate the heaven and earth;
So that none violates my eternal laws."

(Rig.10.125.6)

"I breathe like the wind pervading all the regions;
I go beyond the heavens, beyond the limits of this
    vast earth.
I am invincible; none can defy me."

(Rig.10.125.8)

"I am the possessor of all riches.
Fain would I be a leader of my equals.
The supreme knowledge is my soul.
A friend of man is dear to my heart.
My heart is free from sorrow.
It has the capacity of a sea
A dwelling place for all beloved and friendly."

(Atharva.16.3.1)

"I am a terror to the wicked
As a tiger is to the flock of sheep.
The wicked are stunned to see me
As dogs become stunned when they are face to face
    with a lion."

(Atharva.4.36.6)

"I uphold the moisture-shedding cosmic ocean;
I uphold the effulgent region in the abode of
The eternal order.
Being the preserver of eternity,
I created all the regions of the universe."

(Rig 10.125.2)

No one whether he is Arya or non-Arya
Can break by means of his power
My potent eternal law.

(Atharva.5.11.3)

The four corners of the world pay homage to Me,
The waves of the ocean rise in obedience to Me.

(Atharva.9.2.7)

Within these, O enlightened man, I place heaven
        and earth;
All the centres of receiving wisdom and strength.
Inside thy heart I place celestial luminaries.
Mayest thou develop harmony with all
And enjoy life in full.

(Yajur.7.5.)

———◆———

He fashioneth these worlds and pervadeth them;
He beareth many a lapse of ours
And helpeth the pious in countless ways
This He doeth for the welfare of godly devotees;
He worketh unceasingly.
He guideth His devotee as the Sun
        regulateth seasons;
He is the observer of truth and dispeller of
        evil forces;
He is eternal and omniscient.
May He convey His devotees
Across the turbulent sea of life.

(Rig.3.16.4)

Reverence

Offer reverence to the Lord of Destiny who with
His sharp edge of justice severs the bondages of life
and death, liberates us from it and then delivers us
to Yama, the God of Death, who hands us over
back to destiny. Thus the circle of life and death
continues till ultimate liberation is achieved..

(Atharva.6.63.2)

To Him, the most exalted Supreme Lord,
    we offer reverence,
To Him who has made the wind
    as the life of Creation,
Who has made the Rays of Light as its eyes,
Who has made the Directions of Space
    as the organs of hearing.

(Atharva.10.7.34)

Reverence is to the mighty one.
Reverence sustains earth and heaven.
Reverence is to be offered to Nature's bounties;
Reverence overwhelms all evil
I offer penance in the form of reverence for sins,
Which I might have committed ever in my life.

(Rig.6.51.8)

We offer reverence to that Supreme Lord,
Who is bliss incarnate, peace incarnate,
Reverence to Him who bestows bliss and peace;
Reverence to Him who is benign, evermore benign.

(Yajur.16.41)

We offer obeisance to Thee, O Lord Supreme,
 the Ordainer,
Reverence to Thy fierce form of punitive power,
Obeisance to Thy divine bow and arrow,
By which Thou destroyest the wicked,
Reverence to Thy mighty arms
 that support the pious,
And assail the evil-minded.

(Yajur.16.1)

We offer our reverence to Nature's great bounties,
To those who are old, and to the young,
May we speak with the force at our command,
The glory of all Divine Powers.
May we not overlook any of them,
 however big (or small).

(Rig.1.27.13)

--- ◆ ---

The Supreme Lord is omnipresent like space
And Eternal like His word.
And all Nature's bounties have their repose in Him.
What will be there, who knows not this (divine
 principle)?
What will they do with the Veda?
But those who know it come close to the Lord.

(Atharva.9.10.18)

One God

He knows truth who knows
This God as One.
Neither second nor third
Nor fourth is He called;
Neither fifth nor sixth
Nor seventh is He called;
Neither eighth nor ninth
Nor tenth is He called.
He surveys all that breathes
And that breathes not.
He possesses the Power Supreme
He is the One,
The One Alone.
In Him All divine powers
Become the One Alone.

(Atharva.13.5.14-21)

May it be called Agni, Aditya, Vayu or
   Chandrama.
All are the names of the Supreme Spirit.
He is Brahma and Prajapati, the Supreme Lord of
   all
He is the ultimate power, protector of all beings.

(Yajur.32.1)

The perennial divine flame is one
That alone is kindled in various forms.
The sun is one and one alone, gives us
   warmth and life
It glows in vibrant colours through all that is
And breathes on earth and elsewhere.
The dawn is one, one alone, that beautifies the face
Of the universe, with its multicoloured lustre.

(Rig.8.58.2)

That one supreme reality has been styled
By various names by the learned seers,
They call one by many names.
They speak of Him as Indra, the Lord resplendent;
Mitra, the surveyor; Varuna, the virtuous;
   Agni, the adorable;
Garutaman, the celestial and well-sung;
Yama, the ordainer; Matarishvan, the cosmic breath.

(Rig.1.164.46)

Such is Thy greatness, O Liberal Lord!
   innumerable bodily forms are Thine.
Millions are in Thy million, or Thou art a billion
   in Thyself.

(Atharva.13.4)

He is one and one forever remaineth alone;
   believe it.
There is no second in God.

(Atharva.13.5.20)

That was Supreme in the worlds,
whence sprang the mighty God
of splendid power.

(Rig.10.120.1)

He is the One Lord of all holy service.

(Rig.1.100.7)

God is One the Lord of men,
exceeding far and wide.
We observe His holy laws.

(Rig.8.25.16)

There is no parallel to Him,
Whose glory is truly great.

(Yajur.32.3)

He is one.
Come together, you all, with power of spirit,
   to the Lord of heaven,
Who is the only One, the Guest of the people;
He the ancient desireth to come to the new;
To Him all pathways turn; really, He is One.

(Sama.372)

Glorious Lord

He is void of form, dwelleth in and
   out of everything with form and shape,
He is free from lapses, faults and impurities.
He transcendeth all the bodily facilities,
Being the Divine Poet He is Genius,
Maintaining peace and harmony He manifesteth
He sustaineth Creation in perfect order.

(Yajur.10.8)

He is the creator and controller
Our kith and kin;
He knows all the domains
All the places and origins.
All the enlightened souls
Attain immortal bliss in Him
And they reach the loftiest goal,
The ultimate salvation.

(Yajur.31.10)

He, the Lord of this cosmic energy,
Verily understandeth both, the warp and woof.
And in due time He is to tell what ought to be told.
He is the progenitor of all that is eternal
   and immortal.
He freely moveth hither and thither,
   above or below
With an eye on all dimensions and directions.

(Rig.6.9.3)

It is He who fashioneth the universe.
He possesseth multifaceted knowledge
He pervadeth all effulgent bodies,
He supporteth and sustaineth everything,
    being the Creator.
He seeth all and is exalted above all,
He is called 'The one without a second.'
In Him the soul, by means of the seven vital airs,
    enjoys bliss.
He accomplisheth for the souls things which
    yield happiness.
He, the Supreme Being, is to be worshipped.

(Yajur.17.26)

He is omnipresent and all powerful,
He ruleth over all the three regions,
Earth, mid-region and the celestial.
His one step is rooted in the deep dark mystery,
Beyond knowledge of mankind.

(Atharva.7.26.4)

He preserveth the indomitable universe,
Createth three regions, the earth, mid-region and
    the celestial.
He sustaineth and protecteth the sanctity of all
    vital functions
That keep the constancy of universal life.

(Sama.1670)

Seek Him everywhere
All is within His reach.
He knoweth all the things.
Full of wisdom,
He determineth
What ought to be done,
He is our only recourse,
All powers are vested in Him
He fulfilleth all our aspirations.
He is the source
Of all our nourishment and vigour,
Intelligence and strength.

(Rig.1.145.1)

He is an all-pervading, unchanging supreme being
Is the purest of the pure.
He is there in the hearts of holy men;
He inspireth sacred words like priests at the altar,
He is dear like a guest in the household.

He permeateth all eternal laws
And manifesteth throughout
The universal life forces—
The seas, the earth, and the mountains.

(Rig.4.40.5)

He manifesteth every form and is to be identified
With all Nature's richness.
His manifestation is seen everywhere in creation.
He moveth in forms by his creative charm.
His Divine Energy is the life-force
Which animates all created things.

(Rig.6.47.18)

The Only Path

I now realise the presence of the
Almighty Lord, the universal entity,
the one who is self-illuminated and
radiant like the sun.

He is beyond all darkness; with
this realisation, now I fear not even
death.

I proclaim, this is the path, the
only path to salvation, to the goal of
life, the eternal bliss.

(Yaju.31.18)

His eyes are all-seeing
His arms and feet stretch out in all spaces.
He is omniscient, the creator,
Invested with dynamic energy
He sustaineth the heaven, the earth
And everything else that is therein.

(Atharva.13.2.26)

He alone ruleth over men
The whole universe is His kingdom
He alone controlleth and directeth our five
    cognisant senses.

(Atharva.20.70.15)

He the sovereign of the universe,
Sustaineth the tree's stem (the universe)
    in the baseless region.
Its branches spread downward
Its roots rest high above.

(Rig.1.24.7)

None can ignore Him
None ventures to displease Him.
The obstructions cannot threaten His glory,
Neither those who tyrannize over men can do so
Nor the ones whose minds are bent upon wrong-
    doing.

(Rig.1.25.14)

He rescueth good human impulses
Causeth the spiritual Elixir to flow forcefully
(Love, truth, benevolence, austerity,
Contentment, generosity and knowledge).

(Rig.1.32.12)

Never is he defeated, who has been protected by
The virtuous, wise surveyor and law-giving Lord.

(Rig.1.41.1)

He gets prosperous whom divine powers take in
    their own arms,
And whom they defend from the malignant.
He overcomes all obstructions.

(Rig.1.41.2)

He is never vanquished. He easily gains
    the best treasures
Of the world.
He is also rewarded with brave offspring
    like himself.

(Rig.1.41.6)

Seated amidst all is the most glorious, all-wise
And vigilant Lord, breathing like a swan.
His mouth is immersed under the veil
    of cosmic vapours.

(Rig.1.65.5)

Bearing in his hand all might,
He abides and delegates His strength
    to the true seekers.
The sages realize him through deep meditation
    and sincere devotion.

(Rig.1.67.2)

He is the Resplendent Lord who createth
All this fast-moving universe.
He driveth away to oblivion the dark evil forces.
He snatcheth off the riches of the malicious
Like a hunter striking his prey.

(Rig.2.12.4)

To Him, the most exalted Supreme Lord,
    offer reverence,
To Him, who rules the past, the present
    and the future,
Who presides over the entire universe,

Who is the overall sovereign of the world
   and cosmos,
Who is above the reach of Time and Death,
Who is immutable and absolute bliss.

(Atharva.10.8.1)

God, the Beloved

O most revered and resplendent
And loving adorable Lord;
Surely Thou bestowest on Thy devotees
All the attributes that vest in Thee.
May Thy love fill our body and soul.
Thou alone fillest man's empty life
Turning it into an ocean of fullness.
Let us dedicate the best in us at Thy feet,
And surrender our ego in Thy service.

(Rig.1.1.6)

O Lord of material and spiritual powers,
Thou art powerful and kind as kinsmen.
We solicit friendship and affection from Thee.
Desirous of possessing wisdom, we have
Recourse to Thee for full protection.

(Rig.4.41 7)

O Lord, will I ever be worthy
Of Thy love again, or am I lost? In my dreams
   I converse and pray
Let me be with Thee, face to face, O my beloved
   Lord, let my cup of happiness be filled to
   the brim.
Whenever I search my heart in my dreams
   I encounter and converse with Thee.

(Rig.7.82.6)

Our hearts full of love for Thee
We pray, with all humility for the purity of Thy
    resplendent glory.
The flame in our heart has the soul of
Thy omniscient aurora, the source of all conscience.
We pray to Thee, the progenitor of all that exists,
With hearts full of love.

(Rig.8.43.31)

O Radiant Self, bless that my virtues and deeds
    conform to Thy wishes.
May love for Thee above the selfish ego rise.
Bless me with a vision to transcend the barriers of
    'thine and mine'
Let there be neither me nor mine, only Thou and
    Thine.

(Rig.8.44.23)

The Supreme Lord is too near
To be abandoned,
Too close to be witnessed.
Behold Nature's splendour
And the Lord's divine poetry
Both are beyond decay and death.

(Atharva.10.8.32)

Be Thou our Saviour;
Looking after and showing mercy to the
    worshippers
Friend, Father, Fatherliest of fathers,
Who for the loving worshipper provides all
    comforts.

(Rig.4.17.17)

These offerings have been made by us with
   adoration. May the Goddess of Speech
   be pleased with each of our prayers;
Under Thy protection, Thou most beloved!
   May we approach Thee for shelter.

(Rig.8.95 5)

Supported by Thee, O God! may we answer all who
   defy us.
Thou art ours and we are Thine.

(Rig.8.12 32)

Draw thy Friend to Thee like a cow for milking:
O Singer, wake up God the Lover!
Move the Hero for the gift of bounty
Like the vessel filled brimful with treasure.

(Rig.10.42.2)

O Effulgent One, Thou hast made the sun, ageless
   star to mount the sky conferring light on men.
Thou, O Effulgent One, art the people's Light;
Best and dearest art Thou by our side;
Think of the singer, give him life.

(Rig.10.156.4)

I, the devotee,
Am standing in the midst of
Deep waters,
Yet I feel thirsty.
O Blissful Lord,
Have mercy,
Slake my thirst,
And bless me with happiness and contentment.

(Rig.7.89.4)

Adoration

O Adorable Supreme Lord!
Thou art the Protector of the unprotected
Cosmic sacrifice of the creation.
May Thy blessings from all sides
Assuredly reach the seeker of truth.

(Rig.1.1.4)

O Resplendent Lord, the wielder of adamantine
    justice,
Thou art the co-ordinator of all elements.
At Thy command all cosmic energies are harnessed
To the richly-decorated canopy of the universe,
And they come speedily to our help everywhere.

(Rig.1.7.2)

Great art Thou God, greater than the greatest,
Beyond measure,
Thou art boundless, much beyond the celestial
    space,
Surely, Thou art the source of all greatness.

(Rig.1.8.5)

Infinite are Thy powers and capacity to draw
And discharge like oceans.
Thou protectest the entire creation by Thy radiance.
Like oceans Thou collectest and
Like.the sun-rays Thou disperseth.

(Rig.1.8.7)

O Omniscient God, Thy glory enlightens the
  celestial,
Terrestrial and all the other regions of the universe.

(Rig.1.25.20)

The man whom Thou protectest
In the internal and external conflicts
Becomes free from all vices,
And attains eternal wisdom.

(Rig.1.27.7)

O all-wise and all-seeing God,
Direct the ignorant worshipper;
And help him to revert to acts
Which will reclaim him.
Always Thou protectest in times of conflict—
Those who are feeble, but tread the path of truth;
Against those who are strong but tumble on the
  wrong path.

(Rig.1.31.6)

O adorable God!
Thou liftest up mortal man
To superb immortality
By providing sustenance.
Thou bestowest happiness and sustenance
On the wise
In both the lives,
The present and the one to come.

(Rig.1.31.7)

Creative Fancy

Nature's beauty is an art of God.
Let us feel the touch of God's invisible
hands, in everything beautiful,
By the first touch of His hand rivers
throb and ripple.
When He smiles the sun shines, the
moon glimmers, the stars twinkle, the
flowers bloom,
By the first rays of the
rising sun, the universe is stirred;
The shining gold is sprinkled on the
smiling buds of rose;
The fragrant air is filled with sweet
melodies of singing birds,
The dawn is the dream of God's
creative fancy.

(Rig.1.6.3)

Adorable Supreme Lord,
Thou art so gracious to us that we feel
Thou art our Father, our life-giver,
And we are Thy close kinsmen.
Invincible as Thou art,
Thou lovest brave people.
Defender as Thou art of the pious,
So things most prized—
Speed unto Thee in hundreds,
Why, in thousands.

(Rig.1.31.10)

We call on Thee, Lord of Hosts, the Sage of Sages;
The most reputed of all;
The Supreme King of Spiritual Knowledge,
O Lord of Spiritual Wisdom! Listen to us with
    Thy graces;
And in the place of worship.

(Rig.2.23.1)

I bow down to Thee just like a son
Who bows to greet his father.
Mayest Thou grant Thy healing cures to me.

(Rig.2.33.2)

With Thy excellent guidance
Thou leadest a person and protectest him,
No danger would overtake him
Who offers Thee his offerings.
Thou punishest the one who despises knowledge
Thou doest humble the wrath of a violent man,
Supreme is Thy greatness, O Lord Supreme.

(Rig.2.23.4)

None can break Thy dispensations,
  O Supreme Creator,
Even the wild beasts roaming the desert in search
  of water
Are refreshed by the thirst-allaying rivers
Which Thou hast endowed.
Woods are there for birds to feed on.

(Rig.2.38.7)

With great reverence I proclaim the truth—
That whatever exists exists by Thy blessing.
That Thou art the Master of all this Universe
Of all the wealth that is in Heaven or on Earth.

(Rig.4.5.11)

O Divine Creator, surely first Thou grantest
  immortality
To the highly elevated man, dedicated to learning
  and devotion;
Thereafter, Thou completely shieldest him with
  Thy protection
And continuously showerest Thy blessings on him.

(Rig.4.54.2)

None can ever obstruct or deviate Thee from Thy
  way,
O sustainer of the whole world,
Thy touch is widely visible over the extent of
  the earth,
And the magnitude of the heaven.

(Rig.4.54.4)

Restless Swan

Life is a perennial search for truth.

The restless swan—the human soul—is on the journey infinite to find the truth.

For thousands of years he is flying and flying with his wings outstretched and the will to reach the unscaled heights of heaven, higher and ever higher;

The restless swan is on the journey infinite.

He has all the blessings of the mighty God, his piercing eyes perceive all the universe below, yet he knows no rest, no peace and keeps flying higher and ever higher;

The restless swan is on the journey infinite.

(Rig.10.8.18)

seed growing by the

Thou raisest Thy worshippers to the highest level,
Just as the sun riseth above the vast clouds.
They are provided dwellings filled with all comforts,
The more they rise in their levels, the more
Thou fillest their hearts with devotion;
And the more they are in possession of Thy love,
The more they obey Thy command.

(Rig.4.54.5)

O Inspirer of Benevolent Deeds!
The divine powers honour Thee
As the benefactor of all
Thou art the inspirer of men and mankind.

(Rig.6.16.1)

All the cosmic forces adore Thee, O Lord
The cosmic fire, abiding in mysterious darkness.
Let the Immortal Adorable Divine preserve us with
His protection; afford us all provisions.

(Rig.6.9.7)

O doer of great deeds, performer of cosmic
  sacrifice.
Thou knowest the paths and ways
And also how to travel and function with speed.

(Rig.6.16.3)

Wheresoever and upon whomsoever
Thy kindness is directed,
Thou makest him eminent
And givest uncommon vigour;
And in his heart Thou makest Thine own abode.

(Rig.6.16.17)

Thou blessest this adoration, O Self-sustaining Lord,
Thou art heartily appreciated.
That we succeed in retaining what we have earned
And are able to acquire more through Thy grace.

(Rig.7.86.8)

Thou art divine amongst mortal men, and art
preserver of their sacred deeds. Therefore,
we worship Thee in every benevolent task.

(Rig.8.11.1)

Thou art the same in any place.
Thou art the Supreme Lord
Amid all the people of creation.
In fray and fight we call on Thee.

(Rig.8.11.8)

O Lord, Thou bestowest upon the true seeker the
joys of attainment, a body free of desires, a mind
pure and virtuous and an intellect sharp and
discriminate.

(Sama.306)

We humbly invoked Thee
From far-off places
And besought Thee to protect us everywhere,
And emancipate us from decay and death.
Our invocations were listened to.
And from all directions
Thy blissful benedictions
Were showered on us.

(Atharva.19.52.3)

O Lord of Cosmic Light and Energy,
Thou Thyself bindest Thyself to cosmic orders.

(Yajur.4.16)

Eternity is sky, eternity is mid-air,
Eternity is mother, father and son.
Eternity is all that exists.
Eternal is the social consciousness.
Eternal are all that have been born
And shall be born.

(Rig.1.89.10)

Invocation

Day and night, we approach Thee, with reverential homage through sublime thoughts and noble deeds.

(Rig.1.1.7)

Remember, when God's earnest seeker
Pursues the ultimate salvation.
He ascends from one summit to a higher one.
The Lord firmly supporteth him at every step
    forward.
God's loving care and guidance enlighten his path.
He is bestowed with divine blessings.

(Rig.1.10.2)

With bent head and folded hands
Every hour of the day and night
Surrendering all at the Divine Feet,
The devotee must pray to the Lord:
"O Lord! bless and guide me on the path to
    self-revelation."

(Rig.1.11.1)

O Supreme Lord, speed us on with pure and exalted love, with priceless blessings; bestow upon us wealth abundant, thereby enabling us to tide over all the ills of life; dower us with charming eloquence, good fortune and fair name.

(Rig.3.1.19)

Come, O Lord, towards us and bring along with
Thee the divine powers for participation and
enjoyment.

(Rig.6.16.44)

Come, O Universal Divine Power,
Hear our invocations; and be established in our
    hearts
As if Kusha, the sacred grass, is used as a seat.

(Rig.6.52.7)

We hurry to unite with the Lord divine:
    as rivers unite with the ocean
May we not drift to lands unfertile in search of
    things that are fertile
May we on Thy banks dwell, live and love each
    other well.

(Rig.4.58.6)

At the break of day invoke the Lord Supreme,
Lord of Cosmic Light and Plasma,
    the pair of twin Divines,
The Lord of Riches and Nourishment,
Lord of Bliss and Vitality.

(Atharva.3.16.1)

Pious souls, may you sing sacred hymns with
intense devotion, like flying swans and associated
with Nature's bounties, partake in the sparkling
glory of the Supreme Lord.

(Yajur.6.20)

Friends! Let us with one accord offer reverence and
oblation to the Lord.

(Yajur.36.19)

Dedication

To Him we dedicate our life
Who is the giver of life's breath, power and vigour,
Whose command all the Divine Powers obey.
Who is the Lord of Death whose shadow is
    life immortal.

(Rig.10.121.2)

To Him we dedicate our life who ruleth
whatever breathes, moves, or is still,
Who is the God of man and cattle.

(Rig.10.121.3)

'To Him, to Him alone',
Whose grandeur is reflected in the snow-clad
    mountains,
Whose songs of glory are echoed by the thundering
    ocean waves,
Whose expanse is confirmed by these extended
    directions which are like his arms,
Whose cosmic arms embrace the whole universe,
We dedicate our life and offer obeisance.

(Rig.10.121.4)

May the earth's Creator never harm us,
For He maketh the heavens and observeth the
  norm.
He releaseth the powerful and crystal waters.
To what God other than Him could we dedicate
  our life?

(Rig.10.121.9)

O Father of all creations, Thou alone embracest
  all these created things
And none else granteth the wishes of our prayer.
To what God, other than Him, could we dedicate
  our life?

(Rig.10.121.10)

He maketh the heavens and the earth strong,
He establisheth the dwelling place of the sky
  and of the gods,
He measureth the regions in mid-air.
To what God other than Him, could we dedicate
  our life?

(Atharva.4.2.4)

Firm Resolve

May this mind of mine
Which travels too far,
Which is the light of lights,
The only source of all wisdom
Which wanders to far-off places,
Whether I am asleep or awake,
Resolve on what is noble.

(Yajur.34.1)

May this mind of mine
By which assiduous and intellectual persons
Perform their God-assigned tasks
In all social assemblies and congregations
The spirit that lies in all creatures
Resolve on what is noble.

(Yajur.34.2)

May this mind of mine
Which is the source of highest knowledge
The source of wisdom
The source of the power of memory
The immortal flame of consciousness
Within all living beings
Without which no action whatever is performed
Resolve on what is noble.

(Yajur.34.3)

May this mind of mine
Which guides men like a good charioteer
Who controls fleet-footed horses with the reins
That which abides in the heart
Most swift and vigorous
Resolve on what is noble.

(Yajur.34.6)

May this mind of mine
That immortal spirit
By which all the past and present
World is comprehended
By which all the benevolent works
Are promoted and conducted through
Seven sense-organs
Resolve on what is noble.

(Yajur.34.4)

May this mind of mine
Which imbibes and holds the teachings
Imparted by the Rig, the Sama, the Yajur
Like spokes in the nave of a chariot-wheel
In which all thoughts of the living world
Lie interwoven
Resolve on what is noble.

(Yajur.34.5)

Peace Eternal

O Lord of Peace!
May there be peace in heaven and
earth,

May the waters, plants and herbs give
health and life to us,

May all the divine and material forces
be merciful to us.

May all the forces of material and
spiritual world be benevolent to us.

May peace itself bestow eternal joy on
us.

(Yajur.36.17)

Divine Assurance

All the powers of existence help those who are
involved in good benevolent work.

(Rig.1.3.9)

His bounteous gifts, His divine wisdom and wealth
Are given to His devotees as spontaneously
As ripe fruit drops from a loaded branch.

(Rig.1.8.8)

God is all in all, but only those devotees who
completely and in full faith surrender to Him find
His helping hand ever ready to guide and protect
them.

(Rig.1.95.6)

A firm faith in God is the only ray of hope that
penetrates this gloom of fear and ignorance.

(Rig.2.27.11)

The one who has faith and trust in the Lord
invariably conquers adverse circumstances and
emerges the winner, rich with bounty in the
struggle of life.

(Rig.4.23.4)

The one who dedicates his life to the service of the
Lord, whom the Lord takes in His loving fold, finds
himself twice blessed by the supreme celestial
powers and basks happily in the sunshine of God's
love.

(Rig.5.37.5)

The pious soul who is ever awake in God is loved
    by divine hymns,
The sacred songs seek him;
Addressing him the Blissful Lord assures,
"I shall ever be your friend, fast and true."

(Rig.5.44.14)

The wise innocent man, engrossed in selfless service
to mankind, is ever dear to God. He attains oneness
with God.

(Rig.6.2.2)

Those parents who offer oblations to God are
blessed with the privilege of bringing up brave,
fearless children.

(Rig.8.4.6)

The man who has firm faith that God is abiding
within the heart and soul of every man finds
enough strength to surmount and bear the greatest
of tragedies with a sublime contented smile.

(Atharva.20.17.6)

A mind that is in the state of perpetual worship
is never overshadowed by the dark clouds of
sorrow.

(Rig.10.43.6)

O Resplendent Lord!
Thou never lettest Thy devotee
The philanthropist be humbled,
Thy bounty is showered on him
More and ever more.

(Sama.300)

Blessings

Bless me, O Lord of Resplendence, with prosperity
And lustre of fame and magnificent majesty,
So that I may shine like the blazing sun in the sky.

(Atharva.10.3.17)

O Cosmic Vital Physician, greatest amongst all born,
The mightiest of the mighty,
Wielder of adamantine justice,
Carry us safely beyond danger,
And cure sickness of the body and the mind.

(Rig.2.33.3)

O Divine Architect of Creation, the Dextrous Doer,
The Possessor of Wisdom, the Observer of Truth,
Bestow upon us those things which are necessary
    for our preservation.
O wise sages, associated with vital elements, make
    us joyful.

(Rig.3.54.12)

Bless that we be sinless in Thy judgement,
    O the Supremely Virtuous Lord,
Thou showest mercy even to the sinner.
Bless, that we obey the commandments of
    Mother Eternity.
May She preserve us with Her blessings.

(Rig.7.87.7)

O Glorious Lord, Giver of nourishing food,
Bless us with a happy life, peace and prosperity.
May the Divine Architect with His evermoving
   cosmic chariot
Continue giving wealth, wisdom and
   happiness to us.

(Rig.1.89.6)

O Lord Suprascient, may we master
The well-disciplined wealth of wisdom and vigour.
Bestow on us excellent posterity.
Mayest Thou, the Lord of all, listen to our
   invocations
Addressed to Thee through divine hymns.

(Rig.2.24.15)

May the Lord of Light and Bliss grant us prosperity
May the guiding spirit of the firmament
And Goddess of Riches grant us prosperity
May the Adorable and Resplendent Lord prop us;
O, spirit of invincible fullness,
Thou bestowest all prosperity upon us.

(Rig.5.51.14)

O All-wise Lord, bring us wealth with good posterity.
O performer of benevolent deeds, destroy
the demoniac forces.

(Rig.6.16.29)

Grant infinite happiness and most agreeable
wealth to the person who uses his riches
for the service of others.

(Rig.6.16.33)

O Supreme Lord, of both the earth and heaven,
Bring them to Thy threefold jurisdiction.
Refulgent in Thy undecaying splendour,
Invest both the worlds with brilliance.

(Rig.7.5.4.)

Bless that our prosperity lead us to peace;
The social discipline lead us to harmony;
The intellectual pursuits result in sublimity;
The aim of our riches is harmony varied in all
    nature and society.
May the varied systems of law and order
Result in all round peace, progress and prosperity.

(Rig.7.35.2),

Bless that the people of creative endeavour,
The people in charge of sustenance
Bring in peace for society.
May the wide earth, with all its provisions,
Be productive enough of peace and prosperity.
May the vast heaven and earth be for our peace
    and harmony.
May the mountains inspire peace and reverence.
May our pious invocations of Nature's bounties
    secure us peace.

(Rig.7.35.3)

The fire with the splendour of flames provides peace.
The cosmic light and bliss, and the divine twins
Secure peace.
May the impetuous wind give our body and mind
Peaceful sustenance.

(Rig.7.35.4)

Bless that the heaven and earth,
Invoked from the earliest times
Be helpful to our happiness;
The mid-space be for our happiness
With health and charming appearance;
The herbs and forest trees provide us happiness;
The victorious divine powers of distant regions
Favour us with felicity.

(Rig.7.35.5)

Thou manifestest Thy glory in firmament, waters,
Rocks, forests and plants of the earth,
O self-effulgent Lord of the cosmic world.

(Rig.2.1.1)

Bless that the sun, with extensive radiance,
Rise for peace
May the four quarters of the horizon
Be auspicious for peace and harmony.
May the firm-set mountains bless us with happiness
May the rivers provide us with nourishing water
And make our fields fertile.

(Rig.7.35.8)

Bless that the Mother Infinity, through holy
   observances,
Bring us happiness.
The All-pervading and the Nourishing One,
Bring us happiness.
May the cosmic waters be propitious to us.
May the wind blow for our happiness.

(Rig.7.35.9)

May the Divine Refulgent Lord, the Saviour,
Bless us for our peace.
May the Radiant Lord provide inspiration to us.
May the clouds inspire us to attain harmony.
May the Sovereign Lord of the Universe bless us for
   happiness.

(Rig.7.35.10)

May the divine universal bounties bring us peace,
May the divine speech, with holy thoughts, be
   gracious,
May the priests assist us at our sacred works
And the liberal and large-hearted givers
Be conducive to our peace and stability,
May the celestial, terrestrial and heavenly powers
Provide us with peace and happiness.

(Rig.7.35.11)

May the sustainers of eternal truths
Be conducive to harmony.
May our thoughts and actions
Contribute to our happiness,
May the virtuous men of experience and wisdom
Confer peace and progress on us,
May the ancient sages be kind to us
And respond to our invocations in our social
   ceremonies.

(Rig.7.35.12)

O Divine, Unborn, the One-Footed One
(Whose one foot measures the entire universe)
Bless us for peaceful existence,
Bless that the clouds of mid-space shower prosperity
The cosmic oceans provide harmony;
The heart and power, born of water, be gracious;
The mid-space, the sky, guarded by divine powers
Provide us with happiness.

(Rig.7.35.13)

O Supreme Lord
Endow me to-day
With that divine vision
Which the enlightened and realised
   ancient sages enjoy.

(Yajur.32.14)

Bless that Mother Nature be kind to us;
The heavens give us peace
The earth be gentle;
Gentle be the waters that flow;
Gentle be the plants and herbs that grow.
May the past be kind; the future benign.

(Atharva.19.9.1)

Divine Guidance

Establish Thyself in the innermost chamber of our heart.
Let the smoke of ill-thoughts be dispersed.
Enable us to see Thy spotless spiritual radiance.

(Rig.1.36.9)

O Lord, grant us and our men of faith,
That they be inspired to devote their life to the service of humanity and work for the welfare of mankind.

(Rig.1.61.16)

O Supreme Creator, grant us spiritual strength and purity
That we may never be tempted to commit sin,
And be guided by Thy light.
Help us to rest all our life
In the clasp of Thy everlasting arms.
And earn the right to be the recipients of worldly joys.

(Rig.5.82.6)

Dear Lord, grant us wisdom to enjoy Thy blessings.
These may be showered on us, who obey Thy order.
May the wind filled with fragrance blow softly.
May the rivers flow calmly, echoing sweet melody,
And the plants grow their yield with fresh vitality
For us, the law-abiding devotees.

(Yajur.13.27.29)

O Resplendent Lord, bless us with that divine
vision, which gives valiant spirit, name and fame.

(Rig.7.1.5)

Bless us, that liberated from sin,
We perform diligent service
Like a dedicated servant to Thee,
O Divine Dispenser of Blessings,
O Sagacious Lord, give wisdom to the unwise
Guide Thine worshipper on the path of prosperity.

(Rig.7.86.7)

The sun, the sky, the moon, the stars
    move in celestial harmony,
Never violating the canons
    of the Divine Powers.

Let man learn his lesson from Nature's theme
Live in peace and harmony
No matter how strong or how wise,
Live within the realms of the Divine Scheme.

(Rig.10.33.9)

O God Almighty,
Lead our mind towards the virtuous path.

(Rig.10.20.1)

O Lord of Universe, bless that our speech be
eloquent, vigorous and faultless.

(Rig.10.98.3)

O Resplendent Effulgent Lord!
Lead me whither go the sages
Versed in spiritual knowledge and rigorous
    discipline;
Give me insight to follow the righteous path
Traversed by the sages and seers.
I submit to Thee, O Lord,
Let the kindly light guide me to immortal bliss.

(Atharva.19.43.1

May the luminous sun take me to the realm of
spiritual heights and may it enlighten my mind with
its bright light.

(Atharva.19.43.3)

O divine Agni! Self-refulgent God, please lead
us on the path of virtue for the acquisition of
physical and spiritual wealth.
Please remove the sinful acts from us which
make us stray. Bless us that we remain ever engaged
in uttering Thy praises.

(Yajur.11.16)

Torture us not, O Lord of Strength, by making us
victims to nescience by turning us into cravens.
Doom us not to abject submissiveness and the itch
for unbridled captiousness.

(Rig.3.16.5)

Prayers

We seek Thy protection and grace, O Lord.
Though knowing that Thou rulest over earth
and sky
And commandest the waves and the clouds
we are often gripped by panic and despair.
Mayest Thou ordain all fierce forces to be benign
and merciful towards us.
May nothing evil and untoward befall us
And may we all prosper always. (Yajur.36.22)

O Supreme God, bless us to appreciate the
benevolent wisdom of the divine powers and be
like them;

Help us to imbibe the generosity and their loving
kindness.

Bless us with a long life that we may rejoice with
abundance of their bounteous glory and repose;

Help us to be contented, and filled with love and
peace like them.

(Rig.1.89.2)

O enlightened pious souls,
Let us resolutely hear with our ears
What is good;
Let us see with our eyes
What is good;
Let us enjoy
The divinely ordained term of our life,
With firm limbs and healthy body,
And full satisfaction of mind
In the service of the Supreme Lord.

(Rig.1.89.8)

Endowed with all Thy glories in heaven and earth
On mountains, in plants and in waters
O Illustrious Blissful Lord!
Mayest Thou be considerate, benign, and accept
 our homage.

(Rig.1.91.4)

O Gracious Lord, possessor of all the graces as
 Thou art,
Bless us with Thine graces.
Everyone, verily, invokes Thee repeatedly
O Gracious Lord, be Thou our champion in all
 solemnity.

(Rig.7.41.5)

Bless that the omnipresent cosmic powers,
The abodes of the eternal laws of the Supreme
 Creator,
And the friendly and venerable Divine Powers,
Confer upon us auspicious and honourable wealth
That comprises brave children
And may we possess the ability to accomplish
 noble acts.

(Rig.10.36.13)

Shower on us Thy torrential bliss, O Lord,
Save us by sending us the deluge of Thy
 benedictions;
Thou givest without asking.
We can only pray to Thee;
Thou returnest our helplessness and ingratitude
With nothing but a rainbow of Thy compassion;
Bless us, Master, bless us.

(Rig.1.7.7)

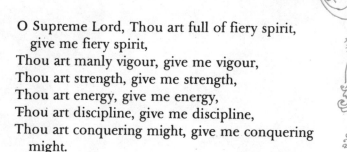

O Supreme Lord, Thou art full of fiery spirit,
  give me fiery spirit,
Thou art manly vigour, give me vigour,
Thou art strength, give me strength,
Thou art energy, give me energy,
Thou art discipline, give me discipline,
Thou art conquering might, give me conquering
  might.

(Yajur.19.9)

O God, bless that the faculties of our mind, intellect
and body function like two wheels of a chariot that
speeds us on the way to perfect fulfilment.

(Rig.1.3.2)

Rise to protect us, like the sun that heals.
Thou art the giver of sustenance,
We invoke Thee with devotion and earnestness.

(Rig.1.36.13)

Youthful and most Resplendent Lord.
Protect us from evil forces
And from our malevolence within.
Protect us from ferocious animal instincts
And blind forces that seek to destroy us.

(Rig.1.36.15)

O Mighty Adorable God, keep us away from the
wicked, voracious and malevolent enemy that
brings us trouble.

(Rig.1.189.5)

Thus protected by Thee,
May we force a way through our enemies,
Like torrents of water.

(Rig:2.7.3)

Surrender

Work and live as an act of offering to
achieve immortal fame and complete
satisfaction of having lived a successful
life.

Remember you are the child of
immortality and that all life is but an
offering;

Never forget that the nectar-honey of
the flower of mercy is for those who
sacrifice, and the life offered is the life
accepted.

Let the sacred flame of divine fire shine
brightly in your soul.

(Atharva.15.17.10)

The Supreme Lord comes to help all in their
   struggle,
Where the flashing arrows of passions are hurled
   all around;
Come with Thy powerful protection, O Lord,
Make us triumphant in our inner conflicts through
   Thy grace.

(Rig.4.41.11)

Guard us from the malignant and preserve us from
   the wicked, O Victorious One.
May our offerings reach Thee free from dishonour.

(Rig.6.15.12)

Preserve us, O Omniscient Lord, from sin;
O Poet of the Divine Verses, protect us from
   the malevolent.

(Rig.6.16.30)

Defend us from sin and from the malevolent
mortal, who threatens us with murderous weapon.

(Rig.6.16.31)

Subject us not, O adorable bounties, to evil
   creatures
Which are like wolves, or robbers, or the ones who
   harm us.
Verily, you alone can guide and rule
Our vigour and speech aright.

(Rig.6.51.6)

God the Rescuer, God the Saviour, Mighty God;
Happily invoked at each invocation;
God powerful, invoked by all;
May God the Bounteous confer on us blessings.

(Sama.333)

Let Him, who is Master of all Knowledge,
Take it on Himself to guard the common man
From evil in every possible way,
From whatever quarter it might come
Like a snake.

(Rig.6.75.14)

May the Divine Powers keep away from me such
of my kinsfolk
Who are full of intolerant jealousy towards me,
Be this heartfelt prayer of mine my invulnerable
armour.

(Rig.6.75.19)

While residing in these earthly dwellings,
O Venerable Lord,
May we enjoy Thy protection,
And win favours from Mother Infinity
And acquire blessings from Thy grace.

(Rig.7.88.7)

Free us from bonds, inherited from our forefathers
And from those for which we are ourselves
responsible.
O Sovereign Lord, liberate us
From our animal passions, like a calf set free from
its tether.

(Rig.7.86.5)

The Supreme Lord is too near
To be abandoned,
Too close to be witnessed.
Behold the nature's splendour
And the Lord's divine poetry
Both are beyond decay and death.

(Atharva.10.8.3)

Free us, O Virtuous Lord, from all snares
That bind us from above
And those that bind us from below;
Keep away from us evil dreams and misfortunes;
And then let us pass into the world of virtue.

(Atharva.7.83.4)

O Lord, protect us from all that we are afraid of;
Drive away our enemies and foes;
In Thy security we seek shelter;
Lead us to ample room, spacious, secure,
Happy and full of sunshine
In Thy mighty arms, we seek fearless shelter.

(Atharva.19.15.4)

Pray grant me freedom from insecurity, depression
and misery, O Lord of the Universe.

(Yajur.5.9)

Enable us to overcome our inner feelings of
enmity.

(Yajur.12.43)

O Lord Supreme, Embodiment of all that is vast
    and benevolent,
Mayest Thou be ever merciful to us;
Mayest Thou leave Thy weapon, the Vajra, the
    thunderbolt, on the lofty summit of this cosmic
    tree;
And come with Thy bow and string on this earth
    for protection of the pious and faithful.

(Yajur.16.51)

O Lord, confer Thy blessing that we suffer no
afflictions or infirmities in the midst of our life-
span.

(Rig.1.89.9)

Keep us away from disease and from those men
who are non-believers and adverse to us.
Bless us with incessant protective bounties.

(Rig.1.189.3)

O Lord, the Sustainer of the Universe,
Do not deprive us of the sight of the sun.
May our brave sons subdue our adversaries.
May we be multiplied with continued progeny.

(Rig.2.33.1)

May the Supreme Creator on our west,
On the east, on the north and
On the south bestow on us
Everything worth having and
Bestow upon us long life.

(Rig.10.36.14)

O Lord of the Vast Universe, grant me capacity to
receive and absorb the strength of those
innumerable divine forces such as the sun, the
moon, the stars and nebulae who are travelling
around in the cosmos assuming various shapes and
forms.

(Atharva.1.1.1)

Bless us that we become pure and pious
And gather divine lustre
Like cosmic luminaries.
Bless us that we overcome all obstacles
And live a hundred years of glorious life
Along with our brave comrades.

(Atharva.12.2.2)

O God among mortals; Thou guardest the holy law
In holy rites, we invoke Thee
Bless my mouth with sweet voice;
Bless my nostrils with pure breath;
Bless my ears with good hearing.
May my hair not turn grey before time.
May my teeth not decay.
May my arms be strong.

(Atharva.19.60.1)

Bless me that I have power in my thighs
Swiftness in my legs
Steadiness in my feet.
May all my limbs be uninjured,
And my soul remain unconquered.

(Atharva.19.60.2)

O God, the Protector
  Protect my body.
Thou art Bestower of long life, bestow on me
  long life.
Thou art the Bestower of intellectual brilliance.
O God! Whatever is wanting in my body make
  that up for me.

(Yajur.3.17)

O God, bless us with a long life so we spread Thy
message of divine aspirations.

(Yajur.4.23)

Enable us to have Thy loving refuge and strength to
do noble deeds.

(Yajur.9.22)

Live a life of a hundred years, a life of self-respect
without being a burden to anyone.
Bless that I be a tree, not a creeper.

(Yajur.36.24)

Forgiveness

Forgive us, O Lord, if immersed in our own affairs,
We have committed sin against divine powers.
Forgive us for our sin against men, sin against
  elders,
And sin against our own conscience.
And for all sins that we have committed knowingly,
And those which we might have committed
  unawares.

(Yajur.8.13)

As rats eat weaver's thread,
Cares are eating inside me,
O God Almighty! Show Thy mercy to Thy devotee.

(Rig.10.33.3)

O God, the Sovereign Lord of the Vast Universe,
Help us to eradicate all our defects and deficiencies.
Of the eyes, of the heart and of the mind.
Be merciful and compassionate to us.

(Yajur.36.2)

Don't let the wicked violent powers harm us,
O Earth, protect us from earthly distress,
O Mid-Air, protect us from heavenly distress.

(Rig.7.104.23)

O Lord, help us in overcoming sin, carry us across
the turbulent river of adversities, as if on a boat.

(Atharva. 1.33.7)

O Merciful Lord,
In as much as all people commit errors,
So do we daily disfigure Thy worship by defaults.
But O Lord of Mercy,
Punish us not by the penalty of death
Through Thy indignation or anger.

(Rig.1.25.1)

To err is human. May we be forgiven our
blunders, men are full of all desires.

(Rig.1.179.5)

All-pervading God!
Whatever heinous sin we may have committed,
Be it one of downright jeering at God—
Or scorn of Him—by tongue, mind or action,
We pray for pardon
For that haughty and perverse God-hater
Who is ever busy tempting us to evil paths.

(Rig.4.54.3)

Harm us not, O Lord of cosmic vitality, abandon
    us not,
Let us not be tormented under Thy bondage
    when Thou art displeased
Make us partakers of the life-sustaining worship,
And may ye, O Nature's bounties, ever shower
    blessings on us.

(Rig.7.46.4)

O Lord, what was my main transgression
That would destroy a singer of Thy glory?
Tell me, O Invincible One, so that sinlessly
I may approach Thee with my devotion.

(Rig.7.86.4)

Forgive us, O Virtuous Lord, it is not our own
  choice,
But our hard environment that betrays us.
It is the vice of intoxication, wrath, gambling and
  carelessness.
And again, it is the handicap of the ill-manners
  of the elder with the young.
Even a dream is provocative to falsehood.

(Rig.7.86.6)

O Saviour, make me immortal
Liberate me from the cycle of birth and rebirth.

(Rig.7.89.1)

When O Lord of Justice, I move along tremulous,
with an inflated ego, bless me, O Saviour, mercy,
my Lord.

(Rig.7.89.2)

———◆———

The face of truth
Is covered by the glittering lid of gold.
The Purusha—the ultimate source of
conscious life,
Who shines in the sun
I am that Aum,
The Supreme Entity.

(Yajur.40.17)

Divine Justice

O Lord of Justice,
Sitting on the pinnacle of the cosmos,
Sustainer of the universe,
Make the arrow, held in Thy hand, tender and
 benign,
Let not the fierce power of Thy bow and arrow
Strike the innocent man and put him
 to death.

(Yajur.16.3)

Only with full faith the devotee is able to declare:
O Lord! We seek Thy divine justice;
Let the deceitful and tyrants and the exploiters
Be defeated at the hands of the honest and virtuous
Their sharp, alert wisdom is backed by Thy
 gracious blessings.

(Rig.1.11.7)

O Effulgent Lord!
May the person who enslaves us
Be crushed under Thy feet,
Whether he is near or far.
Mayest Thou be with us
For our progress and prosperity.

(Rig.1.79.11)

Deprive them of wealth who are hostile towards
Thy faithful devotees. Carry us through all troubles
as a boat carries men across the river against all
hurdles.

(Rig.1.99.1)

The one who incites sinful acts loses the favour and love of the Lord as well as of his fellow-brothers.

(Rig.5.3.7)

O Lord, deplete the wealth of those
Who enjoy the rewards of others' efforts
Without a thought of sharing their wealth with
The less fortunate.
O Sun, with Thy radiance Thou mayest not bless those
Who go astray from the right path and piety,
And those who multiply their progeny unwanted.
They merely indulge in sensual pleasures.

(Rig.5.42.10)

Thou over-spreadest on all the accessible places
Of the earth with its energetic power and impelling force.
Mayest Thou drive away all perils with Thy conquering might,
Fight out against our adversaries
And burn up those who harm us.

(Rig.6.6.6)

With Thy sharp flame, cast away and consume the forces of destruction.

(Rig.6.16.28)

Let us not suffer for the sin of others,
O universal cosmic powers, controllers of the universe,
May the one, who hurts us, be the victim of his own designs.

(Rig.6.51.7)

May the sun in heaven scorch and may the agonies
of burning be inflicted on the unbeliever, who
thinks himself superior and seeks to depreciate the
work of others.

(Rig.6.52.2)

Consume, O Effulgent Lord, all my evils
With that strong flame
Which consumes old worthless things.

(Rig.7.1.7)

Through Thy fear, O Lord,
The dark evil forces come under control.
O Adorable Lord, shine upon all men,
And burn the roots of their vices.

(Rig.7.5.3)

O cosmic God-blessed powers,
Physical and spiritual,
Burn those who plot evil against us.
Direct Thy unyielding strength
Against flesh-eating, cruel infidels.

(Rig.7.104.2)

May the evil-doers fall into the abyss,
Of the endless darkness,
So that not even one would come up again.
Let this angry strength be for the benefit of godly
    people.

(Rig.7.104.3)

Slay the hostile, malicious evil-doers
Who torment pious men.
Let there be no happiness for the evil-doer.

(Rig.7.104.7)

In the eyes of the Lord, no one is big, no one is small; all are alike; all are recipients of Godly love and blessing for prosperity.

(Rig.5.60.5)

Hymns on

Revelation

आ भारती भारतीभिः सजोषा इळा देवैर्मनुष्येभिरग्निः
सरस्वती सारस्वतेभिर्वाक् तिस्रो देवीर्बर्हिरेदं सदन्तु

May the divine speech that
Perfect our understanding and divine knowledge,
And all-satisfying divine culture
Be with us at our faultless yajna and worship
And protect us for our welfare.

(Rig.3.4.8)

The Word

Great streams of divine words flow out
From the minds of sages
With the speed of a gale,
Like rapids rushing down a slope;
Surging with the high waves of wisdom
They beat through all obstacles
As does a courageous war-horse.

(Rig.4.58.7)

The divine words are repositories of wisdom,
They unequivocally draw themselves to God.
Just as loving wives, faithful and smiling, approach
    their husbands.
These solemn words highlight every aspect of God.

(Rig.4.58.8)

May all sons of the immortal ones hear our
    words
And be the source of happiness to us.

(Rig.6.52.9)

Expound to us the three Vedas,
Which are packed with all radiant wisdom,
They are for us an udder, providing a store of
    rare excellent
Milk of unmingled bliss.
Then will He, Who fulfils all desires,
Who makes seeds shoot forth into seedlings and
    saplings
Spring up constantly into our divine awareness,
So much that He voices aloud His presence.

(Rig.7.101.1)

Sarasvati, the Divine Speech

May the divine speech, Sarasvati
The fountainhead of all faculties (mental and
    spiritual)
The purifier and bestower of true vision,
The recompenser of worship,
Be the source of inspiration and accomplishment
For all our benevolent acts!

(Rig.1.3.10)

She sets in motion all the energies of
The soul and intellect.
She imparts deep knowledge to all who are
    seekers of truth.

(Rig.1.3.12)

It is from Her that vast oceans of scriptures
    spring up.
It is because of Her that the Universe is full of life,
Through Her, indeed, the imperishable God unfolds
    Himself
And from Her, verily, the whole Universe draws
    its sustenance.

                                      (Rig.1.164.42)

Four are the definite grades of speech,
The learned and the wise know them.
Three of these are deposited in secret, they
    indicate no meaning to the common man
Men speak the fourth grade of speech, which is
Phonetically expressed.

                                      (Rig.1.164.45)

O Divine Mother of Speech,
That ever-full breast (with inexhaustible vocabulary)
Which is the source of delight
With which Thou bestowest all good things,
Which is the container of wealth
The distributor of riches
The giver of good fortune
That bosom dost Thou lay open at this moment
For our sustenance.

                                      (Rig.1.164.49)

May the divine speech that
Perfects our understanding and divine knowledge,
And all-satisfying divine culture
Be with us at our faultless yajna and worship
And protect us for our welfare.

(Rig.3.4.8)

The divine sages discovered this light of truth,
Enveloped in darkness,
The Vedas present truth in crystal-clear form.

(Rig.4.58.4)

God created speech divine.
Even living creatures of all species utter it.
May this speech, our wish-yielding cow,
Universally extolled as granter of gladness,
Food, strength and fame,
Come to us!

(Rig.8.100.11)

May this most gracious and eternal
Life-giving divine speech
Impart extensive knowledge to us.
May it come to all men.

(Rig.10.31

O Lord of Speech, when humans utter
The first word,
They bring forth to light that
Which is most excellent and pure,
And through love they discover
The secret hidden deep in their hearts.

(Rig.10.71.1)

When men discover the essence of the language
   with wisdom,
As if winnowing paddy through a sieve,
Friends start acknowledging love,
The sign of friendship.
And their talk retains the sentiments
Expressed through it.

(Rig.10.71.2)

There are men who may see with eyes.
But they do not see the source of divine speech.
There are men who hear but have no ability.
To understand the deeper meaning of divine words.
But there are pious sages to whom
The Goddess of Speech reveals her lovely form.

(Rig.10.71.4)

Sudden Showers

God is just behind us when we cry for help,

We feel our prayers might not reach Him.

In our panic we seek the assurance of safety,

In a moment the clouds of gloomy fears are swept away.

My soul, bathed in celestial joy,

The heavens laid bare their blue abyss.

The choicest gifts are showered upon me from all directions,

And I am lost in complete bliss.

(Atharva. 19.52.3)

These words tell about a man,
Too cold in friendship,
Who is never moved to act courageously,
And who is ever engrossed in his futile imaginings,
The word he hears never yields fruit or flower.

(Rig.10.71.5)

They tell all wise things to the ones who deserve
    friendship
Though it was experienced till the end by both.
They do not take advantage of words,
Even though they talk or listen to each other in vain,
For they understand nothing of what the words tell.

(Rig.10.71.6)

When priests jointly chant hymns,
Fashioned by the heart and inspired by the mind,
They all speak the same words.
But in attainment, some are far behind the others,
Though all are equal in status.

(Rig.10.71.8)

Those who move neither forward nor backward,
Neither are they priests nor performers of
    sacred deeds
They are poor craftsmen, misusing words,
Ignorant, they spin out a useless thread for themselves.

(Rig.10.71.9)

May the inner voices lead thee to divine bliss!

(Yajur.6.18)

O Lord of Resplendence, sharpen our intellects
And wake up our thoughts and spirits
So that we may overcome the malice of our enemy.

(Atharva.7.97.9)

Listen to divine words, O sons of the immortal spirit.

(Yajur 11.5)

Likewise, may I speak these beneficent words
To all people assembled here,
To the Brahmana and the Kshatriya,
To the Shudra and the Vaishya
To kin and aliens alike.

(Yajur.26.2)

O Lord of Divine Speech, when we invoke Thee,
With loving hearts and deep faith,
May we sense Thy loving beckonings!
In this mutual love
May we proceed and progress with Thy divine
     blessings!
Under Thy direct inspiration, may we never go against
Thy directions embedded in our conscience!

(Atharya.1.1.4)

Voices that never were, emit from the Spirit Supreme,
Speak truth, each one points to Him
As the one and only source of creation.
To the supreme they return,
Each new voice that emits from Him.

(Atharva.10.8.33)

We pray to the Supreme Lord to be with us.
May peace, quickened by our prayers be with us.
May the Goddess of Divine Speech of the highest
   domain grant us peace;
May the mighty celestial powers grant us peace
By making us pure and virtuous!

(Atharva.19.3.4)

Sing the songs of celestial love, O
singer!

May the divine fountain of eternal
grace and joy enter your soul,
May the Lord stay there forever!

May He pluck the strings of your inner
soul, with His celestial fingers and feel
His own presence within!

Bless us with a divine voice that we
tune the harp-strings of our life to sing
songs of love to Thee.

(Rig.1.91.11)

Eternity

This wheel of eternal time, with its twelve spokes,
Which knows no decay,
Perpetually revolves round the high heavens.
Seven hundred and twenty are the spokes
That comprise this (ever revolving) wheel.

(Atharva.9.9.13)

Born of pure light, Agni, Fire Divine,
Manifests itself as the prime element of creation.
The person who knows the eternal laws of this fire
Flourishes like a tree in bloom.

(Rig.2.5.4)

With fervent devotion, I sing in praise
Of the eternal cosmic order,
Designed to continue from eternity to eternity,
O Lord, enable us to understand its wondrous design,
Help us to know why the cow though dark
Yields rich, sweet and pure white milk.

(Rig.4.3.9)

Glorify eternal truth, but the proof of it is to
Put your creed into your deeds
And practise truth in your action.

(Rig.3.4.7)

One who clings fast to Eternal Truth
Will attain Ultimate Truth itself.
The strength of Rita, Eternal Order, is far-reaching
It brings wisdom to those that pursue it.
Earth and Heaven owe their existence to Rita eternally.
And the Supreme Powers yield their ambrosial milk,
    their treasured contents,
In perfect obedience to the Lord of Eternal Existence.

(Rig.4.23.1)

Infinite are the powers of eternal laws;
Abiding by these ends all afflictions
The contemplation on eternal existence
Dispels all sorrows.
Even an understanding of these laws is
Illuminating and purifying to living beings.
The eternal message impresses and inspires even
the unheeding ears.

(Rig.4.23.8)

Wisdom comes to a man who meditates, acts and
lives according to the true eternal laws of Nature.

(Rig.10.47.6)

God does not spare the one who tells a lie.

(Rig.10.147.1)

Truth, infallible laws, consecration, austerity,
Prayer and sacrifice;
These uphold the earth.
May Mother Earth, the mistress of our past and future,
Confer prosperity on us.

(Atharva.12.1.1)

Teach us, O Radiant Lord,
To follow the path of ascetic austerity
With dedication, diligence and perseverance.
Bless us that we be worthy
Of being loved by preceptors;
Enable us to live the full span of life
Enjoying bright intellect.

(Atharva.7.61.1)

The ever true principles of cosmic order alone
sustain the balance of Mother Earth.

(Atharva.14.1.1.)

Observe and follow the path of virtue leading to
eternal happiness which is sought by the
enlightened sages.

(Atharva.18.4.3)

Enable us to realise that God ever keeps us
In a state of eternal joy;
Inspire us to experience fulfilment of all our
    aspirations.

(Yajur.4.21)

O Lord, bless us that we may realise the fulfilment
of our aspirations in the eternal joy of Thy
proximity.

(Yajur.5.7)

Eternal joy is the ultimate aim of life's pilgrimage.

(Yajur.7.45)

O men of Godly nature! Partake of His divinity and
experience the joy of ecstasy.

(Yajur.9.18)

Let us resolve to offer all at the feet of the Blissful
Lord to obtain His blessings,
To live in the consciousness of eternal joy.

(Yajur.11.39)

Mother Nature descends towards the one
Who suffers for others
And those who deserve help
Then she sets her mind towards the Supreme Lord.

(Rig.5.61.7)

Fire Divine

Kindled and established on the earth,
The Fire Divine rises and spreads over all created
   worlds.
May the Fire Divine, the invoker and purifier,
   eternal, all-wise and adorable,
Establish our relations with Nature's forces.

(Rig.2.3.1)

The fire of penance purifies the soul;
Just as the flame of fire purifies gold;
The pure soul alone is worthy of exaltation.

(Rig.10.16.4)

The 'Ahuti' or oblations for yajna rise into space,
Get mingled with air and beautify the atmosphere.
They soar to the rays of the sun,
And therefrom they bring rain
For our betterment.

(Yajur.2.15)

When you perform yajna
And offer into sacred fire
Oblations of *ghrita* and other substances
They, being mingled and absorbed
In ethereal rays, water and air,
Spread throughout space,
Invigorate the atmosphere,
And give to the people
Rejuvenating rain and warm rays, light and life,
Vigour and vitality.

(Yajur.2.22)

Immense is Thy vastness
And Thy glory unparalleled,
O mighty and magnificent Lord!
Hundreds of earths, suns and planets
within our sight or beyond our
perceptions exist under Thy command,
But Thou art even beyond these.

All the world, existent or non-existent,
born or unborn are just a fraction of
Thy limitless being.
Around Thee move all the planets of
the universe.

(Rig.8.70.5)

May thy life's journey be made in the spirit
   of dedication;
May thy life-breath prosper in the spirit
   of dedication;
May thy eyes prosper in the spirit of dedication,
May thy ears prosper in the spirit of dedication.
May thy backbone prosper in the spirit of
   dedication;
May all thy noble works prosper in the spirit
   of dedication!

(Yajur.9.21)

Enable us to conduct our life yajna, in the spirit of
dedication.

(Yajur.11.8)

The nature's benevolent yajna ever continues for
the welfare of all humanity, overcoming all
obstacles on its path.

(Sama.111)

Let the fire of yajna magnify the commodities,
Let it provide wealth and health
By purifying the firmament.

(Sama.1529)

Ordinary men and women understand not
The threads of the warp and woof of God's
   creation,
No one knows the source of the words that have
   been spoken
By a father in this life and, again, which are
To be spoken by the son in the next life.

(Rig.6.9.2)

Soma

The Blissful Force of Divine Will
Awakens my inner spirit from sleep.
The inspiring Soma, the Divine Love, dispenses
    the six evils,
Lust, anger, greed, attachment, pride and jealousy,
Weaknesses from which no creature is exempt.

(Rig.6.47.3)

Soma, the Elixir of Divine Love, finds
The brilliant colours in the forefront of dawn
Whose dwelling is in the firmament.
This mighty Elixir sustains the heavens
With a mighty pillar, the sender of rains, the leader
    of winds.

(Rig.6.47.5)

O Blissful Lord, fill our hearts with Thy nectar
Which purifies and uplifts the soul on its stream
Of spiritual ecstasy to the highest heavenly bliss.

(Rig.9.1.1)

All impure tendencies are destroyed by this Elixir;
O Lord, Thy supreme love adds a new force to our
    inner self.

(Rig.9.1.2)

This celestial elixir is the source
Of all the lights of wisdom,
And that alone is the bestower
Of all wealth worth having.

(Rig.9.1.4)

The whole colourful panorama of the eastern sky
Derives golden beauty
And owes its charm to Soma, the Divine Elixir,
Which purifies the human soul.

(Rig.9.1.6)

Soma, the Elixir of Divine Love,
Cleanses the hearts of all
Unwanted and undesirable tendencies
The soul then is free of fear, sorrow and ignorance.
Thus liberated, full of divine faith and spiritual joy,
The brave soul discovers God in all His
    splendorous forms.

(Rig.9.1.10)

This exhilarating ambrosia inspires
Deep reverence in the hearts of all sincere devotees,
And fills their bodies with pure,
Serene thoughts and emotions.

(Rig.9.1.7)

The divine and heavenly stream of Soma breathes
    life
Into every grain of this vast universe,
Every drop of the expanse of the seas.
The waves that dance with joy
Sing only of the glory of this divine splendour.

(Rig.9.2.4)

It is this unceasing fountain of life-force
Which, like a benevolent power, shines
Through the golden rays of the sun
And guides us like a true friend
On the path of righteousness.

(Rig.9.2.6)

Soma spreads joyous bliss through pure knowledge,
And uplifts the soul on the stream of spiritual
  ecstasy
To the highest heaven.

(Rig.9.2.7)

This elixir of spiritual light and divine love
Has wings to fly like a bird,
It flies to settle in all the material elements
  of the earth.

(Rig.9.3.1)

Joined to the melody of divine music
It flows swiftly like the waves of a river.

(Rig.9.3.2)

Again, it continues to flow on its journey
Like a warrior
Marching with his brave associates
Eager to win the battle of life.

(Rig.9.3.4)

The law of eternal existence is firm and resistless.
For the good of living beings
The eternal order assumes infinite and beauteous
  forms.
Because of eternity, men hope for long-lasting food.
The Vedas enshrine eternal truths within themselves
By the grace of the order of eternity.

(Rig.4.23.9)

As it flows, it speeds up like a chariot,
Showering gifts on God-loving devotees,
It allows its voice to be heard by all.

(Rig.9.3.5)

This elixir gets ready to be offered
With dedication to the devotees.
It goes upto heaven, across the regions,
Its path remains unobstructed and straight.

(Rig.9.3.7)

It flows towards all virtuous thoughts and blesses
them.
It becomes the soul-force of all righteous thoughts and
actions.
It protects and disperses all divine knowledge
For the benefit of the entire universe.

174

(Rig.9.6.8)

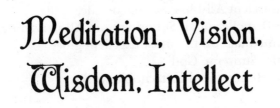

Meditation, Vision, Wisdom, Intellect

He who knows the first vital thread, binding all the things formed in shape, colour and words, knows only the physical form of the universe, and knows very little.

But he who goes deeper and perceives the string inside the string, the thin web binding separate life-forces with cords of unity, knows the real entity.

Only he knows truly the mighty omnipotent and omnipresent God, Who is within and beyond all formulated entities of the vast universe. Penetrate deeper to know the ultimate truth.

(Atharva.10.8.38)

By the grace of the Supreme God, Self-existent,
Omniscient All-bliss, Source of Life,
The Dispeller of all Sufferings and All-pervading.
We meditate on the most excellent glory
Of the Supreme God
That He may lead us to noble works.

(Yajur.36.3)

O Light Divine, the mind preserves thee
To give light
To the sense-organs and vital systems,
Born out of the eternal law
And endowed with divine inspiration
Thou art revered by the people.

(Sama.54)

Walk the divine path to greater wisdom
And divine glory.
This is the path which the divines love.
God escorts and is a constant companion to those
    who are inspired to work hard;
On them does He constantly shower
The joys of His blessings.

(Rig.1.154.5)

He who knows the cosmic brilliance
That grows through the ethereal vapours
Verily he knows the mysterious Lord of Creation.

(Rig.10.8.41)

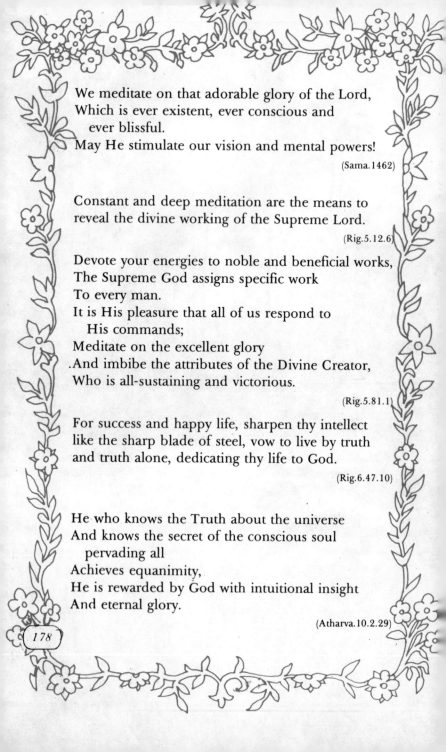

We meditate on that adorable glory of the Lord,
Which is ever existent, ever conscious and
   ever blissful.
May He stimulate our vision and mental powers!

(Sama.1462)

Constant and deep meditation are the means to
reveal the divine working of the Supreme Lord.

(Rig.5.12.6)

Devote your energies to noble and beneficial works,
The Supreme God assigns specific work
To every man.
It is His pleasure that all of us respond to
   His commands;
Meditate on the excellent glory
.And imbibe the attributes of the Divine Creator,
Who is all-sustaining and victorious.

(Rig.5.81.1)

For success and happy life, sharpen thy intellect
like the sharp blade of steel, vow to live by truth
and truth alone, dedicating thy life to God.

(Rig.6.47.10)

He who knows the Truth about the universe
And knows the secret of the conscious soul
   pervading all
Achieves equanimity,
He is rewarded by God with intuitional insight
And eternal glory.

(Atharva.10.2.29)

178

O Lord, teach us that we may know
Thy countless manifestations—
The highest, the lowest and those in between.
Teach us to worship Thee in all Thy manifestations.

(Rig.10.81.5)

O Supreme Lord, grant me that vision
Which the ancient sages were endowed with,
And which made them divine.

(Atharva.6.108.4)

Those who are completely involved
In only spiritual knowledge
Are lost in greater depth of darkness.
Those who are engrossed in material gains
Which do not contribute to the continuity
Of eternal existence and bliss grope in darkness.

(Yajur.40.9)

Knowledge of eternal truth leads to eternal peace
and bliss.

(Yajur.40.14)

Now this body of mine is ready to turn into dust,
The vital breath goes to meet the breath
Of the Universe.
May my immortal Soul blend
With the Universal Soul.
O pious devotee! Meditate on Aum.
Recollect your deeds and pious aspirations.

(Yajur.40.15)

The divine wisdom of the Vedas
Leads to material and spiritual advancement.

(Sama.98)

Mother Nature

Live in complete harmony with Nature, experience the grace of God in the splendour of the universe.

Be blessed by God's reassuring love,

The sweet dawn will sweeten your soul,

The dazzling mid-day will set your hearts aflutter,

And the serene music of your soul will guide you towards peace and prosperity.

And when the day's task is over you will sleep in the lap of Mother Nature,

All the deities will be favourable to you.

(Yajur.34.37)

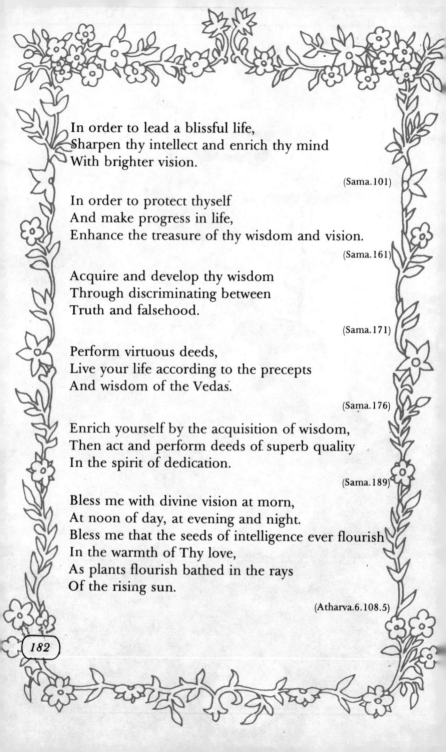

In order to lead a blissful life,
Sharpen thy intellect and enrich thy mind
With brighter vision.

(Sama.101)

In order to protect thyself
And make progress in life,
Enhance the treasure of thy wisdom and vision.

(Sama.161)

Acquire and develop thy wisdom
Through discriminating between
Truth and falsehood.

(Sama.171)

Perform virtuous deeds,
Live your life according to the precepts
And wisdom of the Vedas.

(Sama.176)

Enrich yourself by the acquisition of wisdom,
Then act and perform deeds of superb quality
In the spirit of dedication.

(Sama.189)

Bless me with divine vision at morn,
At noon of day, at evening and night.
Bless me that the seeds of intelligence ever flourish
In the warmth of Thy love,
As plants flourish bathed in the rays
Of the rising sun.

(Atharva.6.108.5)

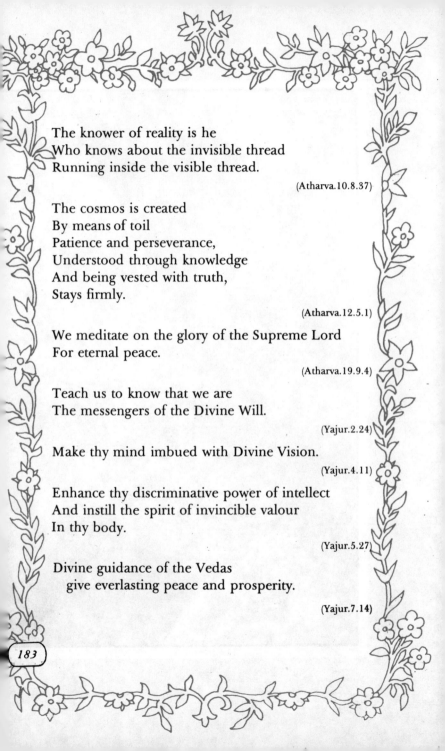

The knower of reality is he
Who knows about the invisible thread
Running inside the visible thread.

(Atharva.10.8.37)

The cosmos is created
By means of toil
Patience and perseverance,
Understood through knowledge
And being vested with truth,
Stays firmly.

(Atharva.12.5.1)

We meditate on the glory of the Supreme Lord
For eternal peace.

(Atharva.19.9.4)

Teach us to know that we are
The messengers of the Divine Will.

(Yajur.2.24)

Make thy mind imbued with Divine Vision.

(Yajur.4.11)

Enhance thy discriminative power of intellect
And instill the spirit of invincible valour
In thy body.

(Yajur.5.27)

Divine guidance of the Vedas
give everlasting peace and prosperity.

(Yajur.7.14)

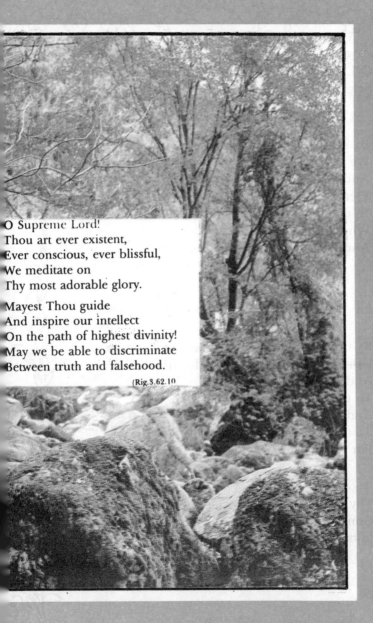

O Supreme Lord!
Thou art ever existent,
Ever conscious, ever blissful,
We meditate on
Thy most adorable glory.

Mayest Thou guide
And inspire our intellect
On the path of highest divinity!
May we be able to discriminate
Between truth and falsehood.

(Rig.3.62.10

O Lord! Enable us to ascend towards heavenly
heights.

(Yajur.9.10)

By means of yoga and meditation
We achieve knowledge, power and beauty,
And are blessed with
Eternal light, might and sight
In the kingdom of the Supreme One
Who is Lord of lords
And Creator of the Universe.

(Yajur.11.2)

Fill thy heart with most ennobling thoughts.

(Yajur.12.113)

By the dint of yoga, union with the Supreme,
I shall rise from the material earth
And sublimate myself
To the loftiest region of heaven;
And from there ascend and rise
To the celestial realm of peace
For achieving perennial bliss, light and life.

(Yajur.17.67)

Thy knowledge protects us from the wrath of sin,
Consumes every malignant spirit,
Lifts us aloft to spiritual heights.

(Rig.1.36.14)

Intellect and faith are the two dependable oars
That bear the wise men safely
Across the tumultuous ocean of life.
Where the fools get drowned in the middle.

(Sama.782)

May your body and mind
(Physical exertion and mental effort)
Work in harmony.
May your mind and actions be in unison.
The gracious Lord of the Universe
Has assembled these two
In the human body to work together
In complete co-ordination.

(Atharva.6.68.1)

He who knows the first vital string
Binding all the things formed in shape,
Colour and words
Knows only the physical form of the universe,
And knows very little.

But he who goes deeper and perceives the string,
The thin web, binding separate life forces
With cords of unity
Knows the ultimate reality.
Only he who realises that the Supreme Lord
Is within and beyond all formulated entities
Of this vast universe
Knows the whole truth.

(Atharva.10.8.38)

Immortality

O Lord, Thou art shining with heavenly radiance
And worshipped with oblations,
May I, though a mortal, become immortal
Even as Thou art, O Lord?

(Rig.8.19.25)

Immortal is the region of celestial bliss,
Where all darkness dissolves
And every wish and yearning,
Every noble aspiration finds fulfilment.
It is the heavenly place where the soul is liberated
And happiness is gained never to be lost again.
Let my heart turn towards the love of
The Resplendent Lord, the source of all light.
Speed fast, then, O mind
And unite with the source of eternal bliss.

(Rig.9.113.5)

Lead me onto that state of eternal light
The light that shows the way to
Perpetual, undecaying and immortal bliss.
May my heart turn towards the love
Of the Resplendent Lord,
The source of all light.
Speed fast, then, O mind,
And unite with the source of eternal bliss.

(Rig.9.113.7)

Make me immortal in that world
Where love of the Lord
And its supreme purity hold sovereign sway,
Before which the heavens themselves are but a
    prison-house.
Where the streams of good deeds flow on and on.
Speed fast, then, O mind,
And unite with the source of eternal bliss.

(Rig.9.113.8)

Make me immortal in that state of eternal bliss
Which is unimaginably
More luminous than heavens,
Where reigns absolute freedom
Of movement and action.
The dwellers whereof are endowed
With eternal light
Speed fast, then, O mind,
And unite with the source of eternal bliss.

(Rig.9.113.9)

Make me immortal in that world
Which forever abounds in joy,
Which is the home of happiness and ecstatic bliss,
Where all things longed for are attained and
All wishes are fulfilled.
Speed fast, then, O mind,
And unite with the source of eternal bliss.

(Rig.9.113.11)

Man's paradise is on earth;
This living world is the beloved place of all;
It has the blessings of Nature's bounties;
Live in a lovely spirit;
Do not die before your assigned time.
Remember anything which is born must die,
But die not a thousand deaths
Before your destiny calls you.

(Atharva.5.30.6)

Fear not, death is imperative
For all men and animals;
For bipeds and quadrupeds,
But, I shall liberate thee from the clutches of death.
Be not afraid, O man, trust me,
Thou shalt not die,
Neither go to the lowest depth of gloom.

(Atharva.8.2.23)

Go away Death, on thy own path of destruction;
Away from the one that the pilgrims
Of Godly men tread;
I speak to those who have eyes and ears
Those who can see and hear;
Great is the number of these wise men around us.
Who are full of love and divine bliss.
For them and none other this plateau is built;
Blessed by God, may they live a full span of life!

(Atharva.12.2.21)

We worship the Mother of three realms,
Renowned to be the granter of eternal glory,
Let the separation of our soul from our body
Be a step to absolute liberation
May She release our soul from the bondage
Of mortal life
As the ripened melon is separated from its stem.
May our death be a step to immortality.

(Atharva.14.1.17)

Having taken the oath to dedicate your life
Towards gaining immortality,
May you know that the path that leads to it
Is that of complete surrender and dedication.
Remember, you are the child of immortality.

(Atharva.15.17.10)

O Lord, liberate our souls
From the shadows of birth and death,
Not from our aspirations of existence, i.e.,
    immortality.

(Yajur.3.60)

O God, help me to put an end
To all physical desires of the maligned body,
Bless that I may qualify to partake
Of the nectar of immortal love.

(Yajur.7.47)

Human Soul

Two birds (God and Soul)
With their beauteous wings
Associate in intimacy,
Perch on the same tree;
Of them, soul, tastes its fruits;
The other, God, enjoys without tasting.

(Rig.1.164.20)

Bless us to be worthy of accepting the valorous deeds
Of the powerful resplendent soul (the lower self).
He casts off the cloud of blind and dark impulses
and evil thoughts.
He lets the stream of wisdom flow to overcome
all obstacles.

(Rig.1.32.1)

He accumulates his strength in three virtuous
directions
Physical, mental and spiritual.
Sharpens his will-power and subdues the first born of
the baser impulses, the physical one.

(Rig.1.32.3)

When the soul is strong, no baser impulses like
  sensuous thoughts,
Passions or any sort of temptations can harm us,
The triumph of the soul in the contest
Becomes full and final over the wicked impulses.

(Rig.1.32.13)

The strong soul, the wielder of powerful spiritual
  power,
Becometh the sovereign of all that is
Movable and immovable, of our impulses and
  emotions.
He becometh monarch of all men.
Then all activities are centred within Him
As the circumference comprehendeth the spokes
  of a wheel.

(Rig.1.32.15)

The spiritualized soul conquers adversaries
With its swift and forceful disintegrating power.
He destroys their sources; reaches the central living
  place of blind instincts
And dismantles the resting-place of these evil impulses
And thereupon rejoices in His victory.

(Rig.1.33.13)

Along with our soul, we invoke Thee from afar
For glory, diligence and fearlessness.
Let our inner strength also carry with it
The idea of progress and vigorous leadership
To do away with our evil desires.

(Rig.1.36.18)

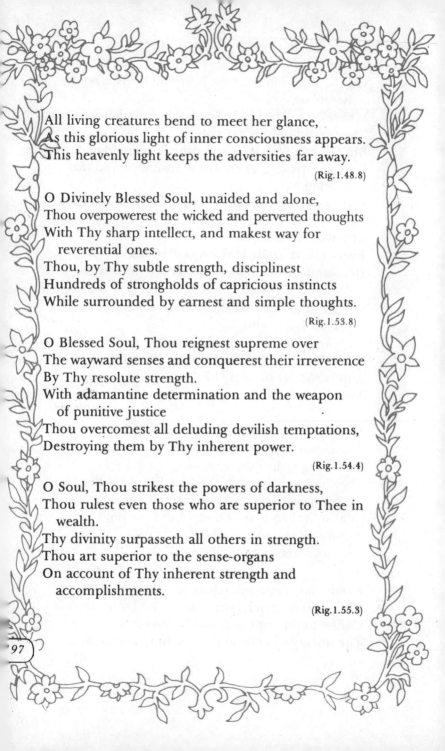

All living creatures bend to meet her glance,
As this glorious light of inner consciousness appears.
This heavenly light keeps the adversities far away.

(Rig.1.48.8)

O Divinely Blessed Soul, unaided and alone,
Thou overpowerest the wicked and perverted thoughts
With Thy sharp intellect, and makest way for
     reverential ones.
Thou, by Thy subtle strength, disciplinest
Hundreds of strongholds of capricious instincts
While surrounded by earnest and simple thoughts.

(Rig.1.53.8)

O Blessed Soul, Thou reignest supreme over
The wayward senses and conquerest their irreverence
By Thy resolute strength.
With adamantine determination and the weapon
     of punitive justice
Thou overcomest all deluding devilish temptations,
Destroying them by Thy inherent power.

(Rig.1.54.4)

O Soul, Thou strikest the powers of darkness,
Thou rulest even those who are superior to Thee in
     wealth.
Thy divinity surpasseth all others in strength.
Thou art superior to the sense-organs
On account of Thy inherent strength and
     accomplishments.

(Rig.1.55.3)

On the tree, whereon the beautiful birds taste the
   sweetness,
Where they all rest and again bring forth their offering.
They say, the fruits are sweet,
But the one who knows not the Supreme Lord
Gets no privilege to enjoy the fruit of devotional
   offering.
(Tree=Supreme Lord; beautiful birds=lower selves).

(Rig.1.164.22)

The soul is immortal
Every mortal body is enlivened by the soul
In accordance with its previous actions (karma).

(Rig.1.164.30)

He, the soul, who was brought to life in the body
Does not know of it.
He who sees it is (now) concealed from it.
It is hemmed in in the womb of the mother
And is subject to many births
And finally it merges into eternity.

(Rig.1.164.32)

The Immortal Soul associated with the mortal body
Ceaselessly takes birth and rebirth,
According to its own actions.
They both go always and everywhere together.
We humans have comprehended the one
(Whilst in the physical body) but have not
   comprehended the other
(The soul free from the body).

(Rig.1.164.38)

Surely, it is the resplendent self, the foremost,
Who, as soon as it is born, excelleth all other faculties.
Owing to the supremacy of its strength,
The duality of body and mind functions well.

(Rig.2.12.1)

198

The resplendent self who makes the trembling
   body firm,
Tranquillises the agitated senses;
Measures out the midvital regions; and
Keeps the celestial mental realm upright.

(Rig.2.12.2)

Exhilarated by sweet spiritual bliss
The soul arms itself with adamantine determination,
Controls the venomous baser tendencies.
The delicious stream of this bliss begins to flow
As birds fly towards their nests.

(Rig.2.19.2)

The powerful soul destroys the vice of
pettimindedness, greed and malice.

(Rig.2.19.6)

For the benefit of the mind, He destroys
The demons of pettiness, greed and malice,
And for the devotees and the enlightened
He demolishes all demonic tendencies whatsoever.

(Rig.2.19.8)

O Inner Self, may your voice be clear and loud; may
you become the oars of the boat of our life; guide us to
the safe shores through the stormy sea of life, avoiding
all calamities.

(Rig.2.42.1)

As the rivers fill up the ocean, in the same way, the
sense-organs milk out the divine happiness, remove
impurities and carry it as an offering to the
Resplendent Lord.

(Rig.3.36.7)

Communion

Live in tune with the universal soul,
Let this be the final craving which you cherish.

Let this be your last prayer.

Cast off your separate ego and merge in the universal entity.

Let there be no distance, no distinction;

Every particle of the human body is a symbol of universal existence.

Creation is the image of the Creator,

The experience of unity is the fulfilment of human endeavours.

(Rig.8.44.23)

Inner Flame

The human body is the temple of God.

One who kindles the light of awareness
within gets true light.

By concentrating the mind the inner vision
is illuminated.

The joys of life are not for those who
keep their minds unclean.

The mysteries of life are revealed to
one who keeps his mind vigilant all the
time.

The sacred flame of your inner shrine
constantly bright and glowing.

(Rig.8 44.15)

The radiant soul gives impetus to the wheel of the
　　intellect,
Controls the vital organs, saves them from inner
　　conflicts.
In times of a conflict between the physical and mental
　　faculties
That give rise to undulating dark clouds
Of confusion and indecision,
The soul with its inner radiance becomes the guiding
　　force.

(Rig.4.17.4)

Even the self-sustaining (autonomous) powers of
　　intellect
And mind bow before the potent self.
And the body resigns to the soul like a submissive
　　wife.
As the soul shares its vigour with all other faculties,
These faculties offer reverence to the soul.

(Rig.5.32.10)

The soul sips the elixir of spiritual joy
Given to it by God and severs the head
Of lust as a hawk does of its victim.
The soul gives protection to the humble,
Flickering and erring human mind,
And makes the person worthy of achieving
　　glorious success.

(Rig.6.20.6)

Spiritual Discipline

May we always look at each other
My eyes to behold Him.
The divine light, placed in my heart,
Is also eager to know Him.
My mind, the receptacle of distant objects,
Hastens towards Him:
What shall I speak?
How shall I comprehend him?

(Rig.6.9.6)

Men often live and follow a beaten path by
imitation, only a few wise men dare to carve out a
new path for themselves.

(Rig.9.23.2)

One ignorant of the land asks of one who knows it;
He travels onward, instructed by the knowing
    guide;
This is the blessing of instruction;
One finds the path that leads straight onward.

(Rig.10.32.7)

A Brahmachari, a spiritually disciplined man of
    divine wisdom,
Performs deeds strengthening both the worlds;
All the divine powers actively bless him in his
    mission;
He upholds the true virtues of earth and heaven;
He satisfies his divine preceptor with the power
    of his ascetic austerity.

(Atharva.11.5.1)

The spiritual teacher, while initiating the disciple,
Takes him in the inmost fold of his loving heart,
As a mother embraces her child and bears the
    child in her womb;
Then all the divine powers come to bless the
    adopted child of the spiritual teacher.

(Atharva.11.5.3)

In this sacred fire, yajna, of spiritual training,
All the divinities of the earth, the heaven and the
    mid-air
Provide fuel to illuminate the path of spiritual
    training.
The disciple, with his austere life,
Learning and hard work,
Serves and pays respects to all, including the
    cosmic powers.

(Atharva.11.5.4)

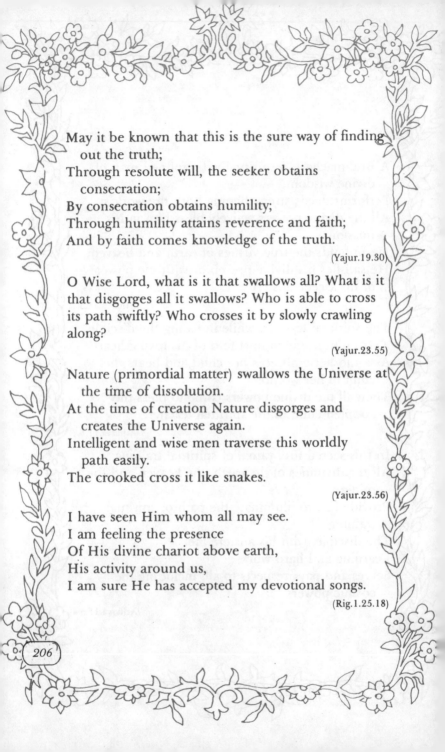

May it be known that this is the sure way of finding
    out the truth;
Through resolute will, the seeker obtains
    consecration;
By consecration obtains humility;
Through humility attains reverence and faith;
And by faith comes knowledge of the truth.

(Yajur.19.30)

O Wise Lord, what is it that swallows all? What is it
that disgorges all it swallows? Who is able to cross
its path swiftly? Who crosses it by slowly crawling
along?

(Yajur.23.55)

Nature (primordial matter) swallows the Universe at
    the time of dissolution.
At the time of creation Nature disgorges and
    creates the Universe again.
Intelligent and wise men traverse this worldly
    path easily.
The crooked cross it like snakes.

(Yajur.23.56)

I have seen Him whom all may see.
I am feeling the presence
Of His divine chariot above earth,
His activity around us,
I am sure He has accepted my devotional songs.

(Rig.1.25.18)

Bless us to proclaim that we feel around us
An unwavering flame of eternal light
Protecting us from all adversities.

(Yajur.2.17)

Bless us to proclaim
That we have attained the everlasting consciousness
Of Supreme Light and Joy.

(Yajur.2.25)

O Lord, may we live perpetually
In a state of everlasting spiritual ecstasy.

(Yajur.4.14)

O Lord, may we resolve
To dedicate our life to the service of mankind;
And uplift them to divinity.

(Yajur.5.4)

I feel liberated from the clutches
Of the material world
And now have reached the highest crest
Of the earth;
Again I ascend above to mid-air;
From there to paradise, to seventh Heaven;
Surely now I am in the domain
Of unlimited ocean of eternal glory.

(Atharva.4.14.3)

O seeker, know the true nature of thy soul
And identify yourself with it completely.

(Yajur.8.22)

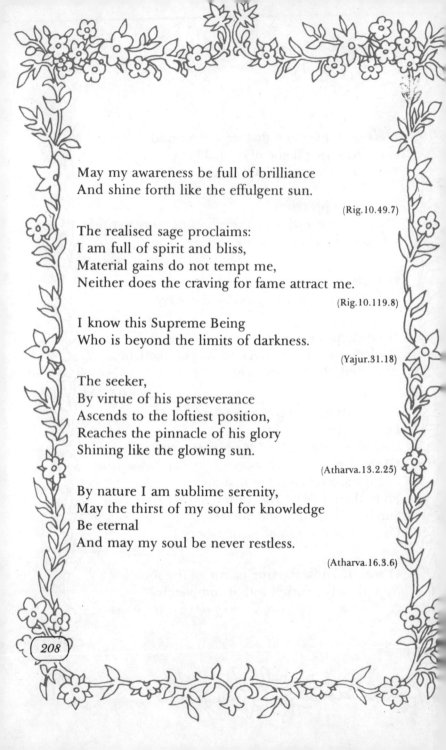

May my awareness be full of brilliance
And shine forth like the effulgent sun.

(Rig.10.49.7)

The realised sage proclaims:
I am full of spirit and bliss,
Material gains do not tempt me,
Neither does the craving for fame attract me.

(Rig.10.119.8)

I know this Supreme Being
Who is beyond the limits of darkness.

(Yajur.31.18)

The seeker,
By virtue of his perseverance
Ascends to the loftiest position,
Reaches the pinnacle of his glory
Shining like the glowing sun.

(Atharva.13.2.25)

By nature I am sublime serenity,
May the thirst of my soul for knowledge
Be eternal
And may my soul be never restless.

(Atharva.16.3.6)

Bondage
and Liberation

In the realisation of spiritual bliss,
The human soul is released from the bondage
Of physical sphere and rises above celestial realm.

(Rig.10.119.7)

Becoming one with Brahman is freedom absolute.

(Atharva.7.100.1)

True devotees through discriminative power
Choose and by right choice attain liberation
From birth and re-birth.

(Rig.4.19.2)

Man has subjected himself
To thousands of self-inflicted bondages.

(Rig.5.2.7)

Free us, O Virtuous Lord,
From each successive bond and tie;
Loosen all binding cords that bind us all over.
May Mother Eternity and Supreme Lord
The resplendent be kind to us.
May we be sinless
Under their motherly kindness and love!

(Atharva.7.83.3)

Salvation

Offer reverence to the punitive power of God,

Like a sharp blade it severs the binding rope of life and death,

The feelings of tender love are hidden beneath this piercing blade,

It liberates us from the bondage of desires and temptations and guides us to the path of righteousness.

The sharp edge of this pain-giving blade cuts the knot of life's entanglements.

Be grateful to the Lord of Death, the destroying power of God, as He delivers us to death once again for ultimate salvation.

(Rig.6.63.2)

The Thirst

Too much wealth makes man greedy
and slave to sensuous pleasures,

It makes him extrovert and darkens his
inner vision;

Desires unfulfilled give rise to grief and
their fulfilment causes greed;

Thus he feels miserably thirsty even
standing in the fathomless sea of
wealth.

The raging waves of wordly
riches surround and submerge his
senses, but he fails to quench the thirst
of his soul.

He runs after countless mirages in
search of peace, but all in vain.

At last he prays for one drop of God's
love which may satisfy all his cravings.

He cries, "Release me, O God, from
these shackles of exhausting sensuous
pleasures and give me lasting peace."

(Rig.7.89.4)

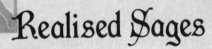

Realised Sages

Like birds of beauteous wings,
Let the poet-sages, possessors of creative intellect,
Dedicate their life to Godly work.

(Rig.10.73.11)

The sages, aspiring for a higher
And better standard,
Work with diligence and devotion;
They inspire people
To do their duty with dedication.
This is the way how nations
And communities grow strong.

(Atharva.19.41.1)

The inspired sages, free of desires
And full of devotional love,
Attain highest glory and everlasting peace.

(Sama.92)

O Supreme Lord, make me firm
And resolute like Thee.
Bless that all may look on me with a friendly eye
And I look on others likewise.
May we experience complete harmony among us.

(Yajur.36.18)

The one who loves all intensely,
Begins perceiving in all living beings
A part of himself
And he who conceiving the self
As a part of the universal soul
Does not look down on anyone.
He never hates anyone and never falls
A victim to hatred, grief or sorrow.
He becomes a lover of all,
A part and parcel of the universal joy.
He flows with the stream of happiness
And is enriched by each loving soul.

(Yajur.40.6)

The devotee who is full of wisdom
And performs all acts
In complete submission is blessed
By the vivid and glorious vision of God.
To him the wide horizon of the universe is filled
With the blazing glow of God.
Such a meditating mind is the noblest of all.

(Rig.1.95.8)

When for a year,
The wise sages procure the barren land
They invest it with fertility;
They continue their efforts
To make it more productive
To achieve glorious success and fame.

(Rig.4.33.4)

Hymns on Action

सं गच्छध्वं सं वदध्वं सं वो मनाँसि जानताम्
देवा भागं यथा पूर्वे संजानाना उपासते

O citizens of the world! Live in harmony and concord.
Be organised and co-operative.
Speak with one voice and make your resolutions
With one mind.
As our ancient saints and seers, leaders and preceptors
Have performed their duties righteously,
Similarly, you will not falter to execute your duties.

(Rig.10.191.2)

The Shore

Perform your duty and leave the rest to God, and have deep faith in His justice.

The world is torn by strifes, enmities and rivalries;

In this dark whirlpool of turbulent stream of life;

Only the all-powerful God may carry us across the ocean of troubles,

Only he can captain our vessel and bring it to the shore of divine fulfilment.

The waves of the stormy sea will become calm at his nod;

Therefore dedicate all your thoughts and desires to God with full faith.

Only He can bless you to conquer your troubles through His divine mercy.

(Rig.8.16.11)

Social Consciousness

Among us there are some who are
Well endowed with sight and hearing,
But are deficient in intelligence;
Some look insignificant like a small pond of water
And some are large like a lake.

(Rig.10.117.9)

May our prayer be one and the same;
May we belong to one fraternity;
May our minds move in accord;
May our hearts work in unison
For one supreme goal;
Let us be inspired by a common ideal;
Let us sing Thy praises in congregation.

(Rig.10.191.3)

May the inmost aspirations of you all
Be perfectly harmonious;
May your hearts beat in unison;
May absolute concord reign in your minds,
May you all be welded
Into strong fellowship and unity.

(Rig.10.191.4)

O people! Those of you who have attained higher,
middle or lower status in your respective fields of
work, enjoy the wealth thus gained together as one.
With the resources for the production of material
goods at your disposal, dedicate your life to
eradicate the evils of society and strive at all times
for the well-being of the people.

(Rig.5.60.6)

In mankind nobody is higher or lower nor is anybody of middle status. Everybody with concerted effort toils along the path of progress. All these men who are naturally diligent and possess outstanding characteristics progress by exploiting the natural resources from the mother earth and utilising them for the welfare of all.

(Rig.5.59.6)

The rich man who does not utilise his wealth for noble deeds or does not offer it for the use of his fellow-beings, but looks after his own needs, is selfish and has earned the wages of sin. It is undeniably true that the wealth of a person becomes meaningless, if it is not distributed and utilised. That hoarded wealth eventually proves to be the cause of his ruin.

(Rig.10.117.6)

The farmer with his plough makes it possible to grow food for the people. Only he who treads each measured step covers the distance and reaches his destination. A teacher who imparts his knowledge is more highly esteemed than a silent sage. A generous individual is far superior to a miserly, wealthy person.

(Rig.10.117.7)

May all the members of society have a common objective! May their hearts beat as one and their minds think alike, so that with their combined energies and diverse skills, they may be able to accomplish their objectives satisfactorily.

(Rig.10.191.4)

O man! May there be conformity in your life-style
and may there be equal share of food and drink for
all in the bounty of Mother Earth. I join you all
to the common yoke of social welfare. As all the
spokes of the wheel joined at the centre give it
acceleration, in the same way be united and equal,
and make progress.

(Atharva.3.30.6)

Love and respect society;
Protect it by feeding the hungry
And helping the distressed.
May you have strength to fight
For noble and righteous causes.
Associated with valiant fighters of diverse qualities,
May you be armed with mighty weapons.
Never succumb to your enemies;
Let your courage soar high
In espousing a great cause;
Summon up your innate greatness.
Lead and guide the wayward straggling masses.

(Rig.6.75.9)

Not one of you is small
Not one a feeble child
All of you are truly great.

(Rig.8.30.1)

The Almighty Lord is pleased
And showereth His blessings and benefits
On the people of that community
Where all the people are well-integrated,
United and offer worship with one faith.

(Rig.10.191.1)

O citizens of the world!
Live in harmony and concord.
Be organised and co-operative.
Speak with one voice
And make your resolutions with one mind,
As our ancient saints and seers,
Leaders and preceptors
Have performed their duties righteously,
Similarly, may you not falter
To execute your duties.

(Rig.10.191.2)

There is no flaw
In this law of karma,
No reservation.
Actions performed in alliance with friends
Are not taken into account.
It is an exact and accurate regulation
Of actions and reactions.
Man eats what he cooks.
That is, he reaps what he sows.

(Atharva.12.3.48)

I bless you to be free from malice
To live in concord and harmony with all.
Love one another as a cow loves
Its new-born calf.

(Atharva.3.30.1)

Let your minds work in harmony.
Let your sentiments be for a common objective.
I shall help you to overcome troubles
And show how to harmonise
Your deeds and thoughts.

(Atharva.6.64.2)

Path of Duty

May we ever unswervingly follow the path of duty as do the sun and the moon!

May we always serve humanity without demanding the price of our service!

May we ever be benevolent, kind, self-sacrificing, detached and adjustable.

May we surrender all and serve humanity like the sun and the moon.

(Rig.5.51.15)

Calm Confidence

The Lord of Bounteousness hath given ample riches to us, still we feel our soul is hollow, and crave for more;

God hath given supreme strength, still we feel weak and emaciated.

Let the stream of God's love flow in our soul, in our veins, freely to enable us to face the the adversities of life with calm confidence.

(Rig.8.32.12)

O mankind! I bind you together towards one objective—the welfare of man. Toil together with mutual love and goodwill. May you share the comforts of life equally. May you accomplish your work with mutual accord and finally may you, in the pursuit of your ambition at all times, engage in working together with goodwill!

(Atharva.3.30.7)

The godly people possess divine virtues
And spread the message of divinity on earth.

(Rig.10.65.11)

May our inward thoughts
Conform to our outward actions.

(Atharva.2.30.4)

Carefully observe the ways
Of those that are virtuous and righteous,
And vigorously follow the path
Laid down by the sages.
This is the path which leads to happiness.
It is here that the enlightened souls
Dwell in sweet blissfulness
And live eternally
In the realm of heavenly bliss.

(Atharva.19.4.3)

O leader among men,
Imbibe godly attributes in thy person.

(Yajur.1.18)

An honest and straightforward man
Easily attains the highest glory.

(Yajur.2.8)

All men are equal in brotherhood,
There is no one small and no one big.

(Yajur.16.15)

Distribute thy wealth to those who deserve it
And seek love of God,
The most precious treasure of life.

(Sama.240)

Verily you win the blessing of the Lord,
If your heart is set on a definite objective,
And you work hard for it.

(Rig.5.44.8)

Keep thy mind and body in perfect condition,
These are the first requisites to achieve the
   desired goal.

(Rig.8.19.20)

Leaders of society should have
The moral strength to proclaim truth fearlessly.

(Rig.8.48.14)

Only the geniuses and scholars speak a pure
language.

(Rig.9.73.7)

As day follows day in close succession;
As the seasons duly follow each other,
May each successor not let down his predecessor.
Similarly, we carry forward the torch of virtues
And live upto the expectations of our elders;
O Ordainer of the Universe,
May this be the order of the day perpetually!

(Atharva.12.2.25)

Marriage and Family Life

May we always look at each other
With love and affection.
May our lives together be happy without malice.
May one spirit dwell in both of us!

(Atharva.7.36.1)

O husband and wife, may you both live the full span
of your life in wedded bliss. Never be separated from
each other. May you always live joyously in your
home with your children and grandchildren.

(Atharva.14.1.22)

O husband and wife; may you be considerate and affectionate towards each other. Follow the path of duty and justice. Beget noble brave children; build your own home to live in.

(Atharva.14.2.43)

O bride, attend to the well-being of all the members of your family, sharing their joys and sorrows. May your coming bring good fortune to your husband, father-in-law, mother-in-law and the rest of the family.

(Atharva.14.2.26)

O bride, entering the house, may you become the guiding light of this family. Endowed with intelligence and understanding, may you observe the rules of good and healthy living in your home. May the Lord shower His blessings upon you.

(Atharva.14.2.75)

I, the father of this girl,
Release her from all ties with this family
And unite her with that of her husband
From whom may she never part.
May my daughter who observed the vows
    of celibacy
Enjoy great happiness
With her handsome and virile husband
And beget noble children.

(Rig.10.85.25)

Having abided by the vows of celibacy earlier, this
girl now accepts this young man to be her husband.
May she bring happiness and prosperity to this
house! Having come to her husband's home, may
she beget noble sons and be honoured as the queen
of the house! May she enjoy the respect and good
wishes of all!

(Atharva.2.36.3)

O bride! looking at your beauty
And hearing about the qualities
Of your head and heart, I embrace you.
I will never seek pleasures outside the home.
I will not even entertain such thoughts.
My behaviour will fully be
In accordance with the scriptures.

(Atharva.14.1.57)

O man, do not be afraid of performing your marital
duties. With courage and conviction, follow the
path of 'Dharma'. Endowed with strength, honour
and valour, may you obey your God-assigned duties
and be happy.

(Yajur.3.41)

O wedded couple, may you in this life
Be wise, benevolent and live to inspire all
To follow the Vedic way of blissful life!

(Yajur.2.19)

Accept my gifts just as I accept yours,
For the world maintains its balance
On this perennial give-and-take,
Which makes life a joyous living.

(Yajur.3.50)

O wedded couple, do not hamper
The life of benevolence and sacrifice
Or go against the inner voice of the soul.
May you live within the dictates
Of your mind.

(Yajur.5.3)

The yajna of the wise surely guides the man
To a happy family life and wedded bliss.
Prayers to the Lord bring joy to all.

(Yajur.8.4)

Let no brother hate his brother,
Let no sister hate her sister,
May you all speak and behave
With harmony and sweetness,
May you all be unanimous
And of one accord.

(Atharva.3.30.3)

Be respectful to elders,
Have a magnanimous heart,
March ahead and progress
With common aim and common goal.
Be not separated from one another,
And talk to each other sweet words.
Come towards Me,
I co-ordinate you
Into inseparable companions
Having common minds
And a common goal.

(Atharva.3.30.5)

He whose mother and father
Are not properly served and honoured
Meet with worries and woes;
While he whose mother and father
Are held in high esteem
Achieves bliss and wins admiration
Among his friends
And virtuous people.

(Rig.4.6.7)

The Supreme Lord, by His mystical powers,
Fills the hearts of wedded couples
With sublime love.

(Rig.5.3.2)

Let married women
Remain in their homes
As noble ladies and ideal wives
Adorned with fragrant balms and collyrium.
May they be
Healthy and happy
Adorned with ornaments and jewels!

(Atharva.12.2.31)

I am what thou art,
Thou art what I am.
I am the psalm,
And thou art the verse.
I am the heaven,
And thou art the earth.
May we live together
To produce progeny!

(Atharva.14.2.71)

O husband and wife, may you always
Be generous and charitable,
May benevolence be the motto of your life!

(Sama.287)

Calm Confidence

In the solitary chambers of my heart,
slumberest Thou, O Supreme Lord.
My sense-organs are mysteriously charged
with Thy cosmic magic.

Unto Thy hands I surrender all my
thoughts and deeds.

Blessed by Thy divine effulgence
enshrined in my soul I become pure
and strong to face all the miseries of
life,

And fortified by the presence in my
conscious realisation,

I bear all the pains with calm
confidence.

(Rig.10.43.6)

Charity

Let us become God's instrument
And distribute fortune to the poor and the needy.

(Rig.1.15.8)

May those who earn honestly and give generously
Be firmly established in the world
And command respect in society.
May they dedicate their work to God!

(Rig.1.15.9)

The liberal giver rises to divine radiance
And attains Godly powers.

(Rig.1.125.5)

These wonderful rewards are for those
Who give generous donations.
They attain immortality
And are blessed with long and glorious lives.

(Rig.1.125.6)

O God! Bestow on us the best treasures;
An efficient mind and spiritual lustre,
The increase of wealth, the health of bodies,
The sweetness of speech and the fairness of days.

(Rig.2.21.6)

The Lord does not favour the dishonest rich
Who refuse to share their wealth
With the needy and the poor.
God snatches away the wealth of the greedy,
While He bestows riches on the generous.

(Rig.5.34.7)

O God, take away the wealth of those
Who exploit others,
Without sharing it with those
Who really toil to earn!

(Rig.5.42.9)

O Lord Almighty, bestow on me
The privilege of enjoying the wealth
Earned by honest, hard labour.

(Rig.8.4.17)

Let a man think well of wealth and strive to win it
By the path of law and by worship;
Let him take counsel with his own inner wisdom
And grasp it with a still greater ability.

(Rig.10.31.2)

Never gamble; be content
And enjoy the fruits of your honest labour.
Take to agriculture and harvest the wealth thereof.
Riches, thus acquired, alone give real happiness.
This is the sacred law of the Divine Lord.

(Rig.10.34.13)

One who is selfish and feeds himself alone,
Refusing to share his food
With his starving brethren,
Is not fit to be a friend.

(Rig.10.117.4)

Let the fortunate rich fulfil
The needs of the poor.
Let his eye see the distant pathway of life;
The wheels of the wealth-chariot are ever rolling.
Riches come today to one, tomorrow to another;
Let everyone realise
That one day he may need the help of someone.

(Rig.10.117.5)

Surely, the law of Providence is such
That the wealth earned through evil means
Is scattered away.
The wealth earned through pious means flourishes;
Those who earn through dishonest means
    are destroyed.

(Atharva.7.115.4)

May you earn as by a hundred hands
And disburse by a thousand!
When you are involved in benevolent work,
Your capacity to earn multiplies,
Increasing a hundredfold;
Those who give in a good cause
Are surely blessed by the Lord.

(Atharva.3.24.5)

O man, work with vigour and vitality
Drive away the devil of poverty and disease.
May your honest earnings support the people,
Engaged in benevolent deeds
For the welfare of society.

(Atharva.6.81.1)

O God, keep away from me
That wealth which brings about my fall,
And results in my defame,
Which entangles me
From all directions,
And withers me like a parasitic plant
That withers away the supporting tree;
O Supreme Lord of Wealth,
Thy hands are golden,
Bless me with that wealth
Which gives peace and joy.

(Atharva.7.115.2)

Death is not caused only through hunger; death is
inevitable even for those who eat to the fullest. The
man who distributes his wealth amongst others is
blessed by God. One who does not share his
possessions with others can make no friends.

(Rig.10.117.1)

One who hoards grain or money, and enjoys all
luxuries of life and remains indifferent to those who
are poor and suffering from starvation, will never
find a true friend.

(Rig.10.117.2)

Only the one who gives or shares food with others,
whether he be an intellectual saint, a poor beggar
or a cripple, eats sacred food. These magnanimous
benefactors will always be blessed by God. He can
make even his enemies his friends.

(Rig.10.117.3)

Those who give charity
And look after the welfare of others
Are ever happy.

(Sama.285)

May a righteous, benevolent devotee
Never suffer a setback.
Even in his days of adversity,
Sorrow does not touch him.
A charitable, truthful man
Has never to repent,
Is never despondent.

(Rig.1.125.7)

Kingship

O King! the people have elected you.
Be a true king, shine in all splendour,
The sole ruler of the people.
All men bow to you,
The heavens bless you;
Be just and merciful
Disburse money to the people.
All bounteous paths lead to your glory
For ten decades may you live
As a strong, kind ruler!
Be just and firm
And share your glory with all.

(Atharva.3.4.2)

O God, strengthen the king of our people,
Leader of us all;
Make him the sole conqueror.
Bless him with riches, impoverish his foes;
May he be the head and chief of all princes.
Like a lion, may he drive away all evil forces;
Blessed by God,
Strengthened by the people,
Allied with all that is pure,
May he conquer his adversaries.

(Atharva.4.22.7)

Out of full-blooded valour was born the first man;
A warrior of royal blood;
He came to the people
Shared his bounties with his kinsmen.
This quality of love and benevolence
Endeared him to the people,
He was the Primeval man, Purusha.

(Atharvă.15.8.1,2)

The king goes to the people majestically,
To the assembly and the army,
Pleasures follow him;
He who thus maintains royal traditions
Becomes beloved of
The assembly and the army.

(Atharva.15.9.1

Neither sin nor sorrow from any quarter,
Neither enemies nor hypocrites and double-dealers
Ever harm the person,
Whom the head of the state defends and protects,
By driving away from him all
That is treacherous and injurious.

(Rig.2.23.5

The sage or the sovereign king,
Whom the Lord blesses, is never vanquished,
Never slain, never perishes,
Never suffers from any anguish,
His riches never dwindle
Nor do the bounties showered on him by the Lord.

(Rig.5.54.7)

O King, be formidable and firm
Like a rock and follow the path of thy duty.

(Yajur.12.17)

Thou art a mighty ruler
Of the Kingdom
Possessest unparalleled strength;
Thou art a destroyer
Of malicious foes;
The devotee who counts Thee
As his friend
Is never defeated
And he remains invincible for ever.

(Rig.10.152.1)

Brave Warriors

O dynamic warriors (kshatriyas),
Possessed of bold spirit,
Formidable like wild beasts,
Reverberating the world by their energies.
Brightly shining like fires
But soft in temperament,
Restore the wealth of the people
By winning over adversaries.

(Rig.2.34.1)

May we win the possessions of the enemies
With our bow.
With the bow may we be victorious in battle.
May we be winners in our hot encounters.
May the bow bring grief and sorrow
To our adversaries.
Armed with the bow may we subdue all hostile
    countries.

(Rig.6.75.2)

This bow-string, drawn tight upon the bow,
And making way in battle,
Repeatedly approaches the ear
As if embracing its friend (the arrow)
And proposing to say something sweet and loving.

(Rig.6.75.3)

May the two extremities of the bow uphold
As a mother nurses her child upon her lap!
And may they, moving concurrently,
And harming the foe, scatter the enemies!

(Rig.6.75.4)

The arrow puts on a feathery wing:
The horn of the deer is its point:
It is bound with the sinews of the cow:
It alights where directed,
Wherever men assemble or disperse,
There may the shafts provide security.

(Rig.6.75.11)

O straight-flying arrow
Defend us; may our bodies be strong as stone
May the blissful Lord give us encouragement
And may Mother Infinity grant us success.

(Rig.6.75.12)

It is the whip,
With which the skilful charioteers
Lash the thighs and the flanks of the steeds;
May it urge the horses in battle to speed on!

(Rig.6.75.13)

The warriors are bearers of bright weapons
And impetuous in their haste.
They deck themselves in shining armour
And their bodies have splendour of their own.

(Rig.7.56.11)

The armour of the warriors
Is bright upon their bodies and
Their lances glitter splendidly.

(Rig.8.20.11)

These warriors are fierce,
Vigorous and strong-armed.
They need not exert
To defend their bodies from attack.
Their bows and arrows are ready in their chariots.
Victory over their enemies makes them glorious.

(Rig.8.20.12)

Homage to Artisans

O expert artisans, skilled in constructive works
And noble citizens possessing wealth
And abundant sustenance,
May you, privileged to be the recipients
Of divine talent,
Grant prosperity to us.
We honour the spirit of selfless service
And charity in you.

(Rig.4.34.10)

O pioneers of road and air communication systems,
Come to inspire us in our benevolent deeds.
These gracious pioneers maintain the tradition
Of doing useful work for securing prosperity
Throughout all time.

(Rig.4.37.1)

O makers of road and air communication systems,
Your threefold transport
Meant for the welfare of the people
Deserves appreciation.
Therefore, affectionate honour is offered to you
Along with other eminent people
Assembled at this solemn ceremony.

(Rig.4.37.3)

O pioneers of air communication system,
We invoke you, the designers of war vehicles,
Which have great utility in war-time.
They are fast-moving, strong, complex in structure
And provided with sensitive components.

(Rig.4.37.5)

Offering

O Supreme Lord, let eminent scholars
Possessing the lustre of spiritual knowledge
Be born in our state
And may brave warriors and statesmen
Capable of ruling the people
Be born in our state.
Let expert archers and marksmen
Be born in our state.
May there be born cows
Giving plentiful milk,
Stout oxen and swift horses.
And many there be born virtuous women
And valorous men.
Heroic youths and charioteers,
Fighters with the will to victory
And fit to shine in assemblies.
May clouds shower rains
Profusely as much as we wish!
May our trees bearing fruit ripen,
May we be able to safeguard
Our earnings and savings!

(Yajur.22.22)

Virtuous Thoughts and Noble Deeds

To be blessed with profound contentment,
Have faith in God and put in your best efforts
Honestly in the beneficial works of society.

(Rig.1.15.7)

One surely and inevitably gains that which
One truly desires
And for which one works honestly and patiently.

(Rig.1.105.2)

Wise men attain salvation
Through their own patient search
And inner vision and adherence to the
Knowledge acquired.

(Rig.1.145.2)

O Lord, mayest Thou fill
Our hearts and minds with sweetness,
May it flow like a stream of honey.

(Rig.9.17.8)

Thy mind goes far away
To heaven and earth,
Call it back to thyself,
So that it may remain
Under thy control.

(Rig.10.58.2)

Thy mind goes far away
To all that occurred in the past
And will occur in future,
Call it back to thyself
So that it may remain
Under thy control.

(Rig.10.58.12)

Teach us, O All-wise Lord, the Lord of Creation,
To purify our vision to behold truth.

(Yajur.4.4)

Stand firm and erect;
Build this body strong like a rock.
And strengthen it to perform your duties
And fulfil your responsibilities;
You will surely live, strong and sturdy
A hundred autumns,
Gaining prosperity and riches,
Warding off all evil.

(Atharva.2.13.3,4)

O Sin, may the fire consume you
The clouds of smoke carry you far away;
May the Lord bless the liberal and pious devotees!

(Atharva.6.113.2)

Remain free of debt of any kind
Throughout all stages of your life.

(Atharva.6.117.3)

Rise O man! To fall is not your nature.
You alone are blessed with
A piercing intellect to avoid pitfalls.

(Atharva.8.1.6)

I resolve to discard all the false values
And accept ever-true ideals of life.

(Yajur.1.5)

Offer reverence to the learned sages and
   your parents,
And treat them with respect.

(Yajur.2.7)

Let Aum — the word—syllable—symbolising
The undiminishing experience of divine light and
   joy
Remain in thy heart for all time to come.

(Yajur.2.13)

Have faith, for thou art invincible
And possessest the strength of an
   unconquerable hero.

(Yajur.5.5)

Never speak harsh words; let not bitter words
Escape thy lips any time;
Keep them far away.

(Yajur.5.8)

Recognise thy own inherent power
That may cause to infuse in thee
All the virtues of the Universe.

(Yajur.5.30)

Let the sublime aura of pure joy
Embrace thee in its fold of intense love forever.

(Yajur.6.2)

Harmony

Give prominence to intellect over emotions.

God has housed your emotional heart and your logical mind in one body.

Do not be swayed by emotions, nor be carried away by mere logic.

Obtain inspiration from the heart, but guidance from the brain and go ahead with steady steps.

The place of reason is higher than the place of the heart!

Try to develop your intellect on the same principles which your enlightened and inspired seers followed.

(Atharva.10.2.26)

Awakening

Awake, divine people, awake!
He who keeps awake is blessed by the
Lord of Soma.

He alone is befriended by the divine
forces who keeps vigilant. In all his
noble deeds God assures him success.

God helps only those who work hard
with vigour and courage.

Worthy of the Lord's association are
not those who are lethargic and sleepy.

None ever comes to the aid of one who
is morbid and fatalistic.

(Rig.5.44.14)

Be self-sufficient, O man!
Be not a slave to any outside help.

(Yajur.6.12)

Listen to such words
That enable thee to conquer thy inner foes.

(Yajur.6.19)

Be so illustrious that all approach thee for guidance.

(Yajur.6.31)

Thou art self-sufficient,
The architect of thy own destiny.

(Yajur.7.3)

O leaders of our nation, resolve to keep
    a strict watch
Over the safety of our motherland.

(Yajur.9.23)

The wisdom of inspired seers is true and effective;
Follow their instructions with full faith.

(Yajur.11.81)

May you, O man!
Realise the virtues of self-reliance
And self-sacrifice.

(Yajur.23.15)

Happiness is acquired through the joy of worship
And the cultivation of virtuous qualities.

(Sama.194)

A true devotee is always soft in speech
And considerate towards others.

(Sama.251)

At all stages of life,
In the beginning, the middle and the end,
Keep away from the evils of violent anger.

(Sama.307)

Bless us with divine fragrance   O God,
And purify our speech,
May we always speak sweetly!

(Sama.358)

While giving charity, may I not be a miser,
May benevolence awaken my spirit of generosity!

(Rig.2.7.2)

The Lord defends and favours
Only those who work hard
And work for a benevolent cause.

(Rig.4.25.6)

Those who perform benevolent works
Become brave and strong
And their minds and bodies
Become free from sin and disease.
God helps them to conquer their adversaries
Like an angry lion
Driving away a herd of elephants.

(Rig.5.15.3)

The Mortal Frame

Continue fighting against sins till the end.

Virtues and sins are eternally bound together in the human body.

When the divine architect planned and fashioned the human form, all the evils and virtues entered the mortal frame and made it their home.

Theft, wickedness, thirst and hunger live there with truth, wisdom, contentment, nobility and faith.

Joy and grief, jealousy and love, amazing darkness and glorious brightness, are all woven in the cloth of one human soul. Thus it becomes complete by opposite qualities.

This soul walled within the mortal body is called Brahman.

(Atharva.11.8.30,32)

I leave here those who are
Not progressive and benevolent,
And take the charitable people
To march forward.

(Rig.10.53.8)

He is desireless, serene, immortal and self-existent;
He is satisfied with essence only, and lacks nothing;
Anyone who knows this serene, ageless
Yet ever youthful Supreme Soul
Fears no one, not even death.

(Atharva.10.8.44)

Ye enlightened men,
Uplift once more
The fallen and the degraded
The lowly and the lorn.
Ye illustrious men,
Uplift him who has sinned
Help him to begin life anew.

(Rig.10.137.1)

Perfect am I
Perfect is my mind,
Perfect are mine eyes,
Perfect are my ears,
Perfect is my breath,
Perfect my entire being,
At peace with myself am I.

(Atharva.19.51.1)

Have no enemies in east, west, north and south!

(Atharva.6.40.3)

Awaken and enhance the progress
Of noble actions.
Now enrich your life
With constant hard work
And virtuous deeds
And live in the spirit of sacrifice.

(Yajur.1.12)

O sage! be seated on this sacred altar
And let the listeners share
Thy spiritual knowledge and experience.

(Yajur.2.18)

May thy body be an unfailing instrument
Engaged in beneficial pursuits.

(Yajur.4.13)

Heal up the wounds of thy fellow-pilgrims
And infuse the spirit of perfect harmony
In their hearts.

(Yajur.12.54)

Through thy nobility and noble deeds
Earn happiness and make others happy.

(Sama.52)

May thy heart be full of generosity,
Kindness and love;
May it flow to the down-trodden
And make them happy!

(Sama.55)

Lead thy life on the ideals of Yajna,
The spirit of sacrifice.

(Sama.56)

Following the path of self-sacrifice,
May you render service to humanity.

(Sama.63)

O man! nurture thy body
And strengthen it with food
That provides vigour and vitality.

(Yajur.6.2)

Watch over and around.
Be wakeful, O godly brave men,
Throw your weapons at the violent,
The cruel and the unbelieving.

(Rig.7.104.25)

Come, march ahead with courage,
Face troubles bravely;
No obstacles can check your progress
While you are on the right path.

(Rig.1.80.3)

O adorable Supreme God,
Grant us wisdom
That we find delight in hard labour
And be convinced that it bears fruit,
Enjoyed only under Thy guardianship
And with Thy blessings.
Thou art the Nourisher, the Giver of all;
Mayest thou guide the hard worker
And bless him to enjoy the fruits of his labour.

(Rig.1.146.3)

True devotees who work diligently
Are amply rewarded.

(Rig.1.168.3)

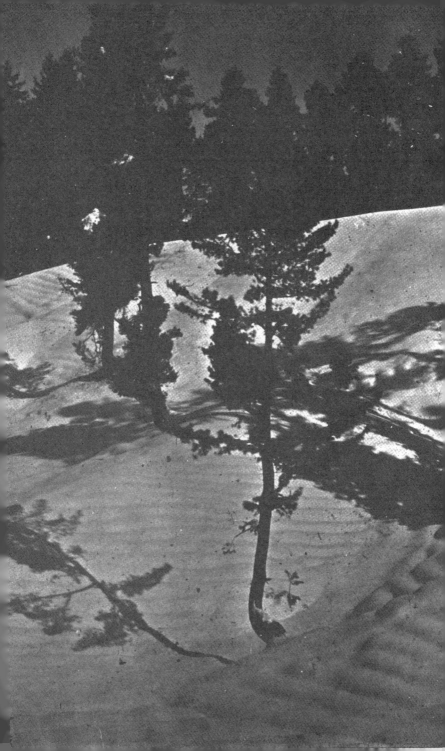

God helps those who help themselves
And work hard under divine guidance.

(Rig.4.23.7)

The dedicated men offer love and respect
To the cosmic divinities;
But remember, offering love alone
Is not enough;
Constant hard work and diligence
Are essential for success.
Then alone the Lord Supreme
Showers His blessings upon them.

(Rig.4.33.11)

One achieves one's objectives
Through one's own efforts.

(Rig.5.44.6)

Live thy full span of life,
Welcome old age with grace,
Mayest thou remain ever active
May the Creator of this splendorous world
Graciously bless thee with good fortune.

(Rig.10.18.6)

May we, with honest efforts
And no consciousness of guilt,
Ascend day by day
Higher and higher summits of
Eternal glory and bliss.

(Rig.10.37.9)

Awake, arise, resolve,
And take the banner
Of truth in thy firm hands;
March forward and annihilate
Those who are evil-spirited
And wicked like serpents.

(Rig.10.103.13)

The dawn comes knocking at your door;
Arise, awake, O divine men,
The glorious sun has risen, the radiant glow is
    flowing from the east, dispersing the darkness
    of the night.
The new bright rays bring in renewed hope.
A new day is ushered in, full of zest and zeal
    and life progresses on its path of glory,
Each dawn brings a bright ray of hope and
    a happy day.

(Rig.10.113.16)

O Soul, may Thy speed be of tempest and
brightness be that of a shining sun! Thy light none
can supersede. Be so bright that it enlightens the
whole Universe.

(Yajur.1.24)

The devotees enjoy riches
Due to their personal efforts
And through the grace of God,
But mainly through their own patience
And perseverance.

(Rig.1.138.3)

O Soul, be brave like a lion;
And strike down thy foes.

(Atharva.4.22.7)

The Supreme Lord abides within the inner self of
all human beings.

(Yajur.5.4)

I resolve to elevate my soul to the highest peak of
spiritual joy.

(Yajur.11.22)

Sublime Peace

Withdraw from all strifes and struggles of your life, as you have reached the last stage of your long journey,

May the earth and heaven be compassionate towards you.

Harbour no enmity for anyone in your heart.

You need fear no one.

May you live the rest of your life in sublime peace!

(Atharva.19.14.1)

All in One, One in All

Behave with others as you would with yourself.

Look upon all the living beings as your bosom friends, for in all of them there resides one soul.

All are but a part of that Universal Soul.

A person who believes that all are his soul-mates and loves them all alike, never feels lonely.

The divine qualities of forgiveness, compassion and service will make him lovable in the eyes of all.

He will experience intense joy throughout his life.

(Yajur.40.6)

Commandments

Let not the wings of thy soul take thee so high that thou losest sight of thy earthly duties.

(Yajur.5.43)

O man, rise up from this lower level of life;
  sink not into the pit of darkness.
Cast away the bonds, the fear of death that holds
  you down;
Be not frustrated in this world.
Shine like the flames of a blazing fire and glow
  like the radiant sun.

(Atharva.12.2.24)

Human life is like a turbulent stream, strewn with rocks and pebbles; the brave step into it; for by sitting on the shore and enumerating hurdles, you shall never get across.

Leave behind the burden of your fears, guilts, weaknesses and cumbersome attachments. Thus freed from all negative forces, smoothly cross over the stream.

(Atharva.12.2.26)

Gather your strength, O human soul.
A stream of eternal life flows on a stony bed;
Leave behind the traits of malignant forces
And move forward with firm steps,
And cross over to the realm of eternal glory.

(Atharva.12.2.26,27)

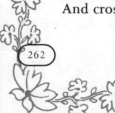

Die not, O men, live on to a ripe old age;
Live with a heroic spirit
Equipped with strong will-power;
And submit not to the fear of death.

(Atharva.19.27.8)

The brave are invincible.

(Atharva.20.47.3)

He who is brave,
Invincible, resolute and steadfast
Wins the battle.

(Atharva.20.53.3)

Attain fortitude and firmness
By obeying the commands of the Supreme Lord;
Never defy them.

(Yajur.1.2)

Brighten thy intellect
For doing divine duties
And unfolding the hidden truth
Behind false values.

(Yajur.1.13)

Let all sages make their fellow-brothers
Partners in sharing the treasures
Of spiritual ecstasy

(Yajur.2.31)

Enable us to dispel our ignorance
Through patience and perseverance.

(Yajur.3.61)

O brave warrior,
Pounce upon your enemy
Like an eagle,
And annihilate him.

(Yajur.4.84)

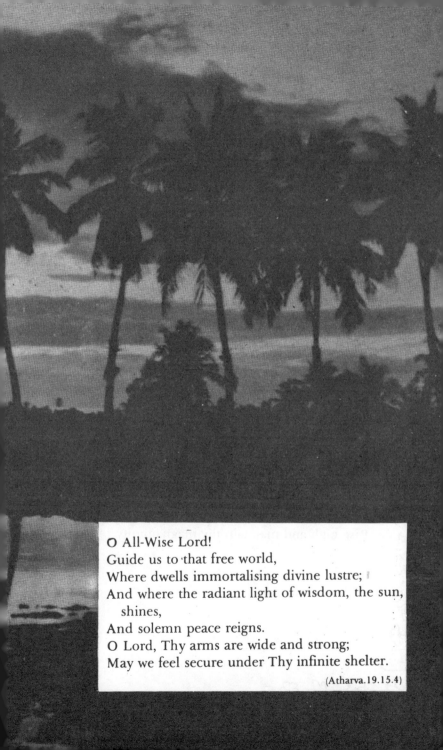

O All-Wise Lord!
Guide us to that free world,
Where dwells immortalising divine lustre;
And where the radiant light of wisdom, the sun,
  shines,
And solemn peace reigns.
O Lord, Thy arms are wide and strong;
May we feel secure under Thy infinite shelter.

(Atharva.19.15.4)

Explore the sky
And be blessed with good fortune.

(Yajur.6.21)

Be brave and overcome evils
With daring courage.
Realise thy own inner strength,
Fear no one,
Be steady and strong.

(Yajur.6.35)

O, brave man,
Crush the violent forces of thy enemy.

(Yajur.9.37)

Warrior! Advance speedily and destroy the enemy.

(Yajur.11.15)

March ahead and ascend high
For reaching the post
Of highest glory and fortune;
March on steadfastly.

(Yajur.11.21)

May thy speed be that of a tempest
And thy strength that of a wild horse.

(Yajur.11.44)

Rise high and maintain thy magnanimity.

(Yajur.13.1)

Overpower thy adversaries
With a heroic spirit.

(Yajur.13.13)

O man, thou hast
Wings of virtue and vitality;
Establish thyself
On the surface of the earth;
Fill the firmament with thy radiance,
Cover the sphere with thy lustre,
Spread thy effulgence in all directions.

(Yajur.17.72)

With prompt, agile action
And wilful offerings,
Attain thy higher aims, O man.

(Sama.47)

Mayest Thou, O Soul, hasten, assail and subdue all
        evils
Thy adamantine determination cannot fail in
        all respects.
O Resplendent Soul, Thy vigour is Thy strength.
Mayest Thou destroy the evil ignorance
With a control over its action,
And thus manifest Thine own sovereignty.

(Sama.413)

Let not the wicked impulses
Destroy our character;
Let them die their natural death.

(Rig.1.38.6)

Never retaliate against any man,
Even if he curses or harms you.
May you invoke the blessings of God
On him by your prayers!

(Rig.1.141.8)

May the rank delusion of the man
Who spins out perilous sophistries
To inveigle us into wrong paths
Die down within him.

(Rig.2.23.6)

The one who harms an innocent person
Is no man but a wolf;
Keep away from him.

(Rig.2.23.7)

In the process of self-realisation,
Evil desires are automatically consumed
And destroyed.

(Rig.2.30.5)

Cultivate the strength of will power
To conquer the passionate urges
Of thy sense-organs.

(Rig.5.31.3)

Dispel the deep dark curtain
Of ignorance, Avidya, non-existence.

(Sama.319)

Destroy the voracious instinct of greed!
For, verily, it is a wolf.

(Rig.6.51.4)

Let the worship of the boastful devotee
Be made humble.

(Rig.6.52.1)

Neither think nor act maliciously;
Tread always the righteous path.

(Rig.10.57.1)

O non-violent seeker! O persistent devotee!
Get rid of the feelings of envy, greed
And other evil impulses.

(Sama.308)

An idle mind is an easy prey to evil thoughts.

(Rig.10.22.8)

We must destroy, completely crush
And burn to ashes those wicked persons
Who are intent upon eliminating
Such brave men
Who fight and vanquish the cruel enemy.

(Atharva.4.36.2)

Cast off anger
From your heart
Like an arrow from the bow,
So that you may again be friends
And live together in harmony.

(Atharva.6.42.1)

As the rising sun takes away
The lustre of other luminaries,
Surely, I'll sap the strength of the wicked,
Who shall fade out into oblivion in no time.

(Atharva.7.13.2)

Grieve not for those departed;
That takes thee backward;
Rise from darkness
To brighter glory,
Come, we grasp thy hands.

(Atharva.8.1.8)

Realisation

Find the eternal object of your quest within your soul.

Enough have you wandered during the long period of your quest!

Dark and weary must have been the ages of your searching in ignorance and groping in helplessness;

At last when you turn your gaze inward, suddenly you realise that the bright light of faith and lasting truth was shining around you.

With rapturous joy, you find the soul of the universe, the eternal object of your quest.

Your searching mind at last finds the object of the search within your own heart.

Your inner vision is illuminated by this new realisation.

(Yajur.32.11)

Those who forsake reverential worship
And pursue the path of material gains
Invite worry and frustration for themselves!

(Atharva.12.2.51)

Overcome thy violent urges with firmness.
Those are thy enemies.

(Yajur.1.19)

O God! Help us to keep evil thoughts far from us.

(Yajur.4.28)

Resolve with courage to crush the deceitful
Or let him be destroyed by his own devices.

(Yajur.6.16)

Rise above material desires
To the heavenly path of spiritual experience;
And behold the light divine
Guiding thee towards eternal joy.

(Yajur.8.52)

Through rigorous discipline and strict austeriy,
Burn thy passionate desires.

(Sama.24)

May we always have noble thoughts in our minds;
May we never express bitter words in our speech!

(Sama.140)

Get rid of jealousy from your heart
And eschew violence.

(Sama.274)

May my motherland
Grant me the lustre of gold

(Atharva.12.1.18)

Hymns on

Splendour

तच्चक्षुर्देवहितं शुक्रमुच्चरत्

पश्येम शरदः शतं जीवेम शरदः शतम्

The sun, the eye of the universe, is divinely placed,
It·rises with bright sunshine;
May we live to see it for a hundred autumns!

(Rig. 7.66.16)

The Universe

The All-controlling,
Immortal wheel of the Universe
Is revolving in infinite space
Ten, yoked together,
Draw it in this wide world.
The wisdom of God,
United with Energy,
Manages the whole Universe.
On this Energy rest
And depend
All regions and planets.

(Atharva.9.9.14)

In the very Infinite,
Are well placed,
The mind, the vital breath
And the name.
All these elements enjoy themselves
At His very approach.

In the self-same Infinite
Are fully established,
The austerity, the grandeur
The vast universe and the Vedic lore.
He is the Lord of all.

(Atharva.19.53.7,8)

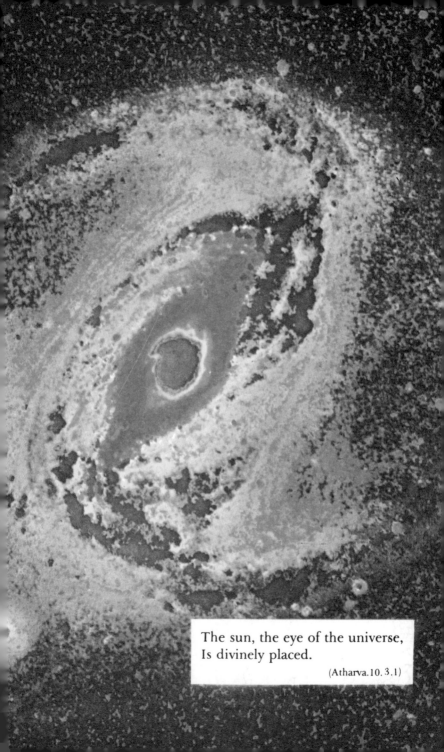

The sun, the eye of the universe,
Is divinely placed.

(Atharva. 10. 3.1)

In Him all divine cosmic powers become one.
He is Father of all hymns and praises.
Messenger of all divines
He purifieth all regions, and from lofty regions
    watcheth all creatures,
All that breathe and all that breathe not.
In Him all deities become One and only One.

(Atharva.13.2.26)

The dynamic universe is the result of intensive
    divine fervour, application of the mind-force to
    matter.
The Supreme Being is described here as the
    Architect of the Universe.
First the oceans were created.
Thereafter the solid land mass was formed.
In this way, the Supreme Sculptor of the Universe,
Chiselled the planetary systems in as great a variety
    of forms
As is perceived and even beyond.
Depending upon his good or evil and sinful deeds,
Mortal man takes birth in this planetary scheme.

(Rig.10.90.17)

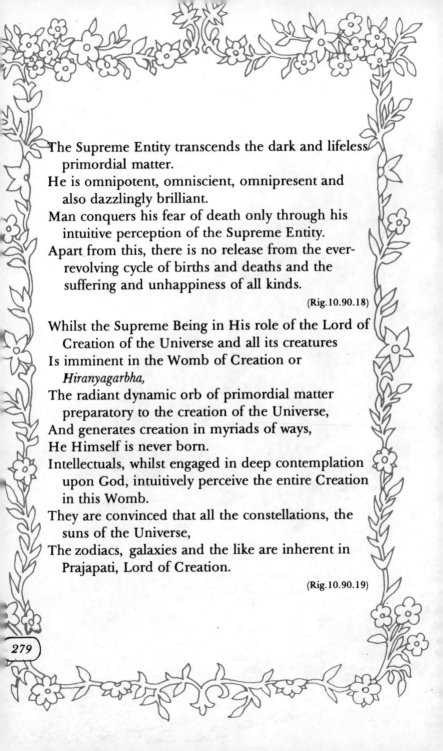

The Supreme Entity transcends the dark and lifeless
    primordial matter.
He is omnipotent, omniscient, omnipresent and
    also dazzlingly brilliant.
Man conquers his fear of death only through his
    intuitive perception of the Supreme Entity.
Apart from this, there is no release from the ever-
    revolving cycle of births and deaths and the
    suffering and unhappiness of all kinds.

(Rig.10.90.18)

Whilst the Supreme Being in His role of the Lord of
    Creation of the Universe and all its creatures
Is imminent in the Womb of Creation or
    Hiranyagarbha,
The radiant dynamic orb of primordial matter
    preparatory to the creation of the Universe,
And generates creation in myriads of ways,
He Himself is never born.
Intellectuals, whilst engaged in deep contemplation
    upon God, intuitively perceive the entire Creation
    in this Womb.
They are convinced that all the constellations, the
    suns of the Universe,
The zodiacs, galaxies and the like are inherent in
    Prajapati, Lord of Creation.

(Rig.10.90.19)

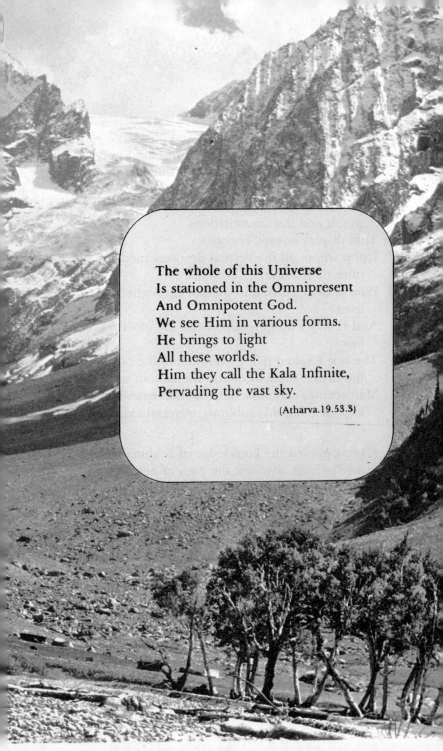

The whole of this Universe
Is stationed in the Omnipresent
And Omnipotent God.
We see Him in various forms.
He brings to light
All these worlds.
Him they call the Kala Infinite,
Pervading the vast sky.

(Atharva.19.53.3)

We offer our sincere homage and obeisance with
    unswerving devotion to the Supreme Entity,
The one omniscient, exalted, illuminated Being,
    who causes the creation of all matter
Comprising the earth, water, fire as well as the sun,
    moon and the constellations
That display cosmic energies;
Upon whom all intellectual devotees meditate and
    offer their prayers;
Who is their guide and mentor throughout their
    lives
And finally who in addition was the most powerful
    force,
The one Exalted Being even before the creation of
    the divine substances and the radiant universe.
Man realises salvation only by understanding and
    experiencing this sublime universal existence.

(Rig.10.90.20)

Having gained the knowledge of Brahman, the
    intellectuals advocate the path of devotion as
    a means of salvation.
These enlightened intellectuals blessed with
    the intuitive perception of Brahman are able to
    control the elemental physical energies
    as well as to discipline their conscious mind
    and faculties.

(Rig.10.90.21)

Spiritual and material splendours symbolise the two
    principal attributes of the Supreme Being,
While day and night symbolically relate to His two
    opposing sides.
The outer space illuminated with suns and galaxies
    proclaims His cosmic existence.
This outer space and the earth correspond to the
    two open jaws of His mouth.
With the strength of His divine fervour the Universe
    is created.
Realising his power we pray:
"O Supreme Being, inspire us and guide us to
    attain Sublime Bliss.
May we progress in every respect in this Universe
    and may we always be blessed with the nectar
    of Thy love!
May this Universe be gloriously beautiful
And finally, may we be blessed with everlasting
    peace and happiness in every way."

(Rig.10.90.22)

First to be created was the celestial region;
The most powerful object in Creation is the Sun;
The most radiant possession of the Universe is
    the Earth;
Night swallows everything.

(Yajur.23.12)

The Golden Dawn

The heaven and the earth
Yield rain for our sustenance.
The bounteous dawns toil for us,
Glittering with dew-drops;
They send down heavenly treasures
For the prosperity of mankind.

(Rig.5.59.8

Right in her movement, sublime by Eternal Law,
    true to Eternal Law, red-tinted, refulgent,
The Divine dawn has come, bringing the light;
    to her the sages sing the welcome of hymns.

(Rig.5.80.1)

The lovely Dawn rouses up the people,
    makes the paths easy to tread, and goes forward;
She, great, all-impelling, rides her great chariot
    and spreads the light before the day's beginning.

(Rig.5.80.2)

She harnesses purple oxen to her chariot
    and, injuring none, makes wealth that lasts forever.
She opens paths to a happy life,
    as, praised of all, she shines with every blessing.

(Rig.5.80.3)

The golden rays of the dawn
Fill one's life with divine lustre.

(Sama.303)

Her colour changing, she, doubly brilliant,
  displays her body from the east,
And follows to perfection the path of Order,
  and, as one who knows all,
  strays not from the quarters.

(Rig.5.80.4)

As if knowing her body is bright, like one
  who has bathed, she stands up, visible to us.
Dispelling all malignity and darkness,
  Dawn, Daughter of Heaven, has come with light.

(Rig.5.80.5)

Like a virtuous woman, the Daughter of Heaven,
  bends her forehead, facing men.
Disclosing her boons to her worshipper,
As before the ever-youthful Dawn brings
  forth the light.

(Rig.5.80.6)

The white and rosy tints
Of the splendorous dawn
Rise up like the waves of the ocean.
She renders all paths easy to travel;
She displays her glory,
Which is benign and friendly.

(Rig.6.63.1)

O divine dawn,
When the birds fly forth
From their nests,
Men must rise to work
And earn their sustenance.

(Rig.6.64.6)

This heaven-born daughter of the sky,
Driving away the darkness,
Wakes up the human beings
From their slumber;
She, with her bright lustre,
Is perceived dissipating the gloom,
Even through the shades of darkness.

(Rig.6.65.1)

May the dawns
Come to bless our worship
With the speed of wind.
May the dawns bring divine grace and **prosperity** !

(Rig.7.41.6)

May the auspicious dawn
Brighten our path
And grant us wealth,
Vitality, wisdom and valiant posterity!
May she come
With all abundance and affection,
And associated with the divine forces
Continue to shower blessings upon us!

(Rig.7.41.7)

I see the paths, innocuous and glorious,
Leading to divine powers.
The glow of dawn reflects
In the east, and moves westward,
Rising to high altitudes.

(Rig.7.76.2

Soothing be our nights
And inspiring the dawns,
Tender be the dust of earth,
May heaven be kind to us!

(Rig.1.90.7)

Night and Dawn

O pair of Divine powers, Night and Dawn,
Come near, like two press-stones,
   with a common aim;
like two zealous men moving to a tree of treasure;
like two hymn-singing Brahmanas to the assembly;
like two people's envoys called at many places.

(Rig.2.39.1)

Like two-charioted heroes going in the morning;
like two leaders, come together to your choice,
like two damsels beautifying themselves,
like a wise married couple among the people.

(Rig.2.39.2)

Like two horns, come earliest to us hither;
like two hoofs, travelling with rapid motion;
like two chakravakas at the day's dawning;
Come towards us, mighty, like charioted heroes.

(Rig.2.39.3)

Like two unaging winds, two confluent rivers,
like two quick-seeing eyes, come towards us;
like two hands, most useful to the body,
like two feet, take us towards our welfare.

(Rig.2.39.5)

Like two lips that speak sweetly with the mouth,
like two breasts that give nurture to our life,
like two nostrils that preserve our being,
like two ears that hear well be you to us!

(Rig.2.39.6)

Like two hands invest us with vigour,
like heaven and earth subduing the atmosphere,
Our songs, O Twin-Divines, that proceed towards
you, sharpen them well, like an axe upon the
whetstone.

(Rig.2.39.7)

These prayers, exalting you, O Twin-Divines,
The poet-sages have made into a hymn of praise.
Be pleased with them, Heroes! and come hither.
Loud may we speak with brave men in the
assembly.

(Rig.2.39.8)

Like two boats, take us across; like two poles,
like axles, like spokes, like fellies, carry us.
Like two dogs ward off all harm to our bodies,
like two crutches protect us against falling.

(Rig.2.39.4)

The Sun

We offer gratitude
To the waters,
Flowing in the rivers;
Kissed by the sun-rays;
As we offer reverence
To the Supreme Creator.

(Rig.1.23.18)

The wheels of the sun
Have two functions;
One imparts knowledge,
The other destroys all evils.

(Rig.5.29.10)

The sun ascends
The shining sky
As soon as he yokes
His bright speedy chariot.
The Almighty draws him
Like a ship across the ocean.

(Rig.5.45.10)

The sun shines and causes to shine
The realms that do not shine.
By dint of the eternal cosmic law
He illuminates the mornings.
He moves with divine rays
Yoked by eternal order.

He furnishes men
With such nerve-centres
That make them feel joyous.

(Rig.6.39.4)

The sun, beholding good and evil
Acts of mortals,
Manifests their intentions.

(Rig.6.51.2)

May the sun
Promptly favour us
With its protection.
May the river, the clouds
And herbs and vegetation
Give us happiness.
May we earnestly
Invoke the Fire Divine
To be a Father to us.

(Rig.6.52.6)

May the sun divine stretch forth
His golden arms to us
And inspire us like an eloquent orator.

(Rig.6.71.5)

The sun divine has diffused
Golden lustre on the sky
From the halo around him;
Verily, the gracious sun is adored
Since he abounds in wealth
Which he distributes amongst men.

(Rig.7.38.1)

Borne by his beams
May the divine sun,
Possessed of precious treasure,
Filling the firmament with radiance,
Bless us with prosperity.
He lulls all beings to slumber
In the shadow of the night
And again awakens them
At the break of dawn.

(Rig.7.45.1)

May the outspread, vast and golden·
Arms of the sun extend to the
Limits of the sky;
May the radiant sun
Instil vigour in our souls.

(Rig.7.45.2)

May the divine sun, the lord of wealth,
Endowed with energy
Bestow treasures upon us!
May he, with his far-spreading lustre,
Provide nourishment to all.

(Rig.7.45.3)

Many are such divine powers
Which are radiant as the sun,
With their fire-like flames
And are worthy of adoration.
They direct universal sacrificial works
With overwhelming strength.

(Rig.7.66.10)

The sun divine, the leader of all
In the solar system
Spreads his immortal, all-benefiting light.
Being the eye
Of all Nature's bounties,
He becomes the source of creativity,
And makes all the regions visible.

(Rig.7.76.1)

May the suns,
The divine self-luminaries,
Offspring of Mother Infinity,
Remove disease
And drive away malignity.
May they ever keep us
Far from sore distress!

(Rig.8.78.10)

The sun is the soul of the world,
Be it static or moving.

(Atharva.13.2.25)

May the rising sun
Liberate us
From the bondage
Of birth and death!

(Atharva.17.1.30)

The solar rays drive away diseases
Dispel malignant thoughts
And keep us away from sins.

(Sama.397

O Sun, on Thy coming,
All living beings are awakened
And the winged birds flock around
From the boundaries
Of skies to greet Thee.

(Rig.1.49.3)

The Full-moon Night

I invoke the splendorous full-moon night
With my well-composed hymns.
May she listen to our prayers
And accept them;
May she blend our thoughts and actions
Into the universal melody.

(Rig.2.33.4)

O bounteous full-moon night,
Possessing grace and charm
Grant peace and prosperity to us.
May you favour us
With thousandfold blessings!

(Rig.2.33.5)

Peering in every corner,
Come, O Goddess of Night,
Wearing your glorious robes;
We welcome you like birds
Resting in their nests;
All beings that walk or fly
Return to their homes at dusk.
Come, O Night,
With your sublime glory.

(Rig.10.127.1)

Divine Clouds and Winds

The bright, fierce and vigorous vital winds,
Cherished by the cosmic order,
Send down the rain
To the barren lands.

(Rig.1.38.7)

May the soft blowing breeze
Refresh and revitalize us
With its healing touch;
And so be the mother earth and father sun;
May the medicinal extracts of the herbs
Be conducive to our health!

(Rig.1.90.6)

Even the fierce-looking clouds
Come to us as benefactors.

(Rig.5.56.2)

Almighty God conveys prayers of men
To the divine winds,
Which send dew-drops to the earth.

(Rig.5.61.17)

O clouds, showerers of rain,
May you send waters
From the firmaments,
O sustainer of the universe,
Mayest Thou enhance the wealth
Of pious men!

(Rig.6.48.6)

O cloud-bearing winds,
Showerers of rain,
May you send waters
From the firmament.
O sagacious vital principles,
Listeners to eulogies,
Sustainers of the world,
May you multiply
The wealth of your praisers.

(Rig.6.49.6)

May the clouds
Lovingly bend down
To lift us up,
And become our helpers
In our difficulties,
Great or small!

(Rig.6.50.4)

May your chariot,
O vital principles,
Be devoid of wickedness.
May this chariot,
Which is without a driver,
Without horses,
Without provender,
And without traces,
Which scatters water
And which accomplishes desires,
Traverse heaven and earth,
And paths of interspace.

(Rig.6.66.7)

The clouds that float
By the whiff of the cool breeze
Descend from the heavens
In all their multicolour glory,
Swaying and surging
To shower the celestial rains
And drench the earth
With life-giving drops
Of Amrita.

(Rig.7.36.7)

O clouds, your bright ornaments
Rest upon your shoulders;
They are like shining necklaces
And are like a pendant hanging
On your bosom.
Glittering with drops of rain
Like lightning flashes,
You whirl about
Your bright weapons
And scatter rain-water.

(Rig.7.56.13)

These swift moving vital winds
Give pleasure to the zealous worshipper,
And humble the strength
Of the strong men;
They protect their adorers
From the angry malignant;
And they show their severe displeasure
To the wicked.

(Rig.7.56.19)

He, the cloud divine,
Is the primary cause
Of impregnation
In the entire universe.

(Rig.7.102.2)

O vital winds,
Leaders of cosmic sacrifice,
Come like swift flying falcons
In your rain-shedding
And strong-horsed chariot
To bestow showers of water.

(Rig.8.20.10)

I invoke such cloud-bearing winds
Which roar like a wild tempest,
Crackle like lightning,
And pierce the depths of the ocean.

(Rig.8.102.5)

Like right-thinking sages with their hymns, like skilled
  invokers of Divines with their offerings,
Like wondrous-looking kings bedecked with ornaments,
  like spotless gallants, leaders of their people.

(Rig.10.78.1)

Shining like fire with gold ornaments on the breast,
  like self-yoked winds, they are bringers of quick aid;
Noble guides, like wise men, most venerable,
  like Soma with good shelter for him who lives by Law.

(Rig.10.78.2)

Like winds they are shakers, swiftly moving;
  like tongues of fire they are resplendent;
Like mighty warriors in their coats of mail,
  and bounteous with gifts like the hymns of
  our ancient sages.

(Rig.10.78.3)

Like spokes of chariot-wheels united in the naves;
  like the ever victorious Heroes of Heaven;
like youthful suitors scattering gracious gifts,
  they raise their musical voice as psalmists their song.

(Rig.10.78.4)

They are like the noblest steeds that are swift of motion,
  like bounteous, charioted heroes seeking the prize,
Like fast-moving waters flowing from a height,
  like omniform fire-priests with Sama hymns.

(Rig.10.78.5)

They are Princes like the grinding stones born of streams,
  like the stones that always crush to pieces,
Like playful children that have beauteous mothers,
  like a mighty host on the march with splendour.

(Rig.10.78.6)

Radiant at sacrifices like the rays of dawn,
  wishing to be lustrous, they shine with ornaments;
Hastening on like rivers with spears that glisten,
  they measure out from afar the vast distances.

(Rig.10.78.7)

Make us happy, O Divines, and masters of wealth.
  Clouds advance us, the singers of your praises;
Be aware of our praise-songs and our friendship;
  from of old there have been your gifts of treasures.

(Rig.10.78.8)

O Divine Cloud,
There lies hidden within Thee
The treasure of immortal joy;
Bestow on us a little of it,
So that we may live a happy life.

(Rig. 10.186.3)

Mother Earth

Truth, Eternal Order, that is great and stern,
Consecration, Austerity, Prayer and Ritual,
Uphold the Earth.
May she, queen of what has been and will be,
provide vast space for us.

(Atharva.12.1.1)

The Earth has many heights and slopes and
   the unconfined plain that bind men together.
The Earth bears plants of various healing powers.
May she provide vast space for us!

(Atharva.12.1.2)

In the Earth lie the sea,
   the river and other waters,
In her food and cornfields have come to be,
In her live all that breathes and moves;
May she confer on us the finest of her harvests!

(Atharva.12.1.3)

The Earth is mistress of four quarters,
In her food and cornfields have come to be;
She bears many forms of creatures
   breathing and moving;
May she give us cattle and crops.

(Atharva.12.1.4)

On the Earth men of old before us
    performed their various works
And overwhelmed the forces of evil;
Earth, the home of kine, horses, birds,
May she give us magnificence and lustre.

(Atharva.12.1.5)

The Earth bears all-sustaining, treasure-bearing places,
    gold-breasted, home of all moving life.
The Earth bears the sacred universal fire.
May the Supreme Lord and talented sages give us
    wealth.

(Atharva.12.1.6)

The Earth, whom never sleeping cosmic powers
    protect without erring,
May she pour on us riches in many forms
    and endow us with lustre.

(Atharva.12.1.7)

At first the Earth was merged
    in the waters of the ocean,
    whose heart was in Eternal Heaven,
Wrapped in Truth immortal.
May she give us lustre and strength.

(Atharva.12.1.8)

The Earth contains rivers common to all
    moving on all sides, flowing day and night.
May she pour on us riches in many forms
    and endow us with lustre.

(Atharva.12.1.9)

Pleasant be thy hills, O Earth,
   thy snow-clad mountains and thy woods!
O Earth—brown, black, ruddy and multi-coloured—
   the firm Earth protected by the supreme Lord
on this Earth I stand, unvanquished, unslain, unhurt.

                        (Atharva.12.1.11)

Set me, O Earth, amidst what is thy centre and thy
   navel, and vitalising forces that emanated from
   thy body.
Purify me from all sides. The Earth is my mother,
   her son am I;
Infinite space is my father, may he fill us with plenty.

                        (Atharva.12.1.12)

The Earth, on which they build the altar,
   and various workers spin the web of yajna,
On which are fixed the tall, bright poles
   before the invocation;
May she, prospering, make us prosper.

                        (Atharva.12.1.13)

The man, O Earth, who hates us, is hostile to us,
   who threatens us by his thoughts and his weapons,
Overwhelm him, O Earth, as thou hast done before.

                        (Atharva.12.1.14)

Born of thee, on thee move mortal creatures;
   thou bearest them—the biped and the quadruped.
Thine, O Earth, are the five races of men to whom,
   mortals, the sun as he rises spreads, with his rays,
   the light immortal.

                        (Atharva.12.1.15)

In concert may all creatures pour out blessings!
Endow me, O Earth, with honied speech.

(Atharva.12.1.16)

Mother of all plants,
   firm Earth is upheld by Eternal Law,
May she be ever beneficent and gracious to us
   as we tread on her.

(Atharva.12.1.17)

A vast abode art thou, and mighty,
   and mighty is thy speed,
   thy moving and thy shaking;
And the mighty Lord protects thee unerringly.
Mayest thou, O Earth, make us shine forth
   with the brightness of gold.
Let no one hate us.

(Atharva.12.1.18)

There lies the fire within the Earth,
   and in plants; the waters carry it;
   the fire is in stone.
There is a fire deep within men;
   a fire in the kine, and a fire in horses.

(Atharva.12.1.19)

The same fire that burns in the heavens;
   the mid-air belongs to this Fire Divine.
Men kindle this fire that bears the oblation
   and loves melted butter.

(Atharva.12.1.20)

May the Earth, clad in her fiery mantle,
   dark-kneed, make me aflame;
May she sharpen me bright.

(Atharva.12.1.21)

We invoke all-supporting Earth
on which trees, lords of forests, stand ever firm.

(Atharva.12.1.27)

Earth on which they offer yajna and oblation
   to divine powers with many decorations,
   on which mortal men live by food and drink;
May she give us breath and life,
   May she make us long-lived.

(Atharva.12.1.22)

The fragrance that rises from thee, O Earth,
   that plants and waters carry,
   and is shared by solar rays,
Make me sweet with that.
   May no one hate me.

(Atharva.12.1.23)

The fragrance that entered the lotus,
   and that the Immortals, O Earth, first brought
   at the ceremonies.
Make me sweet with that.
   May no one hate me.

(Atharva.12.1.24)

Thy fragrance is in men and women,
   and the majesty and lustre in the males
   and the steed, in the wild beast and in the elephant,
Thy radiance unites us with these, O Earth!
   May no one hate me.

(Atharva.12.1.25)

Rock, soil, stone and dust with these
   Earth is held together and bound firm.
My obeisance to gold-breasted Earth.

(Atharva.12.1.26)

Rising or sitting, standing or walking,
May we, either with our right foot or our left,
   never totter on the earth.

(Atharva.12.1.28)

I call to Earth, the purifier,
   the patient Earth, growing strong through
   spiritual might.
May we recline on thee, O Earth,
   who bearest power, plenty and our share of food.

(Atharva.12.1.29)

Pure may the waters flow for our bodies' cleansing.
   To those who trespass against us
   we offer an unpleasant welcome.
I cleanse myself, O Earth, with that which purifies.

(Atharva.12.1.30)

May those that are thy eastern regions,
   and the northern, Earth, and the southern and the
   western, be pleasant for me to tread upon.
May I not stumble while I live in the world.

(Atharva.12.1.31)

So long as I look on thee from around, O Earth,
   with the sun as friend,
So long, as year follows year,
   May not my vision fail.

(Atharva.12.1.33)

Whatever I dig from thee, O Earth,
   may that have quick growth again.
O purifier, may we not injure thy vitals or thy heart.

(Atharva.12.1.35)

May thy summer, O Earth, and thy rains,
   thy autumn, thy dewy months, thy winter and
   thy spring,
May these thy seasons, O Earth, that make the year,
   and day and night
Pour their abundance on us.

(Atharva.12.1.36)

The Earth on which the sacred seat
   and shed are built, and the pole is raised;
On which Brahmanas, versed in Yajur,
   worship in Rig and Sama hymns,
And priests are busy so that the Lord
   may accept the divine juice;
On which, of old, world-building seers
   chanted the sacred words,
And the Seven Sages prayed in session
   with sacrifice and austerity;
May that Earth grant us the wealth that we desire.
May the gracious Lord give the task, and come to
   lead the way.

(Atharva.12.1.38-40)

The Earth on which men sing and dance
   while uttering various words,
Where people meet in battle,
   the war-cry rises, the drum sounds,
May she drive away our enemies,
   May the Earth make us free from foes.

(Atharva.12.1.41)

May Nature's bounties
Uphold us in grace and splendour!

(Atharva.12.1.63)

The Earth on which grow foodgrains—rice and barley,
  on which live all types of men,
Our homage be to her,
  who mellows with the rain.

(Atharva.12.1.42)

May the Earth that bears treasures at many places,
  give me her riches, gems and gold.
May the bounteous mother give us wealth,
  and give it with loving kindness.

(Atharva.12.1.44)

Those forest animals and wild beasts of the woods—
  lions, tigers, man-eaters that prowl about,
and the hyena, the wolf, the bear with its evil ways,
  Drive these out, O Earth, from here away from us.

(Atharva.12.1.49)

The Earth to which the winged bipeds fly together—
  swans, eagles, and other birds of various kinds,
On which the wind blows strongly, raising dust,
  bending trees, and the flame follows the blast
  forward and backward;
The Earth in which Night and Day
  are settled,
Which is covered and canopied by rain—
  May she establish us with bliss in every home.

(Atharva.12.1.51,52)

Heaven, Earth and Mid-air
  have given me this wide space,
And all cosmic powers
  together have endowed me with the intellect.

(Atharva.12.1.53)

318

I am victorious,
 I am called the most exalted on Earth,
A conqueror everywhere, a conqueror of everything,
 I am a victor on every side.

(Atharva.12.1.54)

In villages, in the forest, and in the assemblies on the
 Earth, in congregations and in councils,
We shall speak of thee in lovely terms.

(Atharva.12.1.56)

As a horse scatters dust, so did the Earth,
 since she was born,
 scatter the people who dwelt on the land,
And she joyously sped on, the world's protectress,
 supporter of forest trees and plants.

(Atharva.12.1.57)

What I speak, I speak with sweetness;
 what I look at endears itself to me;
And I am fiery and impetuous:
 others who fly at me with wrath
I smite down.

(Atharva.12.1.58)

Peaceful, sweet-smelling, gracious Earth, filled with
 milk, and bearing nectar in her breast,
May she give with the milk her blessings to me.

(Atharva.12.1.59)

O Mother Earth
Let Thy bosom be free
From sickness and decay.
May we through long life
Be active and vigilant
And serve Thee with devotion.

(Atharva.12.1.62)

Waters and Rivers

Waters contain
All disease-dispelling medicaments,
Useful for the upkeep of our body,
So that we may live long
To enjoy the bright sun.

(Rig.1.23.2)

That there is ambrosia in waters,
There is healing balm in them,
And there are medicinal herbs,
Know this all,
And by their proper use become wiser.

(Rig.1.23.19)

O powerful waters
I might have violated
The laws of Nature
Knowingly or unknowingly,
Foolishly or impudently.
Take away whatever is wrong
Or deficient in me.

(Rig.1.23.22)

Some waters collect together,
Others join them.
As rivers they flow together
To a common reservoir (ocean).
The pure waters have gathered
Round the hydrodynamic power.

(Rig.2.35.3

Down from the lap of mountains, longing,
   like two mares, moving gleefully apart,
Like two white mother-cows licking their calves,
   The two streams rush with their waters.

(Rig.3.33.1)

"Impelled by the Lord, begging that He urge you,
   Seaward you rush, as if charioted,
Flowing two together, swelling with waves,
   each seeking the other, O shining Ones!"

(Rig.3.33.2)

"I have come to the motherliest of Rivers,
   I have reached the river, the broad, the blessed,
Licking the banks as mother-cows the calf,
   both flow together to a common home."

(Rig.3.33.3)

"Even with such waves, we two swelling,
   are moving together to our God-made home;
None can stay the urge that is in motion;
   what would the poet, calling to the Rivers?"

(Rig.3.33.4)

"Stop at my friendly word of request,
   rest for a moment, Observers of the Law,
With a noble hymn, asking for their favour,
   the son of a sage calls to the Rivers."

(Rig.3.33.5)

"The Lord, the thunder-armed, dug out the
   channels, destroying obstructions, which had
   checked our flow;
Mother of Knowledge, the beautiful-handed, led us,
   and with the urge She gave we flow broadening."

(Rig.3.33.6)

"Praised through endless time will be Lord's
    heroic act in removing obstacles,
With thunder He smote all obstructions down,
    and the water flows, yearning for their home."

(Rig.3.33.7)

"Do not forget, O Singer! this speech of thine,
    which after ages will be resounding;
In thy praise-songs, Poet, be loving towards us,
    lower us not amid men; farewell!"

(Rig.3.33.8)

"Sisters! May you listen well to the poet
    who with wagon and chariot has come from afar,
Bow down quite low, be easy to cross,
    Stay with your stream below the axles."

(Rig.3.33.9)

"Yes, Śinger, we will listen to thy words,
    as with wagon and chariot thou comest from afar.
'We will bend before thee like a nursing mother,'
'We will yield to thee as a maiden to her suitor'."

(Rig.3.33.10)

O rivers, let your waves flow
That the pin of my yoke
Remains above the waters.
And may you two together
Proceed with restraint
And stay within limits
For the benefit of all.

(Rig.3.33.13)

The divine waters,
The purifiers of hundreds,
Rejoicing in their innate nature;
Pursue the paths of Nature's forces;
They never violate
The sacred laws
Of the Resplendent Lord:
May you offer to rivers
Your tribute
Rich in affection and love!

(Rig.7.47.3)

In the solitary regions
Of green valleys;
And the confluence of the rivers;
The sages obtain
Divine intuition.

(Rig.8.6.28)

It is for the Resplendent Lord,
That this blissful,
Refreshing divine elixir
Is flowing in hundreds
And thousands of rivulets,
Making everything clean,
Lovely and delightful,
And it is for Him
That fountains burst
Into sweet melodies.

(Rig.9.107.17)

O fast rivers, the venerable Lord cuts easy channels for your onward flow.

Since the land fed by you would be a source of immense food, you speed over the lofty rocks down to the plains. You will thus evidently rule over the world.

(Rig.10.75.2)

The roar of the mighty river goes forth to heaven above the earth.

She with shining waves animates her endless speed, and as the rains issue thundering from the clouds, the fast river advances, bellowing like a bull.

(Rig.10.75.3)

Like mothers crying for their children and like milch cows with their milk for their calves, the other roaring streams run towards the main river.

Irrigating the banks on both sides, you march like a king going to battle carrying the waters of your tributaries along with you like the troops of your army.

(Rig.10.75.4)

The straight-flowing, white-coloured, bright-shining river moves along with her ample volumes through the realms; the inviolable river, most efficacious and speckled like a horse, is beautiful as a comely maiden.

(Rig.10.75.7)

Soul, Thou hast two wings of eagle—wisdom and valour—to carry Thee to heavenly heights.

(Yajur.12.4)

Ploughing

With the Lord of the field,
    we, as with a friend, obtain the food
that nourishes our cows and horses.
    May he, in this way, be gracious to us.

(Rig.4.57.1)

Lord of the field, pour for us,
    like the cow pouring milk, a sweet stream
that drops honey and is pure as holy butter.
    May the Lords of the Holy Law shower on us grace.

(Rig.4.57.2)

Sweet be the herbs to us and waters,
    and for us the mid-air be full of sweetness.
Let the Lord of the field be sweet to us,
    and may we follow him uninjured.

(Rig.4.57.3)

May the draught-bulls work happily.
    and happily our men,
    and happily the plough furrow.
May the traces happily bind,
    Wield the goad happily.

(Rig.4.57.4)

O ploughshare and the plough,
Be pleased with this our hymn,
    and, with the rain water of heaven
    besprinkle this earth.

(Rig.4.57.5)

O graceful furrow, come near us;
We honour thee,
So that thou mayest be gracious and fruitful.

(Rig.4.57.6)

O brave man, take in hand the furrow
Let the Lord of Nourishment direct her.
May she, filled with plenty
    yield it to us year after year.

(Rig.4.57.7)

Happily may the ploughshares turn the soil,
    and happily the ploughman go with the oxen!
May the clouds sprinkle the earth with
    honey and water!
May the ploughshare and plough grant us prosperity!

(Rig.4.57.8)

———◦•◦———

May God come and reside in our
hearts;

May our body be the temple of God!

May He feed freely upon the harvest of
our actions as the cows graze in the
pasture.

May we reap the harvest of our life and
dedicate all at His feet.

May we ever remain His true servants!

(Rig.1.91.13)

Harvest Song

Full of sweetness are the plants,
   and full of sweetness these my words;
And with things that are full of sweetness
   I prosper in a thousand ways.

(Atharva.3.24.1)

I know the Lord who is full of sweetness;
   he has made abundant corn,
We hereby invoke him with our song.

(Atharva.3.24.2)

Let these five quarters of the globe,
   and these five types of men,
Bring us full prosperity
   as, after rains, the river brings up floating wood.

                           (Atharva.3.24.3)

As a fountain rises in a
   hundred thousand streams,
   and remains inexhaustible,
So may our corn flow in a thousand streams
   and remain inexhaustible.

                           (Atharva.3.24.4)

O thou hundred-handed one, gather this!
   O thou thousand-handed one, pour it out!
Bring together the abundant corn
   that is reaped or waits to be reaped.

(Atharva.3.24.5

Three measures are for cosmic powers,
   and four for the mistress of the house;
And with the measure that's the amplest
   of them all, we associate thee.

(Atharva.3.24.6

Cows

The cows have come and brought us good fortune,
May they stay in the stall and be pleased with **us**;
May they live here, mothers of calves, many-coloured,
  and yield milk for worship on many dawns.

(Rig.6.28.1)

The Lord protects and befriends the worshipper, and
  makes gifts and does not take away what is one's own;
Increasing his wealth forever and evermore
  He puts the devout in an impregnable fortress.

(Rig.6.28.2

They are not lost, nor do robbers injure them, nor
  the unfriendly frighten, nor wish to assail them;
The master of the cattle lives together along
  with these, and worships the divines and offers gifts.

(Rig.6.28.3)

The charger, whirling up the dust, does not reach them,
   they never make their way to the slaughtering stool,
The cows of the worshipping man roam about
   over the widespread pastures, free from all danger.

(Rig.6.28.4)

Ye cows, you fatten the emaciated,
   and you make the unlovely look beautiful,
Make our house happy, you with pleasant lowings,
   your power is glorified in our assemblies.

(Rig.6.28.6)

May you have many calves, graze on pastures
   and drink pure water at drinking places;
May not the thief master you, nor the wicked,
   and may the darts of the fierce Lord leave you aside.

(Rig.6.28.7)

May there be a close mixing up,
May Soma, the herbal juice, mix with cows' milk,
And may this manly vigour be,
   O for your heroic might.

(Rig.6.28.8)

Seasons

Rejoice in all the moods of Nature,
Experience the unseen divine glory manifested
in various forms.

Spring is the season of flowers and scented breezes
Which gladden the hearts,

Summer follows and has a beauty of its own,

The rain with its dark clouds and dazzling flashes,
Bathes the entire earth with its splendour,

Autumn and winter too possess their peculiar
charm and beauty.

(Sama.616)

God has set the sun in the midst of heaven. It
attracts rain-water and pours it down, is red,
protects us thoroughly, possesses diverse coloured
rays, rotates, keeps under check the clouds and
different worlds, and guards them. It pervades
lightning, the efficient cause of light.

(Rig.5.47.3)

Maintain us in well-being in Summer, Winter, Dew-
time, Spring, Autumn, and Rainy season. Grant us
happiness in cattle and children. May we enjoy your
unassailed protection.

(Atharva.6.55.2)

Medicinal Herbs

The medicinal herbs of the motherland
Bearing a hundred names,
Uses and locations,
And thousands of germinations
Render a hundredfold benefits,
And transform the ailing patient
Into a healthy and strong man.

(Rig.10.97.2)

The flower- and fruit-bearing herbs
Have beautiful tendrils;
They conquer diseases
Like swift horses,
And prove their efficacy
For the sick
And make them healthy and happy.

(Rig.10.97.3)

The medicinal herbs prepared by
A skilled physician
Relieve us of the disease.
No matter whether
They bear fruit or not
Have flowers or not.

(Rig.10.97.5)

The medicinal herbs
Penetrate and get diffused
Into all limbs
And joints of the sick,
And like a sharp
And strong moderator,
Destroy the disease.

(Rig.10.97.12)

These life-giving medicinal herbs
Are harmless,
Vital and invigorating.
They ever progress
And never regress.
They ever advance
And never obstruct.
They bear flowers,
Sweet juice and kernels.
I bring them here
To cure and purify
This ailing man.

(Atharva.8.7.6)

Mayest Thou, O Lord of Vitality,
Traversing through misty heaven
Listen to our prayers;
Mayest Thou, O circumambient wind,
Listen to our invocations
Mayest Thou, O crystal-clear,
Water-laden cloud,
As Thou floatest around the towering mountains,
Listen to our call.

(Rig.5.41.12)

Motherland

Work for the glory of your country and countrymen speaking different dialects.

Give due respect to the faiths and aspirations of the people.

Countless are the resources of Mother Earth, from whom flow the rivers of wealth in hundreds of streams,

Worship Motherland as you worship God.

From time eternal, the Mother Earth is giving life to her children—you owe debt to Her.

(Atharva.12.1.45)

The One Source

When the earliest of mornings dawned, the Great
  Eternal was manifested in the path of light;
Now the statutes of divines shall be revered
Great is the one source of energy of the cosmic
forces.

(Rig.3.55.1)

May the Divines not allow us to err, nor
  the Fathers of old times who know the path,
Nor the sign set between the two ancient homes.
Great is the one source of energy of the cosmic forces.

(Rig.3.55.2)

My desires fly about in many places,
  I light up the ancient sacrifices;
With the fire lighted let us declare the Law
Great is the one source of energy of the cosmic forces.

(Rig.3.55.3)

The universal King, born in many places,
  sleeps in couches, is spread in the forests.
One Mother feeds the infant, another rests.
Great is the one source of energy of the cosmic forces.

(Rig.3.55 4)

Living in old plants, he is in the new as well,
    being quickly born within the youthful ones.
Unimpregnated, they conceive and bear fruit.
Great is the one source of energy of the cosmic forces.

(Rig.3.55.5)

Now lying far away, he, born of two Mothers
    wanders unobstructed, a solitary child
These are the statutes of the sun and the ocean
Great is the one source of energy of the cosmic forces.

(Rig.3.55.6)

Child of two Mothers, the Invoker,
    the Sovereign at the Assembly,
    he moves, yet rests as the Support.
Speakers of gladdening words bring him sweet
    praise-songs.
Great is the one source of energy of the cosmic forces.

(Rig.3.55.7)

As to the beloved hero engaged in battle
    everything coming near is seen to go over,
So the hymn in the heart joins the milk libation.
Great is the one source of energy of the cosmic forces.

(Rig.3.55.8)

The ancient envoy abides within those,
    and, mighty, he moves about in his splendour,
And, wearing beautiful forms, looks upon us.
Great is the one source of energy of the cosmic forces.

(Rig.3.55.9)

The all-pervading Guardian protects the supreme path,
    upholding the beloved immortal spheres;
The fire divine knows all these created worlds.
Great is the one source of energy of the cosmic forces.

(Rig.3.55.10)

Each different from the other,
  you Two, Day and Night, have made twin
  beauties of yourselves;
  of the Two one is bright, the other dark,
Yet these Two, the dark-coloured and the red, are
  sisters.
Great is the one source of energy of the cosmic forces.

(Rig.3.55.11)

When the two Cows, Mother and Daughter,
  (Heaven and Earth)
  that yield nectar, give suck equally together,
Both I worship in the seat of Eternal Law.
Great is the one source of energy of the cosmic forces.

(Rig.3.55.12)

Licking the calf of the other, One of them lows.
  On what world has the milch cow laid her udder?
The earth fills with the milk of Eternal Law.
Great is the one source of energy of the cosmic forces.

(Rig.3.55.13)

The Earth wears beauties in various forms,
She stands up licking
  her year-and-a-half-old calf, the sun;
Knowing this I seek the seat of Eternal Law.
Great is the one source of energy of the cosmic forces.

(Rig.3.55.14)

The Two, Day and Night, are lodged as if in a
  wondrous place;
  of these One is concealed, the Other manifest;
One common pathway is divided in two.
Great is the one source of energy of the cosmic forces.

(Rig.3.55.15)

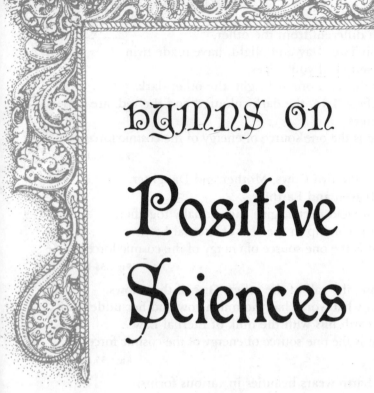

HYMNS ON

Positive
Sciences

यो विद्यात् सूत्रं वित्ततं यस्मिन्त्रोताः प्रजा इमाः
सूत्रं सूत्रस्य यो विद्यात् स विद्यात् ब्राह्मणं महत्

Only he who knows the secret of the visible,
the science of creation,
May glimpse the invisible, the Creator behind the
creation.

(Atharva 10.8.37)

Interstellar Space and Cosmic Rays

The Vayu Group of Cosmic Rays

According to the Vedas, vayu is the chief element pervading space.

(a) This vayu has a lustre. वायुर् अन्तरिक्षे दीप्यते

(Jaimini Brahmana, I, 192)

Yajurveda I, 24, वायुरसि तिग्मतेजा: confirms this, *viz.* thou art vayu, having penetrating lustre.

(b) According to *Shatapatha Brahmana,* this vayu is born of Agni and it is due to Agni that vayu gives out a lustre. Compare what Yajnavalkya says: प्राणेन वा ऽग्निर्दीप्यते । अग्निना वायु: । वायुना आदित्य:... (X, 6, 2, 11)

(c) The same *Brahmana* further testifies that the solar system and the galaxies of stars move, as if in a string, woven by this vayu.

तदसावादित्य इमान् लोकान् सूत्रे समावयते तद् यत् तत् सूत्रं वायु
स: ॥ (VIII, 7, 3, 10)

Heat Waves Called 'Vayansi'

Colloquially this word वयांसि means पक्षी (birds) but in scientific connotation, this word which is often used in the vedas, denotes the interstellar birds or *heat waves* in space. In *Taittiriya-Samhita* V, 7, 6, we read वयो वा अग्नि: 'वय: is indeed Agni (heat).

(a) In *Rigveda* X, 140, 1, we have a reference to these shining heat waves.

अग्ने तव श्रवो वयो महि भ्राजन्ते
अर्चयो विभावसो ।

(Agni ! thou rich in wealth of beams ! thy fires (called श्रव and वय:) blaze mightily.)

And also in *Yajurveda* XII, 106

श्रग्ने तव श्रवो वयो महि भ्राजन्ते ।

The smoke in space is the श्रव: and the वय:., as the *Shatapatha Brahmana* clarifies explanation of this mantra.

घूमो वा श्रस्य (श्रग्ने:) श्रवो वय: (VII, 3, 1, 29)

(b) It is interesting to note that heat became "immortal", and acquired perpetual movement only on account of these वयांसि, or heat waves. Previously, there was no electric effect in heat. मत्यों ह वाऽग्ने देवा श्रासु: and Agni became immortal as an effect of these heat particles called वयांसि. *Rigveda* confirms this in the mantra.

श्रग्नि: श्रमृतोऽभवद् वयोभि: । (X, 45, 8)

The state of mortality to which the *Shatapatha Brahmana* has referred, is the state of instability of planets. With the expansion of the universe, as soon as these heat waves affected space, the sun became effulgent, and when the moon too started shedding light on earth, there was motion, and there was stability.

To modern science. this law is known as *the law of mutual stability* due to heat waves.

(c) These have their characteristic motion. According to *Rigveda* V, 59, 7, they move in group-fields.

वयो न ये श्रेणी: पप्तु: ।

In the cosmic expansion from श्राप: to श्रग्नि:, to वायु: वयांसि, the heat waves emit light, so the earth shines at night.

Rigveda I, 136, 3 refers to this.

ज्योतिष्मती श्रदितिय धारयत् ज्ञितिम् ।

and the *Taittiriya Samhita* V, 6, 4, confirms this.

सर्वा ह वा इयं वयोम्यो नक्तं बृते दीप्यते
तस्माविमा वर्यांसि नक्तं नाध्यास्ते ॥

The Marichi Group of Cosmic Rays

Then we come to the rays called मरीचय: In today's terms of science, these मरीचय: are known collectively as an *aurora*. They are corpuscles from the sun which are caused by the cyclic motion of the Maruts. "They take so many forms—beams of light or glowing arches, stable or changing patterns, long drapes or narrow strips of pulsating light, coloured flames or white sheets."

(a) Like vayu, these are also born out of heat (Agni) and hence emit heat and light. The *Jaimini Brahmana* confirms it thus:

मरीचयो विस्फुलिङ्गा:. (1, 45)

(b) There are 49 such cosmic rays rotating in different fields and giving rise to different shapes, but it is only the rays called मरीचय: that are most uniform and shining in their movement. This is why Lord Krishna gives special importance to them in the *Bhagavad Gita* chapter X verse 21, wherein he describes His excellences :

मरीचि: मरुताम् प्रस्मि

(Of the Maruts, I am Marichi.)

(c) The vedas hold that these 49 rays move in groups.

cf. *Rigveda* V, 53, 10, गणं मारुतम्
    Yajurveda XXXIII, 45, मारुतं गणम्
    Yajurveda VII, 37, सगणो मरुद्भि:

(d) These rays possess an electric charge and are called वातत्विष: in *Rigveda* V, 57, 4. They are similar in effect to the solar rays. Thus *Rigveda* V, 55, 3 calls them

सूर्यस्येव रश्मय:

They move in electric fields. Pointing out this electricity in these maruts, the sage addresses them as विद्युन्मद्भिर्मरुत: while expounding the Rigvedic hymn.

(e) A synonymn for मरीचय: is वातरश्मय:. We read in *Matsya Purana*, the following version.

तस्मात् सर्वेण दृश्यन्ते व्योम्नि देवगणास्तु ते
यावत्यश्चेंब तारास्तु ताबन्तो वातरश्मयः ॥

A particular type of rays belonging to the sun is called मरीचिपा

cf. आदित्यस्य वै रश्मयो देवा मरीचिपाः ॥

These sun-rays protect the मरीचय: (or वातरश्मय:)

(f) These मरीचय: are also called अप्सरा, for which the popular translation is "nymph". In *Yajurveda* XVIII, 38, we have a mention of these अप्सरस: and commenting on that mantra, the *Shatapatha Brahmana* (I, 88, 1) observes,

आः विद्युन्मद्धिर्मरुतः स्वकँः
रथेभिर्यात ऋष्टिमद्धिरश्वपर्णँः ।

(g) The god Rudra is the god of electricity and is the father of these rays called मरुतः. He is called पितर्मरुतां in *Rigveda* II, 33, 1, and in *Rigveda* I, 85, 1. It is interesting to note, these maruts are called the offspring of Rudra— रुद्रस्य सूनवः.

There are other qualifying names given to maruts, according to their characteristic features. For example, *Yajurveda* III, 44 calls them रिशादस: since they consume (burn up) dead particles.

The Pashu (animal) Group of Cosmic Rays

What are these rays that the Vedas refer to as *Animals* in space ? These are the types of cosmic rays which revolve in a field in the configuration of a quadruped. They are types of heat and electric currents in space. As *Jaimini Brahmana* holds, आग्नेयश्च मारुतश्च पशुः. (II, 231)

These are the "dust-and-storm types", says *Rigveda* I, 22, 17:

समूढमस्य पांसुरे ।

(a) They contain heat. This fact is corroborated by *Shatapatha Brahmana* VI, 2, 1, 4.

प्रजापतिः तेषु पशुषु एतम् अग्निम् अपश्यत्
तस्माद्दँबँते पशवः ।

The *Taittiriya Brahmana* holds:

आग्नेयाः पशवः ।   (I, 1, 4, 3)

Shatapatha Brahmana VI, 1, 4, 12, clarifies the heat-component of these types of cosmic rays.

सर्वे पशवो यदिग्नः । तस्मादग्नौ पशवो रमन्ते ।

(b)   That these apparent animals in space are no other than maruts is indisputably confirmed by *Aitareya Brahmana* III, 19 when it holds that पशवो वै मरुत:

and *Shatapatha Brahmana* IX, 3, 3, 7 connects these with व्ग्रांसि, the type of waves about which we have written before at length.

Rigveda X, 90 also connects them with vayu.

cf. पशून्स्तांश्चक्रे वायव्यान्

These rays emit light.

(c) *Jaimini Brahmana* III, 318 holds that there are eight animal shapes moving in space अष्टातयान् पशून्. Of these the horse-form and the bull-form are distinctly visible, moving in the Sagittarius and Taurus signs of the zodiac. In *Rigveda* II, 33, 6 and 8 the bull-type is referred to :

वृषभो मरुत्वान् । प्रबभ्रवे वृषभाय श्वितीचे ॥

And in another text we have

आकाशसम्भवंरश्वं:
—the horses born out of space.

Surely, one who is ignorant of this scientific terminology in the Vedas will stumble at this meaning of अश्व as horse.

These horses are the *cosmic rays* with an electric field of the shape of a horse.

(d) What causes these different shapes ? It is the intermixture of the atoms in आप:, अग्नि: and वायु: in the atmosphere. The *Jaimini Brahmana* affirms this in II, 99:

ऊनातिरिक्तो मिथुनौ प्रजननी ऊनम अन्यस्य

अतिरिक्तम अन्यस्य । ऊनातिरिक्ताद् वै

मिथुनात् प्रजा पशव: प्रजायन्ते ॥

The laws of pressure (सम्पीडन) and atomic friction are responsible for these variations, inspite of which there is a uniformity of motion and affinity of class. This fact is elucidated by the *Shatapatha Brahmana* in VI, 3, 1, 22.

तस्मादु हैतत् पशु: स्वाय रुपाय श्राविर्भवतीति

गौर्वा गवे अश्वो वाश्वाय । पुरुषो वा पुरुषाय ॥

(*Tandya Brahmana* XVI, 6, 2)

The Periodicity of the Cosmic Rays

We have a reference to this periodicity in *Atharvaveda* XIX, 7 which refers to the 27 nakshatras as a luni-solar concept of time. Each nakshatra evinces the relation between the rotations of the sun and the moon. The time taken by the sun to complete one revolution round the zodiac is 365.25 days. The moon completes one revolution round the zodiac in 27.32 days.

$$\frac{\text{Time of sun}}{\text{Time of moon}} = \frac{365.25}{27.32} = 13^0 20'$$

So, while the sun completes one revolution, the moon completes 13 1/3 revolutions approximately. Based on an arc of 13° 20′, the whole zodiac is divided into 27 divisions which are called *nakshatras*. Of the four types of months referred to in Hindu astronomy, there is one type known as the nakshatra-month. **This has a duration of 27 days and**

He is the Lord, before whom bend all
The powers of celestial and terrestrial regions.
He is the cherisher of all benevolent thoughts
and deeds.

(Rig.2 13.13)

the cosmic particles revolve in space with this 27-day periodicity.

Atharvaveda XIX, 8, 1, refers to these nakshatras :

यानि नक्षत्राणि दिव्यन्तरिक्षे
अप्सु भूमौ यानि नगेषु दिक्षु ।
प्रकल्पयं‍श्चन्द्रमा यान्येति
सर्वाणि ममैतानि शिवानि सन्तु ॥

Benign to me all those mansions to which the moon as she moves on, doth honour—all that are in the sky, the air, the waters. on earth, or mountains, in the heavenly regions.

Inhabitants of Space

THE GALAXIES

THROUGH the largest (200 - inch) reflecting telescope on Mount Palomar in California we can look at space upto 2,00,00,00,00,000 (11 zeroes) light years away. This space is almost uniformly populated with about 26,00,00,000 galaxies These galaxies are about 20,00,00,000 light years away from us. Each galaxy is made up of at least 10,00,00,00,000 stars.

Vedic Calculations

Regarding the number of these galaxies which adorn the firmament, we have a calculation in the *Shatapatha Brahmana* in X, 4, 4 :

प्रजापतिं वं प्रजाः सृजमानम् ।
पाप्मा मृत्युरभिपरिजघान् स तपोऽतप्यत ।
सहस्र संवसरान् पाप्मानं विजिहासन् ।

तस्य तवस्तेवमानस्य एभ्यो लोमगर्तेभ्य ।

ऊर्ध्वानि ज्योतींष्यायन ।

तद्यानि तानि ज्योतींषि एतानि तानि नक्षत्राणि ।

यावन्त्येतानि नक्षत्राणि तावन्तो लोकगर्ताः ।

यावन्तो लोमगर्ताः तावन्तः सहस्रसंवत्सरस्य मुहूर्ताः ॥

According to this, the number of stars in our galaxy approximates 1,08,00,000.

THE MARUT GROUP OF COSMIC RAYS

These are referred to in the Vedas as shining ones भ्राजत् ऋष्टयः (*Rigveda* I, 31, 1) with their chests (fields) shining like gold रुक्म-वक्षसः (*Rigveda* II, 34, 2).

Maruts and Magnetism

The *Rigveda* refers to the magnetic power of the Maruts by calling them त्रयोदंष्ट्र in I, 88, 5. All electro-magnetism in space is due to these Maruts.

Modern science believes that there is always a magnetic field surrounding a current of electricity. In certain conditions magnetic fields also induce electric currents.

The term, electro-magnetic field, which is responsible for propagation of light waves, radio waves etc. in space, is well known in modern physics.

Electro-magnetic Field Created by Maruts

Rigveda I, 87, 4 indicates the electro-magnetic field that defines the direction of the Maruts. The 87th hymn is the Marut hymn and the Maruts have been called ईशानः therein i.e. pointing to the north-east. · *Rigveda* I, 64, 5 calls the Marut, ईशान-कृत.

Men-Shaped Maruts

These Maruts possess electricity and therefore, heat. *Rigveda* I, 45, 14 describes the Maruts as अग्निजिह्व.

It is interesting to note the effect of the heat and light of the solar rays that come in contact with these Maruts, in the cosmic atmosphere. This fact is clearly stated in a hymn of the *Rigveda*, which is addressed to the Sun. The specific mantra I, 50, 5 holds :

प्रत्यङ् देवानां विशः प्रत्यङ् ङुदेषि

O Sun, thou goest to the देवविश् i.e. Maruts and thou comest hither, to मानुष (*lit.* mankind). Now what are these "men" in the atmosphere ?

The waves of the electro-magnetic field wherein these man-shaped particles work. A subtle group in the interstellar region is known as the ऋमवः in vedic terminology. *Rigveda* I, 146, 4 refers to "men in the Sun", आविरेभ्यो अमवत् सूर्यो नॄन् and again in I, 110, 6, we have अन्तरिक्षस्य नृम्यः "for the men living in" the interstellar region. Surely, these "men" are no other than Maruts of the shape of men, with reference to the electro-magnetic field in which they move.

The Maruts as Rain-Carriers

The cycle of condensation and evaporation is carried out under the pressure of these Maruts.

The Maruts carry particles of vapour through the interstellar region. *Rigveda* V, 55, 5 confirms this in an invocation to Maruts, to carry rain upwards from the oceans to the sun.

उदीरयथा मरुतः समुद्रतो
यूयं वृष्टिं वर्षयथा पुरीषिणः ।

(The word पुरीषिणः here refers to the special type of Agni particles carried by them.) There is another reference in *Rigveda* I, 164, 47, to the same effect.

THE RIBHAVA-GROUP OF COSMIC RAYS

(ऋभुः) Ribhu is a ray of the Sun, which glows intensely.

Yaskacharya confirms this :

ऋभव उरु भान्तीति वा (*Nirukta* XI, 15).

Rigveda I, 110, 4 holds that the Ribhavas are solar rays

ऋभवः सूरचक्षसः

They had no lustre, originally, and were "mortal" as it were; but they became "immortal gods" by becoming a solar medium. As *Rigveda* I, 110, 4 affirms:

मर्तासः सन्तो अमृतत्वमानशुः

The entire sukta 110 of the *Rigveda* Mandala I relates to ऋभवः ribhus, and their evolution.

Ribhavas are one type of solar ray such as विम्बा and वाज which are frequently mentioned in the Vedas.

THE APSARA GROUP OF COSMIC RAYS

The Apsaras, literally translated as nymphs of the sky, are also types of cosmic rays—types of the मरीचयः which we have already discussed. In support of this conclusion *Yajurveda* XVIII, 38 refers to these Apsaras:

ऋताबाड् ऋतधामाग्निः
गन्धर्वस्तस्यौषधयोऽप्सरसो मुदो नाम ।

While commenting on this verse, the *Shatapatha Brahmana* states:

सूर्यो गन्धर्वः । तस्य मरीचयोऽप्सरस
आयुवो नाम···आयुवान-इव हि मरीचयः
प्लवन्ते ॥ (IX, 4, 1, 8)

The sun is the Gandharva and his rays are the Apsaras.

COSMIC DUST

The dust in space is known as रजः in the vedic connotation. It is a cosmic wind, a constant stream of protons and electrons. *Rigveda* X, 121, 5 alludes to this रज: in

यो अन्तरिक्षे रजसो विमानः ।

—That Prajapati who created *dust* in the interstellar region. *Rigveda* X, 129 speculates on the fact that there was no *dust* at the beginning of the creation (नासीद्रज:). This dust in the interstellar region is distinguished from the dust on the terrestrial sphere which is called पार्थिव रज:. *Yajurveda* XXXIV, 32 refers to this :

श्रा रात्रि पार्थिवँरज:
पितुरप्रायि धामभि: ।

Rigveda I, 154, 1 also draws this distinction by referring to earthly dust in

व: पार्थिवानि विममे रजांसि ।

Colour of the Cosmic Dust

Rigveda I, 35, 4 mentions a dark coloured dust कृष्णा रजांसि and so in *Rigveda* I, 35, 9 the phrase is कृष्णेन रजसा.

पांगुरजोऽरुणप्रमेषु वृष्टिमू । इवेते
ब्राह्मणपीडाम् । लोहिते शस्त्रकोपम्
नीले शस्त्रक्षयम् ॥

Absence of Dust in the Cosmic Rays

Rigveda I, 168, 4 suggests the possibility that the मरुत: type of the cosmic rays do not carry dust. The mantra refers to अरेणव: मरुत:

According to modern science, "the space immediately near the sun is free of dust since here the dust of the sun evaporates all solid particles."

BOUNDARIES IN SPACE

The Magnetic Field of these Boundaries

They move in a circular form (छन्द), as *Shatapatha Brahmana* VIII, 5, 2, 3, certifies दिशो वैं परिभू: छन्द:. The

Shatapatha Brahmana further holds that the gods converted these boundaries into ellipses so as to stabilize the sun and the earth etc.

एतद्वै देवा इमांल्लोकान् उखां कृत्वा
दिग्भिरद्रृं हन् । दिग्भिः पर्यंतन्वन् ॥ (VI, 5, 2, 11)

Scientifically speaking, this stability is due to the electro-magnetic field that these boundaries generate.

And this field extends to include the entire atmosphere. "Although the atmosphere extends, at most, but a few hundred miles upwards, the magnetic field is appreciable upto a distance of 10,000 miles. At 400 miles the magnetic field's intensity is about one eighth that at the surface."

Electro-magnetic density is maximal at the northern boundaries. This fact is stated in the *Brahamana*.

अर्थंतस्याम् उदीच्यां दिशि भूयिष्टं विद्योतते ।

These boundary rays are controlled by other rays called भ्राप्य, साध्य, ग्रन्वाध्य and मरुत. The *Shatapatha Brahmana* affirms this in XIII, 4, 2, 16

अर्थंते देवा: (आशापाला:) भ्राप्या:, साध्या:,
ग्रन्वाध्या:, मरुत: ।

There are 'mountains' to shield these rays and these 'mountains' are the मरुत's. The *Rigveda* refers to these in I, 39, 3

वि यायन वनिन: पृथिव्या वि भ्राशा:
पर्वतानाम् ।

Atharvaveda V, 24, 6 also refers to these 'mountains' called मरुत's

मरुत: पर्वतानामधिपतयः ।

The Sun and Solar Radiation

WHAT is the sun ? The *Aditya*—the indestructible source of energy.

Such is the sun, the *Aditya*, the सहस्ररश्मि:, which the ancient vedic texts investigate together with the solar composition, its hydrogen, approximating the *Apah* (आप:) of the ancient vedic science.

The sun contains Vayu, Apa, and Agni. It is also known as अश्मापृश्नि which is its primary content.

What is this अश्मापृश्नि: ? *Rigveda* V, 47, 3 situates it in mid-heaven.

cf. मध्ये दिव: निहित: पृश्निरश्मा
वि चक्रमे रजसस्पात्यन्तौ ॥

This अश्मापृश्नि: matter is responsible for the sun. The *Shatapatha Brahmana* refers to it as containing विद्युत् electricity. मध्ये दिव्योनिहित पृश्निरश्मा. This substance, as its name implies, generates the prismatic colours that we know as VIBGYOR.

The *Shatapatha Brahmana* confirms this :

पृश्निभंवति । रश्मिभिर्हि मण्डलं पृश्नि: ॥

The Prajapati said "rays" and with this word, were the rays created in the sun, which is called रश्मि: समूह (collection of beams).

The following references from the Vedas deal with the solar constituent of आप:

(i) *Yajurveda* XIII, 30 clearly refers to this :

आपो गर्भन्तसीद मा त्वा सूर्योऽभिताप्सीत् ।

The *Shatapatha Brahmana* comments

एतद् ह आपां गर्भिष्ठं एतत् तपति ।   (VII, 5, 1, 8)

Certainly, the sun is the densest seat of the heavenly *apah*.

(ii) The core of the sun is filled with भ्राप:. It is its vital strength for heat and light. The *Aitareya Brahmana* confirms it in IV, 20 :

एष (भ्रादित्य:) वा प्रब्जा प्रव्स्यो वा एष
प्रातरुवेति भ्रप: सायं प्रविशति ॥

The sun is virtually *Apah* and *Apah* is the sun. There is no distinction between the two. Says *Shatapatha Brahmana* in X, 6, 5, 2

भ्रापो वा ऽ कं:

This original stage was one of great instability. Worlds oscillated forward and backward till they were stabilized by the action of the boundaries and by Vayu.

Stabilization of the Worlds

Rigveda II, 12, 2 clearly speaks of this condition.

य: पृथिवीं व्यथमानामदृं हद्
य: पर्वतान् प्रकुपितां भ्ररम्णात् ।
यो भ्रन्तरिक्षं विममे वरीयो
यो द्यामस्तभ्नात् स जनास इन्द्र: ॥

"He who fixed fast and firm the earth that staggered and set at rest the agitated mountains. Who measured out of the air's wide middle region and gave the heaven support, He men, is Indra."

This is a graphic description of staggering instability in the world's earliest stages and how it was eventually ordered by Indra, *elctro-magnetic waves,* in its later stages.

(d) We find the same thought again in *Rigveda* X, 149, 1

सविता यन्त्रं: पृथिवीमरम्णाद्
भ्रसकम्भने सविता द्यामदृं हत् ॥

(*Savita* fixed the earth with bands to bind it, and made heaven steadfast where no prop supported.)

(e) And this is emphasized in *Rigveda* VII, 99, 3

व्यस्तभ्ना रोदसी विष्णवेते
दाघर्थंपृथिवीमभितो मयूखंः ।

Both these worlds, Vísnu, hast thou stayed asunder and firmly fixed the earth with pegs around it.

(f) Again we have the following texts to support the above view :

महीं चिद् घामातनोत् सूयण
चास्कम्भ चित् कम्भनेन स्कभीयान् । (*Rigveda* X, 111, 5)
यस्तस्तम्भ सहसा वि ज्मो अन्तान्
बृहस्पतिः त्रिषधस्थो रवेण । (*Rigveda* IV, 50, 1)
हविषो गृहीताद् इमे लोका उदवेपन्त
तान् देवा एतेन यजुषा अद्रं हन् । (*Maitreya Samhita* IV, 1, 5)

(g) In the process of stabilization, these worlds arranged themselves from below upwards and on the other side, from above downwards. This is what *Tandya Brahmana* VII, 10, 5 holds,

इतो वा इमे लोका उर्ध्वाः कल्पमाना यन्ति
अमुतोऽर्वाञ्चः कल्पमाना आयन्ति ।

(h) *Rigveda* III, 54, 6 takes the same view of the process :

नाना चक्राते सदनं यथा वेः
समानेन ऋतुना संविदाने ।

The Atomic Nuclei of Contemporary Physics

"ALL light, no matter whether from space, from an electric bulb, or from a glow worm, is emitted by atoms or by the even smaller electrons."

And "even cosmic radiation which rains down on us from outer space with the velocity of light (1,86,000 miles per second) appears to have a similar composition of atomic nuclei."

These atomic nuclei, in vedic terminology, are the रश्मय:. The sun, the moon, the maruts, vayu, nakshatras etc.—all these have the *atomic nuclei* which radiate light; and it is only on account of the balance of radiation that the solar atmosphere is stable.

मासा रश्मय: । रश्मयो मरुत: ।
तेरसावादित्यो घृत: ॥ (*Jaimini Brahmana* I, 137)

These atomic nuclei are responsible for several physical processes on the sun. "Electrons and protons fly about freely and when they rise upto the solar surface where the temperature is much lower, they are recaptured by the protons there. During this process, heat is liberated just as it is during the condensation of water in air.

This gives rise to granular convection currents with a constantly changing field of contiguous whirlwinds. The wind velocities here are well over a thousand miles per hour, while in our own atmosphere, even during the worst hurricanes, they rarely exceed 200 miles an hour."

These atomic nuclei constitute the moon, also the maruts and the vatas that pervade the atmosphere. The technical vedic term for the rays of the maruts, is अभीशव:. A reference to this lies in *Rigveda* I, 38, 12 :

स्थिरा व: सन्तु नेमयो रथा अश्वास एषाम् ।
सुसंस्कृता अभीशव: ॥

and similarly in *Rigveda* V, 61, 2, addressed to maruts :

क्व वो अश्वा: क्वा अभीशव:
कथं शेक कथा यय ।

Of all these radiations, those of the sun are the brightest and the purest. *Yajurveda* II, 26 confirms this :

स्वयंभूरसि श्रेष्ठो रश्मिः ।

The Heat-Wave Nuclei

The heat-wave nuclei are the घर्मसर्जना rays and they are 300 in number. These are also called शुक्ला, शुक्रा, कुहकाः, ककुमः, गावः, विश्वभृतः or गावः.

Rigveda IX, 97, 35 is clear in its reference

सोमं गावो धेनवो वावशानाः ।

and *Nirukta* XIV, 85, commenting on this, translates the word गावः as solar rays. This type of solar rays give nourishment to the whole universe, just as गौः 'the cow' gives nourishment to all that exists on earth.

As *Shatapatha Brahmana* III, 9, 2, 14 affirms : गौर्वा इदं सर्वं विभर्ति. The entire heat of the sun is due to this group of rays called घर्मसर्जना and it is only to this type that *Rigveda* I, 154, 6 refers in यत्र गावो भूरिश्रृङ्गा अयासः. The word गोमातरः is also used in the Vedas, and this is synonymous with the पृश्निमातरः the rays of variegated colour. For instance, *Rigveda* I, 85, 3 states :

गोमातरो यच्छुभयन्ते अञ्जिभिः ।

and *Rigveda* I, 85, 2 holds :

अधिश्रियो दधिरे पृश्निमातरः ।

Seven Principal Rays of the Sun

There are seven principal rays of the sun which are the most excellent of the 1000 rays of the sun. These seven rays are called सप्तऋषयः and of these rays are born all the planets. This is what *Vayu Purana* LX, 99 says:

खे रश्मिसहस्रं यत्
पराङ् मया समुदाहृतम् ।
तेषां श्रेष्ठाः पुनः सप्त
रश्मयो ग्रहयोनयः ॥

They are

(1) सुपुर्ण:
(2) हरिकेश: This name is mentioned, with reference to the sun in *Rigveda* X, 139, 1 सूर्यरश्मिर्यंहरिकेश:
(3) विश्वकर्मा The *Kaushitaki Brahmana* makes a mention of this in V, 5 असौ वै विश्वकर्मा योसौ तपति
(4) विश्वश्रवा: In *Shatapatha Brahmana* the name is given as विश्वव्यचा
(5) संपद्वसु: or संयद्वसु: according to *Shatapatha Brahmana*
(6) अर्वावसु: or अर्वाग्वसु: in another text
(7) स्वराट्

Other Important Rays of the Sun

Apart from the seven primary solar rays, there are other important and effective solar rays each with its own particular colour and intensity as mentioned in the vedic literature. To omit a passing reference to them in this treatise would be to leave incomplete the vedic literature on the sun.

अङ्गिरस rays : *Jaimini Brahmana* 11, 366 refers to these : तद् ये ह वा एत आदित्यस्योदञ्चो रश्मयस्त आदित्या: । ये दक्षिणास्तेऽङ्गिरस: ॥

Those whose electro-magnetic field is directed northward are called the आदित्य rays, and those directed southward are called the अङ्गिरस. The distinction lies in the direction of their field.

आदित्य rays are also called गाव: and गावो वा आदित्या: is the text of the *Aitareya Brahmana* which describes them as snake-like सर्पा वा आदित्या:.

It is interesting to note in this connection a text of the *Yajurveda* (XIII, 8), in which the snake-like field of such rays is mentioned. The text runs thus :

ये वा अमी रोचने दिवो ये वा सूर्यस्य रश्मिषु
ये अप्सु षदांसि चक्रिरे तेभ्य: सर्पेभ्यो नम: ॥

(We bow to those vital rays of the sun, in the form of snakes,...)

हंसा: A reference to this group of solar rays which move in a magnetic field of the form of हंस, is found in the *Rigvedic* text :

हंस: शुचिषद् वसुरन्तरिक्षसद्धोता
वेदिषवतियिदुं रोणसत् ॥ (IV, 40, 5)

On this, Yaskacharya comments :

हंसा सूर्यरश्मय: (*Nirukta* XIV, 31)

On the text of *Yajurveda* XII, 14

हंस: शुचिषद् वसुरन्तरिक्षसद्धोता ।

Shatapatha Brahmana VI, 7, 3, 11 has this clarification :

असौ वा ऽ आदित्यो हंस: शुचिषत् ॥

ऋभव: Yaskacharya refers to this group in *Nirukta* XI, 16, thus : आदित्यरश्मयो ऽपि ऋभव उच्यन्ते. Sayana also in his commentary on the text of *Tandya Brahmana* XIV, 2, 5, translates ऋभव as referring to solar rays.

सुपर्णा: These rays are mentioned in the *Rigvedic* text X, 73, 11 वय: सुपर्ण उप सेदुरिन्द्रम् and *Nirukta* IV, 3 comments on this : सुपतना आदित्यरश्मय:. The same group of rays is mentioned in another text of *Rigveda* I, 105, 11 सुपर्ण एत आसते मध्य आरोधने दिव: ॥

हरित: We have a mention of this group in *Rigveda* I, 115, 4, which is an invocation to the sun.

यदेदयुक्त हरित: सधस्था—
दौद्रात्री वासस्तनुते सिमस्में ॥

and Yaskacharya clarifies in *Nirukta* IV, 11 that these हरित: are the solar rays, (हरित:) हरणात् आदित्यरश्मीन्. The colour of these rays is blue as Skandasvami, the great vedic commentator confirms, in reference to the *Rigvedic* text I, 50, 8 सप्त त्वा हरितो रथे वहन्ति देव सूर्य as follows :

हरित्-शब्दो हरित-शब्दपर्यायः ।
नीलवर्णवचन: ॥

The Vedic Nakshatras and the
Luni-Solar Concept of Time

The Nakshatras

यानि नक्षत्राणि दिव्यन्तरिक्षे अप्सु
भूमौ यानि नगेषु दिक्षु ।
प्रकल्पयंश्चन्द्रमा यान्येति सर्वाणि
ममैतानि शिवानि सन्तु ॥   (*Atharvaveda* XIX, 8, 1)

अष्टाविंशानि शिवानि शम्मानि
सह योगं भजन्तु मे ।
योगं प्र पद्ये क्षेमं च क्षेमं प्र पद्ये
योगं च नमोऽहोरात्राभ्यामस्तु ॥   (*Atharvaveda* XIX, 8, 2)

(1) 'Benign to me be all those Lunar Mansions to which the Moon as she moves on, doth honour—all that are in the sky, the air, the waters, on earth, on mountains, in the heavenly regions.'

(2) 'Propitious, mighty, let the eight and twenty together deal me out my share of profit—profit and wealth be mine, and wealth and profit ! To Day and Night be adoration rendered !'

Names of Nakshatras as mentioned in the Vedas

सुहवमग्ने कृत्तिका रोहिणी
चास्तु भद्रं मृगशिरः शमार्द्रा ।
पुनर्वसू सुनृता चारु पुष्यो
भानुराश्लेषा अयनं मघा मे ॥   (*Atharvaveda* XIX, 7, 2)

पुष्यं पूर्वाफल्गुन्यौ चात्र हस्तादिचित्रा
शिवा स्वाति सुखो मे अस्तु ।
राधे विशाखे सुहवानुराधा
ज्येष्ठा सुनक्षत्रमरिष्ट मूलम् ॥   (*Atharvaveda* XIX, 7, 3)

Plants, increasing physical strength, full of juice,
ever growing, fresh and new, sure, healing, bearing
a thousand names, let them be all collected here.

(Atharva.8.7.8

अन्नं पूर्वा रासतां मे अषाढा
ऊर्जं देव्युत्तरा आ वहन्तु ।
अभिजिन्मे रासतां पुण्यमेव
श्रवणः श्रविष्ठाः कुर्वतां सुपुष्टिम् ॥   (*Atharvaveda* XIX, 7, 4)

आ मे महच्छतभिषग् वरीय
आ मे द्वया प्रोष्ठपदा सुशर्म ।
आ रेवती चाश्वयुजौ भगं म
आ मे रयिं भरण्य आ वहन्तु ॥   (*Atharvaveda* XIX, 7, 5)

'The brilliant lights shining in heaven together, which through the world glide on with rapid motion. And days and firmament with songs, I worship, seeking the twenty-eight fold for its favour.'

1. Krittika, Rohini, be swift to hear me ! Let Mrigasiras bless me, help me Ardra ! Punarvasu and Sunrita, fair Pushya, the Sun, Asleshas, Magha, lead me onward.

2. May bliss be Svati and benign Chitra, Purva Phalguni and Hasta-Radhas, Visakhas, gracious Anuradha, Jyeshtha and happy starred uninjured Mula.

3. Food shall the Purvashadas grant me; let those that follow bring me strength and vigour. With virtuous merit, Abhijit endow me ! Sravana and Sravishthas make me prosper.

4. Satabhishak afford me ample freedom and both the Proshthapadas guard me safely. Revati and the Asvayujas bring me luck and the Bharanis abundant riches !

An asterism (*nakshatra*), as a division of the zodiac, brings out a relation between the sun and the moon and has its basis in the luni solar concept of time.

The Twelve Signs in Astrology

Whatever be the nature and background of planetary symbology, Astrology, the science of stars, derived from the

Greek root, *Astron*, meaning 'a star,' hinges round the twelve signs of the zodiac, which the *Atharvaveda* refers to in the following *mantra* :

द्वादश प्रधयश्चक्रमेकं त्रीणि
नभ्यानि क उ तच्चिकेत ।
तत्राहतास्त्रीणि शतानि शंकवः
षष्टिश्च खीला अविचाचला ये ॥   (*Atharvaveda* X, 8, 4)

"One is the wheel, the tyres are twelve in number, the naves are three. What man has understood it ? Three hundred spokes have thereupon been hammered and sixty pins set firmly in their places."

These twelve signs have been thus named and symbolised :

Aries	...	Ram	...	मेष
Taurus	...	Bull	...	वृष
Gemini	...	Twins	...	मिथुन
Cancer	...	Crab	...	कर्क
Leo	...	Lion	...	सिंह
Virgo	...	Virgin	...	कन्या
Libra	...	Balance	...	तुला
Scorpio	...	Scorpion	...	वृश्चिक
Sagittarius	...	Archer	...	धनु
Capricorn	...	Goat	...	मकर
Aquarius	...	Waterman	...	कुम्भ
Pisces	...	Fishes	...	मीन

These twelve signs, like the twelve tyres of the Wheel of Time, were regarded as glyphs of a universal language, common to seekers of truth, irrespective of caste, creed, and colour and they were the twelve gates of another world, whose beauty and splendour caused the physical realm to appear as a candle in the sunlight. It is for this reason that astrology was regarded as a "divine science", through whose zodiacal symbolism, the spiritual evolution of the whole human race is interpreted.

The zodiac is comparable to a board in which the *nakshatras* form the strings; sun, the regulator, gives it vitality and sustenance, and moon which harps on the strings of the zodiac while passing along the 28 *nakshatras*, produces vibratory currents in creation, which affect humanity at large. References to the moon's phases may be seen in *Rigveda* (X, 85, 19) and *Yajurveda* (XVIII, 40)

We have several references to the year and the division of time, to the additional month, to the twelve days and twelve nights. The *mantras* are quoted below in original.

संवत्सरोऽसि परिवत्सरोसीदवत्सरोऽसीद्वत्सरोऽसि वत्सरोऽसि । उषसस्ते कल्पन्तामहोरात्रास्ते कल्पन्तामर्धमासास्ते कल्पन्तामृतवस्ते कल्पन्ता संवत्सरस्ते कल्पताम् । . . .

(Yajurveda, XXVII, 45)

"Thou art Samvatsara; thou art Parivatsara; thou art Idavatsara; thou art Vatsara. Prosper thy Dawns ! Prosper thy Days-and-Nights ! Prosper thy Half—months, Months, Seasons and Years !"

Additional Month Mentioned

अहोरात्रैर्विमितं त्रिंशदङ्गं त्रयोदशं मास यो निर्मिमीते ॥

(Atharvaveda XIII, 3, 8)

"He who metes out the *thirteenth* month, constructed with days and nights, containing thirty members. This God, etc."

The Planets and Comets

PLANET literally means "wanderer" in Greek, and the planets are so named, in contrast to the fixed stars, because, they travel across the sky, from asterism to asterism following closely the path of the sun, called the ecliptic.

The Comets

The comets are also members of the solar system. In previous ages they were regarded as inauspicious and were held responsible for famine and pestilence. However, they do not look so very startling, today.

According to physical analysis, "they usually look like round clouds with a somewhat brighter centre. In contradistinction to planets, comets revolve round the sun in ellipses with high eccentricities. Their periods range between a few years and a few thousand years, and the total number of comets in the solar system is thought to be greater than a thousand. As a comet approaches the sun, its nucleus consisting of an immense number of small particles, is heated by the sun's rays and begins to exude gases (mainly hydrocarbons). The moment these gases leave the nucleus, they are acted upon by a strong force that drives them away from the sun—hence the notorious tail which generally points away from the sun."

The tails of the comets are formed by gases that are driven away by intense solar radiation.

The Vedic Reference to Comets

There is a reference to 'the comet (धूमकेतु:) in *Rigveda* V, 11, 3, which is addressed to the शुचि: rays of the sun :

असंमृष्टो जायसे मात्रो: शुचि:
मन्द्र: कविरुदतिष्ठो विवस्वत: ।
घृतेन त्वावर्षयन्नग्न आहुत
धूमस्ते केतुरभवद्दिवि श्रित: ॥

Pure, unadorned, from thy two mothers art thou born, thou Comet from Vivasvan as a charming sage. With oil they strengthened thee, O Agni, (Shuchi) worshipped God, thy banner was *the smoke that mounted to the sky* (i.e. thy smoke became the comet).

The Earth

THE EARTH is a planet. It is the largest of the four inner planets. It rotates on its axis once a day and revolves round the sun in 365.256 days, which period is known as a sidereal year. Its axis of rotation is inclined to the plane of its orbit by an angle of $66\frac{1}{2}°$. The earth, in the course of its motion, turns towards the sun periodically, in its northern and southern hemispheres, and this fact causes the change of seasons.

A vedic sage has posed the question of origin in *Rigveda* I, 185, 1 :

कतरा पूर्वा कतरा परायोः कया जाते कवयः को वि वेद ।
विश्वं त्मना बिभृतो यद्ध नाम वि वर्तेते अहनी चक्रियेव ॥

(Which of these is elder? Which latter? How were they born? Who knoweth it, ye sages ?)

Yajurveda XXXVII, 4, however, indicates certainly that earth was born first in the cosmic creation.

देव्यो वन्नयो भूतस्य प्रथमजा ।

On this verse, *Shatapatha Brahmana* XIV, 1, 2, 10 comments:

इयं वै पृथिवी भूतस्य प्रथमजा ।

The same *Brahmana*, further, holds very clearly, that of all the regions, the region of earth was created first.

इयमु पृथिवी वा एषां लोकानां प्रथमाऽसृज्यत । (VI, 5, 3, 1)

The chapter of Genesis in the Bible holds the same view.

The Interior of the Earth

The interior of the earth is extremely hot. *Shatapatha Brahmana* XIV, 9, 4, 21 mentions this by calling it अग्निगर्भा पृथिवी ।

Yajurvedu XI, 57 makes this explicit :

माता पुत्रं यथोपस्थे साग्निं विभर्तुं गर्भ जा ।

(The earth holds fire just as the mother holds the child.) Commenting on this, Yajnavalkya writes: यथा माता पुत्रमुपस्थे बिभृयादेवमग्नि गर्भे विमर्त्विंति । (*Shatapatha Brahmana* VI, 5, 1, 11)

According to scientific researches, "the study of the earth's interior indicates that most of its body is still in a molten state and that the *solid ground* of which we speak so casually, is actually only a comparatively thin sheet floating on the surface of the molten magma."

Rotundity of the Earth

That the earth is round is supported by numerous statements in the vedic literature. *Shatapatha Brahmana* VII, 1, 1, 37 holds:

परिमण्डल उ वा अयं (पृथिबी) लोक: ।

This earth is round in shape.

In the *Kathaka Brahmana*, the same truth is expressed:

मण्डलो ह्यं लोक:

Jaimini Brahmana I, 257 states this fact quite emphatically though in a metaphorical way—not only the earth, but the sun, moon and other planets are all spherical in form.

Earth as a Magnet

The earth, as discovered by Newton, has a powerful gravitational field.

A verse in *Rigveda* VII, 15, 14 points in this direction. It holds that the entire earth contains *magnetic filings* in the interior.

The earth, herein, is called आयसी, containing iron filings which have assumed magnetic properties under the influence of the Maruts.

Aitareya Brahmana I, 23 holds

ते (असुरा) वा अयस्मयीम् एवमां पृथिवीम् अकुर्बंन् ।

Mark the word अयस्मयीम्=लोहयुक्ताम्=magnetic

The *Kaushitaki Brahmana* holds the same view:

(असुराः) त्रयस्मयीं पुरीं अस्मिन् अकुर्बन् । (VIII, 8)

The *Taittiriya Brahmana* also has the same thing to state:

अस्य वं (भू:) लोकस्य रूपम्

त्रयस्मय्य: सूच्य: । (III, 9, 6, 5)

The word त्रयस्मय्य: सूच्य: corresponds to iron filings.

The Vedic View

The vedic scientist seems to have tackled the problem in a different manner. From the vedic standpoint, one thing is clear, that the temperature of the earth's interior, at which the modern science has arrived, is speculative. In fact there is some subtle co-relation between the heat waves in the interior of the earth and the working of the electro-magnetic waves of the Maruts in the firmament, which seems to be responsible for terrestrial magnetism.

This problem needs further research.

Copernican Theory and Vedic View

In the *Yajurveda*, Chapter III, we have a verse to show that this earth moves round the sun.

आयं गौ: पृश्निरक्रमीदसदन् मातरं पुर: ।

पितरं च प्रयन्त्स्व: ॥   (*Yajurveda* III, 6)

"The earth with all its waters revolves round the sun."

"the Earth revolves in space, it revolves with its mother, Water, in its orbit. It moves round its father, the Sun."

"Water is the mother of Earth as Earth is produced by the mixture of the particles of water with its own particles and remains pregnant with water. The Sun is the father of the Earth as from the Sun, it derives all light and sustenance."

पृश्नि:	=Spotted Bull=The Sun.
मातर	=The Mother=The Earth.
पितर	=The Father=The Sky,

Long before Copernicus could say anything about his helio-centric system of astronomy, in his famous *Revolutions of the Heavenly Bodies,* the truth about the revolution of the earth round the sun, was known to the vedic seers.

The Origin, History, and Theory of Indian Medicine

The longevity of man's life up to hundred years जिजीविषेत् शतं समा:—(*Yajurveda* XL, 2) or even more, जीवेम शरद; शतम्-भूयश्र शरद: शतात् can be maintained according to vedic teachings.

And how that span of life can be attained, is given in the Ayurveda, the science of life, with all its therapeutical hints and prescriptions given in the *Atharvaveda* (in a nucleus form). The extent and object of introducing medical knowledge, therefore, in the *Atharvaveda* is abundantly clear.

The starting point of this tradition is the intuitive insight "realized through an introverted awareness of the elements and laws that constitute the fact of life and the characteristics of living beings, the interrelation of the many and various data of the life-process"

को ददर्श प्रथमं जायमानं
अस्थन्वन्तं यदनस्था विभर्ति ।
भूम्या असुर् असृगात्मा क्व स्वित्
को विद्वांसमुपगात् प्रष्टुमेतत् ॥   (*Rigveda* I, 164,4)

"Who beheld life, when it first arose?—Life that formless

in itself, fills all forms.   From earth are fashioned blood and breath but whence the spirit that informs these ?   Who has gone to the ultimate Knower of all things to put the question ?"

Yet, the empirical link of ideas, with vigilant observation followed widening experience.

In the *Atharvaveda* we have a mention of the animals and birds from whom the use of healing herbs and drugs could be learnt.

वराहो वेद वीरुधं नकुलो वेद भेषजीम्
सर्पां गन्धर्वां या विदुस्ता अस्मा अवसे हुवे ।

(*Atharvaveda* VIII, 7, 23)

"The boar knows the plant, the mongoose knows the remedial herb.   What the serpents, the gandharvas know, those I call to aid."

And in the *Atharvaveda* VIII, 7, 24,

याः सुपर्णा आराङ्गरसीदिश्व या रघटो विदुः
वयांसि हंसा या विदुर्यादिच सर्वे पतत्रिणः
मृगा या विदुरोषधीस्ता अस्मा अवसे हुवे ।।

"The herbs of the angirasas that the eagles know, the heavenly ones that the Raghatas know, those that the birds, and the swans know, and what all the winged ones know, these herbs that the wild beasts know—I call them to aid." Again,

यावतीनामोषधीनां गावः
प्राश्नन्तिऽध्न्या यावतींनामजावयः
तावतीस्तुभ्यमोषधीः शर्म यच्छन्त्वाभृताः ।।

(*Atharvaveda* VIII, 7, 25)

"Of how many herbs, the inviolable kine partake, of how many the goats and sheep, let so many herbs, being brought, and extend protection to thee."

It is in such associations, that we find the origin of rational medicine, of the healing art, with a fourfold classifica-tion of vedic therapy which is alluded to in the *Atharvaveda* XI, 4, 16.

Four kinds of remedies are considered to protect life :

(1) The drugs of the Angirasas (Juices of plants and herbs)
(2) The drugs of the Atharvans (a part of tne mantra-therapy.)
(3) The divine drugs in the form of prayers and mental yoga
(4) The drugs of human artifice and contrivance.

The *Atharvaveda* mentions turmeric (हल्दी) and yellow-birds into which jaundice is induced so as to relieve the human patient of that disease. उरो मत्वा क्षतं लाक्षां पयसा मधुसंयुताम् सद्य एव पिबेज्जीर्णे पयसा उद्यात् सशर्करम् ।

In the domain of surgery, it is true that the knowledge of instruments and the operations performed by old Indian physicians has become dim with the passage of time, but there are strange similarities still observable in the names of the some of the surgical instruments used now. For example, सिंह मुख and मकरमुख स्वस्तिक 's' are the prototypes of Lion and the Crocodile forceps of the modern physicians.

यदान्त्रेषु गवीन्योर्योर्द्वरतावधि संश्रितम्
एवा तेमूत्रं मुच्यतां वर्हिवालिति सर्वकम्
प्रतें भिनद्मि मेहनं वर्त्रंवेशन्तिम्राइव
एवा ते मूत्रं मुच्यतां वर्हिवांलितिसर्वकम् ॥

(Atharvaveda I, 3, 6, 7, et. seq.)

Here we have a mention of a certain tubular instrument to relieve the retention of urine and modern surgery continues to employ the catheter and tubal instruments for the dilation of urethral system.

The Injection of solutions was popular in vedic times. The Sanskrit word for injection is अन्तःक्षेप or सूचीबेध We have a reference to this in *Rigveda* X, 97, 12

यस्यौषधी: प्रसर्पथाङ्ग मङ्ग परुष्परः ।
ततो यक्ष्मं वि वाघध्व उग्रो मध्यमशीरिव ॥

The word प्रसर्पसि (penetrates) is thus derived : प्रविश्य अन्त: शिरामुखे व्याप्नोषि referring to the needle entering the body and spreading the medicine.

Who is the Greatest Physician ?

The greatest physician recognised in the vedas is God.

उन्नो वीरां॑ अर्पय॑ भेषजेभिर्भिषक्तमं त्वा भिषजां शृणोमि ॥

Brahma is the physician.

(*Rigveda* II, 33, 4)

Do thou with strengthening balms incite our heroes; I hear thee famed as best of all physicians.

The *Yajurveda* XVI, 5, also states the same thing.

अध्यवोचदधिवक्ता प्रथमो दैव्यो भिषक् ।

The Advocate, the first Divine Physician, hath defended us.

The Ashvini Kumars are considered to be the physicians of the gods. As we read in the *Aitareya Brahmana* I, 18.

अश्विनौ देवानां भिषजौ

and there is a prayer in *Rigveda*. VIII. 18, 8. to these physicians to protect us.

उत त्या दैव्या भिषजा शं नः
करतो अश्विना युयुयातामितो
रपो अप स्रिध: ॥

And may Ashvins, the divine pair of physicians, send us health. May they remove iniquity and chase our foes.

About the surgical and therapeutic skill of the Ashvin twins, the physicians of the gods, it is stated that they worked miracles, they could replace the head of a man with that of a horse.

The *Atharvaveda* V. 29, 1 recites the qualifications of a good physician as

(1) one who knows the preparation of medicines भेषजस्य कर्ता,

(2) one who can understand diagnosis and prescribe the remedy readily क्रियमाणं अग्रेवेत्ति

It is such a physician who is expert in all ways, has good contacts with specialists and cures the ailment in its entirety.

विश्वेभिः देवैः संबिदानः प्रस्य परिधिः पतालि ॥

(*Atharvaveda* V. 29, 2)

A physician has, by virtue of his medicines, the power to increase the longevity of a person who is क्षितायु : i.e. debilitated by age.

यदि क्षितायुर्यदि वा परेतो यदि मृत्योरन्तिकं नींत एव
तमा हरामि निर्ऋतेरुपस्थादस्पार्षमेनं शतशारदाय ॥

(*Atharvaveda* 111, 2, 2)

"Though his days are ended, though he is almost departed, though very near death already, I bring him out of destruction's lap, and save him for life, to last a hundred autumns, and so with the person who is nearing death."

Such was the demand laid on the vedic physician.

Atharvaveda as a Monument of Indian Medicine

The *Atharvaveda* consists of twenty sections called Kandas and has come to us in nine recensions. Two recensions are extant : the शौनकेय: (which is the only popular recension) and the पैप्पलाद: also known as the Kashmiri recension. The 18th kanda is not found in the पैप्पलाद शाखा and is, therefore believed to be of a later date. It is also believed that the 20th kanda is completely borrowed from the *Rigveda*.

The kandas 19 and 20 are ignored in the प्रातिशाख्य of the *Atharvaveda*. Of the nine recensions of the *Atharvaveda*, seven have been lost.

114 hymns in this veda are devoted to medical subjects, in which some of the outstanding topics like fever, consumption, various wounds, leprosy and poisoning are mentioned.

It is on these foundations that the later sages made researches in Ayurveda, with its eight branches and three fundamentals.

The eight branches of this science, as taught and practised in ancient India, are :

(1) Medical therapy,
(2) The science of the diseases of the eye, ear, nose, throat i.e. of supra-clavicular parts.
(3) Surgery शल्यापहतृं कं
(4) Toxicology विषगदवैरोधिकप्रशमनम्
(5) Psycho-therapy भूत विद्या
(6) Pediatrics कौमारभृत्यकम्
(7) Rejuvenation रसायनम्
(8) Virilification वाजीकरणम्

Sushruta observes that a doctor of medicine should not only be well read but equipped with versatile understanding if he wishes to arrive at the correct diagnosis.

एकं शास्त्रमधीयानो न विद्याच्छास्त्रनिश्चर्यम्
तस्माद बहश्रत: शास्त्रं विजानीयात चिकिःमक· ॥

Hydropathy in the Vedas

The *Atharvaveda* VI, 7, and VI, 57, are full of references to diseases which are curable through the various uses of water and vaporisation.

शं चनो मयश्चनो मा चनः किं चनाममत्
क्षमा रपो विश्वं नो प्रस्तु मेषजं सर्वं नो प्रस्तु मेषजम् ॥

(Atharvaveda, VI, 57, 3)

"Let it be health and joy to us. Let nothing vex or injure us. Let water be the universal medicine—Let all to us be balm".

The *Atharvaveda* I,4, I,5 and I,6 have copious references to water therapy, declaring the efficacy of water in so many words.

शिवतम: रस:	(I,5,2) water is the 'Essence'
प्रपो मयोभुव:	(I,5,1) water is beneficial.
प्रप्सु प्रमृतम्	(I,4,4) water contains nectar.

अप्सु भेषजम्   (I,4,4) water is medicinal.

अप्सु विश्वानी भेषजानि   (I,6,2) water contains all
                               medicinal properties.

(i) The *Rigveda* I, 23, 9 says: अप्स्वन्तरमृतमप्सु भेषजम् and
again in *Rigveda* I,23,20, we have,

(ii) अप्सु मे सोमो अब्रवीत् अन्तर्विश्वानि भेषजा ।

"Within the waters, Soma thus hath told me dwell all
balms".

(iii) आपः पृणीत भेषजम्

O waters, teem. with medicine to keep my body safe from
harm; and

(iv) आपः पृणीत भेषजं वर्हषं तन्बे मम   (*Rigveda* I, 23, 21)

Water destroys the diseases of the internal organs.

                               (*Rigveda* VII, 49, 2)

(v) याः शुचयः पावकास्ता आपो देवीरिह मामवन्तु

Bright, purifying, let those water goddeses, protect me.

(vi) अयक्ष्मा अनमीवा: नाभ्रगसः   (*Yajurveda* IV, 12

May the water, that we have drunk, become auspicious,
make us free from all sin and malady and sickness.

(vii) *Atharvaveda* XIX, 2, 8 is full of references to the
healing power of water.

शंत आपो हैमवतीः शमु ते सन्तूत्स्याः

शंते सनिप्यदा आपः शमु ते सन्तु वर्ष्याः: (*Atharvaveda* XIX, 2, 1)

Blest be the streams from hills of snow, sweet be the
spring waters into thee. Sweet be the swift running waters,
sweet to thee be rain-water.

(viii) Rain and the water from waterfalls has electric
power in it that makes the body elastic like that of a
horse.

अपामह दिव्यानामपां स्त्रोतस्यानाम्

अपामह प्रणेजनेऽइवा भवथ वाजिनः ॥   (*Atharvaveda* XIX. 2, 4)

The different kinds of water are distinguished in the
Atharvaveda

The waters are the sovereign remedy,
herbs possess divine efficacy.

(Atharva.8.7.3)

(i) देवी: ग्राप:	(I, 4, 3) Water received from clouds.
(ii) वार्षकी: ग्राप:	(I, 6, 4) Rainy water.
(iii) सिंधु:	(I, 4, 3) Sea water.
(iv) ग्रनूप्या: ग्राप:	(I, 6, 4) Water obtained in watery regions.
(v) धन्वन्या: ग्राप:	(I, 6, 4) Water obtained in desert or regions of scanty rains.
(vi) खनित्रिमा: ग्राप:	(I, 6, 4) Water obtained from wells which are sunk.

The *Atharvaveda* XIX, 2 gives a composite list in terms of usage

(vii) हैमवती	Water from mountains.
(viii) ग्रत्स्या:	Fountain water.
(ix) सनिष्यदा;	Water from streams and canals which flow throughout the year.
(x) वष्यो:	Rainy water.
(xi) धन्वन्या:	Water in desert area
(xii) कुम्भेभिरामृता:	Water stored in pitchers.

The *Atharvaveda* IV, 17, 1 describes how to increase the potency in medicine by a 1000 times.

ईशानां त्वा भेषजानामुज्जेष ग्रा रभामहे
चक्रे सहस्रवीर्यां सर्वस्मा ग्रोषधे त्वा ॥   (*Atharvaveda* IV, 17, 1)

"We seize and hold thee, Conquering One, the queen of medicines that heals. Plant, I have endowed thee with a thousand powers for every man."

Chromopathy in the Vedas

References to treatment of diseases of heart, kidney, liver etc., by means of sun's rays are found in *Atharvaveda* I, 22 and in *Atharvaveda* VI, 83.

(a) In *Atharvaveda* IX, 8, it is mentioned that the rays of the sun absc o the toxic elements of the body which explains its effectiveness in curing disease.

शीर्षक्तिं शीर्षामयं कर्णशूलं विलोहितम्
सर्वं शीर्षण्यं ते रोग वर्हिर्निमंन्त्रयामहे ।   (*Atharvaveda* IX, 8, 1)

394

(b)   Sunlight kills germs.

(i) उत् पुरस्तात्सूर्यं एति विश्वदृष्टो अदृष्टहा   *(Rigveda* I, 191, 8)

Slayer of things unseen, the sun, beheld of all, rises.

(ii) उद्यन्नादित्यः क्रिमीन् हन्तु   *(Atharvaveda* II, 32, 1)

Uprising, let the sun destroy the worms.

(iii) ये सूर्यं न तितिक्षन्त   *(Atharvaveda* VIII, 6, 12)

These worms cannot bear the sun.

(iv) हृद्रोगं मम सूर्यं हरिमाणं च नाशय   *(Rigveda* I, 50, 11)

Sunlight is efficacious regarding heart-disease and jaundice.

The restful harmony which the sun's rays produce through the combination of colours was recognized by the vedic seers and the *Atharvaveda* presents in a nucleus form, this aspect of chromopathy.

Fever Therapy in the Vedas

The *Atharvaveda* V, 22, mentions fevers and their cure.

(a)   There are three types mentioned.

(i) सदहिन: that which occurs daily.

(ii) तृतीयक: that which occurs every third day.

(iii) वितृतीयक: that which occurs on the fourth day.

तृतीयकं वितृतीयं सदन्दिमुत शारदम्

तक्मानं शीतं रूरं ग्रैष्मं नाशय वार्षिकम् ॥ *(Atharvaveda* V, 22, 13)

(b)   Apart from these three types of periodical ague, there are seasonal fevers.

(i) ग्रैष्म: The fever that occurs during the summer season on account of excessive heat.

(ii) शारद: The fever that occurs during the winter monsoons.

(iii) वार्षिक: The fever that occurs during the rainy season.

(iv) शीत: The Malarial fever which is accompanied with fits of shivering.

(v) रूर: The fever that occurs due to dryness.

(vi) वलास: The fever that arises on account of phlegm.

(vii) कास: Fever accompanied by bronchitis.

(viii) उत-युगं Where phlegm and bronchitis occur as parallel symptoms.

(ix) व्याल: High fever, as severe as a snake bite.

(c) *Atharvaveda* V, 22 verses 6,7,12 mentions the classes of people who suffer from attacks of fever.

(i) निष्टक्करीं The thin and lean or those who are dissipated:

वासी निष्टक्करीमिच्छ तां वक्ष्ण े ण समपंय

(ii) प्रफर्व्यम् The obese. (V, 22, 6)

शूद्रामिच्छ प्रफव्य तां तक्मन् वीव बूनुहि (V, 22, 7)

(iii) श्ररणं जनम् The over-indulgent or voluptuary.

पाप्मा भ्रातृव्ध्येण सह गच्छामुमरणं जनम् ॥ (V, 22, 12)

(d) *Atharvaveda* V, 22, 9, holds that fever does not attack the self controlled individual.

भन्यक्षेत्रे न रमसे वशीसन् मृडयासि न: ।

"One who is self controlled among us, fever does not give him pain but leaves him unaffected."

(e) Then in *Atharvaveda* V, 22, 2, V, 22, 4, resistances against fever are suggested.

(i) The one who performs sacrifices will gain immunity. By havan yajna, the air is purified and there is no contamination of atmosphere by germs.

वर्हि: शोशुचाना समिध:
इत: तक्मानं भ्रप बाघताम् ॥ (*Atharvaveda* V, 22, 1)

(ii) The man who is regular in the care of his bowels will protect himself because according to vedic injunction, with no constipation, there will be no fever.

भ्रघा हि तक्मन्नरसो हि भूया
भ्रघा न्यङ् ङ धराङ् वा परेहि ॥ (V, 22, 2)

(iii) Vegetarianism and moderation in eating are a protection against fever.

शकम्भरस्य मुष्टिहा पुनरेतु महावृषान्   (*Atharvaveda* V, 22, 4)

the metaphor is, that the vegetarian will strike the fever away, as if by a fist.   (मुष्टि-हा)

(f)   The vedic word for ague is तक्मा derived from तकि कृच्छ् जीवने, inflicting pain on the body. We have a reference to this in *Atharvaveda* 1, 25, 1

यदग्निरापो अद्रहत् प्रविश्य
यत्र कृष्वन् धर्मधृतो नमांसि ।
तन्न त आहुः परमं जनित्रं स नः
सं विद्वान् परि वृङ्ग्घि तक्मन् ॥

"When Agni blazed, when he has pierced the waters" (the idea is that fevers begin to be prevalent at the commencement of the annual rains, when Agni, the God of Fire, descends in the form of lightning from the waters of the firmament and falls with the rain into the waters of the earth.)

According to their types and season, there are more than forty names listed.

(g)   *The Three Herbs*

There are several remedies suggested in the *Atharvaveda* to counteract agues but there are three most popular herbs. They are जंगिड:

(i)   आशरीकं विशरीकं बलासं पृष्टयामयम्
तक्मानं विश्वशारदमरसां जंगिडस्करत् ॥ (*Atharvaveda* XIX, 34, 10)

"Lumbago and rheumatic pain, consumptive cough, and pleurisy and fever which each autumn brings, may *jangida* make powerless."

(ii) कुष्ट *Kushta* is another remedy given in *Atharvaveda* V, 4, I

कुष्टेहि तक्मनाशन तकमानं नाशयन्नितः ॥

(iii) The third is ग्रांजन

त्रयोदासा ग्रांजनस्य तक्मा बलास ग्रादहि ॥ (*Atharvaveda* IV, 9,8)

The three persistent hazards : fever, phlegm, and burn are controlled effectively by the herb known as *Anjana*.

(h) *Prayer for Healing of a Sick Person*

यमबध्नाद् बृहस्पतिर्मणिफालं (*Atharvaveda* X, 6, 8)

घृतश्चुतमुप्रं स्वदिरमोजसे

तेनोमां मणिना कृषिमश्विनावभिरक्षतः संभिषग्भयां महोदुहे ॥

"The charm Brihaspati hath bound...the Asvins with the Amulet protect this culture of our fields. This may yield power and protection by two physicians."

The Chemistry of Metals

(a)   In Vedic times, gold, silver, copper, iron, lead etc. were used as medicines and we have a reference to this fact in *Yajurveda*, XVIII, 13.

हिरण्यं च मे ज्यश्व मे श्यामं च मे लौहं च मे
सीसं च मे त्रपु च मे यज्ञेन कल्पन्ताम् ॥

(b) Small amounts of Lead are mentioned as a general tonic

सीसेन दुह इन्द्रियम् (*Yajurveda* XXI, 36)

'with lead, yield strength and power !

इदं बाधत्प्रतृत्रिण
जातानि पिशाच्या: (*Atharvaveda* 1, 16, 3)

It kills the germs known as Atri. Pishacha, Yatu, Rakshasa etc.

(c) Mark the emphasis of its efficacy in *Atharvaveda* 1, 16, 4. 'Lead is a remedy against consumption in the cattle, consumption in men.'

यौगोषुयक्षम: पुरुषेषु यक्षम : तेन त्व. साक्रयवराड् परेहि

(*Atharvaveda* XII, 2, 1)

Treatment in Snake Bites

Hypnotic Method.

(i) There is a mention of treatment by hypnosis called संवशी-

करण In *Atharvaveda* V. 13 we have

चक्षुषा ते चक्षुर्हन्मि विषेण हन्मि ते विषम्

अहे म्रियस्व मा जीवी: प्रत्यगस्येतु त्वा विषम् । (*Atharvaveda* V, 13, 4).

"I with this eye destroy thine eye, and with this position conquer thee. Live not, O Snake, but die the death, may thy venom return on thyself."

(ii) *Atharvaveda* VII, 93, reads :

इन्द्रेण मन्युना वयमभिस्याम पृतन्यतः घ्नन्तो वृत्राण्यप्रति ॥

"With Indra's and with Manyu's aid, may we subdue our enemies resistlessly destroying foes."

(iii) *Atharvaveda* VII, 56, 2, refers to the same.

(iv) *Atharvaveda* V, 13, 5, is just a hypnotic way of exorcising *kairat* कैरात, snakes (पृश्न, उपतृण्य, बभ्रु and असित and अलीक,) away from the courtyard.

कैरात पृश्न उपतृण्य बभ्र आम्रे

भृणतासिता अलीका:

मा मे सख्यु:स्ताभानमपिष्ठाता

श्रावयन्तो निविषेरमध्वम् ॥

"Listen to me, Black-snakes, and hateful creatures, Lurker-in-grass, Kairat, and Brown and Spotted. Approach not near the house, my friend inhabits, give warning and rest quiet with your poison."

खनित्रमा : snake emerging out from underground

The medicinal herbs suggested as cure for snake bite are ताबुव and तस्तुव. What these are compounded of remains yet a matter for research. It is conjectured that these may be some kind of stones, rubbing of which cures snake bite. The second method is to control the spreading poison by means of a constrictive bandage tied in three places.

गृह्णामि ते मध्यमम उत्तमम्

अवमन् एतासु विषं अग्रमम् ॥ (*Atharvaveda* V, 13, 2)

Gem Therapy in the Vedas

The Ayurvedic practitioners praise the efficacious use of gems in warding off disease. For example, in *Sushruta* chapter 46, we have

मुक्ताविद्रुमवजरेन्द वैदूर्यं स्फटिकादय:
चक्षुण्या मणय: शीता लेखवना विषेसूदना:
पवित्रा धरणीयाइच्च पाप्मालक्ष्मी मलापहा: ॥

The gems are मोती, मूंग, हीरा, लहसुनिया, and स्फटिक.

Wearing of these gems improves eyesight, has cooling effect, purifies the mind, increases beauty, decreases ugliness and removes poison. Inspite of the fact that wearing of these gems is advocated in Ayurveda as curative for ailments yet it is believed by certain researchers that references to मणिबन्धन (a list of which is given below) in the *Atharvaveda* relate not to gem therapy, but to knowledge of agricultural missiles and other scientific equipment. For example, फालमणिबन्धन in *Atharvaveda* X, 6, is considered to have nothing to do with the particular type of gem known as फालमणि but relates to a certain agricultural implement. The same view is held regarding the references to

आञ्जनमणि:	in *Atharvaveda* IV, 9
शंखमणि:	in *Atharvaveda* IV, 10
अस्ततृमणि:	in *Atharvaveda* 1, 46
जंगिडमणि:	in *Atharvaveda* 11, 4
do	in *Atharvaveda* XIX, 34
पर्णमणि:	in *Atharvaveda* III.5
शतवारमणि:	in *Atharvaveda* XIX, 36
श्रोदुग्धमणि:	in *Atharvaveda* XIX, 31
अभिबर्तंमणि:	in *Atharvaveda* 1, 29
प्रतिसरमणि:	in *Atharvaveda* VIII, 5
दर्भमणि:	in *Atharvaveda* XIX, 28/29/30
श्रौदुम्बरमणि:	in *Atharvaveda* XIX, 31
वरणमणि:	in *Atharvaveda* X, 3

This is a matter for further research and precise clarification.

These मणि : circular, uncut and pierced gems, were taken from dried roots of herbs and used as medicines in the vedic times. Whether they were actually tied round the waist or the arms, as is a custom prevalent even now a days, is not clear. Some scholars, however, infer from a word प्रसते in *Atharvaveda* XIX, 34, 8, that these gems were tied on different parts of the body.

प्रथोपदान भगवोर्जांगडामितवीर्यं
पुरात उग्रा प्रसत उपेन्द्रो वीर्यं ददौ ॥   (*Atharvaveda* XIX, 34, 8)

Then when thou sprangest into life,
Jangida of unmeasured strength,
Indra, O mighty one, bestowed,
Great power upon thee from the first.

Veterinary Science in the Vedas

Veterinary science which has for its nucleus, the *Atharvaveda* VI, 59; 11, 26; 1, 11, 14; expanded under the attention of the postvedic teachers, and we have voluminous treatises, not only on botany and the vegetable kingdom (वृक्षायुर्वेद) but on horses (अश्वायुर्वेद) elephants (हस्त्यायुर्वेद) the cows (गवायुर्वेद) and even on hawks. (श्येनकायुर्वेद)

Charaka devotes chapter II verses 19 to 26 to this science and *Harit Samhita* has several references to this. 'Salihotra is known as the father of the veterinary science and in the Punjabi dialect, the word 'Salotri' means a veterinary surgeon.

Hindu veterinary science possesses a monumental compilation known as "*Hasti-Ayurveda*", the sacred wisdom on the "Longevity of Elephants."

Dairy-Farming

We have references to this in the *Atharvaveda* II, 26. It is essential for cows to roam about, to ensure healthy breeding. (cf. येषां सहचारं वायु: जुजोष *Atharvaveda* II, 26, 1) .and that those animals that have wandered may return safely is indicated in :

ये पशव: परा ईयु: ते इह श्रायन्तु   (*Atharvaveda* II, 27, 1)

Atharvaveda III, 14 is an important hymn on cow-breeding (गोसंवर्धन)

The most efficacious remedy in veterinary diseases is the herb known as श्ररुन्धती   (*Atharvaveda* VI, 59)

It increases milk in the animals such as the cow.

श्रनडूद्वभ्यस्त्वं प्रथमं घेनुभ्यस्त्वमरुन्धति
श्रघेनवे वयसे शर्मं यच्छ चतुष्पदे ॥   (*Atharvaveda* VI, 59, 1)

First, O Arundhati, protect our oxen and our milky kin, protect each one that is infirm-each quadruped that yields no milk.

On Disinfectants

सर्वेषां च क्रिमीणां सर्वासां च क्रिमीणाम्
भिनद्याश्मना शिरो दहाम्यग्निना मुखम् ॥   (*Atharvaveda* V, 23, 13)

Of every worm and insect, of the female and the male alike—I crush the head to pieces with a stone and burn the face with fire.

ग्रामे सुपक्वे शबले विपक्वे
यो मा पिशाचो श्रशने ददम्भ ।
तदात्मना प्रजया पिशाचा
वि यातयन्तामगदोऽयमस्तु ॥   (*Atharvaveda* V, 29, 6)

If some Pishacha, in my food, raw, ready, thoroughly cooked, hath deceived me, let the Pishachas with their lives and off-spring atone for this and let this man be healthy.

Surely these *Pishachas* in the food could not be demons or ghosts, but germs which cause food poisoning.

Hair Diseases

The falling of hair and premature grey hair, are treated in *Atharvaveda* VI, 136. The remedy is the use of the herbs called,

केश दृं हणी (*Atharvaveda* VI, 21, 3)

नितत्नि (*Atharvaveda* VI, 136, 1)

केशवर्धनी (*Atharvaveda* VI, 137, 1)

देदी देवयामधिजाता पृथिव्यामस्योषधे   (*Atharvaveda*, VI 136)

तां त्वा नितत्नि केशेभ्यो दृं हणाय खनामसि

दृं ह प्रत्नान् जनयाजातां जातानु वर्षीय संस्कृधि

यस्ते केशोऽवपद्यते समूलो यश्च वृश्चते

इदं तं विश्मेषज्याभिषिञ्चनामि वीरुधा ॥ (*Atharvaveda*. VI. 136, 3)

Born from the bosom of wide earth, the goddess, godlike plant art thou : So we Nitatni, dig thee up to strengthen and fix fast the hair.

Make the old hair firm, make new hair spring, lengthen what has already grown.

Thy hair where it is falling off and where the roots are torn away, I wet and sprinkle with the plant, the remedy for all disease.

Insanity

देवेनसादुन्मदितमुन्मत्तं रक्षसस्परि

कृणोमि विद्वान् भेषजं यदानुन्मदितौसति   (*Atharvaveda* VI, 111, 3)

Insane through sin against the gods, or maddened by a demon's power, well-skilled I make a medicine, to free thee from insanity.

Eye Diseases

तिस्रो दिवस्तिस्रः पृथिवीः

षट् चेमाः प्रदिशः पृथक्

त्वयाहं सर्वा भूतानि

पश्यामि देव्योषधे ॥   (*Atharvaveda* IV, 20, 2)

Through thee, O god-like plant, may I *behold* all creatures that exist, three several earths and these six regions one by one.

Herb for Beauty

इदं खनामि भेषजं मां पश्यमभिरोहदम्

परायतो निवर्तनमायतः प्रतिनन्दनम् ॥   (*Atharvaveda* VII, 38, 1)

I dig this healing herb that makes my lover look on me and weep. That bids the parting friend return and kindly greets him as he comes.

Sterility

श्रा ते योनिर्भं एतु पुमान् बाण इवेषुधिम्
श्रा वीरो ऽत्र जायतां पुत्रस्ते दशमास्यः ॥ (*Atharvaveda* III, 23, 2)
यासां द्यौः पिता पृथिवी माता समुद्रो
मूलं वीरुधां बभूव
तास्त्वा पुत्रविद्याय देवीः प्रावन्त्वोषधयः ॥ (*Atharvaveda* III, 23, 6)

(i) As arrow to the quiver, so let a male embryo enter thee. Then from thy side, be born a babe a ten month child, thy hero son.

(ii) May those celestial herbs whose sire was heaven, the earth their mother and their root the ocean. May those celestial plants assist thee to obtain a son.

Herb for Pregnancy

शमीमश्वत्थ श्रारूढ तत्र पुंसुवनं कृतम्
तव् वै पुत्रस्य वेदनं तत्स्त्रीष्वा भरामसि ॥ (*Atharvaveda* VI, 11, 1)

Asvattha on the Shami-tree. There a male birth is certified. There is the finding of a son; this bring we to the women-folk.

Female Diseases

यस्ते गर्भममीवा दुर्णामा योनिमाशये
श्रग्निष्ठं ब्रह्मणासह निष्कव्याद मनीनशत् ॥ (*Atharvaveda* XX, 96, 12)

Agni, concurring in the prayer, drive off the eater of thy flesh. The malady of evil-name (दुर्णामा) that hath attacked thy babe and womb.

Contagious Diseases in the Atharvaveda VII, 65, 3

श्यावदता कुनखिना बण्डेन यत् सहासिम
　　　1　　　2　　　3　　　4
श्रपामार्गं त्वया वयं सर्वं तदपमृज्महे ।

If with the cripple we have lived, whose teeth are black and whose nails deformed with thee, O Apamarga the plant.

achyranthes aspera we wipe all that ill away, from us.

Leprosy

नक्त'जातास्योषधे रामे कृष्णे असिक्निच
इदं रजनि रजय किलासं पलितं च यत् ।　　　(*Atharvaveda* I, 23, 1)

Plant, thou sprangest up at night, dusky, dark coloured black in hue ! So Rajni, re-colour thou these ashy spots of this leprosy.

Haemorrhage

(*Atharvaveda* II, 3) This is checked by लाक्ष herb

अरु: क्राणमिदं महृत् पृथिव्या अध्युद्भृतम्
तदास्त्रावस्य भेषजं तदु रोगमनीनशत् ॥　　　(*Atharvaveda* II, 3, 5)

Mighty is this wound-healing balm, from out the earth was it produced. This is the cure for morbid flow this driveth malady away.

Skin Diseases

विद्रधस्य बलासस्य लोहितस्य बनस्पते
विस्लपकस्योषधे मोच्छिष: पिशितं च न ॥ (*Atharvaveda* VI, 127, 1)

Of abscess, of decline, of inflamation of the eyes, O plant of penetrating pain ! thou herb, let not a particle remain.

Sciatica सन्धिवात

दश वृत्र मुञ्चेमं रक्षसो ग्राह्या ।
अधि येनं ज ग्राह पर्वसु
अथो एनं वनस्पते जोबानां लोकमुन्नय ॥　　　(*Atharvaveda* II, 9, 1)

Free this man, Dasa vriksha ! from the demon, from *grahi* who hath seized his joints and members.

And raise him up again, O Tree, into the world of living men.

Birth Control or Family Planning

Atharvaveda VI, 138 refers to birth control by rendering one impotent. The name of the herb is not mentioned but the entire hymn with five verses is worth examination.

त्वं बीरुध्यां श्रेष्ठतमाभिभूतास्योषधे
इमं मे अग्र पुरुषं क्लीबमोपशिनं कृधि ॥ (*Atharvaveda* VI, 138, 1)

Plant, thy fame is spread abroad as best of all the herbs that grow. Unman for me to-day, this man that he may wet the horn of hair——make him a eunuch.

क्लीबं क्लीबं त्वाकरं वध्रेर्बाध्र
त्वाकरमरसारसं त्वाकरम् ।
कुरीरमस्य शीर्षणि
कुम्बं चाधिनिदध्मसि ॥   (*Atharvaveda* VI, 138,3)

Yes, I have unmanned thee eunuch ! yés, impotent ! made thee impotent, and robbed thee, weakling, of thy strength.

Wooing a woman

यथेमे द्यावापृथिवी
सद्यः पर्येति सूर्यः
एवा पर्येमि ते मनो
यथा मां कामिन्यद सो
यथा मन्नापगा असः ॥   (*Atharvaveda* VI, 8, 3)

As round this heaven and earth, the sun goes day by day encircling them. So do I go around thy mind that, woman, thou shalt love me well and shall not turn away from me.

Selection of certain medicines mentioned in the *Atharvaveda*.

दशवृक्ष	*Atharva.* II, 9	wind troubles
प्राशं	*Atharva.* II, 27	general debility
पिप्पली	*Atharva.* VI, 109	fevers
पृश्निपर्णीं	*Atharva.* II, 25	killing vaginal germs
रोहिणी	*Atharva.* IV, 12	fracture of bones
लाक्षा	*Atharva.* V, 5	skin trouble-antiseptic
सहस्रचक्षुः	*Atharva.* IV, 20	general tonic curing 1000 diseases as it were—specific for eyes.
तौरिलिका	*Atharva.* IV, 16	ear diseases

सोमलता. This is a unique herbal extract mentioned in the vedas. The entire book IX of the *Rigveda* with its 114 hymns, praises it. It is described as a nectar to guarantee immortality. It is a panacea for all ills. The *Rigveda* gives us an idea of what kind of herb this is, but the clues are scattered. For instance श्रृंगे शिशानो आर्षति ।

(Rigveda IX, 5, 2)

It is produced on the hill top.

सोममद्रौ (*Rigveda* V. 85, 2)—Soma is born in the mountains.

सोमस्येव मौजवतस्य मक्ष: (*Rigveda* X, 34. 14) It has many branches, but downwards—a tall plant.

अन्तरिक्षेण रारजत् (*Rigveda* IX, 5, 2)—a very tall plant going up the skies.

सहस्रवल्शं (*Rigveda* IX, 5, 10)—of many branches. There are several verses indicating how it may be taken, either alone, (अत्र्यये वारे)

or with curds	सामासो दध्याशिर:	(*Rigveda* I, 5, 5)
		(*Rigveda* IX, 103, 3)
or with cow milk	सोमगवाशिर:	(*Rigveda* I, 137, 1)
or with barley	यवाशिरो मजामहे ।	(*Rigveda* I, 187, 9)

Terms such as the Bhuta, Preta and Rakshasa explained

Atharvaveda IV, 37, is full of what have been known as ghosts and demons. But the error becomes apparent when we examine that the words भूत, प्रेत, राक्षस, गन्धर्व, mean only the "poisonous germs" which cause disease. They are destroyed by the disinfectant fumes of हींग, सरसों, तुलसी, गुग्गुल. These medicinal herbs are also mentioned in the *Atharvaveda*. According to *Raja-Nighantu*, हींग is called रक्षोघ्न

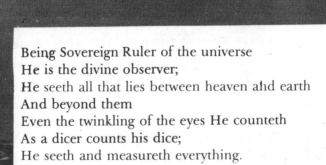

Being Sovereign Ruler of the universe
He is the divine observer;
He seeth all that lies between heaven and earth
And beyond them
Even the twinkling of the eyes He counteth
As a dicer counts his dice;
He seeth and measureth everything.

(Atharva.4.16.5)

"killer of demons" and *Dhanawantri Nighantu* gives a synonym of हींग as जन्तुघ्न 'killer of germs'. हींग is also called भूतनाशिनं हिड्गु 'killer of spirits'. The ayurvedic Nighantus are full of references and classification of these medicinal herbs, that kill the germs, that go by the name of राक्षस, भूत, प्रेत, गन्धर्व etc. etc..

The Germs called Rakshasas

The राक्षस is surely not a demon as is misinterpreted by some.

असृग्भाजानिह वैरक्षांसि—

(*Kaushitaki Brahmana* 17, 4) the blood sucking germs are called Rakshasa.

रक्षो रक्षितव्यमस्मात्   (*Nirukta* IV, 18)

Rakshasa is a germ from which one has to protect oneself. It is the disinfecting Sun alone which can kill these Rakshasas. As the *Shatapatha Brahmana* 1,3,4,8, puts it : सूर्यो हि नाप्ट्राणां राक्षसामपहन्ता.

These rakshasas can be killed by *fire*, too. अग्निर्वै ज्योती रक्षोहा (*Shatapatha Brahmana* VII, 4, 1, 34) अग्निर्वै रक्षसामपहन्ता (*ibid* 1, 2, 1, 6)

The invocation to Agni as protector has been made, because Agni is known to be the germ-killer

अग्ने हंसि न्यत्रिणां दीद्यन्   (*Rigveda* X, 118,1)

Agni, refulgent among men, thou slayest the devouring fiend (germs). Agni kills the germs called *Rakshas*

अदाभ्येन शोचिषाग्ने रक्षस्त्वं दह   (*Rigveda* X, 118,7)

O Agni, burn the Rakshasas with thine unconquerable flame ! सर्वेषाञ्च क्रिमीणां·········दहामृथग्निनामुखम्
(*Atharvaveda* V, 23,13)

I destroy all germs by means of fire'.

प्रति दह यातुधानान् प्रतिदेव किमीदिनः
प्रतीची: कृष्णवर्त्तने सं दह यातुधान्यः ॥   (*Atharvaveda* 1.28,2)

O Agni, burn these germs called यातुधान, these called किमीदिन Kimidina; burn all female Yatudhana germs.

The term 'Durnama' (दुर्णामा) explained

Atharvaveda VIII, 6 makes specific mention of Rakshasa and Pishacha. Let us examine the first verse of this hymn wherein we find the word *durnama* दुर्णामा mentioned.

यौ ते मातोन्ममार्जं जातायाः पतिवेदनौ
दुर्णामा तत्र मा गृधदंलिश उत वत्सपः ॥ (*Atharvaveda* VIII, 6,1)

"Let neither fiend of evil name *Durnama, Alinsa, Vatsapa* desire thy pair of husband wooers which thy mother cleansed when thou wast born."

Psycho-therapy मन्त्र चिता

(a) The *Atharvaveda* abounds in references to curing of diseases by the exercise of will-power; because according to *Atharvaveda* XIX, 52.1, will-power is the very essence of the mind.

(कामस्तदग्रे समवर्तत मनसो रेतः............)

This is scientific approach to the problem of disease. 'It is truly said, 'a peaceful mind generates power.' The mind has to be enriched with vital thoughts, to ensure a rich and strong body.

Let us examine some of the verses in the *Atharvaveda* in which this method of will-power is applied in overcoming ailments.

परो पेहि मनस्पाप विमंशस्तानि शंसति...... (*Atharvaveda* VI, 45.1)

'Sin of the mind, avaunt begone ! why sayest thou what none should say.'

And again, कृतं मे दक्षिणे हस्ते जयो मे सव्य आहित :

(*Atharvaveda* VII, 50.8)

'My right hand holds my winnings fast and in my left is victory."

To acquire valour by increasing one's will power is enjoined in a verse of the *Rigveda*.

वृषा ह्यसि राधसे जज्ञिषे
वृष्णि ते शवः

(*Rigveda* V. 35, 4)

"Mighty to prosper us wast thou born and mighty is the strength, thou hast."

अग्ने यन्मे तन्वा अनंतन्मआ्राापृण (*Yajurveda* III, 17)

is a prayer to Agni to supply all that is wanting in me. (*Wilson*) which is the same as

अपेहि मनसस्पतेपक्राम परश्चर: (*Atharvaveda* XX, 96, 24)

"Avaunt, thou Master af the Mind ! Depart and vanish far away."

Atharvaveda iII, 22, 1.

हस्तिवर्चसं प्रथतां वृहद्यशो अदित्या यत्
तन्व: सम्बभूव —

This mantra corresponds to Patanjali's *Yoga-Sutra* IV, 24, बलेषु हस्तिबलादोनि which assures the yogi, the power of an elephant, through concentration and identification with the might of an elephant.

(b) **Healing by Touch.** This is a part of the science of Mesmerism which was introduced in Europe by Mesmer, but the sages knew this science since the age of the vedas. We have a reference to this application in *Atharvaveda* IV, 13, 6.

अयं मे हस्तो भगवानयं मे भगवत्तर:
अयं मे विश्वाभेषजोऽयं शिवभिमर्शं न:

"Felicitous is this my hand, yet more felicitous is this. This hand contains all healing balms, and this makes whole with *gentle touch*."

The Vedic Chemistry of Gold and Gems

In China and in Egypt, gold was regarded as a magic medicine from very old times. In India we have references to gold as a miracle-cure for many ailments, in *Atharvaveda* XI, 1, 28 :

इमं मे ज्योतिरमृतं हिरण्यम् ।

"This gold is my immortal light." The Hindus, like the Chinese, associated medicinal gold with longevity and immortality.

Chemistry of Gold and Shell in the Atharvaveda

We have several references to the alchemy of shell and gold in the *Atharvaveda* and in this connection, the following hymns are worthy of note :

Atharvaveda IV, 10, 1 says:

वाताङ्जातो अन्तरिक्षाद् विष्णुतो ज्योतिषस्परी ।
स नो हिरण्यजाः शङ्खः कृशनः पात्वंहसः ॥

(Born in the heavens, born in the sea brought on from the river, this shell born of gold, is our life-prolonging amulet.)

Atharvaveda IV, 10, 7 says:

देवानामस्थि कृशनं बभूव तदात्मन्वच्चरत्यप्स्वन्तः ।
तत् ते बध्नाम्यायुषे वर्चसे बलाय दीर्घायुत्वाय
शतशारदाय कार्शनस्त्वाभि रक्षतु ॥

(The bone of the gods turned into pearl that animated, dwells in waters. That do I fasten upon thee unto life, lustre, strength, longevity, unto a life lasting a hundred autumns. May the amulet of pearl protect thee !)

Atharvaveda XIX, 26, 1 says :

अग्ने प्रजातं परियद्धिरण्यममृतं दध्रे अधि मर्त्येषु
य एनद् वेद स इदेनमर्हति जरामृत्युर्भवति यो बिभर्ति ॥

(The gold which is born from fire, the immortal they bestowed upon the mortals. He who knows this deserves it, of old age he does not die who wears it.)

Atharvaveda XIX, 26, 2 adds :

यद्धिरण्यं सूर्येण सुवर्णं प्रजावन्तो मनवः पूर्वे ईषिरे ।
तत् त्वा चन्द्रं वर्चसा सं सृजत्यायुष्मान् भवति यो बिभर्ति ॥

(The gold endowed by the sun with beautiful colour
which the men of yore, rich in descendants, did desire; may
it gleaming envelop thee in lustre.) Long lived becomes he
who wears it and so into the following verse, concluding
with *Atharvaveda* XIX, 26, 4 :

यद् वेद राजा वरुणो वेद देवो बृहस्पतिः ।
इन्द्रो यद् वृत्रहा वेद तत् त आयुष्यं भुवत् ।
तत् ते वर्चस्यं भुवत् ॥

(The gold which king Varuna knows, which god Brihaspati knows, which Indra, the slayer of Vritra knows, may
that become for thee a source of life, may that become for
thee a source of lustre.)

Essence of Soma Filtration in Vedic Chemistry

While the ancient Mediterranean and Indian civilizations
knew the art of refining metals and alloys (particularly
copper, lead and tin), they were as familiar with the manu-
facture of soap, starch, glass, leather, stoneware, wine and
beer.

However, Somalata, the famous herbal tonic of the gods
remains an unanalyzable secret of the Indians. Its decoction in
सोमरस which gave health and longevity was a ritual intoxicant
that was well known to the Indian vedic sages. The entire
ninth book of the *Rigveda* is in praise of that *Soma* and is
known as *Pavamana-Soma-sukta* (the hymn of the pure
Soma).

The vedic sages were familiar with the process of distillation, and went into ecstasy over the exhilarating effects of
the fermented soma juice. Particularly delightful is the

hilarity of the sage marching to the filter, in *Rigveda* X, 97, 1 :

या ओषधीः पूर्वा जाता देवेभ्यस्त्रियुगं पुरा ।
मनै नु बभ्रू णामहं शतं धामानि सप्त च ।।

The History and Scope of Chemistry in the Vedas

Chemistry as Branch of Medicine

From the time of the Vedas, chemistry has been the handmaid of medicine, of which "the oldest literary monument is the *Atharvaveda*."

In that close partnership, we find surprising contributions made by chemists in the field of medicine, obviously disciplined by the compass of their own technique and equipment.

In the ancient Hindu texts, we have lot of information on filtration, solution, crystallization, distillation and sublimation (called ऊर्ध्वंपातन) etc.

And all substances which now go by the name of oxides. of copper or iron or zinc, and those known as the sulphates of iron and copper, gold amalgam, white lead, dyes with a large variety of vegetable products, were fully dealt with by the Hindu texts.

Not only was medicine associated with chemistry, but in ancient times *Astrology* had a definite bearing on chemistry inasmuch as the planets, the sun, the moon, saturn, jupiter, mars, venus and mercury were associated with gold, silver, lead, tin, iron, copper and mercury and these metals were particularly in use in case of gem-therapy, copious references to which are available in the *Atharvaveda*.

Vedic References and the Development of Arithmetic, Geometry and Algebra

THE VEDIC hymns make several references to arithmetical principles:

1.	Consecutivity of numbers from 1 to 10	Atharv. XIII, 4
2.	Additions of numbers with multiple of 10	Atharv. V, 15
3.	Additions of 2	Yaj. XVIII, 24
4.	Additions of 4	Yaj. XVIII, 25
5.	Mention of the digit 99	Rig. I, 84, 13
6.	Multiplication by 11	Atharv. XIX,47
7.	Vedic numerical system	Yaj. XVII, 2
8.	Reference to fractions	Rig. X, 90

य एतं देवमेकवृतं वेद

न द्वितीयो न तृतीयश्चतुर्थो नाप्युच्यते ।

न पञ्चमो न षष्ट: सप्तमो नाप्युच्यते

नाष्टमो न नवमो दशमो नाप्युच्यते ॥ (*Atharvaveda XIII,* 5, 16-18)

To him who knoweth this God as simple and ONE, neither second nor third nor yet fourth is He called, He is called neither fifth nor sixth nor yet seventh, He is called neither eighth nor ninth, nor yet tenth.

एका च मे दश च मे	$1+10=11$
द्वे च मे विंशतिश्च मे	$2+20=22$
तिस्रश्च मे त्रिंशच्च मे	$3+30=33$
चतस्रश्च मे चत्वारिंशच्च मे	$4+40=44$
पञ्च च मे पञ्चाशच्च मे	$5+50=55$
षट् च मे षष्टिश्च मे	$6+60=66$

सप्त च मे सप्ततिश्च मे	$7+70=77$
ब्रष्ट च मे ऽशीतिश्च मे	$8+80=88$
नव च मे नवतिश्च मे	$9+90=99$
दश च मे शतं च मे	$10+100=110$
शतं च मे सहस्त्रं च मे	$100+1000=1100$

(*Atharvaveda V*, 15, 1-11)

One and ten, two and twenty etc., etc.

"Eleven of the hymns, which are a charm for general prosperity, are exactly the same with exception of the numbers which increase by eleven in each stanza (thirty and three, forty and four, and so on) upto one hundred and ten in stanza 10, stanza 11, concluding with one thousand and one hundred."

एका च मे तिस्त्रश्च मे	$1+2=3$
तिस्त्रश्च मे पञ्च च मे	$3+2=5$
पञ्च च मे सप्त च मे	$5+2=7$
सप्त च मे नव च मे	$7+2=9$
नव च मे एकादश च मे	$9+2=11$
एकादश च मे ञयोदश च मे	$11+2=13$
ञयोदश च मे पञ्चदश च मे	$13+2=15$
पञ्चदश च मे सप्तदश च मे	$15+2=17$
सप्तदश च मे नवदश च मे	$17+2=19$
नवदश च मे एकर्विशतिश्च मे	$19+2=21$
एकार्विशतिश्च मे ञयोर्विशतिश्च मे	$21+2=23$
ञयोर्विशतिश्च मे पञ्चर्विशतिश्च मे	$23+2=25$
पञ्चर्विशतिश्च मे सप्तर्विशतिश्च मे	$25+2=27$
सप्तर्विशतिश्च मे नवर्विशतिश्च मे	$27+2=29$
नवर्विशतिश्च मे एकत्रिश्च्च मे	$29+2=31$
एकत्रिश्च्च मे त्रयत्रिश्च्च मे	$31+2=33$

यज्ञेन कल्पन्ताम् ॥ (*Yajurveda* XVIII, 24)

May my one and my three, and my three and my five, and

my five and my seven (and similarly upto thirty-three) prosper
by sacrifice.

चतस्त्रश्च मे ऽस्टौ च मे	4+4=8
अ्रष्टौ च मे द्वादश च मे	8=4=12
द्वादश च मे षोडश च मे	12+4=16
षोडश च मे विशतिश्च मे	16+4=20
विशतिश्च मे चतुर्विशतिश्च मे	20+4=24
चतुर्विशतिश्च में ऽष्टाविशतिश्च मे	24+4=28
अ्रष्टाविशतिश्च मे द्वात्रिंशच्च मे	28+4=32
द्वात्रिंशच्च मे षट्त्रिंशच्च मे	32+4=36
षट्त्रिंशच्च मे चत्वारिंशच्च में	36+4=40
चत्वारिंशच्च मे चतुश्चत्वारिंशच्च मे	40+4=44
चतुश्चत्वारिंशच्च मे ऽष्टाचत्वारिंशच्च मे	44+4=48

यज्ञेन कल्पन्ताम् ॥ (*Yajurveda* XVIII, 25)

May my four and my eight and my twelve (and similarly upto forty-eight) prosper by sacrifice.

इमा मे अ्रग्न इष्टका धेनव:

1   10   100
सन्त्वेका च दश च, दश च शतं च

1000
शतं च सहलं च, सहलं चायुतं च

ग्रायुतं च नियुतं च

नियुतं च प्रयुतं च

अर्बुदं च न्यर्बुदं च

समुद्रश्च मध्यं चान्तश्च परार्धश्चेता मे

अ्रग्न इष्टका धेनव: सन्त्वमुत्रामुष्मिंल्लोके ॥ (*Yajurveda* XVII, 2)

O Agni, may these bricks be mine own milch kine; one
and ten, and ten tens, a hundred and ten hundreds, a thousand, and ten thousands, myriad, and a hundred a thousand
and a million; and a hundred millions, and an ocean, middle
and end, and a hundred thousand millions, and a billion.

May these bricks be mine own milch-kine in yonder world and in this world.

We may compare, also, the reference to this numeral system in *Atharvaveda* VIII, 8, 7.

बृहत् ते जालं बृहत् इन्द्र शूर
सहस्रार्घस्य शतवीर्यस्य
तेन शतं सहस्रमयुतं न्यर्बुदं
जघान शक्रो दस्यूनामभिधाय सेनया ॥

Great ıs thy net, brave Indra, thine the mighty match. for a thousand, Lord of hundred powers holding them with his host, therewith hath Indra slaughtered Dasyus, a *hundred, thousand, myriad, hundred millions.*

The Decimal System

It is admitted by scholars that the modern decimal value notation was known in India in the 4th century B.C.

Vedic References to Hindu Geometry

Conception of the circumference of a circle

कालीत्प्रभा प्रतिमा किं निदानम्
प्राज्यं किमासीत् परिधिः क आसीत् ।
छन्दः किमासीत् प्रउगं किमुक्थं
यद्देवा देवमयजन्त विश्वे ॥   (*Rigveda* X, 130, 3)

(What is the measurer? Who measures and counts all? What is the cause and what the essence, like ghee, in this world? What is the *circumference?* What is the independent and what the praiseworthy object?—The Supreme Lord whom the learned have worshipped.)

Area of a triangle (त्रिभुज)

यो अक्रन्दयत् सलिलं महित्वा
योनिं कृत्वा त्रिभुजं शयानः ।
वत्सः कामदुघो विराजः

स गुहा चक्रे तन्वः पराचेः ॥   (*Atharvaveda* VIII, 9, 2)

He who prepared a *threefold* home and lying there made the water bellow through his greatness—calf of Viraja giving each wish, fulfilment, made bodies for himself far off, in secret.—

'Threefold home' refers to the triangle (त्रिभुज) of heaven, firmament and earth, wherein Agni dwells as sun, lightning and fire.

Surface of a cylinder

त्रितः कूपे ऽवहितो देवान्हवत ऊतये
तच्छुश्राव बृहस्पतिः कृण्वन्नंहूरणादुरु०   (*Rigveda* I, 105, 17)

Trita, when buried in the *well*, calls on the gods to succour him. That call of his, Brihaspati heard and released him from distress—Mark this my woe, ye earth and heaven.

In this mantra, too, the well, which is cylindrical has been sunk defectively, for if the ratio is only ½ then any one will be squeezed in that. Trita was obviously trapped into a three dimensional equivalent of the diagram. The implication is clear, that, if the ratio is more or less than $\frac{22}{7}$ then the diameter will be inexact.

We euolgise Thee, O Lord,
Thou hast caused
The flowers and fruit-bearing herbs
To grow in the fields
And blossom and bear seeds.
Thou hast spread
The streams by eternal order.
Thou hast generated
The various luminaries
Of the celestial region
That surround vast realms.

(Rig.2.13.7)

Astronomy

God agitates Matter. Preparing a threefold home through His greatness, He pervades all objects. God, the Fulfiller of all wishes, the Enveloper of Matter, creates in the atmosphere vast distant worlds.

(Atharva.8.9.2)

The revolving Sun is the breast. Atmosphere is the belly. Jupiter is the hump. Vast quarters are the breast-bone and cartilages of the ribs.

(Atharva.9.7.5)

Whatsoever constellations there are in the heavens, the mid-regions, observed through waters and on the earth, on the mountains and in all quarters, and the moon passes by them, revealing them, may they all be peaceful to me.

(Atharva.19.8.1)

The aforesaid twenty-eight constellations along with the moon may provide peace and happiness to me, so that I may acquire the desired object and be able to keep it intact and may I make the right use of my time all through day and night.

(Atharva.19.8.2)

Soul, Rebirth, Cremation

The Lord's joy manifests through the splendorous
Beauty and serenity of His creations.
The supreme bliss of this divine love is felt
  within the
Soul that is pure and receptive to the sanctity of
God's boundless love.
It kindles the innermost self of devotees.

(Sama.547)

The victorious Soul acclaims:
"I am Indra radiant like the sun;
I am invincible, never to be conquered by
  adversities.
No one can ever wrest my wisdom from me,
Never at any time can even death defeat me.
No one can compel me to withdraw
From the path of truth and justice."

(Rig.10.48.5)

O builder of resolute will power, O Soul,
Both body and intellect, tremble in fear of Thee,
May these remain Thy commands.
When the Soul determines to show its strength to
  the evil mind, the architect of evil desires,
It shivers with fear under the spell
Of Thy sovereignty.

(Rig.10.80.14)

Soul, all-time companion of the Radiant Lord,
Be not sorrowful at your limitations;
Enlightened with light divine, aspire to unite with
    God, and get eternal bliss.
Inspired by divine energy, blessed with all
    worldly gifts,
Rise above them all and aspire to attain ultimate
    salvation.
Ascend upwards to the blissful state;
Sail across through both the worlds.
May Godly powers unite with eternity.

(Atharva.4.14.1,2)

Elevate the soul, that may be a prey to five
passions, equipped with five organs of action and
surrounded by five elements.
After death place on the funeral pyre, the head of
the body of the emancipated soul to the east, and
its right side to the south.

(Atharva.4.14.7)

The charitable deeds of this birth will bless the soul
to attain greater wisdom and a perfect physical
body in the next life.

(Atharva.5.1.2.)

The Lord's joy manifests through the splendorous
Beauty and serenity of His creations.
The supreme bliss of this divine love
Is felt within the Soul, that is pure and receptive
To the sanctity of God's boundless love.
It kindles the innermost self of devotees.

(Atharva.20.137.4)

O Soul, surely Thou hast inner brilliance and
invincible power to shine gloriously.

(Yajur.10.15)

O soul, blazing like the sun after cremation, having
reached the fire and the earth for rebirth, and
residing in the belly of thy mother, thou art born
again!

(Yajur.12.38)

O soul, having reached the womb, again and again,
thou auspiciously liest in thy mother, as a child
sleeps in its mother's lap!

(Yajur.12.39)

Yoga

The pure soul, cleansed through the control of
breath and meditation soon attains salvation
And becomes one with God through yogic samadhi.

(Atharva.6.51.1)

As I am the disciple of my learned preceptor,
I am making an effort to free my soul from
this body for the realisation of God.

O preceptor, I, thy pupil, join my soul
through austerity, spiritual fervour
and the sacred thread.

(Atharva.6.133.3)

She (the sacred thread) hath become Faith's
daughter, through Yoga, the sister of sages,
the preachers of Truth.
As such, O sacred thread, give us wisdom,
religious zeal and mental vigour.

(Atharva.6.133.4)

Whatever evil or sinful act we have committed
with thy help, O Prana, life breath, the
remover of sin and pervader in the body,
we wipe it off.

(Atharva.7.65.2)

The five senses are linked with the five elements.
The five seasons are like the five breaths of the
mind. The five directions are the five organs of
cognition controlled by the soul.
These organs are located in the head and
connected with the soul.

(Atharva.8.9.15)

We, the learned, have heard that the soul is
equipped with seven senses which excite passions,
seven subtle senses which imbibe knowledge,
seven tendencies and seven desires
emanating from the physical organs.

(Atharva. 8. 9. 18)

Seven senses: Skin, Eye, Ear, Nose, Tongue, Mind, Intellect Seven
subtle senses: Sound, Touch, Sight, Taste, Smell, Thought, Meditation.
Seven tendencies: Lust, Anger, Avarice, Infatuation, Pride, Hatred, Self-
praise. Seven desires: Fame, Wealth, Progeny, Happiness, Worldly
position, Heath, Salvation.

Seven apertures in the head are interlinked with the
four higher sentiments. How do these seven
depend upon the four, and how do the four depend
upon the seven?

(Atharva.8.9.19)

Seven apertures: Two eyes, two nostrils, two ears, mouth. Four
sentiments. Dharma, Artha, Kama, Moksha. These forces are linked
with each other. Through the right use of the seven apertures, one
attains these higher sentiments.

How does splendour surround the soul,
possessing the threefold qualities of Satva, Rajas,
Tamas?

How is salvation, attainable through action,
contemplation, knowledge acquired by the soul,
full of fifteen traits?

How is the world created by God, the Master of
thirty-three forces?

How does the soul possessing twenty-one forces
acquire the knowledge of the Vedas?   (Atharva.8.9.20)

Fifteen traits: Prana, Apana, Vyana, Udana, Samana, hearing, touch,
sight, taste, smell, earth, water, fire, air and atmosphere.

Thirty-three forces: Eight Vasus, Eleven Rudras, Twelve Adityas, Indra,
Prajapati. Vasus: Fire, Earth, Air, Atmosphere, Sun, Moon, Heaven, a
Star. Rudras: Prana, Apana, Vyana, Udana, Samana, Naga, Kurma,
Krikla, Deva Dutta, Dhananjaya and Jiv Atma (soul). Adityas: Twelve
months. Indra: Lightning, and Prajapati, i.e. Yajna. Twenty-one forces:
Five Bhutas : Earth, Water, Fire, Air, Atmosphere, Five Pranas, Five
Sense Organs, Five Action Organs and Mind.

Eight elements sprang up, first-born of Matter.
O soul, these are the eight divine forces which
contribute to creation, sustenance and dissolution
of the world.

Eight are the stages for the acquisition of God.
and eight His protecting powers.
His infinite power takes man to salvation.

(Atharva.8.9.21)

Eight elements: Intellect, Ego, Earth, Water, Fire, Air, Atmosphere,
Mind. Eight stages: Yama, Niyama, Asana, Pranayama, Pratyahara,
Dharna, Dhyana, Samadhi. Protecting powers: Minuteness, Lightness,
Acquisition, Freedom of Will, Greatness, Glory, Supremacy, Power.

Sight leaves the yogi not, life breath quits
him not before old age. He attains proximity of
Almighty God, whereby he is named Purusha.

(Atharva.10.2.30)

The citadel of the body is unconquerable, equipped
with eight circles and nine portals, contains the soul
full of a myriad power. It is ever marching on to
blissful God, surrounded by the realisation of the
Supreme Being.

(Atharva.10.2.31)

Eight circles: Eight parts of yoga. Yama, Niyama, Asana, Pranayama,
Pratyahara, Dharna, Dhyana, Samadhi. Nine portals: The orifices of the
human body. Two eyes, two ears, two nostrils, mouth, anus and vital
organs.

The yogi with his soul force realises the supreme
Lord, Who dwells in the human soul. The soul has
three spokes and three supports.

(Atharva.10.2.32)

Three spokes: Capacity, Sign, Existence. Three Supports: Action,
Contemplation, Knowledge.

O man, I yoke thy soul that goes to the next
world through breath, with two carriers,
the Prana and the Apana.
Through their control through Yoga,
seek shelter under God and communion with Him!

(Atharva.18.2.56)

Oh! Yogin, shedding off all ignorance, shining like
the Sun, fully equipped with all powers, rise to the
highest state of bliss by your glory and grandeur.
Those who want to suppress you from flying to the
highest state of beatitude, crush them by your force
of destroying evil. Being fearless and terrible, by
your grandeur, may you rise to the most shining
state of bliss.

(Atharva.19.65.1)

Anatomy

God, the Creator, has put together both these arms,
so that man may show manly strength. Hence the
Refulgent God has set the shoulder-blades upon
the trunk.

(Atharva.10.2.5)

God pierced the seven openings in the head. He
made these ears, these nostrils, eyes and mouth,
through whose surpassing might in various forms,
bipeds and quadrupeds complete their journey of
life.

(Atharva.10.2.6)

God set within the jaws the tongue and thereon
gave the mighty power of speech. He pervades
all the worlds, static or moving. No one can
understand it perfectly.

(Atharva.10.2.7)

God first of all fashioned his skull, brain and
forehead. Who is that Adorable God Who has risen
to the pinnacle of splendour?

(Atharva.10.2.8)

Medicine

Just as light hangs between Earth and Firmament,
so does Munja, a healing medicinal herb, cures
fever and dysentery.

(Atharva.1.2.4)

O patient suffering from a urinary disease, just as the water of the flooded ocean rises up, and flows into streams, so have I unclosed the orifice of thy bladder. May that urine of thine come out completely unchecked.

(Atharva.1.3.8)

Those veins, serviceable like maidens, which run their course clothed in blood, must now stand quiet, like sisters who are brotherless and bereft of power.

(Atharva.1.17.1)

O patient, we control thy jaundice with the seeds of Shuka trees and other strong healing medicines. We cure thy jaundice through the use of efficacious mixtures.

(Atharva.1.22.4)

Rama, Krishna and Asikni medicinal herbs spring up at night. Rajni removes leprosy and whiteness of the body.

(Atharva.1.23.1)

Shyama named medicinal herb,
dug out of the earth, imparts beauty and cures leprosy.

(Atharva.1.24.4)

O woman, from thee we banish and expel the cause of thy sterility. We lay this apart and far removed from thee in another place!

(Atharva.3.23.1)

As arrow to the quiver, so let a male embryo enter thee. Then from thy side be born a babe, a ten-month child, thy heroic son.

(Atharva.3.23.2)

By the use of the auspicious seeds yielded by the
herbs named Rishbhak, do thou, O woman, obtain
thyself a son: be thou a fruitful mother-cow!

(Atharva.3.23.4)

Dawn stimulates the body, the sun lends vigour to
our organs, this imperative word of mine creates an
urge, this semen-enhancing, man-protecting
medicine named Vrisha, through its invigorating
juice lends strength to the body.

(Atharva.4.4.2)

O man, if a hunter with five fingers hath filled
thy body with poison from the crooked arrow, I
ask thee to remove the same through the leaves
of the herb Apaskambh.

(Atharva.4.6.4)

I charm away the poison with the thorn of a
porcupine, with the paint of Parndhi, with
Ajashringhi brought from a distant place, and
by the use of Kulmal herb.

(Atharva.4.6.5)

Rohini named herb is the healer of the broken
bone. May Arundhati, wound-healing herb, heal up
this wound!

(Atharva.4.12.1)

Felicitous is this my left hand, yet more felicitous is
this the right one. This hand contains all healing
properties, its gentle touch brings peace and
welfare.

(Atharva.4.13.6)

With our tenfold fingered hands, with our tongue
that leads and precedes the voice, with these two
healers of disease, we stroke thee with a gentle
fondling touch.

(Atharva.4.13.7)

O King, punish the pharmacists who use a deadly
medicine, those who prepare an adverse injurious
medicine in an unbaked or fully burnt dark red
earthen pot, or inject poisonous matter in raw flesh!

(Atharva.4.17.4)

The Apamarga is the foremost among all plants.
With this we wipe away whatever disease hath
attacked thee, O patient. Get rid of it and live long!

(Atharva.4.17.8)

Let disease-germs in waters be washed down, just
as a stream, filled with water, flows down fast.
Five medicines are helpful in dislodging them
(1) Gulgulu (2) Pila (3) Naladi (4) Aukshagandhi
(5) Pramandani.

(Atharva.4.37.3)

The Sun's rays are blazing like hundreds of iron
weapons. With those let it destroy the germs that
feed on oblations and Blyxa Octandra.

(Atharva.4.37.8)

O female, we shall destroy altogether from this
world the poison or the disease-germ which kills
the sperm in the very act of falling in thy organ of
generation, which kills it in the iambic stage, which
kills it when it has begun its movements in the
womb, which wishes to kill it when it is born.

(Atharva.4.96.13)

Sun is thy grandsire, Night thy mother, and the
Cloud thy sire. Thy name is called Silachi (wax),
thou, thyself, art sister of the learned.

(Atharva.5.5.1)

Thou springest from blest Plaxa, or Ashvattha,
Khadira, Dhava, blest Nyagrodha, Parna, so come
thou to use, O medicine, the filler of wounds.

(Atharva.5.5.5)

God-coloured, lustrous, shining like the Sun, most
lovely, O healing medicine, thou art applied on the
wound or fracture. Healing is thy name!

(Atharva.5.5.6)

O learned person, in consultation with other
physicians, arrange in such a way, that the fort of
this disease may fall, which hath caused us pain,
whichever hath consumed our flesh!

(Atharva.5.29.2)

Whatever of the body of this sick man hath been
taken, plundered, borne off, or eaten by the flesh-
consuming germs, that, O learned physician,
restore to him again through medicine. We give
back flesh and spirit to his body.

(Atharva.5.29.5)

If some flesh-consuming germ, entering my raw,
cooked, half-cooked, thoroughly cooked food, hath
injured me, let the germs with their lives and
offspring be destroyed, so that I may be free
from disease.

(Atharva.5.29.6)

The deadly poison that the enemies mix in thy
food, drinking water or administer it in the raw
fruits, the same do I remove.

(Atharva.5.31.1)

With efficacious medicine do I rub the body of the patient. Streams, mountains, hillocks contain useful medicines. May the nourishing, sleep-inducing medicine be effective. May it bring peace to thy mouth, peace to thy heart.

(Atharva.6.12.3)

Of abscess, of consumption, of inflammation of the eyes, O Plant, of painful itch, thou Herb, let not a particle remain.

(Atharva.6.127.1)

Those two eruptions, Consumption, which stand closely hidden in thy groin, I know the medicine for them. Chipudru is their magic cure.

(Atharva.6.127.2)

I have removed the poison of this scorpion that creeps along low on the earth and is now poisonless.

(Atharva.7.56.5)

Black vein is the mother, we have heard, of red-hued pustules. I pierce and penetrate them, with the aid of a surgical knife.

(Atharva.7.74.1)

I pierce the foremost one of these pustules. I perforate one of medium intensity. Here I cut asunder the pustule of little intensity like a lock of hair.

(Atharva.7.74.2)

O girl, fit for marriage, thy mother rejects as thy husband him who suffers from skin disease of leprosy, and him who is far advanced in age. They should never long to marry thee.

(Atharva.8.6.1)

The mother should reject as her daughter's husband, the meat-eater, the companion of meat-eaters, a man violent in nature, one cruel like a wolf, a thief, a grey-haired person, one who suffers from gonorrhoea, a dandy, one stiff-necked like a bear, one suffering from photophobia.

(Atharva.8.6.2)

O leper, don't try to be married, if married through mistake, cohabit not with this girl. Don't live in her house. For this girl I select a beautiful husband as remedy for one suffering from leprosy.

(Atharva.8.6.3)

All-invigorating, semen-augmenting, health-infusing, highly brittle, highly efficacious, attractive medicines, we use for curing ailments.

(Atharva.8.7.1)

May the herbs, whose father is the Sun, their mother Earth, the water their root, deliver this man from consumption, born of lust.

(Atharva.8.7.2)

Let plants that banish pain, whose soul is water, piercing with their sharp horns, expel the malady.

(Atharva.8.7.9)

Medicines that free us from disease, cure dropsy, are strong in action, are antidotes of poison, remove cough and pneumonia, alleviate pain; let all of them be collected in this medical hall.

(Atharva.8.7.10)

The Durbha grass, fire, the grass sprout, Ashvaivara, Parushawara act as antidotes against the serpents' poison.

(Atharva.10.4.2)

The Kairatika or Kumarika drug is dug on the
high ridges of the hills.

(Atharva.10.4.14)

O plant, thou art named as Taudi, Kauya, or
Ghritachi. I take from underneath thy root, the part
that is poison-killing.

(Atharva.10.4.24)

O medicine! from every member drive away the
venom, and free the heart from it. Thus let the
poison's burning heat pass downward and away
from thee.

(Atharva.10.4.25)

Let the Jangida herb drive away the fatal diseases
like Asharika, Vishrika, asthma, cancer of the
back-bone, consumption which eats up the energy
of the body.

(Atharva.19.34.10)

O lady, let the learned physician, well-versed in the
science of killing germs of all diseases, in
consultation with a Vedic scholar, efface from thee
the malignant disease, which has taken hold of thy
uterus.

(Atharva.20.96.11)

O lady, let the expert physician, with his Vedic
knowledge and learning, thoroughly destroy the
malicious disease, which is lying latent in thy
womb.

(Atharva.20.96.12)

These poisonous plants should remain in a safe
place! The rugged mountain that produces this
herb should remain under the supervision of the
Government.

(Atharva.21.6.8)

Energy

Let the wind protect you with food. Let electricity be of great service to you, through electric machines or contrivances.

(Atharva.19.27.1)

O all learned people, fully realise your conduct towards different objects of the universe, know ye the electricity that maintains all beautiful objects, the sun, the invisible matter brought into creation, the invigorating vital airs, thus ye become the utilisers of all objects.

(Yajur.8.57)

O learned person, may thy displeasure spare the fire that has its being from the heat of the Earth, or from the lightning of the sun, whereby the Omnific Lord engenders creatures!

(Yajur.13.45)

Homage to him who knows the science of clouds, and to him who knows the science of electricity.

(Yajur.16.38)

O masters of the sciences of electricity and air, for ye are all these substances prepared.

(Yajur.33.56)

Electricity carries us the learned to distant places. Just as an ox carries the cart, so we use this electricity for prosperity in preparing planes and seating people therein. May that serve as lightning for you.

(Yajur.35.13)

Industry

May I explore and multiply precious stones
and brilliant gems, refined clay, crops,
mountains and their products, sand thick
and pulverised, silver and gold, iron and
weapons, lead and wax, zinc and brass.

(Yajur.18.13)

O God, create bitter drink for penance; for
sharpening intellect an artificer; for beauty a
jeweller; for welfare a sower; for arrows a maker of
shafts; for destructive weapons a bowyer; for victory
a bowstring-maker; for control a ropemaker. Cast
aside a hunter bent on killing.

(Yajur.30.7)

The many paths which the learned traders are
wont to travel, the paths which go between
the earth and heaven, may they provide me with
milk and ghee, that I may make rich profit by
my trade.

(Atharva.3.15.2)

Architecture

In front and behind thy house, let flowery
Durva grass grow.
Let there be a spring or a tank with
lotuses in bloom.

(Atharva.6.106.1)

Let us construct a beautiful, well-designed,
commodious house.   .
Let us strengthen the ties and fastenings
of the house that has doors on all sides
and holds all precious things.

(Atharva.9.3.1)

An artisan draws close, presses fast, makes secure
thy knotted bands. Just as a skilful surgeon operates
upon the diseased joints, so we strengthen all
thy parts, O house.

(Atharva.9.3.3)

Agriculture

Ye husband and wife, the growers and protectors of
corn, destroy the crow, the swine, the rat, cut off
their heads and crush their ribs. Bind fast their
mouths; let them not eat our barley; so guard,
ye twain, the growing corn from danger.

(Atharva.6.50.1)

Ho! crow, ho! thou locust, ho! obnoxious grasshopper.
As a priest rejects the not well-prepared oblation, so
go hence devouring not, injuring not this corn.

(Atharva.6.50.2)

Hearken to me, lord of the violent birds, lord of the
locusts, sharp-toothed vermin! Whatever ye be,
dwelling in woods or villages, devourers of my
harvest, we crush and mangle all those.

(Atharva.6.50.3)

The fiend who feeds on the flesh of cattle, the flesh
of horses and of human bodies, who steals the
milch-cow's milk away, O King, tear off the heads
of such with fiery fury!

(Atharva.8.3.15)

The fiends who poison the cows, the evil doers who
cut the cow into pieces, let the king, the urger of all,
banish them from his state, and their share of herbs
and plants be denied them.

(Atharva.8.3.16)

Geology

Just as I, the friend of all, perform this yajna, the
giver of kindly power, or have recourse to the
science of geology, so do thou.

(Atharva.8.7.9)

O learned man, just as I with the aid of Vedic
speech, the killer of fiends and infuser of strength,
perform the invigorating sacrifice, so do thou.
Just as my wise and able man, expert in the science
of yajna, performs the sacrifice or unearths this
place to test it geologically, so shouldst thou O
man!
Just as I a geologist resort to strength-giving
agriculture and the science of geology, so do thou.

(Yajur.5.23)

Transportation

O learned person, with the skill of art, thou hast
attained to fame under the sun, thou art connected
with air's mid-realm through electricity, thy asylum
is on earth. Being the master of aeroplanes, go
ahead with nice well-balanced speed!

(Yajur.11.12)

O artisan and his master, ye both, the bestowers of
happiness like the sun and air, harness electricity in
this aeroplane, possessing the speed of fire and
water, seating and taking us afar!

(Yajur.11.13)

For them, who with arrows in their hand and
armed with sword, preach the study of the Vedas
and the use of ships, we send our weapons to places
a thousand leagues afar.

(Yajur.16.61)

Let us honour that aeroplane, each day that passes,
with hearts full of joy, in which are laid necessary
ingredients for propelling it, and gun, cannon,
shield, bow, arrow, armour and military equipment
of this warrior.

(Yajur.29.45)

The skilled mechanics should utilise fire in making
automobiles travel for 3339 miles. Fire and water
should be employed in making them cover the
atmosphere.

(Yajur.33.7)

Index

ॐ

Original Text
of
HYMNS

ॐ

Page 9

एषायुक्त परावतः सूर्यस्योदयनादधि
शतं रथेभिः सुभगोषा इयं वि यात्यभि मानुषान्

ऋ. 1.48.7

Page 19

आ द्वाभ्यां हरिभ्यामिन्द्र याह्या चतुर्भिरा षड्भिर्हूयमानः
आष्टाभिर्दशभिः सोमपेयमयं सुतः सुमख मा मृधस्कः

ऋ. 2.18.4

Page 34

हिरण्यगर्भः समवर्तताग्रे भूतस्य जातः पतिरेक आसीत्
स दाधार पृथिवीं द्यामुतेमां कस्मै देवाय हविषा विधेम

ऋ. 10.121.1

Page 36

पूर्णः कुम्भोऽधि काल आहितस्तं वै पश्यामो बहुधा नु सन्तः
स इमा विश्वा भुवनानि प्रत्यङ्कालं तमाहुः परमेव्योमन्

अ. 19.53.3

Page 38

नासदासीन्नो सदासीत् तदानीं नासीद्रजो नो व्योमा परो यत्
किमावरीवः कुह कस्य शर्मन्नम्भः किमासीद्गहनं गभीरम्

ऋ. 10.129.1

न मृत्युरासीदमृतं न तर्हि न रात्या अह्न आसीत् प्रकेतः
आनीदवातं स्वधया तदेकं तस्मांद्धान्यन्न परः किं चनास

ऋ. 10.129.2

तम आसीत् तमसा गूळहमग्रेऽप्रकेतं सलिलं सर्वमा इदम्
तुच्छ्येनाभ्वपिहितं यदासीत् तपसस्तन्महिनाजायतैकम्

ऋ. 10.129.3

450

Page 39

कामस्तदग्रे समवर्तताधि मनसो रेतः प्रथमं यदासीत्
सतो बन्धुमसति निरविन्दन् हृदि प्रतीप्या कवयो मनीषा
ऋ. 10.129.4

तिरश्चीनो विततो रश्मिरेषामधः स्विदासीदुपरि स्विदासीत्
रेतोधा आसन् महिमान आसन् त्स्वधा अवस्तात् प्रयतिः परस्तात्
ऋ. 10.129.5

को अद्धा वेद क इह प्र वोचत् कुत आजाता कुत इयं विसृष्टिः
अर्वाग्देवा अस्य विसर्जनेनाऽथा को वेद यत आबभूव
ऋ. 10.129.6

इयं विसृष्टिर्यत आबभूव यदि वा दधे यदि वा न
यो अस्याध्यक्षः परमे व्योमन् त्सो अङ्ग वेद यदि वा न वेद
ऋ. 10.129.7

Page 41

शं नः सूर्य उरुचक्षा उदेतु शं नश्चतस्रः प्रदिशो भवन्तु
शं नः पर्वता ध्रुवयो भवन्तु शं नः सिन्धवः शमु सन्त्वापः
ऋ. 7.35.8

Page 42

सहस्रशीर्षा पुरुषः सहस्राक्षः सहस्रपात्
स भूमिं विश्वतो वृत्वा ऽत्यतिष्ठद्दशांगुलम्
ऋ. 10.90.1

पुरुष एवेदं सर्वं यद्भूतं यच्च भव्यम्
उतामृतत्वस्येशानो यदन्नेनातिरोहति
ऋ. 10.90.2

एतावानस्य महिमा ऽतो ज्यायाँश्च पूरुषः
पादोऽस्य विश्वा भूतानि त्रिपादस्यामृतं दिवि
ऋ. 10.90.3

त्रिपादूर्ध्व उदैत् पुरुषः पादोऽस्येहाभवत् पुनः
ततो विष्वङ् व्यक्रामत् साशनानशने अभि
ऋ. 10.90.4

Page 43

तस्माद्विराळजायत विराजो अधि पूरुषः
स जातो अत्यरिच्यत पश्चाद्भूमिमथो पुरः
ऋ. 10-90.5

यत् पुरुषेण हविषा देवा यज्ञमतन्वत
वसन्तो अस्यासीदाज्यं ग्रीष्म इध्मः शरद्धविः
ऋ. 10.90.6

तं यज्ञं बर्हिषि प्रौक्षन् पुरुषं जातमग्रतः
तेन देवा अयजन्त साध्या ऋषयश्च ये
ऋ. 10.90.7

तस्माद्यज्ञात् सर्वहुतः संभृतं पृषदाज्यम्
पशून् ताँश्चक्रे वायव्यानारण्यान् ग्राम्याश्च ये
ऋ. 10.90.8

Page 44

तस्माद्यज्ञात् सर्वहुत ऋचः सामानि जज्ञिरे
छन्दांसि जज्ञिरे तस्माद्यजुस्तस्मादजायत
ऋ.10.90.9

तस्मादश्वा अजायन्त ये के चोभयादतः
गावो ह जज्ञिरे तस्मात् तस्माज्जाता अजावयः
ऋ. 10.90.10

यत् पुरुषं व्यदधुः कतिधा व्यकल्पयन्
मुखं किमस्य कौ बाहू का ऊरू पादा उच्येते
ऋ. 10.90.11

Page 46

ब्राह्मणोऽस्य मुखमासीद्बाहू राजन्यः कृतः
ऊरू तदस्य यद्वैश्यः पद्भ्यां शूद्रो अजायत
ऋ. 10.90.12

चन्द्रमा मनसो जातश्चक्षोः सूर्यो अजायत
मुखादिन्द्रश्चाग्निश्च प्राणाद्वायुरजायत
ऋ. 10.90.13

नाभ्या आसीदन्तरिक्षं शीर्ष्णो द्यौः समवर्तत
पद्भ्यां भूमिर्दिशः श्रोत्रात् तथा लोकाँ अकल्पयन्
ऋ. 10.90.14

Page 47

सप्तास्यासन् परिधयस्त्रिः सप्त समिधः कृताः
देवा यद्यज्ञं तन्वाना अबध्नन् पुरुषं पशुम्
ऋ. 10.90.15

यज्ञेन यज्ञमयजन्त देवास्तानि धर्माणि प्रथमान्यासन्
ते ह नाकं महिमानः सचन्त यत्र पूर्वे साध्याः सन्ति देवाः

ऋ. 10.90.16

पूर्णात् पूर्णमुदंचति पूर्णं पूर्णेन सिच्यते
उतो तदद्य विद्याम यतस्तत् परिषिच्यते

ऋ. 10.8.29

Page 49

आवहन्ती पोष्या वीर्याणि चित्रं केतुं कृणुते चेकिताना
ईयुषीणामुपमा शश्वंतीनां विभातीनां प्रथमोपा व्यश्वैत्

ऋ. 1.113.15

द्यावो न स्तृभिश्चितयन्त खादिनो व्यभ्रिया न द्युतयन्त वृष्टयः
रुद्रो यद् वो मरुतो रुक्मवक्षसो वृषाजनि पृश्न्याः शुक्र ऊर्धनि

ऋ. 2.34.2

उरौ महाँ अनिबाधे ववर्धाऽऽपो अग्निं यशसः सं हि पूर्वीः
ऋतस्य योनावशयद् दमूना जामीनामग्निरपसि स्वसृणाम्

ऋ. 3.1.11

अक्रो न बभ्रिः समिथे महीनां दिद्दक्षेयः सूनवे भार्ऋजीकः
उदुस्रिया जनिता यो जजानाऽपां गर्भो नृतमो यह्वो अग्निः

ऋ. 3.1.12

Page 50

को अद्धा वेद क इह प्र वोचद् देवाँ अच्छा पथ्या रे का समेति
दद्दश्र एषामवमा सदांसि परेषु या गुह्येषु व्रतेषु

ऋ. 3.54.5

अधं जिह्वा पापतीति प्र वृष्णो गोषुयुधो नाशनिः सृजाना
शूरस्येव प्रसितिः क्षातिरग्नेर्दुर्वर्तुर्भीमो दयते बनानि

ऋ. 6.6.5

त्वामग्ने पुष्करादध्यथर्वा निरमन्थत। मूर्ध्नो विश्वस्य वाघतः

ऋ. 6.16.13

या ते दिद्युदवसृष्टा दिवस्परि क्षमया चरति परि सा वृणक्तु नः
सहस्रं ते स्वपिवात भेषजा मा नस्तोकेषु तनयेषु रीरिषः

ऋ. 7.46.3

पुरुष एवेदं सर्वं यद् भूतं यच्च भाव्यम्
पादोऽस्य सर्वा भूतानि त्रिपादस्यामृतं दिवि

सा. 619

ता अल्त वयुनं वीरवक्षणं समान्या वृतया विश्वमा रजः
अपो अपाचीरपरा अपेजते प्र पूर्वाभिस्तिरते देवयुर्जनः

ऋ. 5.48.2

वि या सृजति समनं व्यर्थिनः पदं न वेत्योदंती
वयो नकिष्टे पप्तिवांस आसते व्युष्टौ वाजिनीवति

ऋ. 1.48.6

एषायुक्त परावतः सूर्यस्योदयनादधि
शतं रथेभिः सुभगोषा इयं वि यात्वभि मानुषान्

ऋ. 1.48.7

नि दुरोणे अमृतो मर्त्यानां राजा ससाद विदथानि साधन्
घृतप्रतीक उर्विया व्यद्यौदग्निर्विश्वानि काव्यानि विद्वान्

ऋ. 3.1.18

परि प्रासिष्यदत् कविः सिन्धोरूर्मावधि श्रितः
कारं बिभ्रत् पुरुस्पृहम्

सा. 416

हिरण्यपाणिः सविता सुजिह्वस्त्रिरा दिवो विदथे पत्यमानः
देवेषु च सवितः श्लोकमश्रेरादमभ्यमा सुव सर्वतातिम्

ऋ. 3.54.11

इमा जुहाना युष्मदा नमोभिः प्रति स्तोमं सरस्वति जुषस्व
तव शर्मन् प्रियतमे दधाना उप स्थेयाम शरणं न वृक्षम्

ऋ. 7.95.5

उभे यत् ते महिना शुभ्रे अन्धसी अधिक्षियन्ति पूरवः
सा नो बोध्यवित्री मरुत्सखा चोद राधो मघोनाम्

ऋ. 7.96.2

भद्रमिद् भद्रा कृणवत् सरस्वत्यकवारी चेतति वाजिनीवती
गृणाना जमदग्निवत् स्तुवाना च वसिष्ठवत्

ऋ. 7.96.3

अमी य ऋक्षा निहितास उच्चा नक्तं दद्दृश्रे कुह चिद् दिवेयुः
अदब्धानि वरुणस्य व्रतानि विचाकंशच्चन्द्रमा नक्तमेति

ऋ. 1.24.10

इमं स्तोमं सक्रतवो मे अद्य मित्रो अर्यमा वरुणो जुषन्त
आदित्यासः शुचयो धारपूता अवृजिना अनवद्या अरिष्टाः

ऋ. 2.27.2

अश्विना हरिणाविव गौराविवानु यवंसम्
हंसाविव पततमा-सुताँ उप

ऋ. 6.78.2

अकारि वागन्धसो वरीमन्नस्तारि बर्हिः सुप्रायणतंमम्
उत्तान्नहस्तो युवयुर्वबन्दा ऽ ऽ वां नक्षन्तो अद्रय आञ्ज

ऋ. 6.63.3

Page 56

उदीर्ध्वं जीवो असुर्न आगादप प्रागात् तम आ ज्योतिरेति
आरैक् पन्थां यातवे सूर्यायागन्म यत्र प्रतिरन्त आयुः

ऋ. 1.113.6

Page 58

आदित्यासो अदितयः स्याम पूर्देवत्रा वसवो मर्त्यत्रा
सनेम मित्रावरुणा सनन्तो भवेम द्यावापृथिवी भवन्तः

ऋ. 7.52.1

ब्राह्मणासो अतिरात्रे न सोमे सरो न पूर्णमभितो वदन्तः
सम्वत्सरस्य तदहः परिष्ठ यन्मण्डूकाः प्रावृषीणं बभूवं

ऋ. 7.103.7

आपो यं वः प्रथमं देवयन्त इन्द्रपानमूर्मिमकृण्वतेळः
तं वो वयं शुचिमरिप्रमद्य घृतप्रुषं मधुमन्तं वनेम

ऋ. 7.47.1

Page 59

तमूर्मिमापो मधुमत्तमं वो ऽपां नपादवत्वाशुहेमा
यस्मिन्निन्द्रो वसुभिर्मादयांते तमश्यामदेवयन्तो वो अद्य

ऋ. 7. 47.2

ये अग्नयो न शोशुचन्निधाना द्विर्यत् त्रिर्मरुतो वावृधन्त ।
अरेणवो हिरण्ययांस एषां साकं नृम्णैः पौंस्येभिश्च भूवन्

ऋ. 6.66.2

यदेषां पृषती रथे प्रष्टिर्वहति रोहितः यान्ति शुभ्रा रिणन्नपः

ऋ. 8.7.28

यो अनिध्मो दीदयदप्स्वन्तर्यं विप्रास ईळते अध्वरेषु
अपां नपान्मधुमतीरपो दा याभिरिन्द्रो ववृधे वीर्याय

ऋ. 10.30.4

ब्रह्म सूर्यसमं ज्योतिर्द्यौः समुद्रसमश्च सरः
इन्द्रः पृथिव्यै वर्षीयान् गोस्तु मात्रा न विद्यते

य. 23.48

Page 60

एक एवाग्निर्बहुधा समिद्ध एकः सूर्यो विश्वमनु प्रभूतः
एकैवोषाः सर्वमिदं वि भात्येकं वा इदं वि बभूव सर्वम्

ऋ. 8.58.2

Page 62

माता देवानामदितेरनीकं यज्ञस्य केतुर्बृहती वि भाहि
प्रशस्तिकृद् ब्रह्मणे नो व्युच्छा नो जने जनय विश्ववारे

ऋ. 1.113.19

त आदित्यास उरवो गभीरा अदब्धासो दिप्सन्तो भूर्यक्षाः
अन्तः पश्यन्ति वृजिनोत साधु सर्वं राजभ्यः परमा चिदन्ति

ऋ. 2.27.3

तिस्रो भूमीर्धारयन् त्रीरुत द्यून् त्रीणि व्रता विदथे अन्तरेषाम्
ऋतमादित्या महि वो महित्वं तदर्यमन् वरुण मित्र चारु

ऋ. 2.27.8

Page 63

यस्यां अनन्तो अहुतस्त्वेषश्चरिष्णुरर्णवः । अमश्चरति रोरुवत्

ऋ. 6.61.8

आदित्यासो अदितिर्मादयन्तां मित्रो अर्यमा वरुणो रजिष्ठाः
अस्माकं सन्तु भुवनस्य गोपाः पिबन्तु सोममवंसे नो अद्य

ऋ. 7.51.2

आदित्या विश्वे मरुतश्च विश्वे देवाश्च विश्व ऋभवश्च विश्वे
इन्द्रो अग्निरश्विना यो अपां यो विश्वस्य जगतो देव ईशे

ऋ. 7.51.3

यो वर्धन ओषधीनां यो अपां यो विश्वस्य जगतो देव ईशे
स त्रिधातु शरणं शर्म यंसत् त्रिवर्तु ज्योतिः स्वभिष्ट्यस्मे

ऋ. 7.101.2

आपो हि ष्ठा मयोभुवस्ता न ऊर्जे दधातन। महे रणाय चक्षसे

सा. 1839

धारयन्त आदित्यासो जगत् स्था देवा विश्वस्य भुवनस्य गोपाः
दीर्घाधियो रक्षमाणा असुर्यमृतावानश्रयमाना ऋणानि

ऋ. 2.27.4

स होता विश्वं परि भूत्वध्वरं तमु हव्यैर्मनुष ऋञ्जते गिरा
हिरिशिप्रो वृध्सानासु जर्भुरद् द्यौर्न स्तृभिश्चितयद् रोदसी अनु

ऋ. 2.2.5

यो वामृजवे क्रमणाय रोदसी मर्तो ददाश धिषणे स साधति
प्र प्रजाभिर्जायते धर्मणस्परि युवोः सिक्ता विपुरूपाणि सव्रत

ऋ. 6.70.3

स्तरीरुं त्वद् भवति सूत उ त्वद् यथावशं तन्वं चक्र एष:
पितुः पयः प्रति गृभ्णाति माता तेन पिता वर्धते तेन पुत्र:

ऋ. 7.101.3

अहं मनुरभवं सूर्यश्चाहं कक्षीवाँ ऋषिरस्मि विप्रः
अहं कुत्समार्जुनेयं न्यृञ्जे डहं कविरुशना पश्यता मा

ऋ. 4.26.1

अहं भूमिमददामार्याायाऽहं वृष्टिं दाशुषे मर्ताय।
अहमपो अनयं वावशाना मम देवासो अनु केतमायन्

ऋ. 4.26.2

अहं पुरो मन्दसानो व्यैरं नव साकं नवतीः शम्बरस्य
शततमं वेश्यं सर्वतान दिवोदासमतिथिग्वं यदावम्

ऋ. 4.26.3

अहं राजा वरुणो मह्यं तान्यसुर्याणि प्रथमा धारयन्त
क्रतुं सचन्ते वरुणस्य देवा राजामि कृष्टेरुपमस्य व्रतेः

ऋ. 4.42.2

ममाणि ते वर्मणा छादयामि सोमस्त्वा राजामृतेनानु वस्ताम्
उरोर्वरीयो वरुणस्ते कृणोतु जयन्तं त्वानु देवा मदन्तु

सा. 1870

अयम॑स्मि जरित॒: पश्य॑ मे॒ह विश्वा॑ जा॒तान्य॒भ्य॑स्मि म॒ह्ना ।
ऋ॒तस्य॑ मा प्र॒दिशो॑ वर्धयन्त्यादर्दि॒रो भुव॑ना द॒रीमि ॥

ऋ. 8.100.4

इ॒मं जी॒वेभ्य॑: परि॒धिं द॑धामि॒ मैषां॒ नु गा॒दप॑रो अ॒र्थमे॒तम् ।
श॒तं जी॑वन्तु श॒रद॑: पु॒रूची॑रन्त॒र्मृत्युं॑ दधतां॒ पर्व॑तेन ॥

ऋ. 10.18.4

अ॒हं स यो नव्व॑वास्त्वं बृ॒हद्र॒थं सं वृ॒त्रेव॒ दास॑ं वृत्र॒हारु॑जम् ।
यद्व॑र्धय॒न्तं प्र॒थय॑न्तमानु॒पग्दू॒रे पा॒रे रज॑सो रोच॒नाक॑रम् ॥

ऋ. 10.49.6

अ॒हं रु॒द्रेभि॒र्वसु॑भिश्चराम्य॒हमा॑दि॒त्यैरु॒त वि॒श्वदे॑वैः ।
अ॒हं मि॒त्रावरु॑णो॒भा बि॑भर्म्य॒हमि॑न्द्रा॒ग्नी अ॒हम॒श्विनो॒भा ॥

ऋ. 10.125.1

अ॒हं राष्ट्री॑ सं॒गम॑नी॒ वसू॑नां चिकि॒तुषी॑ प्रथ॒मा य॒ज्ञिया॑नाम् ।
तां मा॑ दे॒वा व्य॑दधुः पुरु॒त्रा भूरि॑स्थात्रां॒ भूर्या॑वे॒शय॑न्तीम् ॥

ऋ. 10.125.3

म॒या सो अन्न॑मत्ति॒ यो वि॒पश्य॑ति॒ यः प्राणि॑ति॒ य ईं॑ शृ॒णोत्यु॒क्तम् ।
अ॒म॒न्तवो॑ मां त॒ उप॑ क्षियन्ति श्रु॒धि श्रु॑त श्र॒द्धि॒वं ते॑ वदामि ॥

ऋ. 10.125.4

अ॒हमे॑व स्व॒यमि॒दं व॑दामि॒ जुष्टं॑ दे॒वेभि॑रु॒त मानु॑षेभिः ।
यं का॒मये॒ तंत॑मु॒ग्रं कृ॑णोमि॒ तं ब्र॒ह्माणं॒ तमृषिं॒ तं सु॑मे॒धाम् ॥

ऋ. 10.125.5

अ॒हं रु॒द्राय॒ धनु॒रा त॑नोमि ब्रह्म॒द्विषे॒ शर॑वे॒ हन्त॒वा उ ।
अ॒हं जना॑य स॒मदं॑ कृणोम्य॒हं द्यावा॑पृथि॒वी आ वि॑वेश ॥

ऋ. 10.125.6

अ॒हमे॑व॒ वात॑ इव॒ प्र वा॑म्या॒रभ॑माणा॒ भुव॑नानि॒ विश्वा॑ ।
प॒रो दि॒वा प॒र ए॒ना पृ॑थि॒व्यैता॑व॒ती म॑हि॒ना सं ब॑भूव ॥

ऋ. 10.125.8

मू॒र्धाहं र॒यीणां॒ मूर्धा॒ समा॑नानां॑ भूयासम् ।

अ. 16.3.1

त॒र्प॒णो अस्मि॑ पिशा॒चानां॑ व्या॒घ्रो गो॒मता॑मिव ।
श्वान॑: सिं॒हमि॑व दृ॒ष्ट्वा ते न वि॑न्द॒न्ते न्य॑ञ्चनम् ॥

अ. 4.36.6

अहं सोममाहनसं बिभर्म्यहं त्वष्टारमुत पूषणं भगम्
अहं दधामि द्रविणं हविष्मते सुप्राव्ये३ यजमानाय सुन्वते

ऋ. 10.125.2

सत्यमहं गंभीरः काव्येन सत्यं जातेनास्मि जातवेदाः
न मे दासो नार्यो महित्वा व्रत मीमाय यदहं धरिष्ये

अ. 5.11.3

अध्यक्षो वाजी मम कामं उग्रः कृणोतु मह्यमसपत्नमेव
विश्वे देवा मम नाथं भवन्तु सर्वे देवा हवमा यन्तु म इमम्

अ. 9.2.7

अन्तस्ते यावापृथिवी दधाम्यन्तर्दधाम्युर्वन्तरिक्षम्
सजूर्देवेभिरवरैः परैश्चान्तर्यामे मघवन् मादयस्व

य. 7.5

चक्रियो विश्वा भुवनाभि सांसहिश्चक्रिर्देवेष्वा दुवः
आ देवेषु यतत आ सुवीर्य आ शंस उत नृणाम्

ऋ. 3.16.4

नमोऽस्तु ते निर्ऋते तिग्मतेजोऽयस्मयान् वि चृता बन्धपाशान्
यमो मह्यं पुनरित् त्वां ददाति तस्मै यमाय नमो अस्तु मृत्यवे

अ. 6.63.2

यस्य वातः प्राणापानौ चक्षुरङ्गिरसोऽभवन्
दिशो यश्चक्रे प्रज्ञानीस्तस्मै ज्येष्ठायब्रह्मणे नमः

अ. 10.7.34

नम इदुग्रं नम आ विवासे नमो दाधार पृथिवीमुत द्याम्
नमो देवेभ्यो नर्म ईश एषां कृतं चिदेनो नमसा विवासे

ऋ. 6.51.8

मीढुष्टम शिवंतम शिवो नः सुमना भव
परमे वृक्ष आयुधं निधाय कृत्तिं वसान आ चर पिनाकं बिभ्रदा गहि

य. 16.51

नमस्ते रुद्र मन्यवं उतो त इषवे नमः । बाहुभ्यामुत ते नमः

य. 16.1

नमो॑ मह॒द्भ्यो नमो॑ अर्भ॒केभ्यो॒ नमो॑ युव॒भ्यो नम॑ आशि॒नेभ्यः॑

ऋ. 1.27.13

ऋ॒चो अ॒क्षरे॑ प॒रमे॒ व्यो॑म॒न् यस्मि॑न् दे॒वा अधि॒ विश्वे॑ निषे॒दुः
यस्तन्न॒ वेद॒ किमृ॒चा क॑रिष्य॒ति य इत् तद् वि॒दुस्त॒ इमी॑ स॒मास॑ते

अ. 9.10.18

कीर्ति॑श्च॒ यश॑श्चाम्भ॒श्च॒ नभ॑श्च ब्राह्मण॒वर्च॑सं चान्नं॑ चा॒न्नाद्यं॑ च
य ए॒तं दे॒वमे॑क॒वृतं॒ वेद॑
न द्वि॒तीयो॒ न तृ॒तीयश्च॒तुर्थो॑ नाप्युच्यते । य ए॒तं दे॒वमे॑क॒वृतं॒ वेद॑
न प॑ञ्च॒मो न॒ षष्ठः॒ सप्त॑मो नाप्युच्यते । य ए॒तं दे॒वमे॑क॒वृतं॒ वेद॑
नाष्ट॑मो न॒ नव॑मो॒ दश॑मो नाप्युच्यते । य ए॒तं देवमे॑क॒वृतं॒ वेद॑
स सर्व॑स्मै॒ वि प॑श्यां॒ते यच्च॑ प्रा॒णिति॒ यच्च॒ न । य ए॒तं दे॒वमे॑क॒वृतं॒ वेद॑
तमि॒दं निर्ग॑तं॒ सहः॒ स ए॒ष ए॒क ए॑क॒वृदे॑क॒ एव॑ । य ए॒तं दे॒वमे॑क॒वृतं॒ वेद॑
सर्वे॑ अस्मि॒न् दे॒वा ए॑क॒वृतो॑ भवन्ति । य ए॒तं दे॒वमे॑क॒वृतं॒ वेद॑

अ. 23.5.14-21

तदे॒वाग्निस्तदा॑दि॒त्यस्तद्वा॒युस्तदु॑ च॒न्द्रमाः॑
तदे॑व॒ शुक्रं॒ तद्ब्रह्म॒ ता आपः॒ स प्र॒जाप॑तिः

य. 32.1

ए॒क ए॒वाग्निर्ब॑हु॒धा समि॑द्धः॒ एकः॒ सूर्यो॒ विश्व॒मनु॒ प्रभू॑तः
एकै॒वोषाः॒ सर्व॑मि॒दं वि भा॒त्येकं॒ वा इ॒दं वि ब॑भूव॒ सर्व॑म्

ऋ. 8.58.2

इन्द्रं॑ मि॒त्रं वरु॑णम॒ग्निमा॑हु॒रथो॑ दि॒व्यः स सु॑प॒र्णो ग॒रुत्मा॑न्
एकं॒ सद् विप्रा॑ बहु॒धा व॑दन्त्य॒ग्निं य॒मं मा॑त॒रिश्वा॑नमाहुः

ऋ. 1.64.46

वि॒द्म शर॑स्य पि॒तरं॑ च॒न्द्रं श॑तवृ॒ष्ण्यम्
तेना॒ ते त॒न्वे 3 शं॒करं॑ पृथि॒व्यां ते॒ निषे॑चनम् ब॒हिष्टे॑ अस्तु बालि॒ति

अ. 1.3.4

तमि॒दं निर्ग॑तं॒ सहः॒ स ए॒ष ए॒कं ए॑क॒वृदे॑क॒ एव॑ । य ए॒तं दे॒वमे॑क॒वृतं॒ वेद॑

अ. 13.5.20

सर्वे॑ अस्मि॒न् दे॒वा ए॑क॒वृतो॑ भवन्ति । य ए॒तं दे॒वमे॑क॒वृतं॒ वेद॑

अ. 13.4.21

तदिदास भुवनेषु ज्येष्ठं यतो जज्ञ उग्रस्त्वेषनृम्णः ।
सद्यो जज्ञानो नि रिणाति शत्रूननु यं विश्वे मदन्त्यूमाः ॥
ऋ. 10.120.1

तमूतयो रणयञ्छूरसातौ तं क्षेमस्य क्षितयः कृण्वत त्राम् ।
स विश्वस्य करुणस्येश एको मरुत्वान्नो भवत्विन्द्र ऊती ॥
ऋ. 1.100.7

अयमेक इत्था पुरूरु चष्टे वि विश्पतिः । तस्य व्रतान्यनु वश्चरामसि ॥
ऋ. 8.25.16

न तस्य प्रतिमा अस्ति यस्य नाम महद्यशः ।
हिरण्यगर्भ इत्येष मा मा हिंसीदित्येषा यस्मान्न जात इत्येषः ॥
य. 32.3

समेत विश्वा ओजसा पतिं दिवो य एक इद्भूरतिथिर्जनानाम् ।
स पूर्व्यो नूतनमाजिगीषं तं वर्तनीरनु वावृत एक इत् ॥
सा. 372

Page 80

इमं नो देव सवितर्यज्ञं प्र णय
य. 10.8

यत्पुरुषं व्यदधुः कतिधा व्यकल्पयन् ।
मुखं किमस्यासीत् किं बाहू किमूरू पादा उच्येते ॥
य. 31.10

स इत् तन्तुं स वि जानात्योतुं स वक्त्वान्यृतुथा वदाति ।
य ई चिकेतदमृतस्य गोपा अवश्चरन् परो अन्येन पश्यन् ॥
ऋ. 6.9.3

Page 82

विश्वकर्मा विमना आद्विहाया धाता विधाता परमोत सन्दृक् ।
तेषामिष्टानि समिषा मदन्ति यत्रा सप्त ऋषीन् पर एकमाहुः ॥
य. 17.26

इदं विष्णुर्वि चक्रमे त्रेधा नि दधे पदा । समूढमस्य पांसुरे ॥
अ. 7.26.4

त्रीणि पदा वि चक्रमे विष्णुर्गोपा अदाभ्यः । अतो धर्माणि धारयन् ॥
सा. 1670

Page 83

तं पृच्छता स जगामा स वेद स चिकित्वाँ ईयते सा न्वीयते ।
तस्मिन्त्सन्ति प्रशिषस्तस्मिन्निष्ट्यः स वाजस्य शवसः शुष्मिणस्पतिः ॥
ऋ. 1.145.1

461

हंसः शुचिषद् वसुरन्तरिक्षसद्धोता वेदिषदतिथिर्दुरोणसत्
नृषद् वरसदृतसद् व्योमसदब्जा गोजा ऋतजा अद्रिजा ऋतम्

ऋ. 4.40.5

रूपंरूपं प्रतिरूपो बभूव तदस्य रूपं प्रतिचक्षणाय
इन्द्रो मायाभिः पुरुरूप ईयते युक्ता ह्यस्य हरयः शता दश

ऋ. 6.47.18

Page 85

वेदाहमेतं पुरुषं महान्तमादित्यवर्णं तमसः परस्तात्

य. 31.18

Page 86

यो विश्वचर्षणिरुत विश्वतोमुखो यो विश्वतस्पाणिरुत विश्वतस्पृथः
सं बाहुभ्यां भरति सं पतत्रैर्द्यावांपृथिवी जनयन् देव एकः

अ. 13.2.26

य एकश्चर्षणीनां वसूनामिरज्यति। इन्द्रः पञ्च क्षितीनाम्

अ. 20.70.15

अबुध्ने राजा वरुणो वनस्योर्ध्वं स्तूपं ददते पूतदक्षः
नीचीनाः स्थुरुपरि बुध्न एषामस्मे अन्तर्निहिताः केतवः स्युः

ऋ. 1.24.7

न यं दिप्सन्ति दिप्सवो न द्रुह्णो जनानाम्। न देवमभिमातयः

ऋ. 1.25.15

अश्व्यो वारो अभवस्तदिन्द्र सृके यत् त्वां प्रत्यहन् देव एकः
अजयो गा अजयः शूर सोममवासृजः सर्तवे सप्त सिन्धून्

ऋ. 1.32.12

Page 87

यं रक्षन्ति प्रचेतसो वरुणो मित्रो अर्यमा
नू चित् स दभ्यते जनः

ऋ. 1.41.1

यं बाहुतेव पिप्रति पान्ति मर्त्यं रिषः। अरिष्टः सर्व एधते

ऋ. 1.41.2

स रत्नं मर्त्यो वसु विश्वं तोकमुत त्मना। अच्छा गच्छत्यस्तृतः

ऋ. 1.41.6

श्वसित्यप्सु हंसो न सीदन् क्रत्वा चेतिष्ठो, विशामुषर्भुत्
सोमो वेधा ऋतप्रजातः पशुर्न शिश्वा विभुर्दूरेभाः

ऋ. 1.65.5

क्षेमो न साधुः क्रतुर्न भद्रो भुवत् स्वाधी होर्ता हव्यवाट्

ऋ. 1.67.2

येनेमा विश्वा व्यर्वना कृतानि यो दासं वर्णमधरं गुहाकः
श्वन्घ्नीव यो जिगीवाँ लक्षमाददर्यः पुष्टानि सं जनास इन्द्रः

ऋ. 2.12.4

Page 88

यो भूतं च भव्यं च सर्वं यश्चाधितिष्ठति
स्वर्घर्यस्य च केवलं तस्मै ज्येष्ठाय ब्रह्मणे नमः

अ. 10.8.1

Page 90

यदङ्ग दाशुषे त्वमग्ने भद्रं करिष्यसि । तवेत् तत् सत्यमङ्गिरः

ऋ. 1.1.6

युवामिद्ध्यर्वसे पूर्व्याय परि प्रभूती गविषः स्वापी
वृणीमहे सख्याय प्रियाय शूरा मंहिष्ठा पितरेव शंभू

ऋ. 4.41.7

महे शुल्काय वरुणस्य नु त्विप ओजो मिमाते ध्रुवमस्य यत् स्वम्
अजामिमन्यः श्नथयन्तमातिरद् दभ्रेभिरन्यः प्र वृणोति भूयसः

ऋ. 7.82.6,

Page 91

अग्निं मन्द्रं पुरुप्रियं शीरं पावकशोचिषम् । हद्विर्मन्द्रेभिरीमहे

ऋ. 8.43.31

यदग्ने स्यामहं त्वं त्वं वा धा स्या अहम् स्युष्टे सत्या इहाशिषः

ऋ. 8.44.23

अन्ति सन्तं न जहात्यन्ति सन्तं न पश्यति
देवस्य पश्य काव्यं न ममार न जीर्यति

अ. 10.8.32

त्राता नो बोधि दट्शान आपिरभिख्याता मर्दिता सोम्यानाम्
सखा पिता पितृतमः पितृणां कर्तेमु लोकमुशते वयोधाः

ऋ. 4.17.17

Page 92

इन्द्रं यस्ते नवीयसीं गिरं मन्द्रामजीजनत
चिकित्विन्मनसं धियं प्रलामृतस्य पिप्युषीम्

ऋ. 8.95.5

यदस्य धामनि प्रिये समीचीनासो अस्वरन्
नाभा यज्ञस्य दोहना प्राध्वरे

ऋ. 8.12.32

दोहेन गामुप शिक्षा सखायं प्र बोधय जरितर्जरिमिन्द्रम्
कोशं न पूर्णं वसुना न्यृष्टमा च्यावय मघदेयाय शूरम्

ऋ. 10.42.2

अग्ने नक्षत्रमजरमा सूर्यं रोहयो दिवि। दधज्ज्योतिर्जनेभ्यः

ऋ. 10.156.4

क्रत्वः समह दीनता प्रतीपं जगमा शुचे। मृळा सुक्षत्र मृळय
अपां मध्ये तस्थिवांसं तृष्णाविदज्जरितारम्। मृळा सुक्षत्र मृळय

ऋ. 7.894

Page 94

अग्ने यं यज्ञमध्वरं विश्वतः परिभूरसि। स इद् देवेषु गच्छति

ऋ. 1.1.4

इन्द्र इद्धर्योः सचा संमिश्ल आ वचोयुजा। इन्द्रो वज्री हिरण्ययः

ऋ. 1.7.2

महाँ इन्द्रः परश्च नु महित्वमस्तु वज्रिणे। द्यौर्न प्रथिना शवः

ऋ. 1.8.5

यः कुक्षिः सोमपातमः समुद्र इव पिन्वते। उर्वीरापो न काकुदः

ऋ. 1.8.7.

Page 95

त्वं विश्वस्य मेधिर दिवश्च ग्मश्च राजसि। स यामनि प्रति शुधि

ऋ. 1.25.20

यमग्ने पृत्सु मर्त्यमवा वाजेषु यं जुनाः। स यन्ता शश्वतीरिषः

ऋ. 1.27.7

त्वमग्ने वृजिनवर्तनिं नरं सक्मन् पिपर्षि विदथे विचर्षणे
यः शूरसाता परितकम्ये धने दभ्रेभिश्चित् समृता हंसि भूयसः

ऋ. 1.31.6

त्वं तमग्ने अमृतत्व उत्तमे मर्तं दधासि श्रवसे दिवेदिवे
यस्तातृषाण उभयाय जन्मने मयः कृणोषि प्रय आ च सूर्ये

ऋ. 1.31.7

Page 97

कं तु कृष्णत्रंकेतवे पेशो मर्या अपेशसे। समुषद्भिरजायथाः

ऋ. 1.6.3

त्वमग्ने प्रमंतिस्त्वं पितासि नस्तुं त्वं वयस्कृत् तवं जामयौं वयम्
सं त्वा रायः शतिनः सं सहस्त्रिणः सुवीरं यन्ति व्रतपामंदाभ्य

ऋ. 1.31.10

गणानां त्वा गणपतिं हवामहे कविं कवीनामुंपमश्रवस्तमम्
ज्येष्ठराजं ब्रह्मणां ब्रह्मणस्पत आ नः शृण्वत्रूतिभिः सीद सादंनम्

ऋ. 2.23.1

आ ते पितर्मरुतां सुम्नमेंतु मा नः सूर्यस्य संदृशो युयोथाः
अभि नो वीरो अर्वति क्षमेत प्र जायेमहि रुद्र प्रजाभिः

ऋ. 2.33.4

सुनीतिभिर्नयसि त्रायसे जनं यस्तुभ्यं दाशान्न तमंहो अश्नवत्
ब्रह्मद्विषस्तपनो मन्युमीरसि वृहस्पते महि तत् ते महित्वनम्

ऋ. 2.23.4

त्वयां हितमप्यमप्सु भागं धन्वान्वा मृगयसो वि तंस्थुः
वनानि विभ्यो नर्किरस्य तानि व्रता देवस्य सवितुर्मिनन्ति

ऋ. 2.38.7

ऋतं वोचे नमंसा पृच्छ्यमानस्तवाशसा जातवेदो यदीदम्
त्वमस्य क्षयसि यद्ध विश्वं दिवि यदु द्रविणं यत् पृथिव्याम्

ऋ. 4.5.11

देवेभ्यो हि प्रथमं यज्ञियेभ्यो ऽमृतत्वं सुवसि भागमुत्तमम्
आदिद् दामानं सवितर्व्यूर्णुषे ऽनूचीना जीविता मानुषेभ्यः

ऋ. 4.54.2

न प्रमिये सवितुर्दैव्यस्य तद् यथा विश्वं भुवनं धारयिष्यति
यत् पृथिव्या वरिमन्ना स्वङ्गुरिर्वर्प्मन् दिवः सुवति सत्यमस्य तत्

ऋ. 4.54.4

सहस्राह्वं वियतावस्य पक्षौ हरेंहंसस्य पतंतः स्वर्गम्
स देवान्त्सर्वानुरस्युपदय संपश्यन् याति भुवनानि विश्वा

अ. 10.8.18

इन्द्रज्येष्ठान् बृहद्द्यः पर्वतेभ्यः क्षयाँ एभ्यः सुवसि पस्त्यावतः
यथायथा पतयन्तो वियेमिर एवैव तंस्थुः सवितः सवायं ते

ऋ. 4.54.5

465

त्वमग्ने यज्ञानां होता विश्वेषां हितः । देवेभिर्मानुषे जने
ऋ. 6.16.1

इयमददाद् रभसमृणच्युतं दिवोदासं वध्यश्वाय दाशुषे
या शश्वन्तमाचखादावसं पृ.गं ता ते दात्राणि तविषा सरस्वति

विश्वे देवा अनमस्यन् भियानास्त्वामग्ने तमसि तस्थिवांसम्
वैश्वानरोऽवतूतये नो अमर्त्योऽवतूतये नः
ऋ. 6.9.7

वेत्था हि वेधो अध्वनः पथश्च देवाञ्जसा । अग्ने यज्ञेषु सुक्रतो
ऋ. 6.16.3

यत्र क्व च ते मनो दक्षं दधस उत्तरम् । तत्रा सदः कृणवसे
ऋ. 6.16.17

Page 103

अयं सु तुभ्यं वरुण स्वधावो हृदि स्तोम उपश्रितश्चिदस्तु
शं नः क्षेमे शमु योगे नो अस्तु यूयं पात स्वस्तिभिः सदा नः
ऋ. 7.86.8

त्वमग्ने व्रतपा असि देव आ मर्त्येष्वा । तं यज्ञेष्वीडयः
ऋ. 8.11.1

पुरुत्रा हि सदृङ्ङसि विशो विश्वा अनु प्रभुः । समत्सु त्वा हवामहे
ऋ. 8.11.8

अयं वा मधुमत्तमः सुतः सोमं ऋतावृधा ।
तमश्विना पिबतं तिरोअह्न्यं धत्तं रत्नानि दाशुषे
सा. 306

दूराच्चंकमानायं प्रतिपाणायाक्षये
आस्मा अशृण्वन्नाशाः कामेनाजनयन्त्स्वः
अ. 19.52.3

रास्वेयंत्सोमा भूयो भर देवो नः सविता वसोर्दाता वस्वंदात्
य. 4.16

Page 105

अदितिर्द्यौरदितिरन्तरिक्षमदितिर्माता स पिता स पुत्रः
विश्वे देवा अदितिः पञ्च जना अदितिर्जातमदितिर्जनित्वम्
ऋ. 1.89.10

Page 106

उप त्वाग्ने दिवेदिवे दोषावस्तर्धिया वयम् । नमो भरन्त एमसि
ऋ. 1.1.7

यत् सानोः सानुमारुहद् भूर्यस्पष्ट कर्त्वम्
तदिन्द्रो अर्थं चेतति यूथेन वृष्णिरेजति
ऋ. 1.10.2

इन्द्रं विश्वा अवीवृधन्त् समुद्रव्यचसं गिरः
रथीतमं रथीनां वाजानां सत्पतिं पतिम्
ऋ. 1.11.1

आ नो गहि सख्येभिः शिवेभिर्महान् महीभिरूतिभिः सरण्यन्
अस्मे रयिं बहुलं संतरुत्रं सुवाचं भागं यशसं कृधी नः
ऋ.3.1.19

अच्छा नो याह्या वहाऽभि प्रयांसि वीतये
आ देवान् त्सोमपीतये
ऋ. 6.16.44

विश्वे देवास आ गंत शृणुता म इमं हवम्। एदं बर्हिर्निषीदत
ऋ. 6.52.7

सम्यक् स्रवन्ति सरितो न धेनो अन्तर्हृदा मनसा श्यमानाः
एते अर्षन्त्यूर्मयो घृतस्य मृगा इव क्षिपणोरीषमाणाः
ऋ. 4.58.6

प्रातरग्निं प्रातरिन्द्रं हवामहे प्रातर्मित्रावरुणा प्रातरश्विना
प्रातभगं पूषणं ब्रह्मणस्पतिं प्रातः सोममुत रुद्रं हवामहे
अ. 3.16.1

ऐन्द्रः प्राणो अङ्गे अङ्गे नि दीध्ययैन्द्र उदानो अङ्गे अङ्गे निधीतः
देव त्वष्टर्भूरि ते सत्थ समेतु सलक्ष्मा यद्विपुरूपं भवाति
देवत्रा यन्तमवसे सखायोऽनु त्वा माता पितरौ मदन्तु
य. 6.2

दृते दृढहं मा। ज्योक्ते सन्दृशि जीव्यासं ज्योक्ते सन्दृशि जीव्यासम्
य. 36.19

य आत्मदा बलदा यस्य विश्वं उपासते प्रशिषं यस्य देवाः
यस्य छायामृतं यस्य मृत्युः कस्मै देवाय हविषा विधेम
ऋ. 10.121.2

यः प्राणतो निमिषतो महित्वैक इद्राजा जगतो बभूव
य ईशे अस्य द्विपदश्चतुष्पदः कस्मै देवाय हविषा विधेम
ऋ. 10.121.3

यस्येमे हिमवन्तो महित्वा यस्य समुद्रं रसया सहाहुः
यस्येमाः प्रदिशो यस्य बाहू कस्मै देवाय हविषा विधेम

ऋ. 10.121.4

Page 109

मा नो हिंसीज्जनिता यः पृथिव्या यो वा दिवं सत्यधर्मा सत्यधर्मा जजानं
यश्चापश्चन्द्रा बृहतीर्जजान कस्मै देवाय हविषा विधेम

ऋ. 10.121.9

प्रजापते न त्वदेतान्यन्यो विश्वां जातानि परि ता बंभूव
यत् कामास्ते जुहुमस्तन्नो अस्तु वयं स्याम पतयो रयीणाम्

ऋ. 10.121.10

यस्य द्यौरुर्वी पृथिवी च मही यस्याद उर्व न्तरिक्षम्
यस्यासौ सूरो विततो महित्वा कस्मै देवाय हविषा विधेम

अ. 4.2.4

Page 110

यज्जाग्रतो दूरमुदैति दैवं तदु सुप्तस्य तथैवैति
दूरङ्गमं ज्योतिषां ज्योतिरेकं तन्मे मनः शिवसंकल्पमस्तु

य. 34.1

येन कर्माण्यपसो मनीषिणो यज्ञे कृण्वन्ति विदथेषु धीराः
यदपूर्वं यक्षमन्तः प्रजानां तन्मे मनः शिवसंकल्पमस्तु

य. 34.2

यत्प्रज्ञानमुत चेतो धृतिश्च यज्ज्योतिरन्तरमृतं प्रजासु
यस्मान्न ऋते किं चन कर्म क्रियते तन्मे मनः शिवसंकल्पमस्तु

य. 34.3

Page 111

येनेदं भूतं भुवनं भविष्यत् परिगृहीतममृतेन सर्वम्।
येन यज्ञस्तायते सप्तहोता तन्मे मनः शिवसंकल्पमस्तु

य. 34.4

यस्मिन्नृचः साम यजूंष्यषि यस्मिन् प्रतिष्ठिता रथनाभाविवाराः
यस्मिंश्चित्तथ सर्वमोतं प्रजानां तन्मे मनः शिवसंकल्पमस्तु

य. 34.5

सुपारथिरश्वानिव यन्मनुष्याःन्रनीयते॥भीशुभिर्वाजिन इव
हृत्प्रतिष्ठं यदजिरं जविष्ठं तन्मे मनः शिवसंकल्पमस्तु

य. 34.6

द्यौः शान्तिरन्तरिक्षꣳ शान्तिः पृथिवी शान्तिराप: शान्तिरोषधय: शान्तिः
वनस्पतय: शान्तिर्विश्वे देवाः शान्तिर्ब्रह्म शान्तिः सर्वꣳ
शान्तिः शान्तिरेव शान्तिः सा मा शान्तिरेधि

य. 36.17

विश्वे देवासो अस्रिध एहिमायासो अद्रुह: । मेधं जुषन्त वह्नय:

ऋ. 1.3.9

एवा ह्यस्य सूनृता विरप्शी गोमती मही । पक्वा शाखा न दाशुषे

ऋ. 1.8.8

उपे भद्रे जोषयेते न मेने गावो न वाश्रा उप तस्थुरेवै:
स दक्षाणां दक्षपतिर्बभूवाञ्जन्ति यं दक्षिणतो हविर्भि:

ऋ. 1.95.6

न दक्षिणा वि चिकिते न सव्या न प्राचीनमादित्या नोत पश्चा
पाक्या चिद् वसवो धीर्या चिद् युष्मानीतो अभयं ज्योतिरश्याम्

ऋ. 2.27.11

कथा सबाध: शशमानो अस्य नशद्भि द्रविणं दीध्यान:
देवो भुवन्नेवेदा म ऋतानां नमो जगृभ्वाँ अभि यज्जुजोषत्

ऋ. 4.23.4

पुष्यात् क्षेमे अभि योगे भवात्युभे वृतौ संयती सं जयाति
प्रिय: सूर्ये प्रियो अग्ना भवाति य इन्द्राय सुतसोमो ददाशत्

ऋ. 5.37.5

यो जागार तमृच: कामयन्ते यो जागार तमु सामानि यन्ति
यो जागार तमयं सोम आह तवाहमस्मि सख्ये न्योका:

ऋ. 5.44.14

त्वां हि ष्मा चर्षणयो यज्ञेभिर्गीर्भिरीळते
त्वां वाजी यात्ववृको रंजस्तूर्विश्वचर्षणि:

ऋ. 6.2.2

सहस्रेणेव सचते यवीयुधा यस्त आनळुप्रस्तुतिम्
पुत्रं प्रावर्ग कृणुते सुवीर्ये दाश्नोति नमउक्तिभि:

ऋ. 8.4.6

विशंविशं मघवा पर्यशायत जनानां धेना अवचाकशद्वृषा
यस्याह शक्र: सर्वनेषु रण्यति स तीव्रै: सोमै: सहते पृतन्यत:

अ. 20.17.6

विशंविशं मघवा पर्यशायत जनानां धेना अवचाकशद्वृषा
यस्याहं शक्रः सवनेषु रण्यति स तीव्रैः सोमैः सहते पृतन्यतः
ऋ. 10.43.6

कदा चन स्तरीरसि नेन्द्र सश्चसि दाशुषे
उपोपेन्नु मघवन् भूय इन्नु ते दानं देवस्य पृच्यते
सा. 300

Page 117

यथा सूर्यो अतिभाति यथास्मिन् तेज आहितम्
एवा मे वरुणो मणिः कीर्तिं भूतिं नि यच्छतु
तेजसा मा समुक्षतु यशसा समनक्तु मा
अ. 10.3.17

श्रेष्ठो जातस्य रुद्र श्रियासि तवस्तमस्तवसां वज्रबाहो
पर्षिणः पारमंहसः स्वस्ति विश्वा अभीतो रपसो युयोधि
ऋ. 2.33.3

सुकृत् सुपाणिः स्ववाँ ऋतावा देवस्त्वष्टावंसे तानि नो धात्
पूषणवन्तः ऋभवो मादयध्व मूर्ध्वग्रावाणो अध्वरमंतष्ट
ऋ. 3.54.12

यो मृळयाति चक्रुषे चिदागो वयं स्याम वरुणे अनागाः
अनु व्रतान्यदितेर्ऋधन्तो यूयं पात स्वस्तिभिः सदा नः
ऋ. 7.87.7

Page 118

स्वस्ति न इन्द्रो वृद्धश्रवाः स्वस्ति नः पूषा विश्ववेदाः
स्वस्ति नस्तार्क्ष्यो अरिष्टनेमिः स्वस्ति नो बृहस्पतिर्दधातु
ऋ. 1.89.6

ब्रह्मणस्पते सुयमस्य विश्वहा रायः स्याम रथ्यो३ वयस्वतः
वीरंपु वीराँ उप पृङ्धि नस्त्वं यदीशानो ब्रह्मणा वेर्पि मे हवम्
ऋ. 2.24.15

स्वस्ति मित्रावरुणा स्वस्ति पथ्ये रेवति
स्वस्ति न इन्द्रश्चाग्निश्च स्वस्ति नो अदिते कृधि
ऋ. 5.51.14

सुवीरं रयिमा भर जातवेदो विचर्षणे । जहि रक्षांसि सुक्रतो
ऋ. 6.16.29

भरद्वाजाय सप्रथः शर्म यच्छ सहन्त्य । अग्ने वरेण्यं वसु
ऋ. 6.16.33

तवं त्रिधातु पृथिवी उत द्यौर्वैश्वानर व्रतमग्ने सचन्त
त्वं भासा रोदसी आ ततन्थाऽजस्रेण शोचिपा शोशुचानः

Page 119

शं नो भगः शमु नः शंसो अस्तु शं नः पुरंधिः शमु सन्तु रायः
शं नः सत्यस्य सुयमस्य शंसः शं नो अर्यमा पुरुजातो अस्तु

शं नो धाता शमु धर्ता नो अस्तु शं न उरूची भवतु स्वधाभिः
शं रोदसी बृहती शं नो अद्रिः शं नो देवानां सुहवानि सन्तु

शं नो अग्निर्ज्योतिरनीको अस्तु शं नो मित्रावरुणावश्विना शम्
शं नः सुकृता सुकृतानि सन्तु शं न इषिरो अभि वातु वातः

शं नो द्यावापृथिवी पूर्वहूतौ शमन्तरिक्षं दृशये नो अस्तु
शं न ओषधीर्वनिनो भवन्तु शं नो रजसस्पतिरस्तु जिष्णुः

Page 121

त्वमग्ने शुभिस्त्वमाशुशुक्षणिस्त्वमद्भ्यस्त्वमश्मनस्परि
त्वं वनेभ्यस्त्वमोषधीभ्यस्त्वं नृणां नृपते जायसे शुचिः

Page 122

शं नः सूर्य उरुचक्षा उदेतु शं नश्चतस्रः प्रदिशो भवन्तु
शं नः पर्वता ध्रुवयो भवन्तु शं नः सिन्धवः शमु सन्त्यापः

शं नो अदितिर्भवतु व्रतेभिः शं नो भवन्तु मरुतः स्वर्काः
शं नो विष्णुः शमु पूषा नो अस्तु शं नो भवित्रं शम्वस्तु वायुः

शं नो देवः सविता त्रायमाणः शं नो भवन्तूषसो विभातीः
शं नः पर्जन्यो भवतु प्रजाभ्यः शं नः क्षेत्रस्य पतिरस्तु शंभुः

शं नो देवा विश्वदेवा भवन्तु शं सरस्वती सह धीभिरस्तु
शमभिषाचः शमु रातिषाचः शं नो दिव्याः पार्थिवाः शं नो अप्याः

शं नः सत्यस्य पतयो भवन्तु शं नो अर्वन्तः शमु सन्तु गावः
शं न ऋभवः सुकृतः सुहस्ताः शं नो भवन्तु पितरो हवेषु

ऋ. 7.35.12

शं नो अज एकपाद् देवो अस्तु शं नोऽहिर्बुध्न्यः शं समुद्रः
शं नो अपां नपात् पेरुरस्तु शं नः पृश्निर्भवतु देवगोपा

ऋ. 7.35.13

याम्मेधान्देवगणाः पितरश्चोपासते
तयामामद्यमेधयाग्नेमेधाविनङ्कुरु स्वाहा

य. 32.14

शान्ता द्यौः शान्ता पृथिवी शान्तमिदमुर्वन्तरिक्षम्
शान्ता उदन्वतीरापः शान्ता नः सन्त्वोषधीः

अ. 19.9.1

सं सीदस्व महाँ असि शोचस्व देववीतमः
वि धूममग्ने अरुषं मियेध्य सृज प्रशस्त दर्शतम्

ऋ. 1.36.9

एवा ते हारियोजना सुवृक्तीन्द्र ब्रह्माणि गोतमासो अक्रन्
ऐषु विश्वपेशसं धियं धाः प्रातर्मक्षू धियावसुर्जगम्यात्

ऋ 1.61.16

अनागसो अदितये देवस्य सवितुः सवे । विश्वा वामानि धीमहि

ऋ. 5. 82.6

मधु वाता ऋतायते मधु क्षरन्ति सिन्धवः । माध्वीर्नः सन्त्वोषधीः
मधु नक्तमुतोषसो मधुमत्पार्थिवँ रजः । मधु द्यौरस्तु नः पिता
मधुमान्नो वनस्पतिर्मधुमाँ२ अस्तु सूर्यः । माध्वीर्गावो भवन्तु नः

य. 13.27-29

दा नो अग्ने धिया रयिं सुवीरं स्वपत्यं सहस्य प्रशस्तम्
न यं यावा तरति यातुमावान्

ऋ. 7.1.5

अरं दासो न मीळ्हुषे कराण्यहं देवाय भूर्णयेऽनागाः
अचेतयदचितो देवो अर्यो गृत्सं राये कवितरो जुनाति

ऋ. 7.85.7

न देवानामति व्रतं शतात्मा चन जीवति । तथा युजा वि वावृते

ऋ. 10.33.9

भद्रं नो अपि वातय मनः

ऋ. 1.21.1

अस्मे धेहि द्युमतीं वाचमासन बृहस्पते अनमीवामिषिराम
यया वृष्टिं शंतनवे वनाव दिवो द्रप्सो मधुमाँ आ विवेश

ऋ. 10.98.3

Page 127

यत्रं ब्रह्मविदो यान्ति दीक्षया तपसा सह
अग्निर्भा तत्रं नयत्वग्निर्मेधा दधातु मे । अग्नये स्वाहा

अ. 19.43.1

यत्रं ब्रह्मविदो यान्ति दीक्षया तपसा सह
वायुर्मा तत्रं नयतु वायुः प्राणान् दधातु मे । वायवे स्वाहा

अ. 19.43.2

यत्रं ब्रह्मविदो यान्ति दीक्षया तपसा सह
सूर्यो मा तत्रं नयतु चक्षुः सूर्यो दधातु मे । सूर्याय स्वाहा

य. 19.43.3

पृथिव्याः सधस्थादग्निं पुरीष्यमङ्गिरस्वदा भरा ग्निं पुरीष्यमङ्गिरस्वदच्छेमो
ऽग्निं पुरीष्यमङ्गिरस्वद्धरिष्यामेँ:

य. 11.16

मा नो अग्नेऽमतये मावीरतायै रीरधः
मागोतायै सहसस्पुत्र मा निदे उप द्वेषांस्या कृधि

ऋ. 3.16.5

Page 129

यतोयतः समीहसे तो नो अभयं कुरु
शं नः कुरु प्रजाभ्योऽभयं नः पशुभ्यः

य. 36.22

देवानां भद्रा सुमतिर्ऋजूयतां देवानां रातिरभि नो नि वर्तताम्
देवानां सख्यमुप सेदिमा वयं देवा न आयुः प्र तिरन्तु जीवसे

ऋ. 1.89.2

भद्रं कर्णेभिः शृणुयाम देवा भद्रं पश्येमाक्षभिर्यजत्राः
स्थिरैरङ्गैस्तुष्टुवांसस्तनूभिर्व्यशेम देवहितं यदायुः

ऋ. 1.89.8

473

या ते धामानि दिवि या पृथिव्यां या पर्वतेष्वोषधीष्वप्सु
तेभिर्नो विश्वैः सुमनाः अहेळन् राजन्त्सोम प्रतिहव्या गृभाय

ऋ. 1.91.4

भग एव भगवाँ अस्तु देवास्तेन वयं भगवन्तः स्याम
तं त्वा भग सर्व इज्जोहवीति स नो भग पुरएता भवेह

ऋ. 7.41.5

ये सवितुः सत्यसवस्य विश्वे मित्रस्य व्रते वरुणस्य देवाः
ते सौभगं वीरवद्गोमदप्नो दधातन द्रविणं चित्रमस्मे

ऋ. 10.36.13

तुञ्जेतुञ्जे य उत्तरे स्तोमा इन्द्रस्य वज्रिणः न विन्ध अस्य सुष्टुतिम्

ऋ. 1.7.7

तेजोऽसि तेजो मयि धेहि वीर्यमसि वीर्यं मयि धेहि
बलमसि बलं मयि धेह्यो –
ओजोऽस्योजो मयि धेहि मन्युरसि मन्युं मयि धेहि
सहोऽसि सहो मयि धेहि

य. 19.9

अश्विना पुरुदंससा नरा शवीरया धिया धिष्ण्या वनतं गिरः

ऋ. 1.3.2

ऊर्ध्व ऊ षु ण ऊतये तिष्ठा देवो न सविता
ऊर्ध्वो वाजस्य सनिता यदञ्जिभिर्वाघद्भिर्विह्वयामहे

ऋ. 1.36.13

पाहि नो अग्ने रक्षसः पाहि धूर्तेरराव्णः
पाहि रीषत उत वा जिघांसतो बृहद्भानो यविष्ठ्य

ऋ. 1.36.15

मा नो अग्नेऽव सृजो अघाया ऽविष्यवे रिपवे दुच्छुनायै
मा दत्वते दशते मादते नो मा रीषते सहसावन् परा दाः

ऋ 1.189.5

विश्वा उत त्वया वयं धारा उदन्या इव
अति गाहेमहि द्विषः

ऋ. 2.7.3

तस्य व्रात्यस्य । एकं तदेषाममृतत्वमित्याहुतिरेव

अ. 15.17.10

आ नो॑ बृह॒न्ता बृ॒ह॒ती॒भिरू॒ती इन्द्र॒ यात॑ वरुण वा॒जसातौ॑
यद्दि॒द्यवः॒ पृत॑नासु प्र॒क्रीळा॒न्तस्य॑ वां स्याम स॒नितार॑ आ॒जेः

ऋ. 4.41.11

त्वम॑ग्ने वनु॒ष्यतो॒ नि पा॑हि त्व॒मु नः॑ सह॒सावन्न॒वद्यात्॑
सं त्वा॑ ध्वस्म॒न्वद॒भ्येतु॒ पाथः॒ सं र॒यिः स्पृ॑ह॒याय्यः॑ सह॒स्री

ऋ. 6.15.12

त्वं न॑: पा॒ह्यंह॑सो जा॒तवे॑दो अ॒घाय॒तः रक्षा॑ णो ब्र॒ह्मणस्कवे

ऋ. 6.16.30

यो नो॑ अग्ने दु॒रेव॒ आ मर्तो॑ व॒धाय॒ दाश॑ति । तस्मा॑न्नः पा॒ह्यंह॑सः

ऋ. 6.16.31

मा नो॒ वृका॑य वृ॒क्ये॑ समस्मा अघा॒यते॑ रीरधता यजत्राः
यू॒यं हि ष्ठा र॒थ्यो॑ नस्त॒नूना॒ यू॒यं दक्ष॑स्य॒ वच॑सो बभूव

ऋ. 6.51.6

३ २१ ३२३१२ ३ २ ३२३२ १३२ २१३ २
त्रा॒तार॒मिन्द्र॑मवि॒तार॒मिन्द्र॒ हवे॑हवे सु॒हव॒ शूर॒मिन्द्र॑म्
३२उ ३१ २ ३१ २र३२ ३ २ ३१ ३ १ २
हु॒वे नु श॒क्रं पु॑रुहू॒तमिन्द्र॒मि॒द हवि॑र्मघवा वेत्विन्द्रः॑

सा. 333

अ॒हि॑रिव भो॒गैः पर्ये॑ति बा॒हुं ज्या॒या हे॒तिं परि॑बाध॒मानः॑
ह॒स्त॒घ्नो विश्वा॑ व॒युना॑नि वि॒द्वान्पुमा॒न्पुमा॑सं॒ परि॑ पातु वि॒श्वतः॑

ऋ. 6.75.14

यो नः॒ स्वो अर॒णो यश्च॒ निष्ट्यो॑ जिघां॑सति
दे॒वास्तं सर्वे॑ धूर्वन्तु॒ ब्रह्म॒ वर्म॒ ममान्त॑रम्

ऋ. 6.75.19

ध्रु॒वासु॑ त्वा॒सु क्षि॒तिषु॑ क्षि॒यन्तो॒ व्य॑स्मत्पाशं॒ वरु॑णो मुमोचत्
अवो॒ वन्वा॑ना अदि॒तेरु॒पस्था॑द्यू॒यं पा॑त स्व॒स्तिभिः॒ सदा॑ नः

ऋ. 7.88.7

अव॑ द्रु॒ग्धानि॑ पि॒त्र्या॑ सृजा नो॒ ऽव॒ या व॒यं च॑कृ॒मा त॒नूभिः॑
अव॑ राजन्पशु॒तृपं॒ न ता॒युं सृ॒जा व॒त्सं न दाम्नो॒ वसि॑ष्ठम्

ऋ. 7.86.5

प्रास्मत्पाशा॑न्वरुण मुञ्च॒ सर्वा॑न्य उ॒त्तमा॑ अ॒धमा॑ वा॒रुणा॒ ये
दुष्प्नय॑ दु॒रितं॒ नि ह्वा॑स्म॒दथ॑ गच्छेम सुकृ॒तस्य॒ लोक॑म्

अ. 7.83.4

उरुं नों लोकमनु नेपि विद्वान्त्स्व१ र्यज्ज्योतिरभयं स्वस्ति

उग्रा तं इन्द्र स्थविरस्य बाहू उप क्षयेम शरणा बृहन्तां

अ. 19.15.4

यत्तेऽनाधृष्टं नाम यज्ञियं तेन त्वा दधे१३ । अनु त्वा देववी॑तये

य. 5.9

युयोध्य्स्मद् द्वेपांथर्सि विश्वकर्मणे स्वाहा३

य. 12.43

मीढुष्टम शिर्वतम शिवो नः सुमनां भव

परमे वृक्ष आयुधं निधाय कृत्तिं वसान् आ चर पिनाकं बिभ्रदा गहि३

य. 16.51

Page 139

शतमिन्नु शरदो अन्ति देवा यत्रा नश्चक्रा जरसं तनूनाम्

पुत्रासो यत्र पितरो भवंन्ति मा नो मध्या रीरिषतायुर्गन्तोः

ऋ. 1.89.9

अग्ने त्वमस्मद् युयोध्य्स्मीवा अनग्निन्रा अभ्यमंत कृष्टीः

पुनरस्मभ्यं सुविताय देव क्षां विश्वेभिरमृतेभिर्यजत्र

ऋ. 1.189.3

समिद्धो अग्निर्निर्हितः पृथिव्यां प्रत्यङ् विश्वानि भुवनान्यस्थात्

होता पावकः प्रदिवः सुमेधा देवो देवान् यजत्वग्निरर्हन्

ऋ. 2.33.1

सविता पश्चातात् सविता पुरस्तात् सवितोत्तरात्तात् सविताधरात्तात्

सविता नः सुवतु सर्वतातिं सविता नों रासतां दीर्घमायुः

ऋ. 10.36.14

ये त्रिषप्ताः परियन्ति विश्वा रूपाणि बिभ्रतः

वाचस्पतिर्बला तेषां तन्वोऽ अद्य दधातु मे

अ. 1.1.1

अघशंसदुःशंसाभ्यां करेणानुकरेण च

यक्ष्मं च सर्वं तेनेतो मृत्युं च निरजामसि

अ. 12.2.2

Page 140

वाङ् मे आसन् नसोः प्राणश्चक्षुरुरक्षणोः श्रोत्रं कर्णयोः

अपलिताः केशा अशोणा दन्तां बहु बाह्वोर्बलम्

अ. 19.60.1

ऊर्वोरोजो जङ्घयोर्जवः पादयोः । प्रतिष्ठा अरिष्टानि मे सर्वात्मानिभृष्टः

अ. 19.60.2

476

अग्ने यन्मे तन्वा ऊनं तन्म आपृण

य. 3.17

अहं तवं वीरं विदेय तव देवि सन्दृशि

य. 4.23

नमो मात्रे पृथिव्यै नमो मात्रे पृथिव्या इयं ते राड्
अस्मे वो अस्तिन्द्रियमस्मे नृम्णुत क्रतुरस्मे वर्चांश्सि सन्तु व:

य. 9.22

प्र ब्रवाम शरदः शतमदीनाः स्याम शरदः शतं

य. 36.24

देवकृतस्यैनसोऽवयजनमसि

य. 8.13

मूषो न शिश्ना व्यदन्ति माध्यः स्तोतारं ते शतक्रतो
सकृत् सु नो मघवन्निन्द्र मृळयाऽधा पितेव नो भव

ऋ. 10.33.3

यन्मे छिद्रं चक्षुषो हृदयस्य मनसो वातितृण्णं बृहस्पतिर्मे तद्दधातु
शं नो भवतु भुवनस्य यस्पतिः

य. 36.2

मा नो रक्षो अभि नड्चातुमावतामपोच्छतु मिथुना या किमीदिना
पृथिवी नः पार्थिवात् पात्वंहसो उन्तरिक्षं दिव्यात् पात्वस्मान्

ऋ. 7.104.23

द्विषो नो विश्वतोमुखातिं नावेव पारय। अप नः शोशुचदघम्

अ. 1.33.7

यच्चिद्धि ते विशो यथा प्र देव वरुण व्रतम्। मिनीमसि द्यविद्यवि

ऋ. 1.25.1

इमं नु सोममन्तितो हृत्सु पीतमुप ब्रुवे
यत् सीमागश्चेकृमा तत् सु मृळतु पुलुकामो हि मर्त्यः

ऋ. 1.179.5

अचिती यच्चकृमा दैव्ये जने दीनैर्दक्षैः प्रभूती पूरुषत्वता
देवेषु च सवितर्मानुषेषु च त्वं नो अत्र सुवतादनागसः

ऋ. 4.54.3

मा नो वधी रुद्र मा परा दा मा ते भूम प्रसितौ हीळितस्य
आ नो भज बर्हिषि जीवशंस यूयं पात स्वस्तिभिः सदा नः

ऋ. 7.46.4

किमागं आस वरुण ज्येष्ठं यत् स्तोतारं जिघांससि सखायाम्
प्र तन्मे वोचो दूळभ स्वधावो 3व त्वानेना नमसा तुर इयाम्

ऋ. 7.86.4

Page 145

न स स्वो दक्षो वरुण ध्रुतिः सा सुरा मन्युर्विभीदको अचित्तिः
अस्ति ज्यायान् कनीयस उपारे स्वप्नश्चवनेदनृतस्य प्रयोता

ऋ. 7.86.6

मो षु वरुण मृन्मयं गृहं राजन्नहं गमम् । मृळा सुक्षत्र मृळयं

ऋ. 7.89.1

यदेमिं प्रस्फुरत्रिव दृतिर्न ध्मातो अद्रिवः । मृळा सुक्षत्र मृळय

ऋ. 7.89.2

हिरण्मयेन पात्रेण सत्यस्यापिहितं मुखम् । योऽसावादित्ये पुरुषः
सोऽसावहम् ओ३म् खं ब्रह्म

य. 40.17

Page 146

यामिषुं गिरिश्न्त हस्ते बिभर्ष्यस्तवे
शिवाङ्गिरित्राताङ्कुरुमाहिंसी पुरुषञ्जगत्

य. 16.3

मायाभिरिन्द्र मायिनं त्वं शुष्णमवर्तारिः ।
विदुष्टे तस्य मेधिरास् तेषां श्रवांस्युत्तिर

ऋ. 1.11.7

यो नो अग्नेऽभिदासत्यन्तिं दूरे पदीष्ट सः । अस्माकमिद् वृधे भव

ऋ. 1.79.11

जातवेदसे सुनवाम सोममरातीयतो नि दहाति वेदः
स नः पर्षदति दुर्गाणि विश्वा नावेव सिन्धुं दुरितात्यग्निः

ऋ. 1.99.1

Page 147

यो न आगो अभ्येनो भरात्यधीदघमघशंसे दधात
जही चिकित्वो अभिशस्तिमेतामग्ने यो नो मर्चयति द्वयेन

ऋ. 5.3.7

विसर्माणं कृणुहि वित्तमेषां ये भुजते अपृणन्तो न उक्थैः
अपव्रतान् प्रसुवे वावृधानान् ब्रह्मद्विषः सूर्यादु यावयस्व

ऋ. 5.42.10

आ भानुना पार्थिवानि जयांसि महस्तोदस्य धृषता ततन्थ
स बाधस्वाप भया सहोभिः स्पृधो वनुष्यन् वनुषो नि जूर्व
॰ ऋ. 6.6.6

अग्निस्तिग्मेन शोचिषा यासद् विश्वं न्यत्रिणम्
अग्निर्नो वनते रयिम्
ऋ. 6.16.28

मा व एनो अन्यकृतं भुजेम मा तत् कर्म वसवो यच्चयध्वे
विश्वस्य हि क्षयथ विश्वदेवाः स्वयं रिपुस्तन्वं रीरिषीष्ट
ऋ. 6.51.7

अति वा यो मरुतो मन्यते नो ब्रह्म वा यः क्रियमाणं निनित्सात्
तपूषि तस्मै वृजिनानि सन्तु ब्रह्मद्विषमभि तं शोचतु द्यौः
ऋ. 6.52.2

विश्वा अग्नेऽप दहारातीर्येभिस्तपोभिरदहो जरूथम्
प्र निस्वरं चातयस्वामीवाम्
ऋ. 7.1.7

त्वद् भिया विश आयन्नसिक्नीरसमना जहतीर्भोजनानि
वैश्वानर पूर्वे शोशुचानः पुरो यदग्ने दरयन्नदीदेः
ऋ. 7.5.3

इन्द्रासोमा समघशंसमभ्यघं तपुर्ययस्तु चरुरग्निवाँ इव
ब्रह्मद्विषे क्रव्यादे घोरचक्षसे द्वेषो धत्तमनवायं किमीदिने
ऋ. 7.104.2

इन्द्रासोमा दुष्कृतो वव्रे अन्तरनारम्भणे तमसि प्र विध्यतम्
यथा नातः पुनरेकश्चनोदयत् तद् वामस्तु सहसे मन्युमच्छवः
ऋ. 7.104.3

ब्राह्मणासो अतिरात्रे न सोमे सरो न पूर्णमभितो वदन्तः
संवत्सरस्य तदहः परि ष्ठ यन्मण्डूकाः प्रावृषीणं बभूव
ऋ. 7.104.7

अज्येष्ठासो अकनिष्ठास एते सं भ्रातरो वावृधुः सौभगाय
युवा पिता स्वपा रुद्र एषां सुदुघा पृश्निः सुदिनां मरुद्भ्यः
ऋ. 5.60.5

सिन्धोरिव प्राध्वने शूघनासो वातंप्रमियः पतयन्ति यह्वाः
घृतस्य धारा अरुषो न वाजी काष्ठा भिन्दन्नूर्मिभिः पिन्वमानः
ऋ. 4.58.7

अभि प्रवन्त समनेव योषाः कल्याण्यः स्मयमानासो अग्निम्
घृतस्य धाराः समिधा नसन्त ता जुषाणो हर्यति जातवेदाः
ऋ. 4.58.8

उप नः सूनवो गिरः शृण्वन्त्वमृतस्य ये । सुमृळीका भवन्तु नः
ऋ. 6.52.9

तिस्रो वाचः प्र वद ज्योतिरग्रा या एतद् दुहे मधुदोघमूधः
स वत्सं कृण्वन् गर्भमोषधीनां सद्यो जातो वृषभो रोरवीति
ऋ. 7.101.1

पावका नः सरस्वती वाजेभिर्वाजिनीवती । यज्ञं वष्टु धियावसुः
चोदयित्री सूनृतानां चेतन्ती सुमतीनाम् । यज्ञं दधे सरस्वती
ऋ. 1.3.11

तस्या समुद्रा अधि वि क्षरन्ति तेन जीवन्ति प्रदिशश्चतस्रः
ततः क्षरत्यक्षरं तद् विश्वमुप जीवति
ऋ. 1.164.42

चत्वारि वाक् परिमिता पदानि तानि विदुर्ब्राह्मणा ये मनीषिणः
गुहा त्रीणि निहिता नेङ्गयन्ति तुरीयं वाचो मनुष्या वदन्ति
ऋ. 1.164.45

यस्तु स्तनः शशयो यो मयोभूर्येन विश्वा पुष्यसि वार्याणि
या रत्नधा वसुविद यः सुदत्रः सरस्वति तमिह धातवे कः
ऋ. 1.164.49

आ भारती भारतीभिः सजोषा इळा देवैर्मनुष्येभिरग्निः
सरस्वती सारस्वतेभिर्वाक् तिस्रो देवीर्बर्हिरिदं सदन्तु
ऋ. 3.4.8

त्रिधा हितं पणिभिर्गुह्यमानं गावे देवासो घृतमन्वविन्दन्
इन्द्र एकं सूर्य एकं जजान वेनादेकं स्वधया निष्टतक्षुः
ऋ. 4.58.4

देवीं वाचमजनयन्त देवास्तां विश्वरूपाः पशवो वदन्ति
सा नो मन्द्रेषमूर्जं दुहाना धेनुर्वागस्मानुप सुष्टुतैतु
ऋ. 8.100.11

अस्येदेषा सुमतिः पप्रथाना ऽभवत् पूर्व्या भूमंना गौः
अस्य सनीळा असुरस्य योनौ समान आ भरणे बिभ्रमाणाः
ऋ. 10.121.6

Page 157

बृहस्पते प्रथमं वाचो अग्रं यत् प्रैरत नामधेयं दधानाः
यदेषां श्रेष्ठं यदरिप्रमासीत् प्रेणा तदेषां निहितं गुहाविः
ऋ. 10.71.1

सक्तुमिव तितउना पुनन्तो यत्र धीरा मनसा वाचमक्रंत
अत्रा सखायः सख्यानि जानते भद्रैषां लक्ष्मीर्निहितादधि वाचि
ऋ. 10.71.2

उत त्वः पश्यन् न ददर्श वाचमुत त्वः शृण्वन् न शृणोत्येनाम्
उतो त्वस्मै तन्वं वि सस्रे जायेव पत्य उशती सुवासाः
ऋ. 10.71.4

Page 158

दूराच्चकमानायं प्रतिपाणायाक्षये
आस्मा अशृण्वत्राशाः कामेनाजनयन्त्स्वः
अ. 19.52.3

Page 160

उत त्वं सख्ये स्थिरपीतमाहुनैनं हिन्वन्त्यपि वाजिनेषु
अधेन्वा चरति मायययैष वाचं शुश्रुवाँ अफलामपुष्पाम्
ऋ. 10.71.5

यस्तित्याज सचिविदं सखायं न तस्य वाच्यपि भागो अस्ति
यदीं शृणोत्यलकं शृणोति नहि प्रवेद सुकृतस्य पन्थाम्
ऋ. 10.71.6

हृदा तष्टेषु मनसो जवेषु यद्ब्राह्मणाः संयजन्ते सखायः
अत्राहं त्वं वि जहुर्वेद्याभिरोहंब्रह्माणो वि चरन्त्यु त्वे
ऋ. 10.71.8

इमे ये नार्वाङ्न परश्चरन्ति न ब्राह्मणासो न सुतेकरासः
त एते वाचमभिपद्य पापया सिरीस्तन्त्रं तन्वते अप्रजज्ञयः
ऋ. 10.71.9

सन्तेमनोमनंसा सम्प्राणः प्राणेनंगच्छताम्
य. 6.18

इयं वां ब्रह्मणस्पते सुवृक्तिर्ब्रह्मेन्द्राय वज्रिणे अकारि
अविष्टं धियो जिगृतं पुरंधीर्जस्तमर्यो वनुषामरांतीः
ऋ. 7.97.9

शृण्वन्तु विश्वे अमृतंस्य पुत्राः
य. 11.5

यथेमां वाचं कल्याणीमावदांनि जनेंभ्यः
ब्रह्मराजन्याभ्याश्च शूद्राय चार्याय च स्वाय चारंणाय च
य. 26.2

उपंहूतो वाचस्पतिरुपास्मान् वाचस्पतिर्ह्वयताम्
सं श्रुतेन गमेमहि मा श्रुतेन वि रांधिषि
अ. 1.1.4

आपूर्वेणोषिता वाचस्ता वंदन्ति यथायथम्
वदंन्तीर्यत्र गच्छंन्ति तदांहुर्ब्राह्मणमहत्
अ. 10.8.33

श्रुत्कर्णाय कवये वेद्याय वचोभिर्वांकैरुपं यामि रांतिम्
वतो भयमभयं तन्नो अस्त्ववं देवानां यज हेडो अग्ने
अ. 19.3.4

सोमं गीर्भिष्ट्वा वयं वर्धयांमो वयोविदः
सुमृळीको न आ विश
ऋ. 1.91.11

द्वादंशारं नहि तज्जरांय वर्वर्ति चक्रं परि द्यामृतस्य
आ पुत्रा अग्ने मिथुनासो अत्र सप्त शतानि विंशतिश्चं तस्थुः
अ. 9.9.13

साकं हि शुचिना शुचिः प्रशास्ता क्रतुनाजनि
विद्वाँ अंस्य व्रता ध्रुवा वया इवानु रोहते
ऋ. 2.5.4

ऋतेन ऋतं नियंतमीळ आ गोरामा सचा मधुमत् पक्वमंग्ने
कृष्णा सती रुशंता धासिनैषा जामर्येण पयसा पीपाय
ऋ. 4.3.9

दैव्या होतारा प्रथमा न्यृंजे सप्त पृक्षासः स्वधया मदन्ति
ऋतं शंसन्त ऋतमित् त आहुरनु व्रतं व्रतपा दीध्यानाः
ऋ. 3.4.7

कथा महामवृधत् कस्य होतुर्यज्ञं जुषाणो अभि सोममूध:
पिबन्नुशानो जुषमाणो अन्धो ववक्ष ऋष्वः शुचते धनाय
ऋ. 4.23.1

Page 165

ऋतस्य हि शुरुधः सन्ति पूर्वीर्ऋतस्य धीतिर्वृजिनानि हन्ति
ऋतस्य श्लोको बधिरा ततर्द कर्णा बुधानः शुचमान आयोः
ऋ. 4.23.8

प्र सप्तगुमृतधीतिं सुमेधां बृहस्पतिं मतिरच्छा जिगाति
य आङ्गिरसो नमसोपसद्यो ऽस्मभ्यं चित्रं वृषणं रयिं दाः
ऋ. 10.47.6

श्रत्तें दधामि प्रथमाय मन्यवे ऽहन्यद्वृत्रं नर्यं विवेरप:
उभे यत्त्वा भवतो रोदसी अनु रेजेते शुष्मात् पृथिवी चिदद्रिवः
ऋ. 10.147.1

सत्यं बृहदृतमुग्रं दीक्षा तपो ब्रह्म यज्ञः पृथिवीं धारयन्ति
सा नो भूतस्य भव्यस्य पत्न्युरुं लोकं पृथिवी नः कृणोतु
अ. 12.1.1

यदग्ने तपसा तप उपतप्यामहे तप:
प्रियाः श्रुतस्य मूयास्मायुष्मन्तः सुमेधस:
अ. 7.61.1

सत्येनोत्तभिता भूमिः सूर्येणोत्तभिता द्यौः
ऋतेनादित्यास्तिष्ठन्ति दिवि सोमो अधि श्रितः
अ. 14.1.1

Page 166

ऋतस्य पन्थामनु पश्य साध्वङ्गिरसः सुकृतो येन यन्ति
तेभिर्याहि पथिभिः स्वर्ग यत्रादित्या मधु भक्षयन्ति तृतीये
नाके अधि वि श्रयस्व
अ. 18.4.3

बृहस्पतिष्ट्वा सुम्ने रंग्णातु
य. 4.21

स्वस्ति ते देव सोम सुत्यामशीय
य. 5.7

वि स्वः पश्य व्युन्तरिक्षं
य. 7.45

वाजे वाजेऽवत वाजिनो नो धनेषु विप्रा अमृता ऋतज्ञाः
अस्य मध्वः पिबत मादयध्वं तृप्ता यात पथिभिर्देवयानैः
य. 9.18

यो देवानां चरसि प्राणथेन कस्मै देव वषडस्तु तुभ्यम्
य. 11.39

वि या जानाति जसुरिं वि तृप्यन्तं वि कामिनम्
देवत्रा कृणुते मनः
ऋ. 5.61.7

Page 167

समिद्धो अग्निर्निहितः पृथिव्यां प्रत्यङ् विश्वानि भुवनान्यस्थात्
होता पावकः प्रदिवः सुमेधा देवो देवान् यजत्वग्निरर्हन्
ऋ. 2.3.1

अजो भागस्तपसा तं तपस्व तं ते शोचिस्तपतु तं ते अर्चिः
यास्ते शिवास्तन्वो जातवेदस्ताभिर्वहैनं सुकृतामु लोकम्
ऋ. 10.64.4

इन्द्राग्नी तमपनुदतां योऽस्मान्द्वेष्टि
य. 2.15

संबर्हिरङ्क्ताथ हविषा घृतेन समादित्यैर्वसुभिः सम्मरुद्भिः
समिन्द्रो विश्वदेवेभिरङ्क्तां दिव्यं नभो गच्छतु यत् स्वाहा
य. 2.22

Page 169

यद्द्यावं इन्द्र ते शतं शतं भूमीरुत स्युः
न त्वा वज्रिन् सहस्रं सूर्या अनु न जातमष्ट रोदसी
ऋ. 8.70.5

Page 170

आयुर्यज्ञेन कल्पतां प्राणो यज्ञेन कल्पतां
चक्षुर्यज्ञेन कल्पताथ श्रोत्रं यज्ञेन कल्पतां
पृष्ठं यज्ञेन कल्पतां यज्ञो यज्ञेन कल्पताम्
प्रजापते प्रजा अभूम स्वर्देवा अगन्माऽमृता
अभूम
य. 9.21

इमं नो देव सवितर्यज्ञं प्र णय
य. 11.8

भद्रो नो अग्निराहुतो भद्रा रातिः सुभग भद्रो अध्वरः
भद्रा उत प्रशस्तयः
सा. 111

आग्ने स्थूरं रयिं भर पृथुं गोमन्तमश्विनम्
अङ्ग्रिः खं वर्तया पणिम्
सा. 1529

नाहं तन्तुं न वि जानाम्योतुं न यं वयन्ति समरेऽतमानाः
कस्य स्वित् पुत्र इह वक्त्वानि परो वदात्यवरेण पित्रा
ऋ. 6.9.2

Page 171
अयं मे पीत उदियर्ति वाचमयं मनीषामुशतीमजीगः
अयं षळुवीर्रमिमीत धीरो न याभ्यो भुवनं कच्चनारे
ऋ. 6.47.3

अयं विदच्चित्रदृशीकमर्णः शुक्रसंदनामुषसामनीके
अयं महान्महता स्कम्भनेनोद् द्यामस्तभ्नाद् वृषभो मरुत्वान्
ऋ. 6.47.5

स्वादिष्ठया मदिष्ठया पवस्व सोम धारया। इन्द्राय पातवे सुतः
ऋ. 9.1.1

रक्षोहा विश्वचर्षणिरभि योनिमयोहतम् । द्रुणा सधस्थमासदत्
ऋ. 9.1.2

अभ्यर्ष महानां देवानां वीतिमन्धसा अभि वाजमुत श्रवः
ऋ. 9.1.4

Page 172
पुनाति ते परिसुतं सोमं सूर्यस्य दुहिता। वारेण शश्वता तना
ऋ.9.1.6

गोषा इन्दो नृषा अस्यश्वसा वाजसा उत
आत्मा यज्ञस्य पूर्व्यः
ऋ. 9.2.10

तमीमण्वीः समर्य आ गृभ्णन्ति योषणो दश। स्वसारः पार्ये दिवि
ऋ. 9.1.7

महान्तं त्वा महीरन्वापो अर्षन्ति सिन्धवः
यद्गोभिर्वासयिष्यसे
ऋ. 9.2.4

अचिक्रदद्वृषा हरिर्महान् मित्रो न दर्शतः सं सूर्येण रोचते

ऋ. 9.2.6

Page 173

गिरस्त इन्द ओजसा मर्मृज्यन्ते॑ अपस्युवः याभिर्मदाय शुभ्रसे

ऋ. 9.2.7

एष देवो अमर्त्यः पर्णवीरिव॑ दीयति। अभि द्रोणान्यासदम्

ऋ. 9.3.1

एष देवो विपा कृतो ऽति हर्वांसि धावति। पवमानो॑ अदाभ्यः

ऋ. 9.3.2

ऋतस्य॑ दृ॰॰हा धरुणानि सन्ति पुरूणि चन्द्रा वपुषे॑ वपूंषि
ऋतेन॑ दीर्घमिषणन्त॑ पृक्षं ऋतेन॑ गावं ऋतमा॑ विवेशुः

ऋ. 4.23.9

एष देवो रंथर्यति पवंमानो दशस्यति। आविष्कृणोति वग्वनुम्

ऋ. 9.3.5

Page 174

एष दिवं वि धावति तिरो रजांसि धारया। पवमानः॑ कनिक्रदत्

ऋ. 9.3.7

आत्मा यज्ञस्य रंह्या॑ सुष्वाणः पवते सुतः
प्रत्नं नि पाति काव्यम्

ऋ. 9.6.8

Page 175

वेदाहं सूत्रं वितंतं यस्मिन्नोताः प्रजा इमाः
सूत्रं सूत्रस्याहं वेदाथो यद् ब्राह्मणं महत्

अ. 10.8.38

Page 176

भूर्भुवः स्वः तत्सवितुर्वरेण्यं भर्गो॑ देवस्य धीमहि
धियो यो नः प्रचोदयात्॑

य. 36.3

नि त्वामग्ने मनुर्दधे ज्योतिर्जनाय शश्वते
दीदेथ कण्वं ऋतजात उक्षितो यं नमस्यन्ति कृष्टयः

सा. 54

तदस्य प्रियमभि पाथो अश्यां नरो यत्र देवयवो मदन्ति
उरुक्रमस्य स हि बन्धुरित्था विष्णोः पदे परमे मध्व उत्सः

ऋ. 1.154.5

उत्तरेणेव गायत्रीममृतेऽधि विचक्रमे ।
साम्नायं सामं संविदुरजुस्तद् ददृशे क्वं ।।
अ. 10.8.41

Page 178
तत् सवितुर्वरेण्यं भर्गो देवस्य धीमहि
धियो यो नः प्रचोदयात्
सा. 1462

यस्ते अग्ने नमंसा यज्ञमीट्ट ऋतं स पात्यरुषस्य वृष्णः
तस्य क्षयः पृथुरा साधुरेतु प्रसर्स्राणस्य नहुषस्य शेषः
ऋ. 5.12.6

युञ्जते मन उत युञ्जते धियो विप्रा विप्रस्य बृहतो विपश्चितः
वि होत्रा दधे वयुनाविदेक इन्मही देवस्य सवितुः परिष्टुतिः
ऋ. 5.81.1

इन्द्र मृळ महयं जीवातुमिच्छ चोदय धियमयसो न धारांम्
यत् किं चाहं त्वायुरिदं वदामि तज्जुषस्व कृधि मां देववन्तम्
ऋ. 6.47.10

यो वै तां ब्रह्मणो वेदामृतेनावृतां पुरंम्
तस्मै ब्रह्म च ब्राह्माश्च चक्षुः प्राणं प्रजां ददुः
अ. 10.2.79

Page 179
या ते धामांनि परमाणि यावमा या मध्यमा विश्वकर्मन्नुतेमा
शिक्षा सखिभ्यो हविषि स्वधावः स्वयं यंजस्व तन्वं वृधानः
ऋ. 10.81.5

यामृषयो भूतकृतो मेधां मेधाविनो विदुः
तया मामद्य मेधयाग्ने मेधाविनं कृणु
अ. 6.108.4

अन्धं तमः प्रविशन्ति येऽसंभूतिमुपासते
ततो भूय इव ते तमो य उ सम्भूत्याथ रताः
य. 40.9

विद्यां चाविद्यां च यस्तद्वेदोभयंथ सह
अविद्यया मृत्युं तीर्त्वा विद्ययाऽमृतमश्नुते
य. 40.14

वायुरनिलममृतमथेदं भस्मान्तꣳ शरीरम्
ओ३म् क्रतो स्मर। क्लिबे स्मर। कृतꣳ स्मर॑
य. 40.15

प्र होत्रे॑ पूर्व्यं॑ वचो॑ ऽग्नये॑ भरता बृह॒त्
विपां॑ ज्योती॑षि बिभ्र॒ते न वेधसे॑
सा. 98

Page 180

उ॒तेदा॒नीं भ॒गवन्तः स्यामो॒त प्र॑पि॒त्व उ॒त मध्ये॒ अह्नाम्
उ॒तोदि॑ता म॒घव॑न्त्सूर्यस्य व॒यं दे॒वानाꣳ सु॒मतौ स्याम॑
य. 34.37

Page 182

ज॒ज्ञा॒न सप्त॑ मा॒तरो॑ वे॒धाम॑शासत श्रि॒ये
अ॒यं ध्रु॒वो र॑यी॒णां चि॑के॒त यत्
सा. 101

अ॒भि त्वा॑ वृषभा सु॒ते सु॒तं सृ॑जामि पी॒तये
तृ॒म्पा व्य॑श्नुही॒ मद॑म्
सा. 161

सद॑स॒स्पति॑भ्द्रुतं॒ प्रि॒यमिन्द्र॑स्य का॒म्यम् स॒निं मे॒धाम॑यासिपम्
सा. 171

न॒किर्दे॑वा मिनीमसि॒ नकि॒रा यो॑पयामसि म॒न्त्रश्रुत्यं॑ चरामसि
प॒क्षेभि॑रपि॒क्षेभिरत्राभि॒ सं र॑भामहे
सा. 176

पा॒व॒का नः॒ सर॑स्वती॒ वाजे॑भिर्वा॒जिनी॑वती। य॒ज्ञं व॑ष्टु धि॒यावसुः॑
सा. 189

मे॒धां सा॒यं मे॒धां प्रा॒तर्मे॒धां म॒ध्यंदि॑नं॒ परि॑
मे॒धां सूर्य॑स्य र॒श्मिभि॒र्वचसा॑ वे॒शयामहे
अ. 6.108.5

Page 183

यो वि॒द्यात् सूत्र॒वित॑तं॒ यस्मि॒न्नेताः॒ प्रजा॑ इ॒माः
सूत्रं॑ सूत्र॒स्य यो वि॒द्यात् स वि॒द्याद् ब्रा॑ह्म॒णं म॒हत्
अ. 10.8.37

श्र॒मेण॑ त॒पसा॑ सृ॒ष्टा ब्रह्म॑णा वि॒त्तर्त॑ श्रि॒ता
अ. 12.5.1

इदं यत् परमेष्ठिनं मनो वां ब्रह्मसंशितम्
येनैव ससृजे घोरं तेनैव शान्तिरस्तु नः
अ. 19.9.4

सं वर्चसा पयसा सं तनूभिरगन्महि मनसा सꣳ शिवेन
त्वष्टा सुदत्रो विदधातु रायोऽनुमार्ष्टु तन्वो यद्विलिष्टम्
य. 2.24

यज्ञवाहसꣳ सुतीर्था नो असद्दशे
ये देवा मनोजाता मनोयुजो दक्षक्रतवस्ते नोऽवन्तु ते नः
पान्तु तेभ्यः स्वाहा
य. 4.11

धर्मणा । ब्रह्मवनि त्वा क्षत्रवनि रायस्पोपवनि पर्यूहामि
ब्रह्म दृꣳह क्षत्रं दृꣳहायुर्दृꣳह प्रजां दृꣳह
य. 5.27

अछिन्नस्यतेदेव सोम सुवीर्यस्यरायस्पोषस्यददितारः स्याम
स प्रथमा संस्कृतिर्विश्ववारा स प्रथमो वरुणो मित्रो अग्निः
य. 7.14

Page 185
तत् सवितुर्वरेण्यं भर्गो देवस्य धीमहि धियो यो नः प्रचोदयात्
ऋ. 3.62.10

Page 186
बृहस्पतेरुत्तमं नाकꣳ रुहेयम्
य. 4.9.10

नक्तोषासा समनसा विरूपे धापयेते शिशुमेकꣳ समीची
द्यावाक्षामा रुक्मो अन्तर्वि भाति देवा अग्निं धारयन्द्रविणोदाः
य. 12.2

सं ते पयांꣳसि समु यन्तु वाजाः सं वृष्ण्यान्यभिमातिपाहः
आप्यायमानो अमृताय सोम दिवि श्रवांꣳस्युत्तमानि धिष्व
य. 12.113

पृथिव्या अहमुदन्तरिक्षमारुहमन्तरिक्षादिवमारुहम्
दिवो नाकस्य पृष्ठात् स्वर्ज्योतिरगामहम्
य. 17.67

ऊर्ध्वो नः पाह्यंहसो नि केतुना विश्वं समत्रिणं दह
कृधी न ऊर्ध्वाञ्चरथाय जीवसे विदा देवेषु नो दुवः
ऋ. 1.36.14

वृष्णस्ते वृष्ण्यं शवो वृषा वनं वृषा मदः। सत्यं वृषन् वृषेदसि

सा. 782

आयमगन्त्सविता धुरेणोऽण्णेन वाय उदकेनेहि
आदित्या रुद्रा वसंव उन्दन्तु सचेतसः सोमस्य राज्ञो वपत प्रचेतसः

अ. 6.68.1

वेदाहं सूत्रं वितंतं यस्मिन्त्रोतांः प्रजा इमाः
सूत्रं सूत्रस्याहं वेदाथो यद् ब्राह्मणं महत्

अ. 10.8.38

यदग्ने मर्त्यस्त्वं स्यामहं मित्रमहो अमर्त्यः। सहसः सूनवाहुत

ऋ. 8.19.25

सत्यमुग्रस्य बृहतः सं स्रवन्ति संस्रवाः
सं यन्ति रसिनो रसाः पुनानो ब्रह्मणा हर इन्द्रायेन्दो परि स्रव

ऋ. 9.113.5

यत्र ज्योतिरजस्रं यस्मिन् लोके स्वंहितम्
तस्मिन् मां धेहि पवमानाऽमृते लोके अक्षित इन्द्रायेन्दो परि स्रव

ऋ. 9.113.7

यंत्र राजा वैवस्वतो यत्रावरोधनं दिवः
यत्रामूर्यह्रतीरापस्तत्र माममृतं कृधीन्द्रोयेन्दो परि स्रव

ऋ. 9.113.8

यत्रानुकामं चरणं त्रिनाके त्रिदिवे दिवः
लोका यत्र ज्योतिष्मन्तस्तत्र माममृतं कृधीन्द्रायेन्दो परि स्रव

ऋ. 9.113.9

यत्रानन्दाश्च मोदाश्च मुदः प्रमुद आसंते
कामस्य यत्राप्ताः कामास्तत्र माममृतं कृधीन्द्रायेन्दो परि स्रव

ऋ. 9.113.11

इहैधि पुरुष सर्वेण मनसा सह। दूतौ यमस्य मानु गा
अधि जीवपुरा इहि

अ. 5.30.6

मृत्युरीशे द्विपदां मृत्युरीशे चतुष्पदाम्
तस्मात् त्वां मृत्योर्गोपंतेरुद् भरामि स मा बिभेः
अ. 8.2.23

परं मृत्यो अनु परेहि पन्थां यस्ते एष इतरो देवयानात्
चक्षुष्मते शृण्वते तै ब्रवीमीहेमे वीरा बहवो भवन्तु
अ. 12.2.21

Page 193

अर्यमणं यजामहे सुबन्धुं पतिवेदनम्
उर्वारुकमिव बन्धनात् प्रेतो मुञ्चामि नामुतः
अ. 14.1.17

तस्य व्रात्यस्य। एकं तदेषाममृतत्वमित्याहुतिरेव
अ. 15.17.10

उर्वारुकमिव बन्धनादितो मुक्षीय मामुतः
य. 3.60

यमाय त्वा मह्यं वरुणो ददातु सोऽमृतत्त्वमंशीय
य. 7.47

Page 194

द्वा सुपर्णा सयुजा सखाया समानं वृक्षं परि षस्वजाते
तयोरन्यः पिप्पलं स्वाद्वत्यनश्नन्नन्यो अभि चांकशीति
ऋ. 1.164.20

इन्द्रस्य नु वीर्याणि प्र वोचं यानि चकार प्रथमानि वज्री
अहन्नहिमन्वपस्ततर्द प्र वक्षणा अभिनत् पर्वतानाम्
ऋ. 1.32.1

वृषायमाणो ऽवृणीत सोमं त्रिकद्रुकेष्वपिबत् सुतस्य
आ सायकं मघवादत्त वज्रमहन्नेनं प्रथमजामहीनाम्
ऋ. 1.32.3

Page 196

नास्मै विद्युन्न तन्यतुः सिषेध न यां मिहमकिरद् ध्रादुनिं च
इन्द्रश्च यद् युयुधाते अहिश्चोतापरीभ्यो मघवा वि जिग्ये
ऋ. 1.32.13

इन्द्रो यातोऽवसितस्य राजा शर्मस्य च शृङ्गिणो वज्रबाहुः
सेद्धु राजा क्षयति चर्षणीनामरान् न नेमिः परि ता बभूव
ऋ. 1.32.15

491

अभि सिध्मो अंजिगादस्य शत्रून् वि तिग्मेन वृषभेणा पुरोऽभेत्
सं वज्रेणासृजद् वृत्रमिन्द्रः प्र स्वां मतिमतिरच्छाशदानः
ऋ. 1.33.13

अग्निनां तुर्वशं यदुं परावतं उग्रादेवं हवामहे
अग्निर्नयत्ववार्वास्त्वं बृहद्रथं तुर्वीतिं दस्यवे सहः
ऋ. 1.36.18

विश्वंमस्या नानाम् चक्षसे जगज् ज्योतिष्कृणोति सूनरी
अप द्वेषों मघोनीं दुहिता दिव उपा उच्छदप सिध्दः
ऋ. 1.48.8

त्वं करंजमुत पर्णयं वधीस्तेजिष्ठयातिथिग्वस्य वर्तनी
त्वं शता वङ्गृदस्याभिनत् पुरों ऽनानुदः परिपूता ऋजिश्वना
ऋ. 1.53.8

त्वं दिवो बृहतः सानु कोपयो ऽव त्मना धृषता शम्बरं भिनत्
यन्मायिनों ऽव्रन्दिनो मन्दिनों धृषच्छितां गभस्तिमशनिं पृतन्यसि
ऋ. 1.54.4

त्वं तमिन्द्र पर्वतं न भोजसे महो नृम्णस्य धर्मणामिरज्यसि
प्र वीर्येण देवताति चेकिते विश्वस्मा उग्रः कर्मणे पुरोहितः
ऋ. 1.55.3

यस्मिन् वृक्षे मध्वदः सुपर्णा निविशन्ते सुवंते चाधि विश्वे
तस्येदाहः पिप्पलं स्वाद्वग्रे तन्नोन्नश्द्यः पितरं न वेद
ऋ. 1.164.22

अनच्छये तुरगातु जीवमेजंद् ध्रुवं मध्य आ पस्त्यानाम्
जीवो मृतस्य चरति स्वधाभिरमर्त्यो मर्त्येना सयोनिः
ऋ. 1.164.30

अपश्यं गोपामनिपद्यमानमा च परा च पथिभिश्चरंन्तम्
स सध्रीचीः स विषूचीर्वसांन आ वरीवर्ति भुवनेष्वन्तः
ऋ. 1.164.32

अपाङ् प्राङेति स्वधया गृभीतो ऽमर्त्यो मर्त्येना सयोनिः
ता शश्वंन्ता विषूचीनां वियन्ता न्यंन्यं चिक्युर्न नि चिक्युरन्यम्
ऋ. 1.164.38

यो जात एव प्रथमो मनस्वान् देवो देवान् क्रतुना पर्यभूषत्
यस्य शुष्माद् रोदसी अभ्यसेतां नृम्णस्य महना स जनास इन्द्रः
उत्तर दिशा. ऋ. 2.12.1

Page 199
यः पृथिवीं व्यथमानामदृंहद् यः पर्वतान् प्रकुपिताँ अरम्णात्
यो अन्तरिक्षं विममे वरीयो यो द्यामस्तभ्नात् स जनास इन्द्रः
ऋ. 2.12.2

अस्य मन्दानो मध्वो वज्रहस्तो ऽहिमिन्द्रो अर्णोवृतं वि वृश्चत्
प्र यद् वयो न स्वसराण्यच्छा प्रयांसि च नदीनां चक्रमन्त
ऋ. 2.19.2

स रन्धयत् सदिवः सारथये शुष्णमशुषं कुयवं कुत्साय
दिवोदासाय नवति च नवेन्द्रः पुरो व्यैरच्छम्बरस्य
ऋ. 2.19.6

एवा ते गृत्समदाः शूर मन्मावस्यवो न वयुनानि तक्षुः
ब्रह्मण्यन्त इन्द्र ते नवीय इषमूर्जं सुक्षितिं सुम्नमश्युः
ऋ. 2.19.8

कनिक्रदज्जनुष प्रब्रुवाण इयर्ति वाचमरितेव नावम्
सुमङ्गलश्च शकुने भवासि मा त्वा का चिदभिभा विश्व्या विदत्
ऋ. 2.42.1

समुद्रेण सिन्धवो यादमाना इन्द्राय सोमं सुपुतं भरन्तः
अंशुं दुहन्ति हस्तिनो भरित्रैरध्वः पुनन्ति धारया पवित्रैः
ऋ. 3.36.7

Page 200
यदग्ने स्यामहं त्वं त्वं वा घा स्या अहम्
स्युष्टे सत्या इहाशेषः
ऋ. 8.44.23

Page 201
यो अग्निं तन्वो ऽ दमे देवं मर्तः सपर्यति
तस्मा इद् दीदयद् वसु
ऋ. 8.44.15

Page 203
सुवीरस्ते जनिता मन्यत द्यौरिन्द्रस्य कर्ता स्वपस्तमो भूत्
य ईं जजान स्वर्यं सुवज्रमनपच्युतं सदसो न भूम
ऋ. 4.17.4

न्यस्मै देवी स्वधितिर्जिहीत इन्द्राय गातुरुशतीव येमे
सं यदोजो युवते विश्वमाभिरनु स्वधावुने क्षितयो नमन्त
ऋ. 5.32.10

प्र श्येनो न मदिरमंशुमस्मै शिरो दासस्य नमुचेर्मथायन्
प्रावन्नमीं साप्यं ससन्तं पृणग्राया समिषा सं स्वस्ति
ऋ. 6.20.6

Page 204

वि मे कर्णा पतयतो वि चक्षुर्वीअदं ज्योतिर्हृदय आहितं यत्
वि मे मनश्चरति दूराआधीः किं स्विद् वक्ष्यामि किमु नू मनिष्ये
ऋ. 6.9.6

अनु प्रलास आववः पदं नवीयो अक्रमुः। रुचे जनन्त सूर्यम्
ऋ. 9.23.2

अक्षेत्रवित् क्षेत्रविदं ह्यप्राट् स प्रैति क्षेत्रविदानुशिष्टः
एतद्वै भद्रमनुशासनस्योत स्रुतिं विन्दत्यञ्जसीनाम्
ऋ. 10.32.7

Page 205

ब्रह्मचारीष्णंश्चरति रोदसी उभे तस्मिन् देवाः संमनसो भवन्ति
स दाधार पृथिवीं दिवं च स आचार्यं तपसा पिपर्ति
अ. 11.5.1

आचार्य। उपनयमानो ब्रह्मचारिणं कृणुते गर्भमन्तः
तं रात्रीस्तिस्र उदरे बिभर्ति तं जातं द्रष्टुमभिसंयन्ति देवाः
अ. 11.5.3

इयं समित् पृथिवि द्यौर्द्वितीयोतान्तरिक्षं समिधा पृणाति
ब्रह्मचारी समिधा मेखलया श्रमेण लोकांस्तपसा पिपर्ति
अ. 11.5.4

Page 206

श्रद्धया सत्यमाप्यते
य. 19.30

का ईमरे पिशङ्गिला का ई कुरुपिशङ्गिला
का ईमास्कन्दमर्षति का ई पन्थां वि सर्पति
य. 23.55

अजारे पिशङ्गिला श्वावित्कुरुपिशङ्गिला
शश आस्कन्दमर्पत्यहिः पन्थां वि सर्पति
य. 23.56

दर्शं नु विश्वदर्शतं दर्शं रथमधि क्षमि । एता जुषत मे गिरः
ऋ. 1.25.18

अग्नेः प्रियं पाथोऽपीतम्
य. 2.17

अगन्म स्वः सं ज्योतिषाभूम
य. 2.25

अग्ने त्वथ सु जागृहि वयथ सु मन्दिषीमहि
य. 4.14

रक्षा णो अप्रयुच्छन् प्रबुधे नः पुनस्कृधि
अग्नावग्निश्चरति प्रविष्ट
य. 5.4

पृष्ठात् पृथिव्या अहमन्तरिक्षमारुहमन्तरिक्षाद् दिवमारुहम्
दिवो नाकस्य पृष्ठात् स्वं ज्योतिरगामहम्
अ. 4.14.3

यज्ञं यज्ञं गच्छ यज्ञपतिं गच्छ स्वां योनिं गच्छ स्वाहा
य. 8.22

अहं सूर्यस्य परि याम्याशुभिः प्रैतशेभिर्वहमान ओजसा
यन्मा सावो मनुष आह निर्णिज ऋधक् कृषे दासं कृत्यं हथैः
ऋ. 10.49.7

अभि द्यां महिना भुवमभीमां पृथिवीं महीम्
कुवित् सोमस्यापामिति
ऋ. 10.119.8

विदित्वाति मृत्युमेति नान्यः पन्था विद्यतेऽयनाय
य. 31.18

रोहितो दिवमारुहत् तपसा तपस्वी
स योनिमैति स उ जायते पुनः स देवानामधिपतिर्बभूव
अ. 13.2.25

असंतापं मे हृदयमुर्वी गव्यूतिः समुद्रो अस्मि विधर्मणा
बृहस्पतिर्म आत्मा नृमणा नाम हृदयः
अ. 16.3.6

नहि मे रोदसी उभे अन्यं पक्षं चन प्रति
कुवित् सोमस्यापामिति

ऋ. 10.119.7

पर्यावर्तं दुःष्वप्न्यात् पापात् स्वप्न्यादभूत्याः
ब्रह्माहमन्तरं कृण्वे परा स्वप्नमुखाः शुचः

अ. 7.100.1

अवासृजन्त जिह्वयो न देवा भुवः सम्राळिन्द्र सत्ययोनिः
अहन्नहिं परिशयानमर्णः प्र वर्तनीररदो विश्वधेनाः

ऋ. 4.19.2

शुनश्चिच्छेपूं निदितं सहस्राद् यूपादमुञ्चो अशमिष्ट हि षः
एवास्मदग्ने वि मुमुग्धि पाशान् होतश्चिकित्व इह तू निषद्य

ऋ. 5.2.7

उदुत्तमं वरुण पाशमस्मदवाधमं वि मध्यमं श्रथाय
अधा वयमादित्य व्रते तवानागसो अदितये स्याम

अ. 7.83.3

अरं मे गन्तं हवनायास्मै गृणाना यथा पिबाथो अन्धः
परि ह त्यद् वर्तिर्याथो रिपो न यत् परो नान्तरस्तुतुर्यात

ऋ. 6.63.2

अपां मध्ये तस्थिवांसं तृष्णाविद्ज्जरितारम् । मृळा सुक्षत्र मृळय

ऋ. 7.89.4

वयः सुपर्णा उप सेदुरिन्द्रं प्रियमेधा ऋषयो नाधमानाः
अप ध्वान्तमूर्णुहि पूर्धि चक्षुर्मुमुग्ध्यस्मान् निधयेव बद्धान्

ऋ. 10.73.11

ब्रह्म होता ब्रह्म यज्ञा ब्रह्मणा स्वरवो मिताः
अध्वर्युर्ब्रह्मणो जातो ब्रह्मणोऽन्तर्हितं हविः

अ. 19.42.1

३३ ३२३१२ ३२ ३१ र
इत एत उदारुहन्निदवः पृष्ठान्या रुहन्
२ ३ २१ १२ ३१ २र
प्र भूर्जयो यथा पथोयामङ्गिरसो ययः

सा. 92

दृते दृंहंह मा मित्रस्य मा चक्षुषा सर्वाणि भूतानि समीक्षन्ताम्
मित्रस्याहं चक्षुषा सर्वाणि भूतानि समीक्षे
मित्रस्य चक्षुषा समीक्षामहे

य. 36.18

Page 213

यस्तु सर्वाणि भूतान्यात्मन्नेवानुपश्यति
सर्वभूतेषु चात्मानं ततो न वि चिकित्सति

य. 40.6

त्वेषं रूपं कृणुत उत्तरं यत् संपृञ्चानः सदने गोभिरद्भिः
कपिर्बुध्नं परि मर्मृज्यते धीः सा देवताता समितिर्बभूव

ऋ. 1.95.8

यत्संवत्समृभवो गामरक्षन् यत् संवत्समृभवो अपिंशन्
यत् संवत्सम भरन् भासो अस्यास्ताभिः शर्मीभिरमृतत्वमांशुः

ऋ. 4.33.4

Page 217

स नः पप्रिः पारयाति स्वस्ति नावा पुरुहूतः
इन्द्रो विश्वा अति द्विषः

ऋ. 8.16.11

Page 218

तं त्वा गीर्भिररुरुक्षया हव्यवाहं समीधिरे । यजिष्ठं मानुषे जने

ऋ. 1.117.9

समानो मन्त्रः समितिः समानी समानं मनः सह चित्तमेषाम्
समानं मन्त्रमभि मन्त्रये वः समानेन वो हविषा जुहोमि

ऋ. 10.191.3

समानी व आकूतिः समाना हृदयानि वः
समानमस्तु वो मनो यथा वः सुसहासति

ऋ. 10.191.4

यदुत्तमे मरुतो मध्यमे वा यद् वावमे सुभगासो दिवि ष्ठ
अतो नो रुद्रा उत वा न्वस्याग्ने वित्ताद्धविपो यद् यजाम

ऋ. 5.60.6

Page 219

मोघमन्नं विन्दते अप्रचेताः सत्यं ब्रवीमि वध इत् स तस्य
नार्यमणं पुष्यति नो सखायं केवलाघो भवति केवलादी

ऋ. 10.117.6

ते अज्येष्ठा अकनिष्ठास उद्भिदो ऽमध्यमासो महसा वि वावृधुः
सुजातासो जनुषा पृश्निमातरो दिवो मर्या आ नो अच्छा जिगातन

ऋ. 5.59.6

कृपन्नित् फाल आशितं कृणोति यन्नध्वानमप वृङ्क्ते चरित्रैः
वदन् ब्रह्मावदतो वनीयान् पृणन्नापिरपृणन्तमभि ष्यात्

ऋ. 10.117.7

समानी व आकूतिः समाना हृदयानि वः
समानमस्तु वो मनो यथा वः सुसहासति

ऋ. 10.191.4

Page 220

समानी प्रपा सह वोऽन्नभागः समाने योक्त्रे सह वो युनज्मि
सम्यञ्चोऽग्निं संपर्यतारा नाभिमिवाभितः

अ. 3.30.6

स्वादुष्संसदः पितरो वयोधाः कृच्छ्रेश्रितः शक्तीवन्तो गभीराः
चित्रसेना इषुबला अमृध्राः सतोवीरा उरवो व्रातसाहाः

ऋ. 6.75.9

नहि वो अस्त्यर्भको देवासो न कुमारकः । विश्वे सतोमहान्त इत

ऋ. 8.30.1

संसमिद्युवसे वृषन्नग्ने विश्वान्यर्य आ
इळस्पदे समिध्यसे स नो वसून्या भर

ऋ. 10.191.1

Page 221

सं गच्छध्वं सं वदध्वं सं वो मनांसि जानताम्
देवा भागं यथा पूर्वे संजानाना उपासते

ऋ. 1.191.2

न किल्बिषमत्र नाधारो अस्ति न यन्मित्रैः समममान एति
अनूनं पात्रं निहितं न एतत् पक्तारं पक्वः पुनरा विशाति

अ. 12.3.48

सहृदयं सांमनस्यमविद्वेषं कृणोमि वः
अन्यो अन्यमभि हर्यत वत्सं जातमिवाघ्न्या

अ. 3.30.1

समानो मन्त्रः समितिः समानी समानं व्रतं सह चित्तमेषाम्
समानेन वो हविषा जुहोमि समानं चेतो ऽभिसंविशध्वम्

अ. 6.64.2

Page 222

स्वस्ति पन्थामनु चरेम सूर्याचन्द्रमसाविव
पुनर्ददताघ्नता जानता सं गमेमहि

ऋ. 5.51.15

Page 223

स नः शक्रश्चिदा शकद् दानवाँ अन्तराभरः
इन्द्रो विश्वाभिरूतिभिः

ऋ. 8.32.12

Page 224

सध्रीचीनान् वः संमनसस्कृणोम्येकश्नुष्टीन्त्संवननेन सर्वान्
देवा इवामृतं रक्षमाणाः सायंप्रातः सौमनसो वो अस्तु

अ. 3.30.7

ब्रह्म गामश्वं जनयन्त ओषधीर्वनस्पतीन् पृथिवीं पर्वताँ अपः
सूर्यं दिवि रोहयन्तः सुदानव आर्या व्रता विसृजन्तो अधि क्षमि

ऋ. 10.65.11

यदन्तरं तद् बाह्यं यद् बाह्यं तदन्तरम्
कन्यानां विश्वरूपाणां मनो गृभायौषधे

अ. 2.30.4

आकूत्या नो बृहस्पत आकूत्या न उपा गहि
अथो भगस्य नो धेह्यथो नः सुहवो भव

अ. 19.4.3

अग्ने ब्रह्म गृभ्णीष्व

य. 1.18

इन्द्रो वीर्यमकृणोदूध्वोंऽध्वर आस्थात्

य. 2.8

Page 225

भा नो महान्तमुत मा नो अर्भकं मा न उक्षन्तमुत मा न उक्षितम्
मा नो वधीः पितरं मोत मातरं मा नः प्रियास्तन्वो रुद्र रीरिषः

य. 16.15

२उ   ३ १२ ३.२उ ३ १२
त्वँ ह्योहि चेरवे विदा भगं वसुत्तये
१२   ३ १२ ३२उ १२
उद्धावृषस्व मघवन् गविष्टय उदिन्द्राश्वमिष्टये

सा. 240

ज्यायाँसमस्य यतुनस्य केतुं ऋषिस्वरं चरति यासु नाम ते
यादृशिन् धायि तमपस्ययां विदद् य उं स्वयं वहते सो अरं करत्

ऋ. 5.44.8

भद्रं मनः कृणुष्व वृत्रतूर्ये येना समत्सु सासहः
अव स्थिरा तनुहि भूरि शर्धतां वनेमा ते अभिष्टिभिः

ऋ. 8.19.20

त्रातारो देवा अधि वोचता नो मा नो निद्रा ईशत मोत जल्पिः
वयं सोमस्य विश्वहं प्रियासः सुवीरासो विदथमा वदेम

ऋ. 8.48.14

सहस्रधारे वितते पवित्र आ वाचे पुनन्ति कवयो मनीषिणः
रुद्रास एषामिषिरासो अद्रुहः स्पशः स्वञ्चः सुदृशो नृचक्षसः

ऋ. 9.73.7

यथाहान्यनुपूर्वं भवन्ति यथर्तवं ऋतुभिर्यन्ति साकम्
यथा न पूर्वमपरो जहात्येवा धातरायूंषि कल्पयैषाम्

अ. 12.2.25

Page 226

अक्ष्यौनौ मधुसंकाशे अनीकं नौ समञ्जनम्
अन्तः कृणुष्व मां हृदि मन इन्नौ सहासति

अ. 7.36.1

इहैव स्तं मा वि यौष्टं विश्वमायुर्व्यश्नु
क्रीडन्तौ पुत्रैर्नप्तृभिर्मोदमानौ स्वस्तकौ

अ. 14.1.22

Page 227

स्योनाद्योनेरधि बुध्यमानौ हसामुदौ महसा मोदमानौ
सुगू सुपुत्रौ सुगृहै तराथो जीवावुषसो विभातीः

अ. 14.2.43

सुमङ्गली प्रतरणी गृहाणां सुशेवा पत्ये श्वशुराय शंभूः
स्योना श्वश्रवै प्र गृहान् विशेमान्

अ. 14.2.26

प्र बुध्यस्व सुबुधा बुध्यमाना दीर्घायुत्वाय शतशारदाय
गृहान् गच्छ गृहपत्नी यथासो दीर्घं त आयुः सविता कृणोतु

अ. 14.2.75

प्रेतो मुञ्चामि नामुतः सुबद्धाममुतस्करम्
यथेयमिन्द्र मीढ्वः सुपुत्रा सुभगासति
ऋ. 10.85.25

इयमग्ने नारी पतिं विदेष्ट सोमो हि राजा सुभगां कृणोति
सुवाना पुत्रान् महिषी भवाति गत्वा पतिं सुभगा वि राजतु
अ. 2.36.3

अहं वि ष्यामि मयि रूपमस्या वेददित् पश्यन् मनसः कुलायम्
न स्तेयमद्मि मनसोदमुच्ये स्वयं श्रथ्नानो वरुणस्य पाशान्
अ. 14.1.57

गृहा मा बिभीत मा वेपध्वमूर्जं बिभ्रत एमसि
ऊर्जं बिभ्रदः सुमनाः सुमेधा गृहानैमि मनसा मोदमानः
य. 3.41

यज्ञस्य शिवे संतिष्ठस्व स्विष्टे मे संतिष्ठस्व
य. 2.19

देहि मे ददामि ते नि मे धेहि नि त दधे
निहारं च हरासि मे निहारं नि हराणि ते स्वाहा
य. 3.50

जातवेदसौ शिवौ भवतमद्य नः
य. 5.3

यज्ञो देवानां प्रत्येति सुम्नमादित्यासो भवता मृडयन्तः
य. 8.4

मा भ्राता भ्रातरं द्विक्षन्मा स्वसारमुत स्वसा
सम्यञ्चः सव्रता भूत्वा वाचं वदत भद्रया
अ. 3.30.3

ज्यायस्वन्तश्चित्तिनो मा वि यौष्ट संराधयन्तः सधुराश्चरन्तः
अन्यो अन्यस्मै वल्गु वदन्त एत सध्रीचीनान् वः संमनसस्कृणोमि
अ. 3.30.5

न यस्य सातुर्जनितोरवारि न मातरापितरा नू चिद्दिष्टौ
अधा मित्रो न सुधितः प वकोऽ उग्निर्दीदाय मानुषीषु विक्षु
ऋ. 4.6.7

त्वमर्यमा भवसि यत् कनीनां नाम स्वधावन् गुह्यं बिभर्षि
अञ्जन्ति मित्रं सुधितं न गोभिर्यद् दंपती समनसा कृणोषि
ऋ. 5.3.2

इमा नारीरविधवाः सुपत्नीराञ्जनेन सर्पिषा सं स्पृशन्ताम्
अनश्रवो' अनमीवाः सुरत्ना आ रोहन्तु जनयो योनिमग्रे'
अ. 12.2.31

या ओषधयो या नद्योऽ यानि क्षेत्राणि या वना
तास्त्वां वधु प्रजावतीं पत्ये' रक्षन्तु रक्षसः
अ. 14.2.71

शचीभिर्नः शचीवसू दिवा नक्तं दशस्यतम्
मा वां रातिरुप दसत् कदा चनास्मद् रातिः कदा चन
सा. 287

आपो न सिन्धुमभि यत् समक्षरन् त्सोमास इन्द्रं कुल्या इव ह्रदम्
वर्धन्ति विप्रा महो' अस्य सादने यवं न वृष्टिर्दिव्येन दानुना
ऋ. 10.43.6

द्रविणोदा ददातु नो वसूनि यानि शृण्विरे । देवेषु ता वनामहे
ऋ. 1.15.8

द्रविणोदाः पिपीषति जुहोत प्र च तिष्ठत । नेष्ट्रादृतुभिरिष्यत
ऋ. 1.15.9

नाकस्य पृष्ठे अधि तिष्ठति श्रितो यः पृणाति स ह देवेषु गच्छति
तस्मा आपो' घृतमर्षन्ति सिन्धवस्तस्मा इयं दक्षिणा पिन्वते सदा
ऋ. 1.125.5

दक्षिणावतामिदिमानि चित्रा दक्षिणावतां दिवि सूर्यासः
दक्षिणावन्तो अमृतं भजन्ते दक्षिणावन्तः प्रतिरन्त आयुः
ऋ. 1.125.6

इन्द्र श्रेष्ठानि द्रविणानि धेहि चित्तिं दक्षस्य सुभगत्वमस्मे
पोषं रयीणामरिष्टिं तनूनां स्वादमानं वाचः सुदिनत्वमह्नाम्
ऋ. 2.21.6

समीं पणेरजति भोजनं मुषे वि दाशुषे' भजति सूनरं वसु
दुर्गे चन ध्रियते विश्व आ पुरु जनो यो अस्य तविषीमचुक्रुधत्
5ऋ. 5.34.7

विसर्माणं कृणुहि वित्तमेषां ये भुञ्जते अपृणन्तो न उक्थैः ।
अर्पव्रतान् प्रसवे वावृधानान् ब्रह्मद्विषः सूर्याद् यावयस्व ॥
ऋ. 5.42.9

वेमि त्वा पूषन्नृञ्जसे वेमि स्तोतंव आवृणे ।
न तस्य वेम्यरंणं हि तद् वसो स्तुषे पज्राय साम्ने ॥
ऋ. 8.4.17

परि चिन्मर्तो द्रविणं ममन्यादृतस्य पथा नमसा विवासेत् ।
उत स्वेन क्रतुना सं वदेत श्रेयांसं दक्षं मनसा जगृभ्यात् ॥
ऋ. 10.31.2

अक्षैर्मा दीव्यः कृषिमित् कृषस्व वित्ते रमस्व बहु मन्यमानः ।
तत्र गावः कितव तत्र जाया तन्मे वि चष्टे सवितायमर्यः ॥
ऋ. 10.34.15

न स सखा यो न ददाति सख्ये सचाभुवे सचमानाय पित्वः ।
अपास्मात् प्रेयान्न तदोको अस्ति पृणन्तमन्यमरणं चिदिच्छेत् ॥
ऋ. 10.117.4

पृणीयादिन्नाधमानाय तव्यान् द्राघीयांसमनु पश्येत पन्थाम् ।
ओ हि वर्तन्ते रथ्येव चक्रा न्यमन्यमुप तिष्ठन्त रायः ॥
ऋ. 10.117.5

एता एना व्याकरं खिले गा विष्ठिता इव ।
रमन्तां पुण्या लक्ष्मीर्याः पापीस्ता अनीनशम् ॥
अ. 7.115.4

शतहस्त समाहर सहस्रहस्त सं किर ।
कृतस्य कार्यास्य चेह स्फातिं समावह ॥
अ. 3.24.5

यत्तासि यच्छंसे हस्तावप रक्षांसि सेधसि ।
प्रजां धनं च गृह्णानः परिहस्तो अभूदयम् ॥
अ. 6.81.1

या मा लक्ष्मीः पतयालूरजुष्टाभिचस्कन्द वन्दनेव वृक्षम् ।
अन्यत्रास्मत् सवितस्तामितो धा हिरण्यहस्तो वसु नो रराणः ॥
अ. 7.115.2

न वा उं॑ दे॒वाः॑ क्षुधमि॒द्ध वधं॑ द॒दुरु॑ता॒शि॑तमु॒प॑ गच्छन्ति मृ॒त्यवः॑
उ॒तो र॒यिः पृ॑ण॒तो नोप॑ दस्य॒त्युता॑पृ॒णन् म॒र्डितारं॑ न विन्दते
ऋ. 10.117.1

य आ॒ध्राय॑ चक॒माना॑य पि॒त्वो ऽन्न॑वा॒न्त्सन् र॑फि॒तायोप॑ज॒ग्मुषे॑
स्थि॒रं मनः॑ कृ॒णु॑ते से॒व॑ते पु॒रोतो चि॒त् स म॒र्डितारं॑ न विन्दते
ऋ. 10.117.2

स इद्भो॒जो यो गृ॒ह्वे द॒दात्यन्न॑का॒माय॒ चर॑ते कृ॒शाय॑
अर॑मस्मै भवति॒ याम॑हू॒ता उ॒ताप॒रीषु॑ कृ॒णु॒ते सखा॑यम्
ऋ. 10. 117.3

सुनो॒ता सोम॒पात्रे॑ सोमि॒न्द्राय॑ व॒ज्रिणे॑
प॒चता प॒क्तीर॑व॒से कृ॒णु॒ध्व॒मित् पृ॒णन्नित् पृ॒णते॑ म॒यः॑
सा. 285

मा पृ॒णन्तो॒ दुरि॒तमेन॒ आर॒न् मा जा॑रिषुः सू॒रयः॑ सु॒व्रता॑सः
अ॒न्यस्तेषां॒ परि॑धि॒रस्तु॒ कश्चिद॑पृ॒णन्तम॒भि सं य॑न्तु शोका॑ः
ऋ. 1.125.7

त्वां विशो॑ वृणतां रा॒ज्या॑य॒ त्वामि॒माः प्र॒दिशः॑ पञ्च दे॒वीः॑
वर्ष्म॒न् रा॒ष्ट्रस्य॑ क॒कुदि॑ श्रयस्व॒ ततो॑ न उ॒ग्रो वि भ॑जा॒ वसू॑नि
अ. 3.4.2

सिंह॒प्रती॑को॒ विशो॑ अ॒द्धि सर्वा॑ व्या॒घ्रप्रती॑कोऽव॑ बाधस्व श॒त्रू॑न्
ए॒क॒वृष॑ इ॒न्द्र॑सखा जिगी॒वां छ॒त्रू॑यता॒मा ख़ि॒दा भोज॑नानि
अ. 4.22.7

सो॑ऽस॑रज्य॒त ततो॑ राज॒न्यो॑ऽजायत
स विशः॑ सब॑न्धू॒नन्रा॒यम॒भ्युद॑तिष्ठत
अ. 15.8.1,2

स विशो॒ऽनु॑ व्याच॑लत्
अ. 15.9.1

तं स॒भा च॒ समि॑तिश्च से॒ना च॑ सु॒रा चा॑नुव्याच॑लन्
अ. 15.9.2

स॒भायाश्च॒ वै स समि॑तेश्च सु॒रायाश्च
प्रि॒यं धाम॑ भवति॒ य ए॒वं वेद॑
अ. 15.9.3

न तमंहो न दुरितं कुतश्चन नारातयस्तिरुन् द्वयाविनः
विश्वा इदंस्माद् ध्वरसो वि बाधसे यं सुगोपा रक्षसि ब्रह्मणस्पते
ऋ. 2.23.5

न स जीयते मरुतो न हन्यते न स्रेधति न व्यथते न रिष्यति
नास्य राय उप दस्यन्ति नोतय ऋषिं वा यं राजानं वा सुषूदथ
ऋ. 5.54.7

शिवो भूत्वा महाँमग्ने अथो सीद शिवस्त्वम्
य. 12.17

शास इत्था महाँ अस्यमित्रखादो अद्भुतः
न यस्य हन्यते सखा न जीयते कदा चन
ऋ. 10.152.1

Page 240

धारावरा मरुतो धृष्ण्वोजसो मृगा न भीमास्तविषीभिरर्चिनः
अग्नयो न शुशुचाना ऋजीषिणो भूमिं धमन्तो अप गा अवृण्वत
ऋ. 2.34.1

धन्वना गा धन्वनाजिं जयेम धन्वना तीव्राः समदो जयेम
धनुः शत्रोरपकामं कृणोति धन्वना सर्वाः प्रदिशो जयेम
ऋ. 6.75.3

वक्ष्यन्तीवेदा गनीगन्ति कर्णं प्रियं सखायं परिष्वजाना
योषेव शिङ्क्ते वितताधि धन्वज्यया इयं समने पारयन्ती
ऋ. 6.75.3

ते आचरन्ती समनेव योषा मातेव पुत्रं बिभृतामुपस्थे
अप शत्रून् विध्यतां संविदाने आर्ती इमे विष्फुरन्ती अमित्रान्
ऋ. 6.75.4

Page 241

सुपर्ण वस्ते मृगो अस्या दन्तो गोभिः संनद्धा पतति प्रसूता
यत्रा नरः सं च वि च द्रवन्ति तत्रास्मभ्यमिषवः शर्म यंसन्
ऋ. 6. 75.11

ऋजीते परि वृङ्धि नो श्मा भवतु नस्तनूः
सोमो अधि ब्रवीतु नो दितिः शर्म यच्छतु
ऋ. 6.75.12

या जंघन्ति सान्वेषां जघनाँ उप जिघ्नते
अश्वाजनि प्रचेतसोऽश्वान्त्समत्सु चोदय

ऋ. 6.75.13

स्वायुधास इष्मिणः सुनिष्का उत स्वयं तन्वः शुम्भमानाः

ऋ. 7.56.11

समानमञ्ज्येषां वि भ्राजन्ते रुक्मासो अधि बाहुषु। दविद्युतत्यृष्टयः

ऋ. 8.20.11

त उग्रासो वृष्णं उग्रबाहवो नकिष्टनूषु येतिरे
स्थिरा धन्वान्यायुधा रथेषु वो ऽनीकेष्वधि श्रियः

ऋ. 8.20.12

Page 242

ये गोमन्तं वाजवन्तं सुवीरं रयिं धत्थ वसुमन्तं पुरुक्षुम्
ते अग्रेपा ऋभवो मन्दसाना अस्मे धत्त ये च रातिं गृणन्ति

ऋ. 4.34.10

उप नो वाजा अध्वरमृभुक्षा देवा यात पथिभिर्देवयानैः
यथा यज्ञं मनुषो विक्ष्वासु दधिध्वे रण्वाः सुदिनेष्वह्नाम्

ऋ. 4.37.1

व्युदायं देवहितं यथा वः स्तोमो वाजा ऋभुक्षणो ददे वः
जुह्वे मनुष्वदुपरासु विक्षु युष्मे सचा बृहद्दिवेषु सोमम्

ऋ. 4.37.3

ऋभुमृभुक्षणो रयिं वाजे वाजिन्तमं युजम्
इन्द्रस्वन्तं हवामहे सदासातममश्विनम्

ऋ. 4.37.5

Page 243

आ ब्रह्मन् ब्राह्मणो ब्रह्मवर्चसी जायतामा राष्ट्रे राजन्या: ÷ शूरं
इष्व्योऽतिव्याधो महारथो जायतां दोग्ध्री धेनुर्वोढानड्वानाशु : सप्ति :
पुरन्धिर्योषा जिष्णू रथेष्ठा : सभेयो युवास्य यजमानस्य वीरो जायता
न्निकामे-निकामे न : पर्जन्यो वर्षतु फलवत्यो न ओषधय : पच्यन्तां
योगक्षेमो नः: कल्पताम्

य. 22.22

Page 245

द्रविणोदा द्रविणसो ग्रावहस्तासो अध्वरे। यज्ञेषु देवमीळते

ऋ. 1.15.7

506

अर्थमिद वा उं अर्थिनं आ जाया युवते पतिम्
तुञ्जाते वृष्ण्यं पयः परिदाय रसं दुहे वित्तं में अस्य रोदसी
ऋ. 1.105.2

तमित् पृच्छन्ति न सिमो वि पृच्छति स्वेनेव धीरो मनसा यदग्रभीत्
न मृष्यते प्रथमं नापरं वचो ऽस्य क्रत्वा सचते अप्रदृपितः
ऋ. 1.145.2

मधोर्धारामनु क्षर तीव्रः सधस्थमासदः । चारुर्ऋताय पीतये
ऋ. 9.17.8

यत् ते दिवं यत् पृथिवीं मनो जगाम दूरकम्
तत् त आ वर्तयामसीह क्षयाय जीवसे
ऋ. 10.58.2

यत् ते भूतं च भव्यं च मनो जगाम दूरकम्
तत् त आ वर्तयामसीह क्षयाय जीवसे
ऋ. 10.58.12

चित्पतिर्मा पुनातु
य. 4.4

परीदं वासो अधिथाः स्वस्तयेऽभूर्गृष्टीनामंभिशस्तिपा उं
शतं च जीवं शरदः पुरूची रायश्च पोषमुपसंव्ययस्व
अ. 2.13.3

एह्यश्मानमा तिष्ठाश्मा भवतु ते तनूः
कृण्वन्तु विश्वे देवा आयुष्टे शरदः शतम्
अ. 2.13.4

मरीचीर्धूमान् प्र विशानु पाप्मन्नुदारान् गंछोत वां नीहारान्
नदीनां फेनाँ अनु तान् वि नश्य भ्रूणघ्नि पूषन् दुरितानि मृक्ष्व
अ. 6.113.2

अनृणा अस्मिन्ननृणाः परस्मिन् तृतीये लोके अनृणाः स्याम
ये देवयानाः पितृयाणांश्च लोकाः सर्वान् पथो अनृणा आ क्षियेम
अ. 6.117.3

उद्यानं ते पुरुष नावयानं जीवातुं ते दक्षतातिं कृणोमि
अ. 8.10.6

इदमहमनृतात्सत्यमुपैमि
य. 1.5

नमो॑ दे॒वेभ्य॑ स्व॒धा पि॒तृभ्य॑ः सु॒यमे॑ मे भूयास्तम्
य. 2.7

वि॒श्वे॑ दे॒वास॑ इ॒ह मा॑दयन्ता॒मोऽम्प्रतिष्ठ
य.2.13

अना॑धृष्टमस्यनाधृ॒ष्यं॑ दे॒वाना॒मोजो
य. 5.5

उ॒ग्रं वचो॑ अपा॑वधीत्ते॒षं वचो॑ अपा॑वधीत्स्वाहा॑
य. 5.8

इ॒न्द्र॑स्यूरसीन्द्र॑स्यद् ध्रु॒वोसि
ऐ॒न्द्र॑सिवैश्वदेव॑सि
य. 5.30

दे॒वस्त्वा॑ स॒विता॑ मध्वा॑नक्तु॒ सुपिप्प॒लाभ्य॒स्त्वौषधीभ्य॑ः
य 6.2

Page 248

मू॒र्धान॑मस्य सं॒सीव्याथर्वा॑ हृ॒दयं च॒ यत्
म॒स्तिष्का॒दूर्ध्वः॑ प्रैर॑य॒त् पव॑मानो॒धि शी॒र्ष॑तः
अ. 10.2.26

Page 249

यो जा॒गार॒ तमृच॑ः कामयन्ते॒ यो जा॒गार॒ तमु॑ सामा॑नि यन्ति
यो जा॒गार॒ तम॒यं सोम॑ आह॒ तवाह॑मस्मि स॒ख्ये न्योका॑ः
ऋ. 5.44.14

Page 250

उप॑ ऋ॒तस्य॒ पथ्या॒ऽनु
य. 6.12

वसां॑ वसापावानः॑ पिबतान्तरि॑क्षस्य ह॒विर॒सि स्वाहा॑
य. 6.19

मनो॑ मे तर्पय॒त वाच॑ मे तर्पयत
य. 6.31

स्वाङ्कृ॒तोऽसि॒ विश्वे॑भ्य इन्द्रि॑येभ्यो॑
य. 7.3

व॒यꣳ रा॒ष्ट्रे जा॑गृयाम पुरोहि॒ता॑ः स्वाहा॑
य. 9.23

508

सथश्शितं मे ब्रह्म सथश्शितं वीर्यं बलम्
सथश्शितं क्षत्रं जिष्णु युस्याहमस्मि पुरोहितः
य. 11.81

स्वयं वाजिँस्तन्वं कल्पयस्व स्वयं यंजस्व स्वयं जुषस्व
य. 23.15

उदु् त्वां मन्दन्तु स्तोमाः कृणुष्व राधो' अद्रिवः
अवं ब्रह्मद्विषो' जहि
सा. 194

Page 251

उदु् त्ये मधुमत्तमा गिरः स्तोमांस ईरते
सत्राजितो' धनसा अक्षितोतयो वाजयन्तो रथां इव
सा. 251

२   ३   १२३ १२३ २३ १२३१   २
आ त्वा सोमस्य गल्दया सदा याचत्रहं ज्या
१ २ ३१   २र   ३ १ २र २ २
भूर्णि मृगं न सवनेषु चुक्रुधं क ईशानं याचिषत्
सा. 207

दधिक्राव्णो' अकारिषं जिष्णोरश्वंस्य वाजिनः
सुरभि नो मुखां करत् प्र 'ण आयूँषि तारिषत्
सा. 338

मा नो अरांतिरीशत देवस्य मर्त्यस्य च
पर्षि तस्यां उत द्विषः
ऋ. 2.7.2

सुप्राव्यः प्राशुषाळेष वीरः सुष्वें पंक्तिं कृंणुते केवलेन्द्रः
नासुष्वेरांपिर्न सखा न जामिर्दुष्प्राव्योंऽवहन्तेदवांचः
ऋ. 4.25.6

अंहोयुवंस्तन्वंस्तन्वते वि वयो' महद् दुष्टरं पूर्व्यायं
स संवतो नवंजातस्तुतुर्यात् सिंहं न क्रुद्धमभितः परिं ष्ठुः
ऋ. 5.15.3

Page 252

या आपो याश्च देवता या विराड् ब्रह्मणा सह
शरीरं ब्रह्म प्राविशच्छरीरेऽधि प्रजापतिः
अ. 11.8.30

सूर्यचक्षुर्वर्तिं: प्राणं पुरुषस्य वि भेजिरे
अथास्येतरमात्मानं देवाः प्रायच्छन्नग्नये
अ. 11.8.31

तस्माद् वै विद्वान् पुरुषमिदं ब्रह्मेति मन्यते
सर्वा ह्यास्मिन् देवता गावो गोष्ठ इवासंते
अ. 11.8.32

Page 254

अश्मन्वती रीयते सं रभध्वमुत्तिष्ठत प्र तरता सखायः
अत्रा जहाम ये असन्नशेवाः शिवान् वयमुत्तरेमाभि वाजान्
ऋ. 10.53.8

अकामो धीरो अमृतः स्वयंभू रसेन तृप्तो न कुतश्चनोनः
तमेव विद्वान् न बिभाय मृत्योरात्मानं धीरमजरं युवानम्
अ. 10.8.44

उत देवा अवहितं देव उन्नयथा पुनः
उतागश्चक्रुषं देवा देवा जीवयथा पुनः
ऋ. 10.137.1

अयुतोऽहमयुतो म आत्मायुतं मे चक्षुरयुतं मे श्रोत्रमयुतो मे प्राणोऽयुतो
मेऽपानोऽयुतो मे व्यानोऽयुतोऽहं सर्वः
अ. 19.51.1

अनमित्रं नो अधरादनमित्रं न उत्तरात्
इन्द्रानमित्रं नः पश्चादनमित्रं पुरस्कृधि
अ. 6.40.3

Page 255

देवीरापो अग्रेगुवो अग्रेपुवोऽग्र इममद्य यज्ञं नयताग्रे
यज्ञपतिथ सुधातु यज्ञपतिं देवयुवम्
य. 1.12

इमां वाचमभि विश्वे गृणन्त आसद्यास्मिन् बर्हिषि
मादयध्वंछ स्वाहा वाट्
य. 2.18

इयं ते यज्ञिया तनूरपो मुञ्चामि न प्रजाम
य. 4.13

लोकं पृण छिद्रं पृणाथो सीद ध्रुवा त्वम्
इन्द्राग्नी त्वा बृहस्पतिरस्मिन् योनावसीषपदन्
य. 12.54

अया वर्धस्व तन्वां गिरा ममा ऽऽ जाता सुक्रतो पृण
सा. 52

देवो वो द्रविणोदाः पूर्णा विवष्ट्यासिचंम्
उद् वां सिञ्चध्वमुप वा पृणध्वमादिद् वो देव ओहते
सा. 55

देवा यज्ञं नयन्तु नः
सा. 56

Page 256
वृणीध्वं हव्यवाहनम्
सा. 63

देवस्त्वां सविता मध्वानक्तु
य. 6.2

प्रति चक्ष्व वि चक्ष्वेन्द्रश्च सोम जागृतम्
रक्षोभ्यो वधमस्यतमशनिं यातुमद्भ्यः
ऋ. 7.104.25

प्रेह्यभीहि धृष्णुहि न ते वज्रो नि यंसते
इन्द्र नृम्णं हि त शवो हनो वृत्रं जयां अपो ऽर्चन्ननु स्वराज्यम्
ऋ. 1.80.3

समानं वत्समभि संचरन्ती विष्वग्धेनू वि चरतः सुमेके
अनपवृज्याँ अध्वनो मिमाने विश्वान् केताँ अधि महो दधाने
ऋ. 1.146.3

सोमांसो न ये सुतास्तृप्तांशवो हृत्सु पीतासो दुवसो नासते
ऐषामंसेषु रम्भिणीव रारभे हस्तेषु खादिश्च कृतिश्च सं दधे
ऋ. 1.168.3

Page 258
न रेवतां पणिनां सख्यमिन्द्रो ऽसुन्वता सुतपाः सं गृणीते
आस्य वेदः खिदति हन्ति नग्नं वि सुष्वये पक्तये केवलो भूत
ऋ. 4.25.7

इदाह्नः पीतिमुत वो मदं धुर्न ऋते श्रान्तस्य सख्याय देवाः
ते नूनमस्मे ऋभवो वसूनि तृतीये ऽस्मिन् सवने दधात
ऋ. 4.33.11

यादृगेव ददृशे तादृगुच्यते सं छायया दधिरे सिध्रयाप्स्वा
महीमस्मभ्यमुरुषामुरु ज्रयो बृहत् सुवीरमनपच्युतं सहः
ऋ. 5.44.6

आ रोहतायुर्जरसं वृणाना अनुपूर्वं यतमाना यति ष्ठ
इह त्वष्टा सुजनिमा सजोषा दीर्घमायुः कति जीवसे वः
ऋ. 10.18.6

यस्य ते विश्वा भुवनानि केतुना प्र चेरते नि चं विशन्ते अक्तुभिः
अनागास्त्वेन हरिकेश सूर्याह्नाह्नां नो वस्यंसावस्यसोदिहि
ऋ. 10.37.9

प्रेता जयता नर इन्द्रो वः शर्म यच्छतु
उग्रा वः सन्तु बाहवो ऽनाधृष्या यथासथ
ऋ. 10.103.13

Page 259

देवस्य त्वा सवितुः प्रसवेऽश्विनोर्बाहुभ्यां पूष्णो हस्ताभ्याम्
आददेऽध्वरकृतं देवेभ्य इन्द्रस्य बाहुरसि दक्षिणः सहस्रभृष्टिः
ऋ. 10.113.16; अ. 19.51.2

शततेजा वायुरसि तिग्मतेजा द्विपतो वधेः
य. 1.24

अहेळमान उरुशंस सरी भव वाजेवाजे सरी भव
ऋ. 1.138.3

सिंहप्रतीको विशो अद्धि सर्वा व्याघ्रप्रतीकोऽवं बाधस्व शत्रून्
एकवृष इन्द्रसखा जिगीवां छत्रूयतामा खिदा भोजनानि
अ. 4.22.7

वाक्पतिर्मा पुनातु देवो मा सविता पुनात्वच्छिद्रेण पवित्रेण
य. 4.4

उदक्रमीद् द्रविणोदा वाज्यर्वाकः सुलोकंऽथ सुकृतं पृथिव्याम्
ततः खनेम सुप्रतीकंमग्निंऽथ स्वो रुहाणा अधि नाकमुत्तमम्
य. 11.22

Page 260

इदमुच्छ्रेयोऽवसानमागां शिवे मे द्यावापृथिवी अभूताम्
असपत्नाः प्रदिशो मे भवन्तु न वै त्वां द्विष्मो अभयं नो अस्तु
अ. 19.14.1

Page 261

यस्तु सर्वाणि भूतान्यात्मन्नेवानु पश्यति
सर्वभूतेषु चात्मानन्ततो न विचिकित्सति
य. 40.6

द्यां मा लेखीरन्तरिक्षं मा हिं%सीः पृथिव्या सम्भव
य. 5.43

आ रोहतायुर्जरसं वृणाना अनुपूर्वं यतमाना यति स्थ
तान् वस्त्वष्टा सुजनिमा संजोषाः सर्वमायुर्नयतु जीवनाय
अ. 12.2.24

अश्मन्वती रीयते सं रभध्वं वीरयध्वं प्र तरता सखायः
अत्रा जहीत ये असन् दुरेवा अनमीवानुत्तरेमाभि वाजान्
अ. 12.2.26

उत् तिष्ठता प्र तरता सखायोऽश्मन्वती नदी स्यन्दत इयम्
अत्रा जहीत ये असत्रशिवाः शिवान्त्स्योनानुत्तरेमाभि वाजान्
अ. 12.2.27

आयुरपायुःकृतां जीवायुष्मान् जीव मा मृथाः
प्राणेनात्मन्वतां जीव मा मृत्योरुदगा वशम्
अ. 19.27.3

गिरा वज्रो न संभृतः सबलो अनपच्युतः ववक्ष ऋष्वो अस्तृतः
अ. 20.47.3

य उग्रः सत्रनिष्टत स्थिरो रणाय संस्कृतः
यदि स्तोतुर्मघवा शृणवद्धवं नेन्द्रो योषत्या गमत्
अ. 20.53.3

परमेण धाम्ना दृंहस्व मा ह्वार्मा ते यज्ञपतिर्हार्षीत्
य. 1.2

दैव्याय कर्मणे शुन्धध्वं
य. 1.13

अत्र पितरो मादयध्वं
य. 2.31

तेन परो मूजवतोऽतीहि
य. 3.61

श्येनोभूत्वापरापतयजमानस्य गृहात् गच्छतन्नौ संस्कृतम्
य. 4.34

उरुं नो लोकमनु नेपि विद्वान्त्स्वर्ग्यज्ज्योतिरभयं स्वस्ति
उग्रा तं इन्द्र स्थविरस्य बाहू उप क्षयेम शरणा बृहन्ता
अ. 19.15.4

समुद्रं गंछ्ह स्वाहां उ्न्तरिक्षं गंछ्ह स्वाहां

य. 6.21

मा भेर्मा सं विक्था ऊर्जं धत्स्व धिषणे

य. 6.35

प्रागपागुदंगधराक्स्वर्वतंस्त्वा दिश आ धांवन्तु

य. 6.36

प्रतूर्वन्नेहंवक्रामत्रशंस्ती

य. 11.15

उल्क्रांम महते सौभंगायांस्मादास्थानांद्

य. 11.21

स्थिरो भंव वीड्वङ्ग आशुर्भव वाज्यर्वन्

य. 11.44

मयिं गृह्णाम्यग्रें अग्निंठ्ठ रांयस्पोषांय सुप्रजांस्त्वांय सुवीर्यांय

य. 13.1

प्र मृंणीहि शत्रूंनूं

य. 13.13

सुपर्णोऽसि गरुत्मांन् पृष्ठे पृथिव्याः सीद
भासाऽन्तरिक्षमा पृंण ज्योतिषा दिवमुत्तंभान् तेजंसा दिश उद्दृंह्ह

य. 17.72

अदंर्शि गातुविंत्तंमो यस्मिन् व्रतान्यादंधुः। पदीष्ट तृष्णंया सह

सा. 47

प्रेह्यभीहि धृष्णुहि न ते वज्रो नि यंसते
इन्द्रं नृम्णं हि ते शवंो हनों वृत्रं जयां अपो ऽच्चत्रनुं स्वराज्यंम्

सा. 413

मो षु णः परांपरा निर्ऋंतिर्दुर्हणां वधीत्

ऋ. 1.38.6

मा वंो घ्नन्तं मा शर्पन्तं प्रति वोचे देवयन्तंम्
सुम्नैरिद् व आ विवासे

ऋ. 1.41.8

त्वं नों गोपाः पंथिकृद् विचक्षणस्तवं व्रतांय मतिभिर्जरामहे
बृहस्पते यो नों अभि ह्वरों दधे स्वा तं मर्मर्तु दुच्छुना हरंस्वती

ऋ. 2.3.6

उत वा यो नो᳚ मर्चयादनांगसो ᳚रातीवा मर्तः सानुको वृकः ।
बृहस्पते अप तं वर्तया पथः सुगं नो᳚ अस्यै देवतीतये कृधि

ऋ. 2.3.7

अव क्षिप दिवो अश्मानमुच्चा येन शत्रुं मन्दसानो निजूर्वाः ।
तोकस्य सातौ तनयस्य भूरेर्स्माँ अर्धं कृणुतादिन्द्र गोनाम्

ऋ. 2.30.5

उदयत् सहः सहस आजनिष्ट देदिष्ट इन्द्रं इन्द्रियाणि विश्वा ।
प्राचोदयत् सुदुघा वव्रे अन्तर्वि ज्योतिषा संववृत्वत् तमोऽवः

ऋ. 5.31.3

अप ध्वान्तमूर्णुहि पूर्धि चक्षुर्मुमुग्ध्यस्मान् निधयेव बद्धान्

सा. 319

रिशादसः सत्पतीँरदब्धान् महो राज्ञः सुवसनस्य दातॄन् ।
यूनः सुक्षत्रान् क्षयतो दिवो नॄनादित्यान् याम्यदितिं दुवोयु

ऋ. 6.51.4

न तद् दिवा न पृथिव्यानु मन्ये न यज्ञेन नोत शमीभिराभिः ।
उब्जन्तु तं सुभ्वः पर्वतासो नि हीयतामतियाजस्य यष्टा

ऋ. 6.52.1

मा प्र गाम पथो वयं मा यज्ञादिन्द्र सोमिनः । मान्तः स्थुर्नो अरातयः

ऋ. 10.57.1

अध्वर्यो द्रावया त्वं सोममिन्द्रः पिपासति

सा. 308

अकर्मा दस्युरभि नो᳚ अमन्तुरन्यव्रतो अमानुषः ।
त्वं तस्यामित्रहन् वर्धर्दासस्य दम्भय

ऋ. 10.22.8

यो नो दिप्सदर्दिप्सतो दिप्संतो यश्च दिप्संति ।
वैश्वानरस्य दंष्ट्रयोरग्नेरपि दधामि तम्

अ. 4.36.2

अव ज्यामिव धन्वनो मन्युं तनोमि ते हृदः ।
यथा संमनसौ भूत्वा सखायाविव सचावहै

अ. 6.42.1

उद्यन्त्सूर्य इव सुप्तानां द्विषतां वर्च आ ददे

अ. 7.13.2

515

मा गतानामा दीधीथा ये नयन्ति परावतम्
आ रोह तमसो ज्योतिरेह्या ते हस्तौ रभामहे
अ. 8.1.8

Page 271

परीत्य भूतानि परीत्य लोकान् परीत्य सर्वाः प्रदिशो दिशश्च
उपस्थाय प्रथमजामृतस्यात्मनाऽऽत्मानमभि सं विवेश
य. 32.11

Page 272

येऽश्रद्धा धनकाम्या क्रव्यादां समासते
ते वा अन्येषां कुम्भीं पर्यादधति सर्वदा
अ. 12.2.51

शर्मास्यवधूतश्च रक्षोऽवधूता अरातयो
य. 1.19

परि माऽग्ने दुश्चरितादुबाधस्वा मा सुचरिते भज
य. 4.28

रक्षसां भागोऽसि निरस्तᳩ रक्षं
य. 6.16

सत्रस्य ऋद्धिरस्यगन्म ज्योतिरमृता अभूम
दिवं पृथिव्या अध्याऽरुहामाविदाम देवान्त्स्वर्ज्योतिः'
य. 8.52

अग्ने रक्षा णो अंहसः प्रति ष्म देव रीषतः । तपिष्ठैरजरो दह
सा. 24

बोधिन्मना इदंस्तु नो वृत्रहा भूर्यासुतिः । शृणोतु शक्र आशिषम्
सा. 140

वि द्विषा वि मृधो जहि
सा. 274

Page 273

सा नो भूमे प्र रोचय हिरण्यस्येव संदृशि मा नो द्विक्षत कश्चन
अ. 12.1.18

Page 275

तच्चक्षुर्देवहितं शुक्रमुच्चरत
पश्येम शरदः शतं जीवेम शरदः शतम्
ऋ. 7.66.16

सनेमि चक्रमजरं वि वांवृत उत्तानायां दश युक्ता वहन्ति
सूर्यस्य चक्षू रजसैत्यावृतं यस्मिन्नातस्थुर्भुवनानि विश्वा

अ. 9.9.14

काले मनः काले भूतानि प्राणः काले नाम समाहितम्
कालेन सर्वा नन्दन्त्यागतेन प्रजा इमाः

अ. 19.53.7

काले तपः काले ज्येष्ठं काले ब्रह्म समाहितम्
कालो ह सर्वस्येश्वरो यः पितासीत् प्रजापतेः

अ. 19.53.8

यो भूतं च भव्यं च सर्वं यश्चाधितिष्ठति
स्वर्ऱ्यस्य च केवलं तस्मै ज्येष्ठाय ब्रह्मणे नमः

अ. 10.8.1

यो विश्वचर्षणिरुत विश्वतोमुखो यो विश्वतस्पाणिरुत विश्वतस्पृथः
सं बाहुभ्यां भरति सं पतत्रैर्द्यावापृथिवी जनयन् देव एकः

अ. 13.2.26

ऋतं च सत्यं चाभीद्धात् तपसोऽध्यजायत
ततो रात्र्यजायत ततः समुद्रो अर्णवः

ऋ. 10.190.1

समुद्रादर्णवादधि संवत्सरो अजायत
अहोरात्राणि विदधद्विश्वस्य मिषतो वशी

ऋ. 10.190.2

सूर्याचन्द्रमसौ धाता यथापूर्वमकल्पयत्
दिवं च पृथिवीं चान्तरिक्षमथो स्वः

ऋ. 10.190.3

पूर्णः कुम्भोऽधि काल आहितस्तं वै पश्यामो बहुधा नु सन्तः
स इमा विश्वा भुवनानि प्रत्यङ्कालं तमाहुः परमे व्योमिन्

अ. 19.53.3

Page 283

द्यौरासीत्पूर्वचित्तिरश्वं आसीद् बृहद्दयः

अर्विरासीत्पिलिप्पिला रात्रिरासीत्पिशङ्गिला
य. 23.12

Page 284

मिमांतु द्यौरदितिर्वीतये नः सं दानुनिचित्रा उषसो यतन्ताम्

आचुच्यवुर्दिव्य कोशमेत ऋषे रुद्रस्य मरुतो गृणानाः
ऋ. 5.59.8

द्युतद्यामानं बृहतीमृतेनं ऋतावरीमरुणप्सुं विभातीम्

देवीमुषसं स्वरावहन्तीं प्रति विप्रासो मतिभिर्जरन्ते
ऋ. 5.80.1

एषा जनं दर्शता बोधयन्ती सुगान् पथः कृण्वती यात्यग्रे

बृहद्रथा बृहती विश्वमिन्वोषा ज्योतिर्यच्छत्यग्रे अह्नाम्
ऋ. 5.80.2

एषा गोभिररुणेभिर्युजाना स्त्रेधन्ती रयिमप्रायु चक्रे

पथो रदन्ती सुविताय देवी पुरुष्टुता विश्ववारा वि भांति
ऋ. 5.80.3

Page 285

प्रत्यु अदर्श्यायत्युप्ंच्छन्तीं दुहिता दिवः

अपो महिं व्ययति चक्षसे तमो ज्योतिष्कृणोति सूनरी
सा. 303

Page 286

एषा व्येनी भवति द्विबहां आविष्कृण्वाना तन्वं पुरस्तात्

ऋतस्य पन्थामन्वेति साधु प्रजानतीव न दिशो मिनाति
ऋ. 5.80.4

एषा शुभ्रा न तन्वो विदानोर्ध्वेव स्नाती दृशये नो अस्थात्

अप द्वेषो बाधमाना तमांस्युषा दिवो दुहिता ज्योतिषागात्
ऋ. 5.80.5

एषा प्रतीची दुहिता दिवो नून् योषेव भद्रा नि रिणीते अप्सः

व्यूर्ण्वती दाशुषे वार्याणि पुनर्ज्योतिर्युवतिः पूर्वथाकः
ऋ. 5.80.6

क्वं त्या वल्गू पुरुहूताद्य दूतो न स्तोमोंऽविद्त्रमंस्वान्

आ यो अर्वाङ्नासत्या ववर्त प्रेष्ठा ह्यसथो अस्य मन्मन्
ऋ. 6.63.1

उत् ते वयश्चिद् वसतेरपप्तन नरश्च ये पितुभाजो व्युष्टौ
अमा सुते वहसि भूरि वाममुषो देवि दाशुषे मर्त्याय
                                                    ऋ. 6.64.6

Page 287

एषा स्या नो दुहिता दिवोजाः क्षितीरुच्छन्ती मानुषीरजीगः
या भानुना रुशता राम्यास्वज्ञायि तिरस्तमंसश्चिदक्तून्
                                                    ऋ. 6.65.1

समध्वरायोषसो नमन्त दधिक्रावेव शुचये पदाय
अर्वाचीनं वसुविदं भगं नो रथमिवाश्वा वाजिन आ वहन्तु
                                                    ऋ. 7.41.6

अश्वावतीर्गोमतीर्न उषासो वीरवतीः सदमुच्छन्तु भद्राः
घृतं दुहाना विश्वतः प्रपीता यूयं पात स्वस्तिभिः सदा नः
                                                    ऋ. 7.41.7

प्र मे पन्था देवयाना अदृश्रन्नमर्धन्तो वसुभिरिष्कृतासः
अभूदु केतुरुषसः पुरस्तात् प्रतीच्यागादधि हर्म्येभ्यः
                                                    ऋ. 7.76.2

Page 288

मधु नक्तमुतोषसो मधुमत् पार्थिवं रजः। मधु द्यौरस्तु नः पिता
                                                    ऋ. 1.90.7

Page 289

ग्रावाणेव तदिदर्थं जरेथे गृध्रेव वृषं निधिमन्तमच्छं
ब्रह्माणेव विदथ उक्थशासां दूतेव हव्या जन्या पुरुत्रा
                                                    ऋ. 2.39.1

प्रातर्यावाणा रथ्येव वीरा जेव यमा वरमा सचेथे
मेने इव तन्वाउ शुम्भमाने दंपतीव क्रतुविदा जनेषु
                                                    ऋ. 2.39.2

शृङ्गेव नः प्रथमा गन्तमर्वाक् छफाविव जभुराणा तरोभिः
चक्रवाकेव प्रति वस्तोरुस्रा उर्वाञ्चा यातं रथ्येव शक्रा
                                                    ऋ. 2.39.3

वातेवाजुर्या नद्येव रीतिरक्षी इव चक्षुषा यांतमर्वाक्
हस्ताविव तन्वे उ शंभविष्ठा पादेव नो नयतं वस्यो अच्छं
                                                    ऋ. 2.39.5

ओष्ठाविव मध्वास्ने वदन्ता स्तनाविव पिप्यतं जीवसे नः
नासेव नस्तन्वो रक्षितारा कर्णाविव सुश्रुता भूतमस्मे
ऋ. 2.39.6

हस्तेव शक्तिमभि सददी नः क्षामेव नः समजतं रजांसि
इमा गिरो अश्विना युष्मयन्तीः क्ष्णोत्रेणेव स्वधितिं सं शिशीतम्
ऋ. 2.39.7

एतानि वामश्विना वर्धनानि ब्रह्म स्तोमं गृत्समदासो अक्रन्
तानि नरा जुजुषाणोप यातं बृहद् वदेम विदथे सुवीराः
ऋ. 2.39.8

नावेव नः पारयतं युगेव नभ्येव न उपधीव प्रधीव
श्वानेव नो अरिषण्या तनूनां खृगलेव विस्रसः पातमस्मान्
ऋ. 2.39.4

अपो देवीरुप ह्वये यत्र गावः पिबन्ति नः । सिन्धुभ्यः कर्त्वं हविः
ऋ. 1.23.18

प्रान्यच्चक्रमवृहः सूर्यस्य कुत्सायान्यद् वरिवो यातवेऽकः
अनासो दस्यूँरमृणो वधेन नि दुर्योण आवृणङ् मृध्रवाचः
ऋ. 5.29.10

आ सूर्यो अरुहच्छुक्रमर्णो ऽयुक्त यद्धरितो वीतपृष्ठाः
उद्धा न नावमनयन्त धीरा आशृण्वतीरापो अर्वागतिष्ठन्
ऋ. 5.45.10

अयं रोचयदरुचो रुचानोऽ ज्यं वासयद् व्यृतेन पूर्वीः
अयमीयत ऋतयुग्भिरश्वैः स्वर्विदा नाभिना चर्षणिप्राः
ऋ. 6.39.4

वेद यस्त्रीणि विदथान्येषां देवानां जन्म सनुतरा च विप्रः
ऋजु मर्तेषु वृजिना च पश्यन्नभि चष्टे सूरो अर्य एवान्
ऋ. 6.51.2

इन्द्रो नेदिष्ठमवसागमिष्ठः सरस्वती सिन्धुभिः पिन्वमाना
पर्जन्यो न ओषधीभिर्मयोभुरग्निः सुशंसः सुहवः पितेव
ऋ 6.52.6

उद्दू अयाँ उपवक्तेव बाहू हिरण्ययां सविता सुप्रतीका
दिवो रोहांस्यरुहत्पृथिव्या अरीरभत्सतयत्कच्चिदभ्वम्
ऋ 6.71.5

उदु ष्य देवः सविता ययाम हिरण्ययीममतिं यामशिश्रेत
नूनं भगो हव्यो मानुषेभिर्वि यो रत्ना पुरूवसुर्दधाति

ऋ. 7.38.1

Page 294

आ देवो यातु सविता सुरत्नोऽन्तरिक्षप्रा वहमानो अश्वैः
हस्ते दधानो नर्या पुरूणि निवेशयञ्च प्रसुवञ्च भूम

ऋ. 7.45.1

उदस्य बाहू शिथिरा बृहन्ता हिरण्यया दिवो अन्ताँ अनष्टाम्
नूनं सो अस्य महिमा पनिष्ट सूरश्चिदस्मा अनु दादपस्याम्

ऋ. 7.45.2

स घा नो देवः सविता सहावा ऽऽ साविषद् वसुपतिर्वसूनि
विश्रयमाणो अमतिमुरूचीं मर्तभोजनमध रासते नः

ऋ. 7.45.3

बहवः सूरचक्षसो उग्निजिह्वा ऋतावृधः
त्रीणि ये येमुर्विदथानि धीतिभिर्विश्वानि परिभूतिभिः

ऋ. 7.66.10

Page 295

उदु ज्योतिरमृतं विश्वजन्यं विश्वानरः सविता देवो अश्रेत
क्रत्वा देवानामजनिष्ट चक्षुराविरकर्भवनं विश्वमुषाः

ऋ. 7.76.1

तवेदिन्द्राहमाशसा हस्ते दात्रं चना ददे
दिनस्य वा मघवन् त्संभृतस्य वा पूर्धि यवस्य काशिना

ऋ. 8.78.10

रोहितो दिवमारुहत् तपसा तपस्वी
स योनिमैति स उं जायते पुनः स देवानामधिपतिर्बभूव

अ. 13.2.25

अग्निर्मा गोप्ता परि पातु विश्वत उद्यन्त्सूर्यो नुदतां मृत्युपाशान्
व्युच्छन्तोरुषसः पर्वता ध्रुवाः सहस्रं प्राणा मय्या यतन्ताम्

अ. 17.1.30

अपामीवामप स्रिधमप सेधत दुर्मतिम्
आदित्यासो युयोतना नो अंहसः

सा. 397

वयश्चित् ते पतत्रिणो द्विपच्चतुष्पदर्जुनि
उपः प्रारन्नृतूँरनु दिवो अन्तेभ्यस्परि

ऋ. 1.49.3

मा त्वां रुद्र चुक्रुधामा नमोभिर्मा दुष्टुती वृषभ मा सहूती
उन्नो वीराँ अर्पय भेषजेभिर्भिषक्तमं त्वा भिषजां शृणोमि

ऋ. 2.33.4

हवीमभिर्हवंते यो हविर्भिरव स्तोमेभी रुद्रं दिषीय
ऋदूदरः सुहवो मा नो अस्यै बभ्रुः सुशिप्रो रीरधन्मनायै

ऋ. 2.33.5

रात्री व्यख्यदायती पुरुत्रा देव्यक्षभिः। विश्वा अधि श्रियोंऽधित

ऋ. 10.127.1

तं घेमित्था नमस्विन उप स्वराजमासते
होत्राभिरग्निं मनुषः समिन्धते तितिर्वांसो अति स्रिधः

ऋ. 1.36.7

मधु वाता ऋतायते मधु क्षरन्ति सिन्धवः। माध्वीर्नः सन्त्वोषधीः

ऋ. 1.90.6

मधु नक्तमुतोषसो मधुमत् पार्थिवं रजः। मधु द्यौरस्तु नः पिता

ऋ. 1.90.7

मधुमान्नो वनस्पतिर्मधुमाँ अस्तु सूर्यः। माध्वीर्गावो भवन्तु नः

ऋ. 1.90.8

यथा चिन्मन्यसे हृदा तन्दिमे जग्मुराशसः
ये ते नेदिष्ठं हवनान्यागमन् तान् वर्ध भीमसंदृशः

ऋ. 5.56.2

एतं मे स्तोममूर्मे दाभ्याय परा वह। गिरो देवि रथीरिव

ऋ. 5.61.17

आ यः पप्रौ भानुना रोदसी उभे धूमेन धावते दिवि
तिरस्तमो ददृश ऊर्म्यास्वा श्यावास्वरुपो वृषा श्यावा अरुषो वृषा

ऋ. 6.48.6

पर्जन्यवाता वृषभा पृथिव्याः पुरीषाणि जिन्वतमप्यानि
सत्यश्रुतः कवयो यस्य गीर्भिर्जगतः स्थातर्जगदा कृणुध्वम्
ऋ. 6.49.6

आ नो रुद्रस्य सूनवो नमन्तामद्या हुतासो वसवोऽधृष्टाः
यदीमर्भे महति वा हितासो बाधे मरुतो अह्वाम देवान्
ऋ. 6.50.4

अनेनो वो मरुतो यामो अस्त्वनश्वश्चिद यमजत्यरथीः
अनवसो अनभीशू रजस्तूर्वि रोदसी पथ्या याति साधन्
ऋ. 6.66.7

उत त्ये नो मरुतो मन्दसाना धियं तोकं च वाजिनोऽवन्तु
मा नः परि ख्यदक्षरा चरन्त्यवीवृधन् युज्यं ते रयिं नः
ऋ. 7.36.7

अंसेष्वा मरुतः खादयो वो वक्षःसु रुक्मा उपशिश्रियाणाः
वि विद्युतो न वृष्टिभी रुचाना अनु स्वधामायुधैर्यच्छमानाः
ऋ. 7.56.13

इमे तुरं मरुतो रामयन्तीमे सहः सहस आ नमन्ति
इमे शंसं वनुष्यतो नि पान्ति गुरु द्वेषो अररुषे दधन्ति
ऋ. 7.56.19

यो गर्भमोषधीनां गवां कृणोत्यर्वताम् । पर्जन्यः पुरुपीणाम्
ऋ. 7.102.2

वृषण्श्वेन मरुतो वृषप्सुना रथेन वृषनाभिना
आ श्येनासो न पक्षिणो वृथा नरो हव्या नो वीतये गत
ऋ. 8.20.10

हुवे वातस्वनं कविं पर्जन्यंक्रन्दं सहः
अग्निं समुद्रवाससम्
ऋ. 8.102.5

विप्रासो न मन्मभिः स्वाध्यो देवाव्योरे न यज्ञैः स्वप्नसः
राजानो न चित्राः सुसंदृशः क्षितीनां न मर्या अरेपसः
ऋ. 10.78.1

अग्निर्न ये भ्राजसा रुक्मवक्षसो वातासो न स्वयुजः सद्यऊतयः
प्रज्ञातारो न ज्येष्ठाः सुनीतयः सुशर्माणो न सोमा ऋतं यते

ऋ. 10.78.2

वातासो न ये धुनयो जिगत्नवो ऽग्नीनां न जिह्वा विरोकिणः
वर्मण्वन्तो न योधाः शिमीवन्तः पितॄणां न शंसाः सुरातयः

ऋ. 10.78.3

रथानां न येऽराः सनाभयो जिगीवांसो न शूरा अभिद्यवः
वरेयवो न मर्या घृतप्रुषो ऽभिस्वर्तारो अर्क न सुष्टुभः

ऋ. 10.78.4

अश्वासो न ये ज्येष्ठास आशवो दिधिषवो न रथ्यः सुदानवः
आपो न निम्नैरुदभिर्जिगत्नवो विश्वरूपा अङ्गिरसो न सामभिः

ऋ. 10.78.5

ग्रावाणो न सूरयः सिन्धुमातर आदर्दिरासो अद्रयो न विश्वहा
शिशूला न क्रीळयः सुमातरो महाग्रामो न यामन्नुत त्विषा

ऋ. 10.78.6

Page 306

उषसां न केतवोऽध्वरश्रियः शुभंयवो नाञ्जिभिर्व्यश्वितन्
सिन्धवो न ययियो भ्राजदृष्टयः परावतो न योजनानि ममिरे

ऋ. 10.78.7

सुभागान्नो देवाः कृणुता सुरत्नानस्मान् स्तोतॄन् मरुतो वावृधानाः
अधि स्तोत्रस्य सख्यस्य गात सनाद्धि वो रत्नधेयानि सन्ति

ऋ. 10.78.8

यददो वात ते गृहेऽमृतस्य निधिर्हितः । ततो नो देहि जीवसे

ऋ. 10.186.3

Page 307

सत्यं बृहदृतमुग्रं दीक्षा तपो ब्रह्म यज्ञः पृथिवीं धारयन्ति
सा नो भूतस्य भव्यस्य पत्न्युरुं लोकं पृथिवी नः कृणोतु

अ. 12.1.1

असंबाधं बध्यतो मानवानां यस्यां उद्वतः प्रवतः समं बहु
नानावीर्या ओषधीर्या बिभर्ति पृथिवी नः प्रथतां राध्यतां नः

अ. 12.1.2

यस्यां समुद्र उत सिन्धुरापो यस्यामन्नं कृष्टयः संबभूवुः
यस्यामिदं जिन्वति प्राणदेजत् सा नो भूमिः पूर्वपेये दधातु

अ. 12.1.3

यस्याश्चतस्रः प्रदिशः पृथिव्या यस्यामन्नं कृष्टयः संबभूवुः
या बिभर्ति बहुधा प्राणदेजत् सा नो भूमिर्गोष्वप्यन्ने दधातु

अ. 12.1.4

Page 308

यस्यां पूर्वे पूर्वजना विचक्रिरे यस्यां देवा असुरानभ्यवर्तयन्
गवामश्वानां वयसश्च विष्ठा भगं वर्चः पृथिवी नो दधातु

अ. 12.1.5

विश्वंभरा वसुधानीं प्रतिष्ठा हिरण्यवक्षा जगतो निवेशनी
वैश्वानरं बिभ्रती भूमिरग्निमिन्द्रंऋषभा द्रविणे नो दधातु

अ. 12.1.6

यां रक्षन्त्यस्वप्ना विश्वदानीं देवा भूमिं पृथिवीमप्रमादम्
सा नो मधु प्रियं दुहामथो उक्षतु वर्चसा

अ. 12.1.7

याऽर्णवेऽधि सलिलमग्र आसीद् यां मायाभिरन्वचरन् मनीषिणः
यस्या हृदयं परमे व्योमन्त्सत्येनावृतममृतं पृथिव्याः
सा नो भूमिस्त्विषिं बलं राष्ट्रे दधातूत्तमे

अ. 12.1.8

यस्यामापः परिचराः समानीरहोरात्रे अप्रमादं क्षरन्ति
सा नो भूमिर्भूरिधारा पयो दुहामथो उक्षतु वर्चसा

अ. 12.1.9

Page 310

गिरयस्ते पर्वता हिमवन्तोऽरण्यं ते पृथिवि स्योनमस्तु
बभ्रुं कृष्णां रोहिणीं विश्वरूपां ध्रुवां भूमिं पृथिवीमिन्द्रगुप्ताम्
अजीतोऽहतो अक्षतोऽध्यष्ठां पृथिवीमहम्

अ. 12.1.11

यत् ते मध्यं पृथिवि यच्च नभ्यं यास्त ऊर्जस्तन्वः संबभूवुः
तासु नो धेह्यभि नः पवस्व माता भूमिः पुत्रो अहं पृथिव्याः
पर्जन्यः पिता स उ नः पिपर्तु

अ. 12.1.12

यस्यां वेदिं परिगृह्णन्ति भूम्यां यस्यां यज्ञं तन्वते विश्वकर्माणः
यस्यां मीयन्ते स्वरवः पृथिव्यामूर्ध्वाः शुक्रा आहुत्याः पुरस्तात्
सा नो भूमिर्वर्धयद् वर्धमाना

अ. 12.1.13

यो नो द्वेषत् पृथिवि यः पृतन्याद् योऽभिदासान्मनसा यो वधेनं
तं नो भूमे रन्धय पूर्वकृत्वरि

अ. 12.1.14

त्वज्जातास्त्वयि चरन्ति मर्त्यास्त्वं बिभर्षि द्विपदस्त्वं चतुष्पदः
तवेमे पृथिवि पञ्च मानवा येभ्यो ज्योतिरमृतं मर्त्येभ्य
उद्यन्त्सूर्यो रश्मिभिरातनोति

अ. 12.1.15

Page 311

ता नः प्रजाः सं दुह्तां समग्रा वाचो मधु पृथिवि धेहि मह्यम्

अ. 12.1.16

विश्वस्वं मातरमोषधीनां ध्रुवां भूमिं पृथिवीं धर्मणा धृताम्
शिवां स्योनामनु चरेम विश्वहा

अ. 12.1.17

महत् सधस्थं महती बभूविथ महान् वेग एजथुर्वेपथुष्टे
महांस्त्वेन्द्रो रक्षत्यप्रमादम्
सा नो भूमे प्र रोचय हिरण्यस्येव संदृशि मा नो द्विक्षत कश्चन

अ. 12.1.18

अग्निर्भूम्यामोषधीष्वग्निमापो बिभ्रत्यग्निरश्मसु
अग्निरन्तः पुरुषेषु गोष्वश्वेष्वग्नयः

अ. 12.1.19

अग्निर्दिव आ तपत्यग्नेर्देवस्योर्वन्तरिक्षम्
अग्निं मर्तास इन्धते हव्यवाहं घृतप्रियम्

अ. 12.1.20

अग्निवासाः पृथिव्यासितजूस्त्विषीमन्तं संशितं मा कृणोतु

अ. 12.1.21

Page 313

यस्यां वृक्षा वानस्पत्या ध्रुवास्तिष्ठन्ति विश्वहा
पृथिवीं विश्वधायसं धृतामच्छावदामसि

अ. 12.1.27

सा नो भूमिः प्राणमायुर्दधातु जरदष्टिं मा पृथिवी कृणोतु

अ. 12.1.22

यस्ते गन्धः पृथिवि संबभूव यं बिभ्रत्योषधयो यमापः
यं गन्धर्वा अप्सरसश्च भेजिरे तेन मा सुरभिं कृणु मा नो द्विक्षत कश्चन

अ. 12.1.23

यस्ते गन्धः पुष्करमाविवेश यं संजभ्रुः सूर्यायां विवाहे
अमर्त्याः पृथिवि गन्धमग्रे तेन मा सुरभिं कृणु मा नो द्विक्षत कश्चन

अ. 12.1.24

यस्ते गन्धः पुरुषेषु स्त्रीषु पुंसु भगो रुचिः। यो अश्वेषु वीरेषु यो मृगेषु हस्तिषु
कन्यायां वर्चो यद् भूमे तेनास्माँ अपि सं सृज मा नो द्विक्षत कश्चन

अ. 12.1.25

शिला भूमिरश्मा पांसुः सा भूमिः संधृता धृता
तस्यै हिरण्यवक्षसे पृथिव्या अकरं नमः

अ. 12.1.26

उदीराणा उतासीनास्तिष्ठन्तः प्रकामन्तः
पद्भ्यां दक्षिणसव्याभ्यां मा व्यथिष्महि भूम्याम्

अ. 12.1.28

विमृग्वरीं पृथिवीमा वंदामि क्षमां भूमिं ब्रह्मणा वावृधानाम्
ऊर्जं पुष्टं बिभ्रतीमन्नभागं घृतं त्वामि नि पीदेम भूमे

अ. 12.1.29

शुद्धा न आपस्तन्वे क्षरन्तु यो नः सेदुरप्रिये तं नि दध्मः
पवित्रेण पृथिवि मोत् पुनामि

अ. 12.1.30

यास्ते प्राचीः प्रदिशो या उदीचीर्यास्ते भूमे अधराद् याश्च पश्चात्
स्योनास्ता मह्यं चरते भवन्तु मा नि पप्तं भुवने शिश्रियाणः

अ. 12.1.31

यावत् तेऽभि विपश्यामि भूमे सूर्येण मेदिना
तावन्मे चक्षुर्मा मेष्टोत्तरामुत्तरां समाम्

अ. 12.1.33

527

यत् ते' भूमे विखनामि क्षिप्रं तदपि रोहतु
मा ते मर्म' विमृग्वरि मा ते हृदयमर्पिषम्

अ. 12.1.35

Page 316

ग्रीष्मस्ते' भूमे वर्षाणि शरद्धेमन्तः शिशिरो वसन्तः
ऋतवस्ते विहिता हायनीरंहोरात्रे पृथिवि नो दुह्यताम्

अ. 12.1.36

यस्यां सदोहविर्धाने यूपो यस्यां निमीयते'
ब्रह्माणो यस्यामर्चन्त्यृग्भिः साम्ना' यजुर्विदः
युज्यन्ते यस्यामृत्विजः सोममिन्द्राय पातवे

अ. 12.1.38

यस्यां पूर्वे भूतकृत ऋषयो गा उदानृचुः
सप्त सत्रेण वेधसो' यज्ञेन तपसा सह

अ. 12.1.39

सा नो भूभिरा दिशतु यद्धनं कामयामहे
भगो' अनुप्रयुङ्क्तामिन्द्र एतु पुरोगवः

अ. 12.1.40

यस्यां गायन्ति नृत्यन्ति भूम्यां मर्ता व्यैलबाः
युध्यन्ते यस्यामाक्रन्दो यस्यां वदति दुन्दुभिः
सा नो भूमिः प्र णुदतां सपत्नांनसपत्नं मा पृथिवी कृणोतु

अ. 12.1.41

Page 317

भूमे' मातर्नि धेहि मा भद्रया सुप्रतिष्ठितम्
संविदाना दिवा कवे श्रियां मा धेहि भूत्याम्

अ. 12.1.63

Page 318

यस्यामन्नं ब्रीहियवौ यस्यां इमाः पञ्च कृष्टयः
भूम्यै' पर्जन्यपत्न्यै नमोऽस्तु वर्षमेदसे

अ. 12.1.42

निधिं बिभ्रती बहुधा गुह्य वसु मणिं हिरण्यं पृथिवी दंदातु मे
वसूनि नो वसुदा रासमाना देवी दधातु सुमनस्यमाना

अ. 12.1.44

ये त आरण्याः पशवो मृगा वने हिताः सिंहा व्याघ्राः पुरुषादश्चरन्ति
उलं वृकं पृथिवि दुच्छुनामित ऋक्षीकां रक्षो अप बाधयास्मत्

अ. 12.1.49

यां द्विपादः पक्षिणः संपतन्ति हंसाः सुपर्णा शकुना वयांसि
यस्यां वातो मातरिश्वेयंते रजांसि कृण्वंश्च्यावयंश्च वृक्षान्
वातस्य प्रवामुपवामनु वात्यर्चिः

अ. 12.1.51

यस्यां कृष्णमरुणं च संहिते अहोरात्रे विहिते भूम्यामधि
वर्पेण भूमिः पृथिवी वृतावृता सा नो दधातु भद्रया प्रिये धाम निधामनि

अ. 12.1.52

द्यौश्च म इदं पृथिवी चान्तरिक्षं च मे व्यचः
अग्निः सूर्य आपो मेधां विश्वे देवाश्च सं ददुः

अ. 12.1.53

Page 319
अहमस्मि सहमान उत्तरो नाम भूम्याम्
अभीषाडस्मि विश्वापाडाशामाशां विपासहिः

अ. 12.1.54

ये ग्रामा यदरण्यं याः सुभाअधि भूम्याम्
ये संग्रामाः समितयस्तेषु चारु वदेम ते

अ. 12.1.56

अश्वं इव रजो दुधुवे वि तान् जनान् य आक्षियन् पृथिवीं यादजायत
मन्द्राग्रेत्वरी भुवनस्य गोपा वनस्पतीनां गृभिरोषधीनाम्

अ. 12.1.57

यद् वदामि मधुमत् तद् वदामि यदीक्षे तद् वनन्ति मा
त्विषीमानस्मि जूतिमानवान्यान् हन्मि दोधतः

अ. 12.1.58

शन्तिवा सुरभिः स्योना कीलालोधनी पयस्वती
भूमिरधि ब्रवीतु मे पृथिवी पयसा सह

अ. 12.1.59

उपस्थास्ते अनमीवा अयक्ष्मा अस्मभ्यं सन्तु पृथिवि प्रसूताः
दीर्घं न आयुः प्रतिबुध्यमाना वयं तुभ्यं बलिहृतः स्याम

अ. 12.1.62

उभा देवा दिविस्पृशेन्द्रवायू हंवामहे
अस्य सोमस्य पीतये॑

ऋ. 1.23.2

अप्स्वं॑न्तरमृतंमप्सु भेषजमपामुत प्रशंस्तये। देवा॑ भवंत वाजिनः॑

ऋ. 1.23.19

इदमांपः प्र वंहत यत् किं च॑ दुरितं मयि
यद् वाहमंभिदुद्रोह यद् वा॑ शेप उतानृंतम्

ऋ. 1.23.22

समन्या यन्त्युप यन्त्यन्याः समानमूर्वं नद्यः॑ पृणन्ति
तमू शुचिं॑ शुचयो दीदिवांसंमपां नपांतं परिं तस्थुरापः॑

ऋ. 2.35.3

Page 322

प्र पर्वतानामुशंती उपस्थांदश्वे॑ इव विषिंते हासंमाने
गावेव शुभ्रे मातरा॑ रिहाणे विपाट्छुतुद्री पयसा जवेते

ऋ. 3.33.1

इन्द्रेषिते प्रसवं॑ भिक्षंमाणे॑ अच्छा समुद्रं रथ्येव याथः
समाराणे ऊर्मिभिः॑ पिन्वंमाने अन्या वां॑मन्यामप्येति शुभ्रे

ऋ. 3.33.2

अच्छा॑ सिन्धुं॑ मातृतंमामयासं विपांशमुर्वीं॑ सुभगां॑मगन्म
वत्समिव मातरा॑ संरिहाणे समानं॑ योनिमनु संचरंन्ती

ऋ. 3.33.3

एना वयं॑ पयंसा पिन्वंमाना अनु योनिं॑ देवकृंतं चरंन्तीः
न वर्तवे प्रसंवः सर्गतंक्तः किंयुर्विप्रो॑ नद्यो॑ जोहवीति

ऋ. 3.33.4

रमध्वं मे॑ वचंसे सोम्याय॑ ऋतांवरीरुप मुहूर्तंमेवैः॑
प्र सिन्धुमच्छा॑ बृहती मनींषा ऽवस्युरंह्वे कुशिकस्यं सूनुः॑

ऋ. 3.33.5

इन्द्रो॑ अस्माँ अरदद् वज्रबाहुरपांहन् वृत्रं परिंधिं नदीनाम्॑
देवोंऽनयत् सविता सुपाणिस्तस्यं वयं प्रंसवे यां॑म उर्वीः॑

ऋ. 3.33.6

530

प्रवाच्यं शश्वधा वीर्यं१ तदिन्द्रस्य कर्म यदहिं विवृश्चत्
वि वज्रेण परिषदो१ जघानाऽऽत्रापोऽयनमिच्छमानाः

ऋ. 3.33.7

एतद् वचो१ जरितर्मापि मृष्ठा आ यत् ते घोषानुत्तरा युगानि
उक्थेषु कारो प्रति नो जुषस्व मा नो नि कः पुरुषत्रा नमस्ते

ऋ. 3.33.8

ओ षु स्वंसारः कारवे१ शृणोत ययौ वो१ दूरादनसा रथेन
नि षू नंमध्वं भर्वता सुपारा अंधोअक्षाः सिन्धवः स्रोत्याभिः

ऋ. 3.33.9

आ ते१ कारो शृणवामा वर्चांसि ययाथ दूरादनसा रथेन
नि ते१ नंसै पीप्यानेव योषा मयायीव कन्यां शश्वचे ते१

ऋ. 3.33.10

उद् वं१ ऊर्मिः शम्या हन्त्वापो योक्त्राणि मुञ्चत
मादुष्कृतौ व्येनसा ऽघ्न्यौ शूनमारंताम्

ऋ. 3.33.13

शतपंवित्राः स्वधया मदंतीर्देवीर्देवानामपि यन्ति पाथः
ता इन्द्रस्य न मिनन्ति व्रतानि सिन्धुभ्यो हव्यं घृतवंज्जुहोत

ऋ. 7.47.3

उपह्वरे गिरीणां संगथे च नदीनाम्। धिया विप्रो१ अजायत

ऋ. 8.6.28

इन्द्राय पवते मदः सोमो१ मरुत्वंते सुतः
सहस्रधारो अत्यव्यं१मर्षति तमी१ मृजन्त्यायवः

ऋ. 9.107.17

प्र ते१ऽरदद्वरुणो यातंवे पथः सिन्धो यदाजाँ अभ्यद्रवस्त्वम्
भूम्या अधि प्रवतां यासिं सानुना यदेषामग्रं जगतामिरज्यसि

ऋ. 10.75.2

दिवि स्वनो यंतते भूम्योपर्यन्नंतं शुष्ममुदियर्ति भानुना
अभ्रादिव प्र स्तनयन्ति वृष्ट्यः सिन्धुर्यदिति वृषभो न रोरुवत्

ऋ. 10.75.3

अभि त्वा सिन्धो शिशुमिन्न मातरो वाश्रा अर्षन्ति पयसेव धेनवः
राजेवयुध्वां नयसि त्वमित् सिचौ यदासामग्रं प्रवतामिनंक्षसि

ऋ. 10.75.4

ऋजीत्येनी रुशती महित्वा परि ज्रयांसि भरते रजांसि
अदब्धा सिन्धुरपसामपस्तमा श्वा न चित्रा वपुषीव दर्शता

ऋ. 10.75.7

Page 329
सुपर्णोऽसि गरुत्मान्दिवं गच्छ स्वः पतं

य. 12.4

Page 330
क्षेत्रस्य पतिना वयं हितेनेव जयामसि
गामश्वं पोषयित्वा स नो मृळातीदृशे

ऋ. 4.57.1

क्षेत्रस्य पते मधुमन्तमूर्मिं धेनुरिव पयो अस्मासु धुक्ष्व
मधुश्चुतं घृतमिव सुपूतमृतस्य नः पतयो मृळयन्तु

ऋ. 4.57.2

Page 331
मधुमतीरोषधीर्द्याव आपो मधुमन्नो भवत्वन्तरिक्षम्
क्षेत्रस्य पतिर्मधुमान् नो अस्त्वरिष्यन्तो अन्वेनं चरेम

ऋ. 4.57.3

शुनं वाहाः शुनं नरः शुनं कृषतु लाङ्गलम्
शुनं वरत्रा बध्यन्तां शुनमष्ट्रामुदिङ्गय

ऋ. 4.57.4

शुनासीराविमां वाचं जुषेथां यद् दिवि चक्रथुः पयः
तेनेमामुप सिञ्चतम्

ऋ. 7.57.5

Page 332
अर्वाची सुभगे भव सीते वन्दामहे त्वा
यथा नः सुभगासि यथा नः सुफलासि

ऋ. 4.57.6

इन्द्रः सीतां नि गृह्णातु तां पूषानु यच्छतु
सा नः पयस्वती दुहामुत्तरामुत्तरां समाम्

ऋ. 4.57.7

शुनं नः फाला वि कृषन्तु भूमिं शुनं कीनाशा अभि यन्तु वाहैः
शुनं पर्जन्यो मधुना पयोभिः शुनासीरा शुनमस्मासु धत्तम्

ऋ. 4.57.8

सोमं रारन्धि नो हृदि गावो न यवसेष्वा । मर्य इव स्व ओक्ये

ऋ. 1.91.13

Page 334

पयस्वतीरोषधयः पयस्वन्मामकं वचः
अथो पयस्वतीनामा भरेऽहं सहस्रशः

अ. 3.24.1

वेदाहं पयस्वन्तं चकार धान्यं बहु
संभृत्वा नाम यो देवस्तं वयं हवामहे यो यो अपज्ञो गृहे

अ. 3.42.2

Page 335

इमा याः पञ्च प्रदिशो मानवीः पञ्च कृष्टयः
वृष्टे शापं नदीरिवेहि स्फातिं समावहान्

अ. 3.24.3

उदुत्सं शतधारं सहस्रधारमक्षितम्
एवास्माकेदं धान्यं सहस्रधारमक्षितम्

अ. 3.24.4

Page 336

शतहस्त समाहरसहस्रहस्त सं किर
कृतस्य कार्यस्य चेह स्फातिं समावह

अ. 3.24.5

तिस्रो मात्रा गन्धर्वाणां चतस्रो गृहपत्न्याः
तासां या स्फातिमत्तमा तया त्वाभिमृशामसि

अ. 3.24.6

Page 338

आ गावो अग्मन्नुत भद्रमक्रन् त्सीदन्तु गोष्ठे रणयन्त्वस्मे
प्रजावतीः पुरुरूपा इह स्युरिन्द्राय पूर्वीरुषसो दुहानाः

ऋ. 6.28.1

इन्द्रो यज्वने पृणते च शिक्षत्युपेद् ददाति न स्वं मुषायति
भूयोभूयो रयिमिदस्य वर्धयन्नभिन्ने खिल्ये नि दधाति देवयुम्

ऋ. 6.28.2

न ता नँशन्ति न दंभाति तस्करो नासांमामित्रो व्यथिरा दधर्षति
देवाँश्च याभिर्यज्ञते दर्दाति च ज्योगित् ताभिः सचते गोपतिः सह

न ता अर्वा रेणकंकाटो अश्नुते न संस्कृतत्रमुपं यन्ति ता अभि
उरुगायमभयं तस्य ता अनु गावो मर्तस्य वि चरन्ति यज्वनः

ऋ. 6.28.4

यूयं गावो मेदयथा कृशं चिदश्रीरं चित् कृणुथा सुप्रतीकम्
भद्रं गृहं कृणुथ भद्रवाचो बृहद् वो वयं उच्यते सभासु

ऋ. 6.28.6

प्रजावतीः सूयवसं रिशन्तीः शुद्धा अपः सुप्रपाणे पिबन्तीः
मा वः स्तेन ईशत माघशंसः परि वो हेती रुद्रस्य वृज्याः

ऋ. 6.28.7

उपेदमुपपर्चनमासु गोषूपं पृच्यताम्
उपं ऋषभस्य रेतस्युपेन्द्र तव वीर्ये

ऋ. 6.28.8

वसन्त इनु रन्त्यों ग्रीष्मं इनु रन्त्यैः
घर्षाण्यनुं शैरदौ हेमन्तः शिशिरं इनुं रन्त्यैः

सा. 616

उक्षा समुद्रो अरुषः सुपर्णः पूर्वस्य योनिं पितुरा विवेश
मध्ये दिवो निहितः पृश्निरश्मा वि चक्रमे रजसस्पात्यन्तां

ऋ. 5.47.3

ग्रीष्मो हेमन्तः शिशिरो वसन्तः शरद् वर्षाः स्विते नो दधात
आ नो गोषु भजता प्रजायां निवात इद् वः शरणे स्याम

अ. 6.55.2

शतं वो अम्ब धामानि सहस्रमुत वो रुहः
अधा शतक्रत्वो यूयमिमं मे अगदं कृत

ऋ. 10.97.2

ओषधीः प्रति मोदध्वं पुष्पवतीः प्रसूवरीः
अश्वा इव सजित्वरीर्वीरुधः पारयिष्णवः

ऋ. 10.97.3

अश्वत्थे वो निषदनं पर्णे वो वसतिष्कृता
गोभाज इत् किलासथ यत् सनवथ पूरुषम्
ऋ. 10. 97.5

यत्रौषधीः समग्मत राजानः समिताविव
विप्रः स उच्यते भिषग् रक्षोहामीवचातंनः
ऋ. 10.97.6

यस्यौषधीः प्रसर्पथाङ्गमङ्गं परुष्परुः
ततो यक्ष्मं वि बाधध्व उग्रो मध्यमशीरिव
ऋ. 10.97.12

जीवलां नघारिषां जीवन्तीमोषधीमहम्
अरुन्धतीमुन्नयन्तीं पुष्पां मधुमतीमिह हुवे ऽस्मा अरिष्टतातये
अ. 8.7.6

शृणोतु न ऊर्जा पतिर्गिरः स नभस्तरीयाँ इषिरः परिज्मा
शृण्वन्त्वापः पुरो न शुभ्राः परि स्रुचो बबृहाणस्याद्रेः
ऋ. 5.41.12

जनं बिभ्रती बहुधा विवाचसं नानाधर्माणं पृथिवी यथौकसम्
सहस्रं धारा द्रविणस्य मे दुहां ध्रुवेव धेनुरनपस्फुरन्ती
अ. 12.1.45

उषसः पूर्वा अध यद् व्यूषुर्महद् वि जज्ञे अक्षरं पदे गोः
व्रता देवानामुप नु प्रभूषन् महद् देवानामसुरत्वमेकम्
ऋ. 3.55.1

मो षू णो अत्र जुहुरन्त देवा मा पूर्वे अग्ने पितरः पदज्ञाः
पुराण्योः सद्मनोः केतुरन्तर्महद् देवानामसुरत्वमेकम्
ऋ. 3.55.2

वि मे पुरुत्रा पतयन्ति कामाः शम्यच्छा दीध्ये पूर्व्याणि
समिद्धे अग्नावृतमिद् वदेम महद् देवानामसुरत्वमेकम्
ऋ. 3.55.3

समानो राजा विभृतः पुरुत्रा शये शयासु प्रयुतो वनानु
अन्या वत्सं भरति क्षेति माता महद् देवानामसुरत्वमेकम्
ऋ. 3.55.4

आक्षित् पूर्वास्वपरा अनूरुत् सद्यो जातासु तरुणीष्वन्तः ।
अन्तर्वतीः सुवते अप्रवीता महद् देवानांमसुरत्वमेकम् ॥
ऋ. 3.55.5

शयुः परस्तादध नु द्विमाता ऽबन्धनश्चरति वत्स एकः ।
मित्रस्य ता वरुणस्य व्रतानि महद् देवानांमसुरत्वमेकम् ॥
ऋ. 3.55.6

द्विमाता होतां विदथेषु सम्राळन्वग्रं चरति क्षेति बुध्नः ।
प्र रण्यानि रण्यवाचो भरन्ते महद् देवानांमसुरत्वमेकम् ॥
ऋ. 3.55.7

शूरस्येव युध्यतो अन्तमस्य प्रतीचीनं ददृशे विश्वमायत् ।
अन्तर्मतिश्चरति निष्पिधं गोर्महद् देवानांमसुरत्वमेकम् ॥
ऋ. 3.55.8

नि वेवेति पलितो दूत आस्वन्तर्महांश्चरति रोचनेन ।
वपूंषि बिभ्रदभि नो वि चष्टे महद् देवानांमसुरत्वमेकम् ॥
ऋ. 3.55.9

विष्णुर्गोपाः परमं पाति पाथः प्रिया धामान्यमृता दधानः ।
अग्निष्टा विश्वा भुवनानि वेद महद् देवानांमसुरत्वमेकम् ॥
ऋ. 3.55.10

नानां चक्राते यम्याऽ वपूंषि तयोरन्यद् रोचते कृष्णभन्यत् ।
श्यावी च यदरुषी च स्वसारौ महद् देवानांभसुरत्वमेकम् ॥
ऋ. 3.55.11

माता च यत्र दुहिता च धेनू सबर्दुघे धापयेते समीची ।
ऋतस्य ते सदसीळे अन्तर्महद् देवानामसुरत्वमेकम् ॥
ऋ. 3.55.12

अन्यस्यां वत्सं रिहती मिमाय कया भुवा नि दधे धेनुरूधः ।
ऋतस्य सा पयसापिन्वतेळां महद् देवानांभसुरत्वमेकम् ॥
ऋ. 3.55.13

पद्या वस्ते पुरुरूपा वपूंष्यूर्ध्वा तस्थौ त्र्यविं रेरिहाणा ।
ऋतस्य सद्म वि चरामि विद्वान् महद् देवानांमसुरत्वमेकम् ॥
ऋ. 3.55.14

पदे इव निहिते दस्मे अन्तस्तयोरन्यद् गुह्यमाविरन्यत् ।
सध्रीचीना पथ्याऽ सा विष्पूची महद् देवानांमसुरत्वमेकम् ॥
ऋ. 3.55.15

यः पुष्पिणीश्च प्रस्वश्च धर्मणा ऽधि दाने व्यऽवनीरधारयः

यश्चासा मा अर्जनो दिद्युतो दिव उरुरुर्वीं अभितः सास्युक्थ्यः

ऋ. 2.13.7

यो अक्रन्दयत् सलिलं महित्वा योनिं कृत्वा त्रिभुजं शयानः

वत्सः कामदुघो विराजः स गुहा चक्रे तन्वाः पराचैः

अ. 8.9.2

श्येनः क्रोडोऽन्तरिक्षं पाजस्यं१ बृहस्पतिः ककुद् बृहतीः कीकसाः

अ. 9.7.5

यानि नक्षत्राणि दिव्यऽन्तरिक्षे अप्सु भूमौ यानि नगेषु दिक्षु

प्रकल्पयंश्चन्द्रमा यान्येति सर्वाणि ममैतानि शिवानि सन्तु

अ. 19.8.1

अष्टाविंशानि शिवानि शग्मानि सह योगं भजन्तु मे

योगं प्र पद्ये क्षेमं च क्षेमं प्र पद्ये योगं च नमोऽहोरात्राभ्यामस्तु

अ. 19.8.2

सुतासो मधुमत्तमाः सोमा इन्द्राय मन्दिनः

पवित्रवन्तो अक्षरन् देवान् गच्छन्तु वो मदाः

सा. 547

अहमिन्द्रो न परा जिग्य इद्धनं न मृत्यवेऽव तस्थे कदा चन

सोममिन्मा सुन्वन्तो याचता वसु न मे पूरवः सख्ये रिषाथन

ऋ. 10.48.5

अभिष्टने ते आद्रिवो यत् स्था जगच्च रेजते

त्वष्टा चित् तव मन्यव इन्द्र वेविज्यतेऽभियार्चन्ननु स्वराज्यम्

ऋ. 1.80.14

अजोऽह्याऽग्निरजनिष्ट शोकात् सो अपश्यज्जनितारमग्ने

तेन देवा देवतामग्र आयन् तेन रोहान् रुरुहुर्मेध्यासः

अ. 4.14.1

क्रमध्वमग्निना नाकमुख्यान् हस्तेषु बिभ्रतः

दिवस्पृष्ठं स्व र्गत्वा मिश्रा देवेभिराध्वम्

अ. 4.14.2

पञ्चौदन पञ्चभिरङ्गुलिभिर्दव्योद्धर पञ्चधैतमोदनम्

प्राच्यां दिशि शिरो अजस्य धेहि दक्षिणायां दिशि दक्षिणं धेहि पार्श्वम्

अ. 4.14.7

आ यो धर्माणि प्रथमः ससाद ततो वपूंषि कृणुषे पुरूणि
धास्युर्योनिं प्रथम आ विवेश यो वाचमनुदितां चिकेत
अ. 5.1.2

सुतासो मधुमत्तमाः सोमा इन्द्राय मन्दिनः
पवित्रंवन्तो अक्षरन्देवान्गच्छन्तु वो मदाः
अ. 20.137.4

Page 425

सोमस्य त्विषिरसि तेवेव मे त्विषिर्भूयात्
मृत्योः पाह्योजोऽसि सहोऽस्यमृतमसि
सा. 10.15

प्रसद्य भस्मना योनिमपश्च पृथिवीमग्ने
सःसृज्य मातृभिष्ट्वं ज्योतिष्मान् पुनरा ऽसदः
सा. 12.38

पुनरासद्य सदनमपश्च पृथिवीमग्ने
शेषे मातुर्यथोपस्थेऽन्तरंस्यांऽ शिवतमः
य. 12.39

वायोः पूतः पवित्रेण प्रत्यङ् सोमो अति द्रुतः
इन्द्रस्य युज्यः सखा
अ. 6.51.1

मृत्योरहं ब्रह्मचारी यदस्मिं नियर्चन् भूतात् पुरुषं यमाय
तमहं ब्रह्मणा तपसा श्रमेणानयनैनं मेखलया सिनामि
अ. 6.133.3

श्रद्धायां दुहिता तपसोऽधि जाता स्वस ऋषीणां भूतकृतां बभूव
सा नों मेखले मतिमा धेहि मेधामथों नो धेहि तप इन्द्रियं च
अ. 6.133.4

Page 426

यद् दुष्कृतं यच्छमलं यद् वा चेरिम पापया
त्वया तद् विश्वतोमुखापामार्गप मृज्महे
अ. 7.65.2

पञ्च व्युष्टीरनु पञ्च दोहा गां पञ्चनाम्नीमृतवोऽनु पञ्च
पञ्च दिशः पञ्चदशेन क्लृप्तास्ता एकमूर्ध्नीरभि कोकमेकम्
अ. 8.9.15

सप्त होमाः समिधों ह सप्त मधूनि सप्तर्तवों ह सप्त
सप्ताज्यानि परि भूतमायन् ताः सप्तगृध्रा इति शुश्रुमा वयम्
अ. 8.9.18

सप्त छन्दांसि चतुरुत्तराण्यन्यो अन्यस्मित्रध्यापितानि
कथं स्तोमाः प्रति तिष्ठन्ति तेषु तानि स्तोमेषु कथमार्पितानि
अ. 8.9.19

Page 427
कथं गायत्री त्रिवृतं व्यापि कथं त्रिष्टुप् पंञ्चदशेन कल्पते
त्रयस्त्रिंशेन जगती कथमनुष्टुप् कथमेकविंशः
अ. 8.9.20

अष्ट जाता भूता प्रथमजर्तस्याष्टेन्द्रत्विजो दैव्या ये
अष्टयोनिरदितिरष्टपुत्राष्टमीं रात्रिमभि हव्यमेति
अ. 8.9.21

न वै तं चक्षुर्जहाति न प्राणो जरसः पुरा
पुरं यो ब्रह्मणो वेद यस्याः पुरुष उच्यते
अ. 10.2.30

Page 428
अष्टाचक्रा नवद्वारा देवानां पूरयोध्या
तस्यां हिरण्ययः कोशः स्वर्गो ज्योतिषावृतः
अ. 10.2.31

तस्मिन् हिरण्यये कोशे त्र्यरि त्रिप्रतिष्ठिते
तस्मिन् यद् यक्षमात्मन्वत् तद् वै ब्रह्मविदों विदुः३
अ. 10.2.32

इमौ युनज्मि ते वह्नी असुनीताय वोढवे
ताभ्यां यमस्य सादनं समितीश्चावं गच्छतात्
अ. 18.2.56

हरिः सुपर्णो दिवमारुहोऽर्चिषा ये त्वा दिप्सन्ति दिवमुत्पतन्तम्
अव तां जहि हरसा जातवेदोऽर्बिभ्यदुग्रोऽर्चिषा दिवमा रोह सूर्य
अ. 19.65.1

Page 429
को अस्य बाहू समभरद् वीर्यं करवादिति
अंसौ को अस्य तद् देवः कुसिन्धे अध्या दधौ
अ. 10.2.5

कः सप्त खानि वि ततर्द शीर्षणि कर्णाविमौ नासिके चक्षणी मुखम्
येषां पुरुत्रा विजयस्य महिना चतुष्पादो द्विपदो यन्ति यामम्
अ. 10.2.6

हन्वोर्हि जिह्वामदधात् पुरूचीमधा महीमधि शिश्राय वाचम्
स आ वरीवर्ति भुवनेष्वन्तरपो वसानः क उ तच्चिकेत

अ. 10.2.7

मस्तिष्कमस्य यतमो ललाटं ककाटिकां प्रथमो यः कपालम्
चित्वा चित्यं हन्वोः पूरुषस्य दिवं रुरोह कतमः स देवः

अ. 10.2.8

यथा द्यां च पृथिवीं चान्तस्तिष्ठति तेजनम्
एवा रोगं चास्रावं चान्तस्तिष्ठतु मुञ्ज इत्

अ. 1.2.4

Page 430

विषितं ते वस्तिबिलं समुद्रस्योदधेरिव
एवा ते मूत्रं मुच्यतां बहिर्बालिति सर्वकम्

अ. 1.3.8

अमूर्या यन्ति योषितो हिरा लोहितवाससः
अभ्रातर इव जामयस्तिष्ठन्तु हतवर्चसः

अ. 1.17.1

शुकेषु ते हरिमाणं रोपणाकासु दध्मसि
अथो हारिद्रवेषु ते हरिमाणं नि दध्मसि

अ. 1.22.4

नक्तंजातास्योषधे रामे कृष्णे असिक्नि च
इदं रजनि रजय किलासं पलितं च यत्

अ. 1.23.1

श्यामा सरूपंकरणी पृथिव्या अध्युद्भृता
इदमू पु प्र साधय पुना रूपाणि कल्पय

अ. 1.24.4

येन वेहद् बभूविथ नाशयामसि तत् त्वत्
इदं तदन्यत्र त्वदप दूरे नि दध्मसि

अ. 3.23.1

आ ते योनिं गर्भ एतु पुमान् बाण इवेषुधिम्
आ वीरोऽत्र जायतां पुत्रस्ते दशमास्यः

अ. 3.23.2

Page 431

यानि भद्राणि बीजान्यृषभा जनयन्ति च
तैस्त्वं पुत्रं विन्दस्व सा प्रसूर्धेनुका भव

अ. 3.23.4

उदुषा उदु सूर्य उदिदं मामकं वचः
उदेजतु प्रजापतिर्वृषा शुष्मेण वाजिनां

अ. 4.4.2

यस्त आस्यत् पञ्चाङ्गुरिर्विक्राच्चिदधि धन्वनः
अपस्कम्भस्य शल्यान्निरवोचमहं विषम्

अ. 4.6.4

शल्याद् विषं निरवोचं प्राज्ञनादुत पर्णधेः
अपाष्ठाच्छृङ्गात् कुल्मलान्निरवोचमहं विषम्

अ. 4.6.5

रोहण्यसि रोहण्यस्थिच्छिन्नस्य रोहणी। रोहयेदमरुन्धति

अ. 4.12.1

अयं मे हस्तो भगवानयं मे भगवत्तरः
अयं मे विश्वभेषजोऽयं शिवाभिमर्शनः

अ. 4.13.6

हस्ताभ्यां दशशाखाभ्यां जिह्वा वाचः पुरोगवी
अनामयिल्लुभ्यां हस्ताभ्यां ताभ्यां त्वाभि मृशामसि

अ. 4.13.7

यां ते चक्रुरामे पात्रे यां चक्रुनींललोहिते
आमे मांसे कृत्यां यां चक्रुस्तयां कृत्याकृतों जहि

अ. 4.17.4

अपामार्ग ओषधीनां सर्वासामेक इद् वशी
तेन ते मृज्म आस्थितमथ त्वमगदश्चर

अ. 4.17.8

गुल्गुलूः पीला नलद्यौईक्षगन्धिः प्रमन्दनी
तत् परेताप्सरसः प्रतिबुद्धा अभूतन

अ. 4.37.3

भीमा इन्द्रस्य हेतयः शतमृष्टीरयस्मयीः
ताभिर्हविरदान् गन्धर्वान्वकादान् व्यृषितु

अ. 4.37.8

यस्ते हन्ति पतयन्तं निषत्स्नु यः सरीसृपम्
जातं यस्ते जिघांसति तमितो नाशयामसि

अ. 20.96.13

रात्री माता नभः पितार्यमा तें पितामहः
सिलाची नाम वा असि सा देवानांमसि स्वसां
अ. 5.5.1

भद्रात् प्लक्षात्रिस्तिष्ठस्यश्वत्थात् खदिराद्धवात्
भद्रान्न्यग्रोधात् पर्णात् सा न एह्वरुन्धति
अ. 5.5.5

हिरण्यवर्णे सुभगे सूर्यवर्णे वपुष्टमे
रुतं गच्छासि निष्कृते निष्कृतिर्नाम वा असि
अ. 5.5.6

तथा तदग्ने कृणु जातवेदो विश्वेभिर्देवैः सह संविदानः
यो नों दिदेव यतमो जघास यथा सो अस्य परिधिष्पतांति
अ. 5.29.2

यदस्य हृतं विहृतं यत् परांभृतमात्मनों जग्धं यंतमत् पिशाचैः
तदग्ने विद्वान् पुनरा भर त्वं शरीरें मांसमसुमेरंयामः
अ. 5.29.5

आमे सुपक्वे शबले विपक्वे यो मां पिशाचो अशने ददम्भ
तदात्मनां प्रजयां पिशाचा वि यांतयन्तामगदोऽयमस्तु
अ. 5.29.6

यां ते चक्रुरामे पात्रे यां चक्रुर्मिश्रधान्ये
आमे मांसे कृत्यां यां चक्रुः पुनः प्रति हरामि ताम्
अ. 5.31.1

मध्वां पृष्ठे नद्यः पर्वता गिरयो मधु
मधु परुष्णी शीपाला शमास्ने अस्तु शं हृदे
अ. 6.12.3

विद्रधस्य बलासस्य लोहितस्य वनस्पते
विसल्पकस्योषधे मोञ्छिपः पिशितं चन
अ. 6.127.1

यौ ते बलास तिष्ठतः कक्षे मुष्कावर्पश्रितौ
वेदाहं तस्य भेपजं चीपुद्रुरभिचर्क्षणम्
अ. 6.127.2

अरसस्य शर्कोटस्य नीचीनस्योपसर्पतः
विषं ह्ऽस्यादिष्वथों एनमजीजभम्
अ. 7.56.5

542

Page 440

यः पौरुषेयेण क्रविषां समङ्क्ते यो अश्व्येन पशुनां यातुधानः
यो अव्न्याया भरति क्षीरमग्ने तेषां शीर्षाणि हरसापि वृश्च

अ. 8.3.15

विषं गवां यातुधानां भरन्तामा वृश्चन्तामदितये दुरेवाः
परैणान् देवः संविता ददातु परां भागमोषधीनां जयन्ताम्

अ. 8.3.16

अवकोल्बा उदकात्मान ओषधयः। व्यृषिन्तु दुरितं तीक्ष्णशृङ्गर्यः

अ. 8.7.9

रक्षोहणं वलगहनं वैष्णवीमिदमहं तं वलगमुत्किरामि
यं मे निष्ट्यो यममात्यों निचखानेदमहं

य. 5.23

Page 441

प्रतूर्तं वाजिन्ना द्रव वरिष्ठामनु संवतम्
दिवि ते जन्म परममन्तरिक्षे तव नाभिः पृथिव्यामधि योनिरित

य. 11.12

युञ्जाथाश्च रासभं युवमस्मिन् यामे वृषण्वसू। अग्निं भरन्तमस्युमं

य. 11.13

ये तीर्थानि प्रचरन्ति सृकाहस्ता निषङ्गिणः
तेषां सहस्रयोजनेऽव धन्वानि तन्मसि

य. 16.61

रथवाहणश्च हविरस्य नाम यत्रायुधं निहितमस्य वर्म
तत्रा रथमुप शग्मश्च संदें विश्ववाहां व्यथश्च सुमनस्यमानाः

य. 29.45

त्रीणि शता त्री सहस्राण्यग्निं त्रिंशच्च देवा नव चासपर्यन्

य. 33.7

Page 435

अपचितां लोहिनीनां कृष्णा मातेति शुश्रुम
मुनेर्देवस्य मूलेन सर्वां विध्यामि ता अहम्

अ. 7.74.1

विध्याम्यासां प्रथमां विध्याम्युत मध्यमाम्
इदं जघन्या मासामा च्छिनद्मि स्तुकामिव

अ. 7.74.2

यौ ते मातोन्ममार्ज जातायाः पतिवेदनौ
दुर्णामा तत्र मा गृधदलिंशं उत वत्सपः

अ. 8.6.1

पलालानुपलालौ शर्कुं कोकं मलिम्लुचं पुलीजकम्
आश्रेषं व त्रिवांससमृक्षग्रीवं प्रमीलिनम्

अ. 8.6.2

मा सं वृतो मोप सृप उरु मावं सृपोऽन्तरा
कृणोम्यस्यै भेषजं वज दुर्णामचातनम्

अ. 8.6.3

या बभ्रवो याश्च शुक्रा रोहिणीरुत पृश्नयः
असिक्नीः कृष्णा ओषधीः सर्वा अच्छावदामसि

अ. 8.7.1

त्रायन्तामिमं पुरुषं यक्ष्माद् देवेपितादधि
यासां द्यौष्पिता पृथिवी माता समुद्रो मूलं वीरुधां बभूव

अ. 8.7.2

अवकोल्बा उदकात्मान ओषधयः। व्यृषिन्तु दुरितं तीक्ष्णशृङ्गर्यः

अ. 8.7.9

उन्मुञ्चन्तीर्विवरुणा उग्रा या विषदूषणीः
अथो बलासनाशनीः कृत्यादूषणीश्च यास्ता इह यन्त्वोषधीः

अ. 8.7.10

दर्भः शोचिस्तरुणकमश्वस्य वारः परुषस्य वारः। रथस्य बन्धुरम्

अ. 10.4.2

Page 436

कैरातिका कुमारिका सका खनति भेषजम्
हिरण्ययीभिरभ्रिभिगिरीणामुप सानुषु

अ. 10.4.14

तौदी नामासि कन्या धृताची नाम वा असि
अधस्पदेन ते पदमा ददे विषदूषणम्
अ. 10.4.24

अङ्गादङ्गात् प्र च्यावय हृदयं परि वर्जय
अधा विपस्य यत् तेजोऽवाचीनं तदेतु ते
अ. 10.4.25

आशरीकं विशरीकं बलासं पृष्ट्यामयम्
तक्मानं विश्वशारदमरसां जेङ्गिडस्करत्
अ. 19.34.10

ब्रह्माणाग्निः संविदानो रक्षोहा बाधतामितः
अमीवा यस्ते गर्भं दुर्णामा योनिमाशयें
अ. 20.96.11

यस्ते गर्भममीवा दुर्णामा योनिमाशयें
अग्निष्टं ब्रह्माणा सह निष्क्रव्यादमनीनशत्
अ. 20.96.12

वर्धयस्ते खनितारो वद्धिस्त्वमस्योपधे
वद्धिः स पर्वतो गिरिर्यतो जातमिदं विषम्
अ. 21.6.8

Page 437
वायुष्ट्वा ब्रह्माणा पातिविन्द्रस्त्वा पातिविन्द्रियैः
अ. 19.27.1

विश्वें देवा अथशुपु न्युप्तों विष्णुराप्रीतपा आप्याय्यमानों
यमः सूयमानों विष्णुः सम्भ्रियमाणों वायुः पूयमानः
शुक्रः पूतः शुक्रः क्षीरश्रीर्मन्थी संक्तुथीः
य. 8.57

यो अग्निरग्नेरध्यजायत शोकात्पृथिव्या उत वा दिवस्परि
येन प्रजा विश्वकर्मा जजान तमग्ने हेड्ः परि ते वृणक्तु
य. 13.45

नमो मेघ्याय च विद्युत्याय च नमो वर्ष्याय चावर्ष्याय च
य. 16.38

इन्द्रवायू इमे सुता उप प्रयोभिरा गतम्। इन्दवो वामुशन्ति हि
य. 33.56

अनड्वाहमन्वारभामहे सौरभेयश्च स्वस्तयें
स न इन्द्र इव देवेभ्यो वह्निः सन्तारणो भव
य. 35.13

Page 438
अश्मा च मे मृत्तिका च मे गिरयश्च मे पर्वताश्च मे
वनस्पतयश्च मे हिरण्यं च मे ऽयश्च मे श्यामं च मे
सीसं च मे त्रपु च मे यज्ञेन कल्पन्ताम्

तपसे कौलालं मायायै कर्मारथं रूपाय मणिकारथं
शुभे वपथं शर्व्याया इषुकारथं हेत्यै धनुष्कारं व
दिष्टाय रज्जुसर्जं मृत्यवे मृगयुमन्तकाय श्वनिनम्

ये पन्थानो बहवो देवयानां अन्तरा द्यावापृथिवी
ते मा जुषन्तां पयसा घृतेन यथा क्रीत्वा धनमाह

आयने ते परायणे दूर्वा रोहतु पुष्पिणी:
उत्सो वा तत्र जायतां हृदो वा पुण्डरीकवान्
अ. 6.106.1

Page 439
उपमिता प्रतिमितामथो परिमितामुत
शालाया विश्ववाराया नद्धानि वि चृतामसि
अ. 9.3.1

आ यन्याम सं वंवह ग्रन्थींश्चकार ते दृढान्
परूंषि विद्वांस्तेवेन्द्रेण वि चृतामसि
अ. 9.3.3

हतं तर्द संङ्गमाखुमश्विना छिन्तं शिरो अपि पृ
यवात्रेददानर्पि नह्तं मुखमथाभयं कृणुतं धान्या

तर्द है पतङ्ग है जभ्य हा उपक्वस
ब्रह्मेवासंस्थितं हविरन्दन्त इमान् यवानहिंसन्तो

तदीपते बर्घापते तृप्तंजम्भा आ शृणोत मे
च आरुण्या व्याद्वरा ये के च स्थ व्याद्वरास्तान्

अपचितां लोहिनीनां कृष्णा मातेति शुश्रुम
मुनेर्देवस्य मूलेन सर्वा विध्यामि ता अहम्
अ. 7.74.1

विध्याम्यासां प्रथमां विध्याम्युत मध्यमाम्
इदं जघन्यामासामा च्छिनद्मि स्तुकामिव
अ. 7.74.2

यौ ते मातोन्ममार्जं जातायाः पतिवेदनौ
दुर्णामा तत्र मा गृधदलिंशं उत वत्सपः
अ. 8.6.1

Page 435

पलालानुपलालौ शर्कुं कोकं मलिम्लुचं पलीजकम्
आश्रेषं वत्रिवांससमृक्षग्रीवं प्रमीलिनम्
अ. 8.6.2

मा सं वृतो मोपं सृप उरु मार्व सृपोऽन्तरा
कृणोम्यस्यै भेषजं बजं दुर्णामचातनम्
अ. 8.6.3

या बभ्रवो याश्च शुक्रा रोहिणीरुत पृश्नयः
असिक्नीः कृष्णा ओषधीः सर्वा अच्छावदामसि
अ. 8.7.1

त्रायन्तामिमं पुरुषं यक्ष्माद् देवेपितादधि
यासां द्यौष्पिता पृथिवी माता समुद्रो मूलं वीरुधां बभूव
अ. 8.7.2

अवकोल्वा उदकात्मान ओषधयः। व्यृषन्तु दुरितं तीक्ष्णशृङ्गयः
अ. 8.7.9

उन्मुञ्चन्तीर्विवरुणा उग्रा या विषदूषणीः
अथो बलासनाशनीः कृत्यादूषणीश्च यास्ता इहा यन्त्वोषधीः
अ. 8.7.10

दर्भः शोचिस्तरुणकमश्वंस्य वारः परुषस्य वारः। रथस्य बन्धुरम्
अ. 10.4.2

Page 436

कैरातिका कुमारिका सका खनति भेषजम्
हिरण्यययीभिरभ्रिभिगिरीणामुप सानुषु
अ. 10.4.14

तौदी नामांसि कन्याधृताची नाम वा असि
अधस्पदेनं ते पदमा दंदे विषदूषणम्
अ. 10.4.24

अज्ञांदज्ञात् प्र च्यावय हृदयं परिं वर्जय
अर्धा विषस्य यत् तेजोऽवाचीनं तदेतु ते
अ. 10.4.25

आशरीकं विशरीकं बलासं पृष्ट्यामयम्
तक्मानं विश्वशारदमरसां जङ्गिडस्करत्
अ. 19.34.10

ब्रह्मणाग्निः संविदानो रक्षोहा बांधतामितः
अमींवा यस्ते गर्भं दुर्णामा योनिमाशयें
अ. 20.96.11

यस्ते गर्भममींवा दुर्णामा योनिमाशयें
अग्निष्टं ब्रह्मणा सह निष्क्रव्यादंमनीनशत्
अ. 20.96.12

वध्रयस्ते खनितारो वध्रिस्त्वमंस्योपधे
वध्रिः स पर्वतो गिरिर्यतों जातमिदं विषम्
अ. 21.6.8

Page 437

वायुष्ट्वा ब्रह्मणा पात्विन्द्रंस्त्वा पात्विन्द्रियैः
अ. 19.27.1

विश्वें देवा अथ्श्शुषु न्युप्तों विष्णुराप्रीतपा आप्यायमानों
यमः सूयमानों विष्णुः सम्भ्रियमाणों वायुः पूयमानंः
शुक्रः पूतः शुक्रः क्षीरश्रीमन्थी सक्तुश्रीः
य. 8.57

यो अग्निरग्नेरध्यजायत शोकात्पृथिव्या उत वां दिवस्परिं
येन प्रजा विश्वकर्मा जजान तमग्ने हेडः परिं ते वृणक्तुं
य. 13.45

नमो मेघ्याय चं विद्युत्याय चं नमो वष्याय चांवर्ष्याय चं
य. 16.38

इन्द्रंवायू इमे सुता उपं प्रयोंभिरा गंतम् । इन्दंवो वामुशन्ति हिं
य. 33.56

अनड्वाहंमन्वारंभामहे सौरंभेयथ्श स्वस्तयें
स न इन्द्रं इव देवेभ्यों वह्निः सन्तारंणो भवं
य. 35.13

544

अश्मा च मे मृत्तिका च मे गिरयश्च मे पर्वताश्च मे सिकताश्च मे

वनस्पतंयश्च मे हिरण्यं च मेऽयश्च मे श्यामं च मे लोहं च मे

सीसं च मे त्रपु च मे यज्ञेन कल्पन्ताम्

य. 18.13

तपसे कौलालं मायायै कर्मारंथ्ठै रूपाय मणिकारंथ्ठै

शुभे वपथ्ठे शर्व्याया इषुकारथ्ठै हेत्यै धनुष्कारं कर्मणे ज्याकारं

दिष्टायं रज्जुसर्जं मृत्यवे मृगयुंमन्तकाय श्वनिनम्

य. 30.7

ये पन्थांनो बहवो देवयाना अन्तरा द्यावांपृथिवी संचरन्ति

ते मां जुषन्तां पयसा घृतेन यथा क्रीत्वा धनमाहरांणि

अ. 3.15.2

आयंने ते परायंणे दूर्वां रोहतु पुष्पिणीः

उत्सो वा तत्र जायतां ह्रदो वा पुण्डरीकवान्

अ. 6.106.1

उपमिंतां प्रतिमितामथो परिमितांमुत

शालाया विश्ववाराया नद्धानि वि चृतामसि

अ. 9.3.1

आ यं याम सं वबर्ह ग्रन्थींश्चकार ते दृढान्

परूंषि विद्वांठस्तेवेन्द्रेण वि चृतामसि

अ. 9.3.3

हतं तद् संङ्कमाखुमश्विना छिन्तं शिरो अपि पृष्टीः शृंणीतम्

यवानेददानिपि नह्यतं मुखमथाभयं कृणुतं धान्याय

अ. 6.50.2

तद् ह पतंङ्ग है जभ्य हा उपंक्वस

ब्रह्मेवासंस्थितं हविरनंदन्त इमान् यवानहिंसन्तो अपोदित

अ. 6.50.2

तदीपते वर्षांपते तृष्टंजम्भा आ शृंणोत मे

य आरण्या व्याद्रुरा ये के च स्थ व्याद्ध्रास्तान्त्सर्वान् जम्भयामसि

अ. 6.50.3

यः पौरुषेयेण क्रविषां समङ्क्ते यो अश्व्येन पशुनां यातुधानः
यो अघ्न्याया भरति क्षीरमग्ने तेषां शीर्षाणि हरसापि वृश्च
अ. 8.3.15

विषं गवां यातुधानां भरन्तामा वृश्चन्तामदितये दुरेवाः
परैणान् देवः सविता ददातु परा भागमोषधीनां जयन्ताम्
अ. 8.3.16

अवकोल्बा उदकात्मान ओषधयः। व्यृष्षिन्तु दुरितं तीक्ष्णशृङ्ग्यः
अ. 8.7.9

रक्षोहणं वलगहनं वैष्णवीमिदमहं तं वलगमुत्किरामि
यं मे निष्ट्यो यममात्यो निचखानेदमहं
य. 5.23

प्रतूर्तं वाजिन्रा द्रव वरिष्ठामनु संवतंम्
दिवि ते जन्म परममन्तरिक्षे तव नाभिः पृथिव्यामधि योनिरित्
य. 11.12

युञ्जाथाश्व रासभं युवमस्मिन् यामे वृषण्वसू। अग्निं भरन्तमस्मयुम्
य. 11.13

ये तीर्थानि प्रचरन्ति सृकाहस्ता निष्ङ्गिणः
तेषांश्व सहस्रयोजनेऽव धन्वानि तन्मसि
य. 16.61

रथवाहणश्व हविरस्य नाम यत्रायुधं निहितमस्य वर्म
तत्रा रथमुप शग्मश्व सदेम विश्ववाहा वयश्व सुमनस्यमानाः
य. 29.45

त्रीणि शता त्री सहस्राण्यग्निं त्रिंश्च्च देवा नव चासपर्यन्
य. 33.7